THE EUROPEAN UNION AND DEVELOPING COUNTRIES

Also by Carol Cosgrove-Sacks

ACP FOREIGN TRADE

A FRAMEWORK FOR DEVELOPMENT: The EEC and the ACP

A READER'S GUIDE TO BRITAIN AND THE EUROPEAN COMMUNITIES

BUILDING EUROPE: Britain's Partners in the EEC (*with K. J. Twitchett*)

EC AID YEARBOOK

EUROPE AND AFRICA: From Association to Partnership

HARMONISATION IN THE EEC (*editor*)

THE EUROPEAN COMMUNITY AND DEVELOPING COUNTRIES
Strategies for the Future (*with J. Jamar*)

THE NEW INTERNATIONAL ACTORS: The United Nations and the European Economic Community (*with K. J. Twitchett*)

TRADE FROM AID: A Business Guide to EC Contracts

The European Union and Developing Countries

The Challenges of Globalization

Edited by

Carol Cosgrove-Sacks
Professor
College of Europe, Bruges
and
Director of Trade
United Nations Economic Commission for Europe

Assistant Editor

Gioia Scappucci
College of Europe, Bruges

Foreword by Jacques Delors

in association with

College of Europe
Collège d'Europe

First published in Great Britain 1999 by
MACMILLAN PRESS LTD
Houndmills, Basingstoke, Hampshire RG21 6XS and London
Companies and representatives throughout the world

A catalogue record for this book is available from the British Library.

ISBN 0–333–71835–6

First published in the United States of America 1999 by
ST. MARTIN'S PRESS, INC.,
Scholarly and Reference Division,
175 Fifth Avenue, New York, N.Y. 10010

ISBN 0–312–21189–9

Library of Congress Cataloging-in-Publication Data
The European Union and developing countries : the challenges of globalization / edited by Carol Cosgrove-Sacks, assisted by Gioia Scappucci ; foreword by Jacques Delors.
p. cm.
Includes bibliographical references and index.
ISBN 0–312–21189–9 (cloth)
1. European Union countries—Foreign economic relations––Developing countries. 2. Developing countries—Foreign economic relations—European Union countries. 3. Competition, International. I. Cosgrove-Sacks, Carol, 1943– II. Scappucci, Gioia.
HF1532.15.D44E87 1997
337.40172'4—dc21 97–40582
CIP

This book is printed on paper suitable for recycling and made from fully managed and sustained forest sources.

10 9 8 7 6 5 4 3
06 07 06 05 04 03 02 01 00

Printed and bound in Great Britain by
Antony Rowe Ltd, Chippenham, Wiltshire

For the students at the College of Europe, Bruges

Contents

List of Tables

Annexes

List of Figures

List of Abbreviations

ACP	African, Caribbean and Pacific States
AEEMTRC	EU–ASEAN Energy Management Training and Research Centre
AFTA	ASEAN Free Trade Area
ALA	Asia and Latin America
ALAMED	Asia, Latin America and Mediterranean Countries
ALCAS	Area de Libre Comercio de America del Sur
ANC	African National Congress
ARTM	Transmediterranean Networks Agency
ASEAN	Association of South East Asian Nations
ATC	Agreement on Textiles and Clothing
CACM	Central American Common Market
CAMU	Central Africa Monetary Union
CAP	Common Agricultural Policy
CCP	Common Commercial Policy
CEECs	Central and Eastern European Countries
CET	Common External Tariff
CFSP	Common Foreign and Security Policy
COREPER	Permanent Representatives Committee
CSCE	Conference on Security and Cooperation in Europe
DAC	Development Assistance Committee
DG	Directorate-General
EBICs	European Business Information Centres
EC	European Community
ECHO	European Community Humanitarian Office
ECIP	European Community Investment Partners
ecu	European Currency Unit
EEA	European Economic Area
EEC	European Economic Community
EGCI	Export Group for the Construction Industries
EIB	European Investment Bank
EMU	European Monetary Union
EP	European Parliament
EU	European Union
FI	financial institution
FTA	free trade area

GATT	General Agreement on Tariffs and Trade
GDP	gross domestic product
GMP	Global Mediterranean Policy
GSP	General System of Preferences
IDA	International Development Association
IGC	1996 Intergovernmental Conference
IMF	International Monetary Fund
JOPP	Joint Venture PHARE Programme
LAFTA	Latin American Free Trade Association
LDC	least developed country
LTA	Long-Term Arrangement on Cotton Textiles
mecu	million ecu
MERCOSUR	Southern Cone Common Market of Argentina, Brazil, Paraguay and Uruguay
MFA	Multifibre Arrangement
MFN	most favoured nation
MFTA	Mediterranean Free Trade Area
MNMCs	Mediterranean Non-Member Countries
MS	member states of the EU
NAFTA	North American Free Trade Area
NGOs	non-governmental organizations
NICs	newly industrialized countries
NTBs	non-tariff barriers
OCT	Overseas Countries and Territories
oda	overseas development assistance
ODA	Overseas Development Administration
OECD	Organization for Economic Cooperation and Development
PHARE	EU Programme for Central and Eastern Europe
R&D	research and development
RMP	Redirected Mediterranean Policy
SAARC	South Asian Association for Regional Cooperation
SACU	Southern African Customs Union
SADC	Southern African Development Community
SEM	Single European Market
SMEs	small and medium-sized enterprises
STA	Short-Term Arrangement on Cotton Textiles
TARIC	Integrated Tariff of the European Communities
TEU	Treaty on the European Union
TMB	Textile Monitoring Body

TRIPS	Trade Related Aspects of Intellectual Property Systems
TSB	Textile Surveillance Body
UNCTAD	United Nations Conference on Trade and Development
UNHCR	United Nations High Commission for Refugees
UNIDO	United Nations Industrial Development Organisation
VAT	value added tax
VERs	Voluntary Exports Restraints Textile Surveillance Body (TSB)
WAMU	West Africa Monetary Union
WEU	Western European Union
WFP	World Food Programme
WTO	World Trade Organization

Foreword

As President of the Council of Administration of the College of Europe, Bruges, I am pleased to write the foreword to this book which results from the 1996 interdisciplinary course on the European Union and developing countries, supervised by Dr Carol Cosgrove-Sacks. The papers examine the forces shaping EU responses to the Third World and demonstrate an acute awareness of fundamental changes taking place in European policies. This book is not only a testimony to the hard work and commitment of the students and staff of the College; it is also a practical guide to future prospects for the European Union's development policies.

The European Union of fifteen member states commands an authoritative position in world affairs. The EU itself is highly dynamic and has convincingly demonstrated its capacity to respond positively and constructively to external change while at the same time expanding its own membership. The EU's development cooperation programmes, its technical assistance to the countries of Eastern and Central Europe, its major role in trade negotiations with the United States and Japan, and the emergence of its common foreign and security policy means that the Union has become the critical reference point for the great nations of Europe to share their sovereignty.

Strategic shifts in the geopolitics of Europe are taking place in a world where imbalances are getting worse, with worldwide competitive pressures and advances in technologies deepening afresh the economic and social inequalities between nations. In other words, the North–South problem is still with us. The EU has a special duty to respond to this problem in an era of increasing globalization. The traditional focus of EU development policy, dating from the origins of the Treaty of Rome in the 1950s, was on Africa and the Mediterranean – a North–South geopolitical axis which in the 1990s has metamorphosed into lateral, global links spanning Eastern and Central Europe, Asia and Latin America. In the course of this metamorphosis, Africa is in danger of being increasingly marginalized and excluded.

Globalization rests on interdependence. For Europe, this means recognition of its major role in the world to promote stability and solidarity. During my time as President of the European Commission

I worked to promote greater solidarity within the Union and to combat social exclusion, especially to ameliorate the conditions of that hitherto sheltered strata of society which in recent years had been plunged into insecurity and almost total lack of income. In international relations I hope that the EU will similarly be an effective instrument to combat the threatened exclusion of Africa and other very poor parts of the world from the benefits of the globalization process. This book will help the reader to understand the forces and factors shaping EU relations with developing countries and will, I trust, focus the resolve of individual European citizens to ensure that the Union uses its enormous economic power to promote sustainable development and stability throughout the world.

JACQUES DELORS

Preface

'The European Union and Developing Countries' is the title of an interdisciplinary course at the College of Europe, Bruges, and since 1983 I have had the privilege and pleasure of teaching it. As part of the Master's Degree in Advanced European Studies, it brings together postgraduate students for whom a special interest – Americans would use the term 'major'– may lie in economics, law, political science or human resources. The course is deliberately designed so that its contents are flexible in response to the constant shifts in European and world events and so encourages students to develop horizontal, multidisciplinary analytical techniques. The aim is that they may come to appreciate the benefits of pluralistic approaches to the study of the European Union and especially its external relations.

This book resulted from the 1996 course, on which twenty-eight students from fifteen countries worked together, producing high level analyses of contemporary trends in EU policies towards the Mediterranean, Africa, Asia and Latin America. The principal background events considered included the inauguration of the World Trade Organization, the implementation of the Uruguay Round agreements, the revision of the Lomé Convention between the EU and seventy African, Caribbean and Pacific States and the implications of the major conferences at Barcelona (November 1995) and Bangkok (March 1996). Respectively, they focused the EU leaders' attention on Mediterranean and Asian trade relations. Globalization became a keynote theme of the 1990s, while at the same time, the emergence of new regional blocks, such as the Asia–Pacific Economic Community and MERCOSUR – the southern common market of Latin America – challenged the newly established rhetoric of worldwide trade liberalization.

Gioia Scappucci, the teaching assistant assigned to the course, was a great help and encouragement to the students and an invaluable aid to me as the course professor. Together, we directed the students to explore the exciting highways and byways of EU relations with developing countries. By the end of the course the students had a sophisticated appreciation of the impact of the EU in the world and, I hope, were better able to take account of the interests of developing countries in their future work as policy shapers throughout European institutions, both at the EU and at national levels.

Geneva 1997 CAROL COSGROVE-SACKS

Acknowledgements

We wish to thank all those at the College of Europe, Bruges, who have made this book possible. The College is a unique centre of excellence for European studies; its reputation is supported by highly qualified and dedicated staff who contribute significantly to its high academic status.

We would like particularly to mention Mr Otto von der Gablentz, the Rector, Mr Thierry Montforti, the Academic Secretary and Head of the Admissions Office, Mr Pierre-Olivier Bergeron, the Director of Communications, Mrs Rosamie Arnout, Programme Coordinator, and Professor Robert Picht, Director, European, General and Interdisciplinary Studies, also, Director, Deutsch-Französisches Institut, Ludwigsburg, Germany, all of whom encouraged and also facilitated the organization and production of this book. Special thanks are due to Jeffrey Sacks in Geneva, who cheerfully and bravely undertook the text editing.

Finally, the opinions expressed in this volume are those of the authors and do not in any way purport to be those of the United Nations or the College of Europe.

CAROL COSGROVE-SACKS
GIOIA SCAPPUCCI

Notes on the Contributors

Emma Ascroft obtained a master's degree at the College of Europe in European politics and administration in 1996, with a thesis on EU/South Africa trade relations. She is a graduate of the University of Edinburgh and has an MA in European studies with French. Emma is now an EU public policy consultant working in the Brussels office of a British company specializing in European public affairs.

Audunn Arnórsson studied modern history and political science at the University of Freiburg, where he finished his first MA degree in 1994 and went on to graduate from the College of Europe in 1996 with a master's degree in Advanced European Studies. He is now a journalist on Iceland's biggest newspaper in Reykjavik.

Ben Atkinson took his MA at the College of Europe in European economic studies in 1996. Prior to that, he graduated from the University of Newcastle upon Tyne with a degree in agricultural economics. He is currently working in London as an economist.

Mercedes Bonet obtained a master's degree in advanced European economic studies at the College of Europe in 1996. She is a graduate of the University of Alicante and obtained an honours degree in commerce at Edinburgh University. She is now writing her PhD thesis on applied economics at the University of Frankfurt.

Ana de Castro is a graduate of the Portuguese Catholic University of Oporto. She worked as a trainee for the European Commission in Brussels before attending the College of Europe, where she graduated as a Master of Law. She now works in the Brussels office of a leading Spanish law firm.

Benedicte Claes took a master's degree in European legal studies in 1996 at the College of Europe. A graduate of the Catholic University of Leuven, she is now a lawyer based in Brussels, working for Van Bael & Bellis.

Carol Cosgrove-Sacks, the editor, is a Professor at the College of Europe, Bruges, and Director of the Trade Division of the United Nations Economic Commission for Europe. A graduate of the London School of Economics (BSc (Econ), MSc (Econ), PhD), she was formerly a consultant on trade and enterprise development and has advised the European Commission, the Commonwealth Secretariat, the ACP Secretariat, many United Nations agencies, governments and corporate clients throughout the world. Her publications include *The EC Aid Yearbook*; *Trade from Aid: A Business Guide to EC Contracts*; *The European Community and Developing Countries – Strategies for the Future*; *A Framework for Development: the EEC and the ACP*; *Building Europe: Britain's Partners in the EEC*; *Harmonisation in the EEC*; *ACP Foreign Trade*; *Europe and Africa: From Association to Partnership*; *A Reader's Guide to Britain and the European Communities* and *The New International Actors: the United Nations and European Economic Community*.

Cathryn Costello gained a master's degree in advanced European legal studies in 1996 at the College of Europe. She is a law graduate of University College, Cork and also studied German law at the University of Cologne. Since graduating, she has worked in the Brussels office of a major international law firm and in the European Commission.

Emanuele Giaufret graduated in political science at the University of Florence, in 1994. He gained a master's degree in advanced European studies in 1996 at the College of Europe. He is currently completing a doctorate in the history of international relations at Florence University, researching EEC development policy from the Rome Treaty to the Yaoundé Convention.

Cybèle-Bénédict Haupert gained a master's degree at the College of Europe in the Administrative and Political Department in 1996. She graduated in political studies and obtained a master's degree in international administration from Panthéon-Sorbonne University, Paris. She is now project coordinator for Portuguese speaking countries in Africa, in a development NGO in Lisbon.

Andrzej Kosnikowski graduated from the College of Europe with a master's degree in advanced European studies in 1996, having previously graduated at the Katowice Academy of Economics, where he was awarded a master's degree in economics. He is now an economic expert based in Warsaw, working in the Government Office of the Committee for European Integration.

Karoline Kowald read for a master's degree in advanced European studies at the College of Europe in 1996. She is a graduate of Innsbruck University and has a master's degree in law and in Spanish philology.

Her doctoral thesis deals with the commercial and cooperation agreements of the EC with Latin American countries and regional groupings.

Sarah Lamigeon read for a master's degree in advanced European studies in the Department of Human Resources at the College of Europe in 1996. She graduated in economics of the University of Bordeaux I with a master's degree in European economics.

Jessica Larson gained a master's degree in advanced European legal studies in 1996 at the College of Europe. She holds a master's degree in law from Stockholm University and is now a lawyer in Luxembourg.

Marc Lemaître read for a master's degree in advanced European studies at the College of Europe in the Economics Department in 1996. He is a graduate of l'Université Libre de Bruxelles and is now a diplomat, working for the Luxembourg Ministry of Foreign Affairs.

Annalisa Oddone graduated in diplomatic and international sciences at the University of Trieste, in Italy and then obtained a master's degree in advanced European studies in 1996, in the Political and Administrative Department at the College of Europe. She is presently working for a consulting company in Brussels.

Maria Pia Pace recently obtained her MA in European political and administrative studies at the College of Europe and read her first degree in business management at the University of Malta. She is currently Second Secretary in the Diplomatic Corps at the Ministry of Foreign Affairs, Malta.

Kai Radtke graduated in 1995 from the Free University of Berlin with a master's degree in political science. He then attended the Political Science and Administration Department of the College and received a master's degree in European politics at the College of Europe. He now works at the European Commission's Delegation in Damascus.

Janick Rajoharison has a double specialization in law and languages. She has a postgraduate degree in European Community law from the Law Faculty of Sceaux, Paris XI, and a diploma in linguistic studies (French, English, German) from the Interpretation and Translation Institute in Paris. She studied for one year at the Law Faculty of Edinburgh University where she gained a diploma in English law. She earned a master's degree in European Community law at the College of Europe in June 1996.

Francisco-Javier Raya is currently working as an associate lawyer at the Brussels office of a leading Spanish law firm. He graduated from the University of Valladolid, then obtained a diploma in advanced European studies at the College of Europe in 1996. He has previously worked as a lawyer in the United States and as a *stagiaire* at the Delegation of the European Commission to the United Nations in New York, where he monitored meetings of both the Security Council and ECOSOC.

Gioia Scappucci, the editorial assistant, graduated in political sciences at 'La Sapienza' University in Rome in 1994 with a thesis on 'The UN Protection of Ethnic, Religious and Cultural Minorities'. In 1995 she obtained the College of Europe master's degree in European political and administrative studies. Currently she is a Teaching Assistant at the College's Political and Administrative Department. Her fields of research include EU policy on development cooperation, social, justice and home affairs. She is preparing a PhD on EU food aid. She has written *The Humanitarian Aid of the EU: 'Alibi, Smokescreen or Solidarity Action?' The Response of the EU to the Humanitarian Disaster in Rwanda and* a chapter on 'Italy and European Integration', in *The Governmental Conference 1996.*

Philip Tod graduated with a master's degree in European political and administrative studies in 1996 at the College of Europe. He is a graduate in government from the London School of Economics and Political Science and is now a consultant with Hill & Knowlton, a leading public affairs company in Brussels.

Joost Vandenborre gained a master's degree in advanced European studies in 1996 at the College of Europe and holds a master's degree in history from the University of Ghent and a diploma in international relations from the University of Leuven. A former research fellow at the Jawaharlal Nehru University in New Delhi, he is now a research assistant at the College and is attached to the Secretariat General of the Commission in Brussels.

Part 1

Forces Shaping EU Development Policy

1 EU Development Cooperation in Perspective

Carol Cosgrove-Sacks

SETTING THE SCENE

The globalization of the world economy and the elimination of the Cold War has fundamentally changed the geopolitical context of Europe's relations with developing countries. Moreover, the European Union itself has undergone profound transformation in the process of enlargement to fifteen member states. The myriad network of 'special relationships' contracted with more than a hundred countries in Africa, the Mediterranean, Asia and Latin America has created a pyramid of preferences within which Europe's obligations to one region often seem incompatible with those to another. These obligations, in terms of both aid and trade concessions, cumulatively constitute the threads from which the tapestry of European development cooperation is woven.

Europe has a colonial legacy that continues to shape these relationships. The original Treaty of Rome establishing the European Economic Community (EEC) recognized the African colonial legacies of the then six member states.[1] During the last forty years the principal participants in the European integration process have exerted varying degrees of influence, often in contradictory directions, on Europe's relations with developing countries. The result is an essentially regional set of relationships that has become, according to Enzo Grilli of the International Monetary Fund, 'both an anachronism and a straightjacket of EC Europe'.[2]

The European Community (EC) remains in strict legal terms the partner of the developing countries rather than the European Union (EU). It is the EC treaties that define the competence of the Community institutions and those of the member states regarding trade and common aid provisions. In the late 1990s, however, the Union dominates both the conceptual high ground and the perception of third countries towards the now fifteen member states. To what extent does the EU have an active development cooperation policy? What are the main influences that shape its aid and trade relations with developing countries? Will the twenty-first century usher in a major metamorphosis of these relations? This volume of essays addresses these important questions, focusing especially on EU–developing country links in the mid 1990s, within the overall historical perspective of forty years of common endeavour in external economic relations.

THE CONTENT OF THIS BOOK

This volume contains the written papers presented by the students at the College of Europe, Bruges, who participated in the interdisciplinary course 'The European Union and Developing Countries' during the academic semester January–June 1996, which is part of the course leading to the Masters Degree in European Studies. The students work mainly within one of three major disciplines – law, economics and political science – and come together for selected classes where they bring their common analytical skills to bear regarding important aspects of the EU's development. External relations in general and relations with developing countries in particular demand a knowledge of all three major analytical approaches and the essays collected here display a unique mix of both academic and national backgrounds. The authors of the papers come from fifteen countries – Austria, Belgium, France, Germany, Hungary, Iceland, Ireland, Italy, Luxembourg, Malta, Poland, Portugal, Spain, Sweden and the United Kingdom. Working closely together, they have succeeded in creating a varied and interesting survey of contemporary developments in this important area of EU external relations.

The volume comprises five parts: Part 1, on The Forces Shaping EU Development Policy; Part 2, on the Lomé Convention; Part 3, on the Mediterranean challenge; Part 4, on EU cooperation with Asia and Latin America and Part V on commercial instruments of EU development policy.

Part 1, which includes this opening chapter, examines the forces shaping the macroeconomic and political determinants of EU priorities towards developing countries. It goes on to analyse the respective roles of the European Commission and the European Court of Justice in development cooperation. Chapter 2 indicates that this area of common endeavour has afforded the European Commission a unique opportunity to play a role in international diplomacy, albeit in the less dramatic field of external economic relations rather than the high-profile aspect of foreign policy. Article 113 of the Treaty of Rome allocated clear competence to the Commission regarding a common commercial policy, which has enabled the Commission to play a dynamic role as the motor mechanism of development cooperation. By 1996 it had established more than 140 delegations in third countries and was operating in effect as a major international aid and trade development agency, being acknowledged as the initiator of common EU development policies and responsible for implementing them throughout the world. Chapter 3 examines the role of the European Court of Justice in this area, where it has had a significant but often underestimated influence on the form of EU policies. The chapter analyses the Court's role in interpreting the treaties and in determining institutional competencies, concluding that the Court has been very important in defining the external powers and guiding principles of Europe's relations with developing countries.

The priorities of the member states have so far proved to be the most powerful set of forces shaping the Community's development cooperation. During different periods of the European integration process, individual states or alliances between two or three states have exerted crucial pressure to move the relationship forwards. France and French policy priorities have dominated this process since the mid 1950s, although in the 1990s German interests, centred more on Central and Eastern Europe, have successfully counterbalanced the perspective from Paris of the EU's role in the world. Chapter 4 examines the record of French commitment to Africa as the core of Europe's concern with developing countries, which first prompted the inclusion of association of overseas countries and territories in the Rome Treaty and subsequently led to the Yaoundé Conventions and the Lomé Conventions with the African, Caribbean and Pacific (ACP) states. It analyses the evolution of policy from President de Gaulle to President Chirac, which has demonstrated remarkable continuity throughout forty years. Nevertheless, contemporary French policy espouses the goals of democracy, stable institutional development and sustainable economic growth in its former client states, emphasizing the role of EU aid and trade instruments in promoting structural adjustment,[3] private sector enterprise and investment in viable, export-oriented projects. The chapter demonstrates that France still maintains its historical commitment to Africa and continues to promote active EU policy towards that continent, but at the same time French initiatives regarding the Euro-Mediterranean partnership and the Euro-Asian Summit in Bangkok in 1996 presage fundamental changes in future reorientations.

Chapter 5 looks at the United Kingdom and the Lomé Convention, tracing the often contradictory pressures at work in shaping British policy towards EU cooperation with developing countries. The Lomé Convention itself represents a recognition of British obligations in the post-colonial period to the weaker members of the Commonwealth, and London's willingness to exclude the Asian countries from the special relationship with Europe. This chapter focuses especially on aid relations, the increasing role of multilateral commitments in British aid and the political controversies in the 1990s regarding the decline in British bilateral aid. In recent years the concern over aid effectiveness and the introduction of market reforms in recipient countries has guided British policy towards the Lomé Convention, with an increasing insistence on conditionality regarding democracy, human rights and good government in the ACP states. In the 1990s the United Kingdom has limited its commitment to the Lomé Convention and has sought the freedom to maintain its own bilateral aid budget as an instrument of foreign policy, albeit that the British government also remains an advocate of the development of EU common foreign and security policies – but negotiated on the basis of national interests.

The Mediterranean states, specifically Italy, Spain and Portugal, have exerted an increasingly significant influence on EU policies towards developing countries in the 1990s. Chapter 6 examines each of these national policies, attempting to define priorities with respect to both the Lomé Convention and to the wider area of EU development cooperation. Italy's historical interests in Eastern Africa, particularly in Somalia, Ethiopia and Eritrea, have prompted close coordination between Italian bilateral aid and the Lomé Convention. At the same time, Italy has long supported the development of a more dynamic and better focused European policy towards Latin America and the Mediterranean. In this regard, Spain is a close ally of Italy, although it should be remembered that both Spain and Portugal are relatively new EU members, having joined in 1986. Only Portugal brought an extension of colonial legacies to the EU, although its erstwhile African colonies were in any event within the ACP group. The analysis identifies these three countries as the bridge for new areas of common EU policies towards the Middle East, the Mediterranean and Latin America.

The contribution of the Nordic countries to EU development cooperation is examined in Chapter 7. While Denmark joined alongside the United Kingdom and Ireland in 1973, Finland and Sweden have participated in the EU only since January 1996. Development policy has proved to be fertile ground for a common Nordic approach, with a commitment to coordinated multilateralism and a focus on poverty alleviation strategies. The Nordic group meet at least twice a year[4] and have reached a high degree of correlation between their collective goals in development cooperation and those of the Lomé Convention. They place priority on good governance, democracy and respect for human rights, together with strict standards of accountability and efficiency in the use of public funds. They also stress the potential role for non-governmental organizations (NGOs) in stimulating sustainable economic development. The author argues that the influence of the Nordic countries is likely to be for the positive benefit of the developing countries and will improve the quality of EU aid.

Part 2 has six chapters on the Lomé Convention and the various instruments of EU–ACP policies. With its origins in the mid 1970s, the Lomé Convention was a product of the oil crisis and the aspirations towards a new international economic order. It mirrored Europe's concern with interdependence, the perceived need to protect raw material and commodity supplies, and, in the words of the former President of the European Commission Jacques Delors, the need also to 'promote an original and more balanced relationship with the South'.[5] Lomé I was signed in 1975, Lomé II in 1979, Lomé III in 1985 and Lomé IV in December 1989, in the immediate aftermath of the collapse of communism in East Germany but before its wider implications became clear. Twenty years ago the Lomé Convention really was an innovative response to the challenge of North–South relations, providing a structured framework of institutions based on parity and a comprehensive trade and aid deal. Successive Lomé Conventions have included progressively more ACP states – increasing from 46 in 1975 to 70 in 1996 and possibly 71 in 1998 depending on how one classifies the arrangements under negotiation between the EU and South Africa.

Chapter 8 examines the review of Lomé IV in 1995 and the resulting Lomé IVB, scheduled to enter into force early in 1997. It comments on the continuity of the Lomé relationship, based on an international legal framework agreed between the European countries on the one side and the ACP states on the other on a formal basis of parity, with comprehensive cooperation covering trade development and preferences, stabilization of export earnings,[6] maintenance of mineral production[7] and a wide variety of financial instruments channelled through the European Development Fund (EDF) and the European Investment Bank (EIB). This chapter examines the revision of the aid arrangements, including the debate within the EU on financing the EDF, which remains outside the European budget and hence beyond the control of the European Parliament; measures to promote the private sector; revised conditions governing access to the European market, particularly in the aftermath of the achievement of the Single European Market for most goods and services; and the examination of new priorities in the wake of the Maastricht Treaty with its unambiguous message that the ACP states need to be assisted to be more fully integrated in the global economy.

The record of the trade provisions of the Lomé Convention is examined in Chapter 9. In 1975 at the time of the signature of the first convention, the ACP accounted for 3.4 per cent of total EC imports; by 1985 this had declined to 3.2 per cent and by 1995 to 1.4 per cent.[8] Average EC import growth between 1985 and 1995 was more than 12 per cent, while EC imports from the ACP grew at only 7 per cent over the same period. For the ACP states as a group, revenue from trade is significantly more important for their economic growth than their aid receipts.[9] The chapter analyses the record of ACP–EC trade, examines the allegations that the Lomé Convention has 'failed' and attempts to define the various factors that account for the poor export development record of the ACP, many of which are far beyond the scope of the Lomé arrangements, especially price instability on global commodity markets. The analysis looks at the new focus on trade development on Lomé IVB and briefly assesses the likely impact of the Uruguay Round on the ACP's special relationship with Europe.

The European Development Fund is investigated in Chapter 10. Established by the Rome Treaty, the EDF has proved to be one of the most durable and flexible instruments of assistance to developing countries. The European member states collectively assume responsibility for the regular replenishment of the Fund in accordance with successive financial protocols negotiated alongside the conventions and it is managed by the European Commission Directorate-General VIII subject to the supervision of the EDF Committee which comprises the member states and the Commission. This chapter examines the judicial basis of the Fund, its structure and financing procedures, the management and supervision of its operations,and the negotiations for EDF VIII that will support the aid provisions of Lomé IVB.

The European Investment Bank, the subject of Chapter 11, also contributes to ACP economic development and manages some aspects of the EDF programme where its expertise of loan operations is particularly relevant. The EIB, which obtains its capital from the member states and from international capital markets, enjoys a credit rating of 'AAA' and is a cautious institution. Its operations in the ACP states comprise loans from its own resources and the management of the risk capital allocated by the EDF. Under Lomé IVB, the EIB has made a provisional allocation to each of the ACP states. However, it remains to be seen whether viable projects with a sufficient rate of return will be identified; the ACP states should remember that above all, the EIB is a *bank* which expects both capital and interest to be reimbursed, even if the latter is at subsidized rates.

The possible accession of South Africa to Lomé IVB is the subject of Chapter 12; at the time of writing this is under negotiation in a rather limited form. The potential solution – known quaintly as 'Lomé Minus' – would make South Africa a signatory of the Convention and thus a participant in the ACP Group and in ACP–EU institutions, but would exclude South Africa from both the aid and trade provisions. The relative level of development of some sectors of the South African economy and its trade structure with the EU have combined to prompt a somewhat protectionist response from some of the member states, who have successfully insisted that a free trade area would be the most appropriate solution. Moreover, the GATT refused to recognize developing country status for South Africa, so full participation in the Lomé Convention trade provisions could have prompted objections from other major trading partners in the World Trade Organization (WTO). A special European Programme for Reconstruction and Development (EPRD) is under negotiation, with a provisional budget of 500 million ecu for 1996–9.

The role of the EU in humanitarian aid is the subject of Chapter 13, which examines the operations of the European Community Humanitarian Office (ECHO), which reports to the European Commission separately from both DG IB and DG VIII. ECHO was set up in 1992 with a flexible mandate to respond to disasters and emergencies throughout the world, including in the former Yugoslavia and the former Soviet Union. The objective is to permit ECHO to use a simplified form of financial decision-making which enables it to respond fast to emergency situations where humanitarian assistance is required. ECHO has established operational partnerships with several major relief agencies, especially the United Nations High Commission for Refugees (UNHCR) and the International Committee of the Red Cross and Red Crescent, but also with many smaller, more local NGOs. The ECHO budget rose from 353 million ecu in 1993 to 840 million ecu in 1995, making it one of the principal funding agencies in the world dealing with humanitarian relief operations.

Part 3 assesses the record of EU cooperation with the Mediterranean countries that are not so far members. Chapter 14 analyses the emerging 'Mediterranean partnership' boosted by the Barcelona Conference of November 1995. It comments on the stark contrasts between the northern and southern shores of the Mediterranean basin, the imbalance of economic activity in the region, the dependence of the South on the North, especially on access to the EU market, and the threats posed to stability and security by civil wars, such as in Algeria, and by social unrest, as in Egypt. The EU's so-called Global Mediterranean Policy, launched in the 1970s, failed to deliver a comprehensive framework for EU relations with the countries of the region and the new Euro-Mediterranean partnership is designed to redress these problems and create a dynamic vehicle for aid and trade flows. It is also designed to play a part in the Organization for Security and Cooperation in Europe (OSCE), boosting security and aiming to build a 'zone of shared prosperity' by 2010. A wide range of EU-funded cooperation programmes and the goal of establishing a Mediterranean free trade area are seen as a response to the challenge of potentially increased emigration from the southern shore to the EU.

The intensive EU cooperation with Cyprus, Malta and Turkey is reviewed in Chapter 15. These three countries share the goal of accession to the EU and their individual relations are analysed in terms of the historical development and the key issues in the separate sets of negotiations. In the case of Cyprus, the divided island presents severe political problems for the EU, in which Greece in particular is committed to blocking any measures that would prolong what it and the United Nations sees as Turkish occupation of the northern part of the island. Cyprus applied for EU membership in 1990 and the European Commission reported favourably in 1993 but also identified some severe problems, not least its small size. Nevertheless, the European Summit meeting in Corfu in 1994 made a commitment that the next phase of EU enlargement would include Cyprus and Malta. The latter has enjoyed a preferential association agreement with the EU since

1970, and in 1995 the EU declared that membership negotiations could begin with Malta six months after the conclusion of the EU Intergovernmental Conference (IGC), currently scheduled to end in 1997.[10]

Turkey has been associated with the European Community since 1963 and in 1996 a customs union with the EU came into operation. Turkey's long-term goal still remains membership of the EU, but major political and economic obstacles need to be overcome before serious negotiations could even commence.

Future prospects depend ultimately on Israel, the other major economy in the region, which has enjoyed a preferential trade agreement with the EC since 1970, revised in 1975 and again in 1995. The new agreement will provide an association based on political dialogue and the gradual establishment of a free trade area within the overall context of the Euro-Mediterranean Partnership, examined in Chapter 16.

Part 4 directs attention from the centre to the periphery, to EU relations with Asia and Latin America. It is instructive to recall that in the late 1950s at the time of the establishment of the European Community, Africa and European–African trade was viewed as more important than these two continents. At that time Asia was largely regarded as chronically poor and underdeveloped, with problems on a scale that no European grouping could hope to alleviate. The threat of communism throughout South-East Asia and the racial and religious problems besetting both that region and South Asia were real deterrents to the infant EC institutions, and even after British membership in 1973 there was no significant revision of priorities. Similarly, Latin America was seen as part of the American sphere of influence, with exports that would compete either with those of the African states (such as cocoa, coffee and copper) or with the embryonic European Common Agricultural Policy (wheat, beef and vegetable oils). Apart from some non-preferential trade agreements in the 1960s and 1970s, it was not until the late 1980s that a more strategic approach was developed by the EU towards these fast-growing regions.

The European Community Investment Partners (ECIP) scheme is an attempt to respond to the dynamism of these economies. Chapter 17 examines its origins in 1988 and its focus on promoting foreign direct investment from Europe to Asia, Latin America and the Mediterranean together with its avowed private sector and enterprise development goals. It reflects the conviction of the Delors Commission that job creation and economic growth can best be stimulated by a private–public sector partnership, with the promotion of joint ventures between EU firms and those in the beneficiary countries as the principal initial objective. The ECIP scheme is targeted to small and medium-sized enterprises (SMEs), although larger companies have in practice been best equipped to use its somewhat cumbersome financing techniques. Between 1988 and 1995 some 173 million ecu was provided by the EU to support the scheme, which is judged to be a success.

EU relations with the Association of South-East Asian Nations (ASEAN) are the subject of Chapter 18. The founding ASEAN countries were Indonesia, Malaysia, Philippines, Singapore and Thailand and they have been joined by Brunei and most recently by Vietnam and Burma. This chapter analyses the evolution of institutional and trade relations between the two blocs and traces its shift from what began essentially as a donor–recipient relationship to a partnership of equals. The 1980 EC–ASEAN Cooperation Agreement remains the basis for trade relations, which have expanded hugely, although the EU has run a deficit with ASEAN since 1985 despite protectionist measures like the Common Agricultural Policy, the Multifibre Arrangement (MFA) and ceilings on the Generalized System of Preferences (GSP). The EU has also funded regional technology centres in several ASEAN countries and encouraged European–Asian joint ventures, including the ECIP scheme. The first Euro-Asian Summit held in 1996 in Bangkok included the ASEAN countries together with China, Japan and South Korea, marking a new era in these multilateral relations. India was not invited to the summit meeting, despite a long-established commercial cooperation agreement with the EU. Chapter 19 examines EU relations with India, which is currently the fifth largest economy in the world and is forecast to enjoy spectacular growth in the final years of the twentieth century. The 1973 Agreement provided a framework for India to benefit from the EC's GSP, but it did not enjoy preferential access to the European market. In 1981 a revised agreement was signed that extended cooperation and encouraged more private sector involvement. In 1994 a new agreement was ratified by the EU, intensifying institutional cooperation and designed to stimulate foreign direct investment in India and support sustainable development, not least by assisting India to improve its industrial environment and to aid India's training and human resources programmes.

Chapter 20 examines the EU's relations with the Andean Group Bolivia, Columbia, Ecuador, Peru and Venezuela.[11] The result of the analysis is that Latin America is still on the periphery of EU external relations and that these countries do not command priority attention in Brussels. The Andean Group was founded in 1969 and revised in 1987 in an attempt to strengthen intra-regional trade; a free trade area has existed among four of the signatories, other than Peru, since 1987. In 1995 the trade arrangements were revised again to take account of MERCOSUR (Argentina, Brazil, Paraguay and Uruguay) and a customs union will gradually be established between the two organizations. The 'political dialogue' between the EU and the Andean Group dates back to 1984, having been aimed at supporting the promotion of peace and stability in Central America and was extended to the Rio Group, including both Andean and MERCOSUR together with Mexico, Chile and Panama. This process is underpinned by a range of Euro-Latin American parliamentary conferences. In the context of economic relations, the GSP remains the principal instrument of EU–Latin America trade cooperation and the Latin American countries bitterly oppose the EU's Common Agricultural Policy, hoping that the reforms agreed in the Uruguay Round and incorporated into the new WTO regime will gradually open the European market to their principal exports.

Part 5 examines the commercial instruments of EU policies towards developing countries. Chapter 21 focuses on the common external tariff and preferential access to the EU market, especially the GSP. The analysis presents the EU's pyramid of preferences and the relative importance of the EU's major trading partners, EFTA and the USA being by far the most important, with Japan together accounting for more than 50 per cent of it external trade. The common external tariff has been reduced by each successive GATT round of trade negotiations and after the Uruguay Round it was calculated to have an average of only 3 per cent.[12] However, this low average obscures some high tariffs for sensitive products and the wide range of non-tariff barriers, especially in such sectors as temperate agriculture, textiles and clothing, coal, steel and shoes. The GSP provides a means for eligible developing countries to gain reduced tariff access to the EU market. The EU scheme was revised after the completion of the Single European Market and the Uruguay Round, and the new arrangements came into force in January 1995; at the time of writing it is too soon to assess the results. Key characteristics of the revised GSP are modulation of tariffs in four groups, more generous cumulation of the rules on originating products and the concept of graduation whereby countries which derive major advantages of the scheme are 'graduated' out of it as they become more competitive. There is a separate and more limited arrangement for agricultural products.

A more detailed analysis of EU–developing country trade in the textiles and clothing sector is found in Chapter 22 on the MFA and the Uruguay Round. The EU has worked with other industrialized countries to limit the market penetration of textiles and clothing from developing countries through a series of international arrangements imposed on exporting countries. The MFA has been the most comprehensive and long-lasting set of restrictions, but it is due to be dismantled as part of the Uruguay Round agreements. The heart of the MFA is a series of bilateral deals between importing and exporting countries, and the European Commission has negotiated them on behalf of the member states. By 1993 the EU had imposed MFA restrictions on 23 developing countries, but it is important to note that the 70 ACP states are exempt from the MFA by virtue of the trade provisions of the Lomé Convention.

The WTO as a new framework for trade relations between the EU and developing countries is examined in Chapter 23. The WTO came into existence in 1995, with its Geneva-based secretariat replacing the GATT secretariat. Its members are the signatories of the Uruguay Round agreements, so excluding many developing countries and most of the countries with transition economies which were formerly part of the Soviet bloc. The WTO rests on reciprocal most-favoured-nation treatment between its members, with derogations permitted only under special circumstances, such as the creation of a customs union, a free trade area or a very low level of economic development. It is a rules-based organization, perhaps best suited to managing trade between the principal industrialized countries who have shaped its structure so decisively. The WTO has left the GATT Anti-Dumping Code almost intact, making it possible for the EU and others to impose restrictions on exports of developing countries on grounds of unfair competition. The analysis focuses on the implications for the ACP and other developing countries of the Uruguay Round reforms, and looks ahead to how the EU might deal with the interests of developing countries regarding the new issues of intellectual property, trade-related investment measures and the regulation of trade in services.

The book concludes with a chapter on globalization and the prospects for integrating EU trade with developing countries into the world economy, and the likely evolution of European development cooperation policies by the end of the century. The globalization of trade and the marginalization of the poorest countries, including most of the ACP states, is forecast as having a fundamental impact on the future shape and direction of EU relations with developing countries. The final chapter examines the driving forces of globalization and the response of the EU. The search for competitiveness in world markets and increasing liberalization through the WTO have highlighted the uneven impact of globalization. The EU has recognized the need to adapt its predominantly regionalist network of special relationships with developing countries to the overriding demands of globalization. However, there is a lack of consensus in both the EU and the ACP regarding a possible successor treaty to the Lomé Convention, which is due to expire in the year 2000, and this demonstrates the difficulty of creating a sufficiently flexible framework for EU cooperation with developing countries.

Bibliography

Cosgrove, Carol, *A Framework for Development: The EEC and the ACP* (Allen & Unwin, London, 1981).

Deardon, S., 'The European Union and the Third World', in McDonald, F., and Deardon S., *European Economic Integration*, 2nd edn (1994).

Jacques Delors, *Our Europe* (Verso Press, London and Paris, 1992).

Grilli, E., *The European Community and the Developing Countries* (Cambridge University Press, 1993).

Tsoukalis L., *The New European Economy* (Oxford University Press, 1993).

Notes

1. For an analysis of the origins and early development of EEC relations with developing countries, see Cosgrove (1981).
2. Grilli (1993) p. 343.
3. The 50 per cent devaluation of the CFA franc in January 1994 is the most spectacular evidence of this hard-fought battle.
4. Including Norway, which is a member of the European Economic Area but not in the EU.
5. Delors (1992) p. 20.
6. The STABEX scheme.
7. The SYSMIN scheme.
8. Calculated from Eurostat statistics.
9. Deardon (1994) pp. 234–270.
10. See *EU Bulletin*, 3/95, p. 72.
11. Colombia, Peru, Ecuador, Venezuela and Bolivia, and MERCOSUR – Brazil, Argentina, Paraguay and Uruguay.
12. Tsoukalis (1993) p. 278.

2 The Role of the European Commission

Benedicte Claes

Development policy is a cornerstone of European integration. Today it is a manifestation of Europe's identity in the world at large and a major plank in the Community's external policies generally. (Commission's Memorandum on Community Development Policy, 1992)

INTRODUCTION

The European Community was set up primarily as a means to strive towards an integration of internal interests, but the Community's development cooperation policy came into being at the same time. As development policy forms part of the more general context of the Community's external relations, it helps to enhance the Community's presence on the world stage.

The Treaty of Rome and successive policy developments and treaties, culminating in the agreements reached at Maastricht in 1991, gave the Commission a pivotal function in this field. It is regarded both as a source and as a channel for policy-making.[1]

This chapter begins by exploring the legal foundations and general principles laid down in the Treaty of Rome and its successors. Second, it examines the structure of the competent Commission bodies and the resulting coordination problems. Third, it identifies the key elements in policy formation and implementation. Finally, after assessing its important role in negotiating international agreements, it looks at the ways the Commission carries out its representation role.

LEGAL ASPECTS AND GUIDING PRINCIPLES

The importance of the appropriate legal basis is not merely formal, taking into account that the decision-making procedure sets forth totally different rules when it deals with art. 113 or with art. 235. Article 235 requires unanimity and compulsory consultation with the European Parliament, whereas art. 113 asks for a qualified majority but does not provide for consultation. On this legal basis, the Community has developed a range of multilateral, bilateral and regional agreements that include almost all the developing countries in the world.

With the insertion of Title XVII (Development Cooperation) into the Treaty of Rome by the TEU, things changed radically. Articles 130u–130y finally established the Community with an explicit competence to elaborate an EC development and cooperation policy, which complements the policies of the individual member states. In most cases it will not be necessary to rely on art. 235. Qualified majority and compulsory consultation with the European Parliament are becoming the common rule in adopting the major instruments of development policy. These include: cooperation and partnership agreements with the developing countries of Asia and Latin America, programmes of financial and technical assistance to these countries, the food aid programme of the Community, etc. From now on, those measures are founded on art. 130w or 130y and art. 228. Article 238 continues to govern the relations between the Community and the ACP countries. The Overseas Countries and Territories still fall within the scope of art. 131–136a.[2]

The guiding principles of EC development policy are listed in the Maastricht Treaty and have been explained in more detail in a Commission communication on development cooperation in the run-up to 2000.[3] These principles are: complementarity (art. 130u), coordination (art. 130x), coherence between different EC policies (art. 130v) and geographical weighting.

THE ROLE OF THE COMMISSION IN DEVELOPMENT POLICY: A CLOSER LOOK

The Commission: Structure

Although the Commission is the main actor in coordinating common policies, the structure of the body itself reflects little coordination. The bipolar structure of the external relations of the Union, divided into Common Foreign and Security Policy (CFSP) and Community issues, sometimes creates a lack of coherence on the international scene. The problems of harmonizing different external relations of the Union can also be seen in the organization of the several Directorates-General responsible for external policy and in particular in those responsible for development policy.

The current Santer Commission divides external relations into four different services: Directorate General (DG) IA, DG IB, DG I and DG VIII.[4] Two DGs are discussed here. DG IB (South), is under the management of Manuel Marin and deals with relations between the Community and the Southern Mediterranean, the Middle and Near East, Latin America, Asia (apart from Japan, China, South Korea, Hong Kong, Macao and Taiwan), and with issues of development aid. The other is DG VIII, under the management of João de Deus Pinheiro, which is competent for relations with the ACP countries, South Africa, and the Lomé Conventions.

Management of the many different policies which influence developing countries is scattered among several DGs and consequently several commissioners. This makes adequate resolution of the problems more difficult to achieve. If we take the case of Ruanda as an example, where does development cooperation end and where does CFSP start? If we were dealing with a single decision-making framework, it would not matter that much if a policy, set up in a Third World country like Ruanda, pertains to the domain of development cooperation or to CFSP. Since we are dealing with the Union, there are two different voting requirements: qualified majority in the first case and unanimity in the second.

Even then, the real problem is to be found elsewhere, in particular in the fact that an action undertaken in the field of development policy has consequences at the level of CFSP and vice versa. If the Council decides to take action at CFSP level (by unanimity) and at the same time the Community intervenes with a measure of development aid as part of the Lomé Convention, what is then the significance of that measure on the international scene? And what if the Council fails to obtain a decision because of an active veto in the field of CFSP – how will this look to the outside world if the only measure taken is one at the level of development aid?

After this analysis, it is quite clear that initiatives should be taken to realise a global and single context on different levels: first of all on the decision-making level and afterwards in the field of concrete implementation of the decisions taken. In its preparatory report on the Intergovernmental Conference of 1996, the Commission stressed the importance of better coordination between the interventions of the Union and its member states in order to render all EU development cooperation more credible.[5]

Also relevant is the setting up of the European Community Humanitarian Office, better known as ECHO. On 24 July 1991, the Commission decided to create ECHO. Following Council approval in December 1991, it was officially created in April 1992. Before January 1995, ECHO fell under the responsibility of the commissioner for development, cooperation and humanitarian aid, Manuel Marin. Since the installation of the new Santer Commission, a special commissioner for humanitarian aid was appointed (Emma Bonino).

Her office has the task of managing humanitarian aid to all countries outside the Union and its specific working areas are: general humanitarian aid, emergency humanitarian aid, emergency food aid, aid for refugees and displaced persons and disaster response. ECHO being a tool of the foreign policy of the EU and its member states, we may ask whether it has anything to do with development policy. What is more, in the need for humanitarian aid to developing countries, we could see evidence of the failure of the development policy of the developed countries, more particularly of the EU and its member states.

The Commission: Competencies

Coordination and Complementarity

In every task the Commission fulfils, it tries to implement to the fullest extent the development cooperation principles of complementarity and coordination between the Community's development policy and those of the member states.

Complementarity Between the Community's Development Cooperation and those of the member states. Article 130u of the EC Treaty stipulates, among other things, that Community policy shall be 'complementary to the policies pursued by the member states'. In order to avoid further inefficiencies between member states' development aid, the Commission seemed to propose in its communication of May 1992; 'Development Cooperation Policy in the Run-up to 2000', a harmonization of aid policies within the Community in order to achieve a gradual transfer towards a common approach to development cooperation.

But the ambitions of the Commission were strongly tempered by the reluctance of the member states to engage in a common development policy. Most of them still consider external policy as pertaining to national sovereignty. Others are worried by the EU administration's lack of institutional capacity and by the problems of transparency and the lack of sufficient democratic control of aid management. Consequently, the main instrument for complementarity is better coordination at political, operational and national levels.[6]

Coordination between the European Community and its member states. This need for coordination has also been officially introduced by the TEU in art. 130x. It stipulates that the Community and the member states shall co-ordinate their policies and consult one another on their aid programmes, and generally act together in international organizations and at international conferences. While the Commission may take any useful initiative to promote coordination of national efforts in this field, the Treaty emphasizes in art. 130 y the double-sided nature of the arrangements envisaged under this title, so that the member states' competence in negotiating with international bodies and concluding international agreements is safeguarded.[7]

Although coordination has already increased considerably over the last decade, the situation is still far from perfect. First of all, the chances of progress are limited as long as there is a lack of consensus on the scope of CFSP, of which development cooperation forms a part. Second, complementarity sometimes appears to be just a handy tool to avoid sponsors hindering one another. Third, when it comes to coordinating those sponsors, the results are not very hopeful; they all agree on the need for coordination but none of them wants to be coordinated. Finally, priority should be given to internal coordination problems within the Commission (i.e. integration of the several aid instruments of the EU should be achieved, and the fusion of DG VIII with DG I South is desirable).

The Influence of the Commission in Different Phases of the Decision-making Process in Development Cooperation

The Initiator of Policy Formation. According to art. 155 s. 3, 'the Commission shall have its own power of decision and participate in the shaping of measures taken by the Council and by the European Parliament ...'. In bestowing on the Commission this initiator role regarding common policies, the interests of the Communities are safeguarded. In assisting in the formulation of policy the Commission first engages in consultations with interested parties at political and civil service levels in the developing countries, with the other Community institutions and with the administrations of the member states. As such they are able to exchange views and to focus the discussion on urgent needs. Then the development expertise of DG IB and DG VIII proceeds to consideration of policy proposals until the Commission reaches its final position, which is submitted to the Council.[8]

The inter-institutional coordination process between the Commission and the member states on the one hand and the administrations of the developing countries on the other is most intensive when decisions on concrete programmes and projects are taken. In support of the Commission, several committees were established in which the member states are represented (management committees, implementation committees, *ad hoc* committees). According to the 1995 budget, there are four standing committees in the area of development policy, viz. a food aid committee, a committee on financial and technical assistance and economic cooperation with developing countries in Asia and Latin America, a European Development Fund committee and a committee on the Southern and Eastern Mediterranean. The rules of procedure and their influence in the decision-making process vary from committee to committee, but in all cases their influence is decisive and not purely consultative.[9]

Implementation of Common Policies. In theory, the Commission alone is responsible for the implementation of Community aid. But the practice of cooperation under the Lomé Conventions makes clear that the implementation of projects is done by national authorities of the developing countries in close cooperation with the Commission's delegate on the spot. Each ACP country appoints a representative, the national authorizing officer (NAO), who is responsible for the implementation and works with the Commission, the national administrations and private firms.

The Commission delegates carry out the field research for the implementation of the indicative programmes and liaise with the necessary authorities. It has been argued, however, that such delegations should be given more individual decision-making powers. As they have constantly to pass the power of decision to Brussels, this prolongs the implementation phase of projects which often results in a loss of project revenue in real terms.

As regards the implementation of Community financial aid (consisting of aid from the European Development Fund, the general

Community budget and loans from the European Investment Bank), the Commission and the European Investment Bank cooperate closely, because they jointly administer the resources of the European Development Fund (the main aid instrument for ACP countries, which is financed through national contributions). The Commission is in charge of grants, special loans, STABEX (the scheme for stabilising export earnings) and SYSMIN (loans for mining companies) while the EIB takes the interest rate subsidies and risk capital for its account. The Commission also has an influence on the general budget of the EU because art. 203 para, 2 bestows on the Commission the task of making the preliminary draft budget. The latter is then sent to the Council, which is obliged to consult the Commission when it intends to depart from the Commission's proposals. This general budget contains also a chapter entitled 'Cooperation with Developing and Non-member Countries', and most of these resources go to non-ACP countries, i.e. countries in the Mediterranean area and developing countries in Asia and Latin America.

The Negotiator of International Agreements

Article 130y, as introduced by the TEU, refers to international cooperation in the field of development policy. It provides that:

> Within their respective spheres of competence, the Community and the member states shall cooperate with third countries and with the competent international organizations. The arrangements for Community cooperation may be the subject of agreements between the Community and the third parties concerned, which shall be negotiated and concluded in accordance with Article 228.

According to art. 228 of the TEU, the preliminary phase in negotiating agreements consists of informal contacts and conversations carried out by the Commission, mostly at the request of third parties. The Commission makes recommendations to the Council, which is required to authorize the Commission to open the necessary negotiations. The Commission has to conduct these negotiations in consultation with a special committee appointed by the Council to assist it in this task and within the framework of such directives as the Council may issue. In exercising its powers in this respect, the Council acts by a qualified majority on a proposal from the Commission, as required by the Treaty. However the Council acts unanimously where the agreement covers a field for which unanimity is required for the adoption of internal rules or for association agreements governed by art. 238. The negotiations end with an exchange of letters. These are formalities which authenticate the substance of the draft agreement.

Except in the case of trade agreements under art. 113, the Council concludes agreements after consultation or in some cases after the assent of the European Parliament has been obtained.

This revised art. 228 copies the procedure laid down in the former art. 113 (trade agreements) and extends its scope to the association agreements of art. 238. These articles served as a basis for all the agreements entered into by the EC with developing countries.[10] Agreements based on Art. 113 and 235 are with Asian and Latin American countries

Representation of the European Community

Walter Hallstein made the representative role of the Commission clear in a speech in 1965 when he said, '*La Commission est l'agent diplomatique de la Communauté pour les relations avec le monde extérieur.*'[11] On the basis of its autonomous power (and with the tacit approval of the Council, which was willing to provide the necessary credits) the Commission has set up delegations in several third countries. These numbered 142 delegations at the beginning of 1997, which means that in quantitative terms the Community has more overseas representation than many member states.[12] Each delegation is a quasi-embassy headed by a representative who has no uniform status from country to country, ranking between an ambassador and a consul. Generally each delegation is afforded the same treatment as the diplomatic mission of a member states.

From the standpoint of the active right of legation, there is a difference, because the diplomatic missions of states represent them in all aspects of their activity, whereas Commission delegations are naturally restricted to matters within Community competence.

The member states, in turn, collectively entrust a number of diplomatic functions to the mission of whichever country is holding the presidency of the Council at a given time. This is particularly true of questions concerning 'political cooperation'. However the ill-defined distribution of powers within the Community can lead to conflicts in the allocation of duties between the Commission delegate and the delegate of the State holding the presidency.[13]

The delegations represent the Commission outside the member states and communicate its different policies. They are also responsible for promoting EU information to the public and/or to interest groups in those countries.

The delegations under the responsibility of DG VIII exist in almost every ACP country and form a special case in that a provision of a protocol annexed to the Lomé Convention (art. 31 of Protocol no. 2) provides for the establishment of Commission delegations. Not only do these delegations play the usual role of liaison but they also help 'on the ground' with the implementation of Community policy towards these States. Their essential role in this respect is to oversee the proper execution of projects financed by the European Development Fund (EDF) and so they focus more on development aid. Delegations administered and coordinated by DG IB are less numerous. They are set up in large regional centres and fulfil a more political role.[14]

The Commission also has the task of representing the Community to international organizations in general (art. 229) and more specifically to the OECD (art. 231). Equally, the Community and in particular the Commission has been active in contributing to the work of several United Nations organizations such as the Conference on Trade and Development (UNCTAD), the Industrial Development Organization (UNIDO) and the World Food Programme (WFP).

CONCLUSION

After this analysis of the role of the Commission in development policy, it is clear that the Commission plays the role of an independent actor in development policy relations. More specifically, it has the means to do so because it disposes both of the decision-making facilities in order to prepare policy for the Community as such and of the instruments to implement policy decisions.

The TEU provided development cooperation with a solid legal basis and stressed the importance of the principles of complementarity and coordination. Although some progress has been realised in implementing those principles, major changes are necessary. Coordination at different levels has to be improved. First, efforts should be made to create more coherence between development policy and other policies affecting developing countries such as the Common Agricultural Policy (CAP) and GATT. Secondly, actions undertaken in the field of CFSP and development policy measures should be harmonized. A better division of tasks between the EU and its member states could be a solution. It would allow the Commission to concentrate more effectively on areas in which it has a comparative advantage over the member states (such as trade policy issues), thereby streamlining the effort on both sides. Finally, a fusion between DG IB and DG VIII is desirable in order to remedy the actual 'institutional chaos' reigning in Brussels.

On the other hand, the Commission proved to be successful in negotiating international agreements owing to its long development tradition and technical expertise. Moreover, it played a major role in improving transparency of the Union by setting up delegations in developing countries.

We can end with the words of Robert Lemaignen:

'Le temps a passé; les modes d'action de la Commission ont dû s'infléchir. Mais elle garde constamment les yeux fixés sur l'objectif que le traité lui a imposé, et respecte la ligne de conduite choisie dès les premiers jours de son existence.'[15]

Bibliography

Aptel, C., *La Politique d'aide humanitaire de l'Union Européenne: la création d'ECHO et les enjeux* (Presses Interuniversitaires Européennes et Collège d'Europe, Bruxelles, 1995).

Bossuyt, J., Laporte, G. and Brigaldino, G., *La Politique européenne de développement après le Traité de Maastricht* (ECDPM, Maastricht, 1994).

Church, C. H. and Phinnemore, D., *The European Union and European Community: A Handbook and Commentary on the Post-Maastricht Treaties* (Harvester-Wheatsheaf, Hartford, 1994).

Colla, C. and Monar, J. (supervisor), 'La nouvelle dimension de la cooperation au développement de l'Union Européenne après le Traité de Maastricht', thesis, College of Europe, Bruges, 1995.

Cosgrove, C. and Jamar, J., *The European Community's Development Policy: The Strategies Ahead* (De Tempel, Bruges, 1986).

Davignon, E. *What Future for the European Commission?* (Philip Morris Institute for Public Policy Research, Brussels, 1995).

Dietz, W. A. and Glatthaar, C., *Das Räderwerk der Europäischen Kommission* (Economica Verlag, Bonn, 1994).

Edge, D. and Lintner, V., *Lomé IV Convention: New Dawn or Neo Colonialism* (University of North London Press, 1993).

Edwards, G. and Spence, D., *The European Commission* (Longmans, Harlow, 1994).

Gordon, T. and Monar, J. (supervisor), 'Empire-building within the Commission: a Case Study of DGI/DG I A Relationship', thesis, College of Europe, Bruges, 1995.

Grilli, E. R., *The European Community and the Developing Countries* (Cambridge University Press, 1993).
Groux, J. and Manin, P., *The European Communities in the International Order* (Office for Official Publications of the European Communities, Luxembourg, 1985).
Hartley, T. C., *The Foundations of European Community Law* (Clarendon, Oxford, 1994).
Jacque, J. P., *La Participation de la CEE aux Organisations Internationales Universelles*, (AFDI, Strasbourg, 1975).
Lasok, D., *Law and Institutions of the European Union* (Butterworths, London, 1994).
Lebullenger, J., '*La Rénovation de la politique communautaire du développement*', *Revue Trimestrielle de Droit Européen* (Paris, 1994).
Lemaignen, R., *L'Europe au Berceau*, (Librairie Plon, Paris, 1964).
Lenaerts K. and Van Nuffel, *Europees Recht in Hoofdlijnen* (Maklu, Antwerp, 1995).
Lister, M., *The European Community and the Developing World: the Role of the Lomé Convention*, (Avebury, Aldershot, 1988).
Schmuck, O. and Wessels, W., 'The Community's Development Policy: the Problem of Inter- (Intra-) Institutional Coordination', in Cosgrove, C. and Jamar, J. (eds), *The European Community's Development Policy: The Strategies Ahead* (De Tempel, Bruges, 1986).
Weatherill, S. and Beaumont, P., *EC Law* (Penguin, New York, 1993).

Notes

1. Hereafter 'EC' is used to point out the activities of the Commission in the field of development cooperation in general and 'EU' when alongside the Commission, when the member states participate in the framework of the Common and Foreign Security Policy.
2. For an overview of the countries and territories to which Articles 131–136a currently apply, see Council Decision 91/482/EEC of 25 July 1991 on the association of the overseas countries and territories with the European Economic Community, OJ L263, 19 September 1991.
3. European Commission Doc. SEC(92) 915 final 16 September 1992.
4. This allocation has been made since 25 November 1994. Hans van den Broek is the commissioner in charge of DG IA: he deals with external relations with the Central and Eastern European Countries, the states belonging to the former Soviet Union, Turkey, Cyprus, Malta and other European countries as well as the external service, the CFSP and human rights (with the EU President, Jacques Santer).

   Sir Leon Brittan is in charge of DG I (North) and controls external relations with North America, Australia, New Zealand, Japan, China, South Korea, Hong Kong, Macao, Taiwan, the Common Commercial Policy and relations with the OECD and the WTO.
5. Doc. SEC(95) 731 Final, 10 May 1995.
6. Bossuyt *et al.* (1994).
7. Lasok (1994) p. 769.

8. A revealing example is the fact that the Commission embarked on a wide-ranging process of consultation to consider the actions necessary to remedy the insufficiency of the available resources for cooperation with the Mediterranean partners, in view of the challenges posed. In particular, coordination meetings have taken place with the World Bank including one in February 1995. On this basis the Commission proposed, in its Communication of 8 March 1995, that Community action should be based on support for economic transition, better socio-economic balance and regional integration.
9. Schmuck and Wessels (1986).
10. Agreements based on arts 238 are:
    the four Lomé Conventions;
    the cooperation agreements with Algeria, Egypt, Lebanon, Jordan and Syria;
    the association agreements with Malta and Cyprus; and
    the new agreements entered into by Tunisia (July 1995) and Morocco (February 1996).
11. Jacque (1975) p. 24.
12. Member states with more diplomatic missions are: France (290), Italy (237), Germany (234) and Spain (194). The United Kingdom has fewer (139).
13. Groux and Manin (1985) p. 35.
14. Examples of those regional centers are: Caracas for Latin America (with a branch office in Santiago), Bangkok for South-East Asia and New Delhi for South Asia (with a branch office in Dhaka).
15. Lemaignen (1964) p. 41.

3 The Role of the European Court of Justice

Jessica Larsson

INTRODUCTION

The representation and relations of the Community with Third World countries concerning development cooperation depend on the division of powers between the Community and its member states in the field of external relations. Complexity and dispute over the scope of the Community's external powers derive from the absence of clear provisions in the Treaty regarding the Community's treaty-making powers. In relation to Third World countries, we may ask who is competent for what, and to what extent the competence is exclusive or concurrent. The problem is that the Treaty does not confer upon the Community a general external competence at all.

This short chapter is intended to examine a few of the areas where the European Court of Justice has come to play a major role in the definition of relations between the European Union (EU) and the Third World countries and therefore has had a significant impact on development cooperation. First, the role of the Court will be examined with regard to the special provisions on interpretation of international agreements. The following chapters will define the Court's impact on development cooperation by determining the scope and nature of the Community's external competencies. Since the Court has a particular role in concluding association agreements, this will be dealt with in a separate chapter.

According to art. L in the Treaty on the European Union, the Court's jurisdiction only covers the first pillar under the EU roof. Therefore reference will be made to the European Community (EC) instead of to the EU.

THE ROLE OF THE COURT

Article 164 of the Treaty states that the Court shall ensure the law is observed in the interpretation and application of the Treaty. The main functions of the Court are:

1. to ensure that the law is enforced,
2. to act as a referee between the member states and the EC as well as between the EC institutions and
3. to ensure the uniform interpretation and application of EC law within the EC.[1]

With the Court's jurisdiction in the first pillar in mind, how can it have any role at all regarding the EU acting in the external field? The answer is to be found with the Court itself. In numerous cases it has declared itself competent to deal with international agreements because they are acts by the EC institutions and produce their effects within the scope of the Community. The international agreements are seen to be, and form as such, an integral part of EC law.[2]

The area in which the Court has played a crucial role is in defining and limiting the scope of the Community competencies to conclude international agreements, an issue still very much disputed today by the member states and the Community. The member states mostly claim that their sovereign competencies are retained as long as the Treaty does not specifically provide for an international agreement to be concluded. The Community, being based on the principle of attribution of powers, would then not have the necessary legal base for an action. The way the Court can be invited to pronounce on the compatibility of an international agreement with the Treaty is to be found in art. 228.

ARTICLE 228

Article 228 regulates the procedure whereby agreements can be entered into between the Community and one or more non-member states or international organizations. Before such a draft agreement enters into force, 'the Council, the Commission or a member state may obtain the opinion of the Court as to whether the agreement is compatible with the provisions of the Treaty.' The opinion of the Court is binding.

When the Court gives an unfavourable opinion, the agreement can enter into force only if the Treaty is amended in accordance with art. N. This means that an intergovernmental conference must be held at which amendments are agreed unanimously, followed by ratification of the member states. The practical consequences are that an adverse opinion by the Court will lead to adjustments of the agreement in question, and the Court can be said to possess a 'veto power'.[3]

Extended Application of the Article 228 Procedure

In practice, the procedure is often used to make the Court clarify the division of external powers between the Community and the member states. In declaring such requests admissible, the Court has extended the application of art. 228 not only to cover areas where the question is whether an international agreement is in conformity with the Treaty but also to prevent the member states from encroaching upon the Community sphere of competencies.

An example of this is the opinion on the Natural Rubber Agreement.[4] The International Agreement on Natural Rubber was a draft agreement drawn up within the framework of UNCTAD and negotiated by the Commission and the member states jointly, acting for the Community. This was contested by the Commission, which thought that the agreement fell under art. 113 (the common commercial policy) and therefore belonged to the area of exclusive Community competence. The Agreement, concerning natural rubber from several developing countries, was a commodity agreement giving the Community the possibility of solving problems regarding excess or shortage of supply.

The Commission made an application under art. 228 and asked the Court for an opinion as to whether it would be compatible with the Treaty to conclude the Agreement in the mixed form. Since art. 228 applies only where the agreement is to be concluded by the Community, the member states raised objections of admissibility. Despite the fact that the issue before the Court was not whether the Community could enter into the Agreement, the Court held the application admissible. The substance of the case will be discussed later.

INTERPRETATION OF INTERNATIONAL AGREEMENTS

As mentioned previously, the Court itself has declared its jurisdiction to interpret international agreements concluded by the Community institutions.

In *Haegeman* v. *Belgium*[5] the Court decided it had jurisdiction under art. 177 to give a preliminary ruling on the 1961 Association Agreement between the Community and Greece:

> The Athens Agreement was concluded by the Council under Articles 228 and 238 of the Treaty as appears from the terms of the Decision dated 25 September 1961. This Agreement is therefore, in so far as it concerns the Community, an act of one of the institutions of the Community within the meaning of subparagraph (b) of the first paragraph of Article 177.

The same approach was adopted in *Bresciani*[6] concerning interpretation of the 1963 Yaoundé Convention and in *Razanatsimba*[7] regarding the interpretation of the first Lomé Convention. Both conventions were concluded by the Council under arts 131 and 228 of the Treaty.

The approach by the Court to the question of direct effect of an international agreement is on an *ad hoc* basis. Provisions of such an agreement will be *directly effective* only if they meet the general conditions for direct effect; the requirements of unconditionality and if they are sufficiently precise. Even where the wording in an international agreement is identical to Treaty provisions having direct effect, the purposes are different because the EC is aiming for an ever closer union.[8]

THE COURT'S ROLE IN DETERMINING THE SCOPE OF COMMUNITY COMPETENCIES IN THE EXTERNAL FIELD

International agreements forming part of EC law can be divided into three categories:

- agreements between the EC acting alone and one or more non-member states;
- agreements between the EC and the member states acting jointly and non-member states;
- agreements between member states acting alone and non-member states.[9]

The first category is possible when the Community has the exclusive treaty-making power, while recourse to the second must be made when the competencies are shared between the EC and the member states and thus a mixed agreement must be concluded. The third category normally does not involve Community law.

As mentioned above, the 'principle of attributed powers' applies to all Community measures. This means that all Community powers in the Treaty derive from a transfer of powers from the member states and have been granted for specific fields of activity. The question must therefore be whether the Community has the required external powers for dealing with the matter. If the field is covered by the Treaty then it belongs to the category of express powers. Where no specific provision exists in the Treaty, the field can be covered by implied powers, a theory developed by the Court. Finally, art. 235 can serve as a legal base for the external power.

EXPRESS POWERS

The express powers granted to the Community in respect of common commercial policy under art. 113 are of particular interest for development policy.[10]

Those who drafted the Treaty made it clear when they agreed on art. 113 that an external relations power in the field of EEC trade relations was included, but not in respect of other matters within the EEC's jurisdiction. Article 113 gives no definition of the common commercial policy and the listed examples are indicative, not exhaustive.[11]

For a long time there has been a divergence of views between the Council and the Commission as to what falls within the scope of art. 113.[12] The Commission favours a broad interpretation[13] and argues that the nature of the Community competence depends on the character of the instrument and not the objective which the agreement seeks to achieve, while the Council wants to narrow the scope to the objective of the proposed agreement.

The Court has shown itself willing to adopt a dynamic approach to the concept of external trade and what falls within the scope of art. 113. In its opinion on the Agreement on Natural Rubber, the Court acknowledged that the existence of a link with development problems did not cause a measure to be excluded from the sphere of art. 113. It stated that

> it would no longer be possible to carry on any worthwhile common commercial policy if the Community were not in the position to

avail itself also of more elaborate means devised with a view to furthering the development of international trade.[14]

The Court chose to interpret art. 113 in a dynamic sense, not limited to the traditional forms of trade like customs duties and quotas, and declared the Agreement to fall under art. 113.

In respect of a dispute on the legal base for Community Regulations concerning generalized tariff preferences,[15] the Court again proved its openness towards the concept of a common commercial policy. The Commission brought an action for annulment of two Council regulations applying generalized tariff preferences in respect of certain industrial and textile products originating in developing countries. The Commission had proposed the two regulations to be adopted under art. 113, but the Council had departed from this and did not specify the legal basis for the regulations at all. The Council defended itself by arguing that not only common commercial policy aims were in question but also development aid policy, and that this necessitated recourse to art. 235.

Referring to the opinion on the Natural Rubber Agreement, the Court stressed that the link between trade and development had become progressively stronger in modern relations. It considered it had been recognized in the context of the United Nations, notably by the United Nations Conference on Trade and Development (UNCTAD) and in the context of the GATT, in particular through the incorporation in the GATT of Part IV, entitled 'Trade and Development.'[16] It was also held by the Court that in defining the characteristics and the instruments of the common commercial policy in arts 110 etc. the aim of contributing to the harmonious development of world trade is among the objectives.[17] This is the background for the Community system of generalized tariff preferences and reflects a new concept of international trade relations in which development aims play a major role. The Court declared that art. 113 should have been used as the legal base, and that because this was not the case the regulations were void.

Divergent positions were again taken by the Commission and the Council regarding the Community competencies to conclude the agreement establishing the World Trade Organization and, in particular, the General Agreement on Trade in Services (GATS) and the Trade Related Intellectual Property Systems (TRIPs).[18] The Commission claimed exclusive Community competence under art. 113 because of the objective of the agreements and also the instruments applied by them. This wide interpretation of the concept of common commercial policy was strongly disputed by the Council, which instead claimed shared competencies and thus a mixed agreement to be concluded.

The Court ruled that in relation to trade in goods the Community had exclusive competence, but that with regard to services and TRIPs the agreements went beyond the scope of art. 113 (except in the case of services involving cross-frontier supplies without movement of persons).

The conclusion must be that the Court examines whether the object and content of the measure aims at regulation of trade, defined broadly, and if it does then the measure will fall under the express power of art. 113.[19] This seems to suggest that commercial policy objectives and instruments will be adapted to changes in the international relations. The predominant criterion appears to be the reference to the concept of 'world trade' when the Court is defining the scope of the common commercial policy.

Implied Powers

In general, the Court has interpreted the sources of Community law teleologically, and the field of external relations is not an exception. It is obvious that the Treaty provisions regulate the need for external Community competencies only in a limited way, and that they do not satisfy the needs for external activities. The implied powers theory is developed and used by the Court as a complementary device to express powers.

In the ERTA case[20] the Court ruled that Community power to enter into international agreements exists not only when such a right is expressly provided for by a Treaty provision: the external power may 'flow from other provisions of the Treaty and from measures adopted, within the framework of those provisions, by the Community institutions'.[21]

An additional rule to the ERTA doctrine was given in Opinion 1/76.[22] Here the Court pronounced the Community's power to act externally although it had not acted internally, in so far as participation of the Community was necessary for obtaining the Community objectives. This precondition of *necessity* means that without external Community action it is not possible effectively to achieve the objective for which the powers were given internally.[23] The test of necessity was broadly applied,[24] because the Court ruled that the application of implied powers was not limited to cases where internal powers have been exercised already by the Community.

This broad approach to the theory of implied powers was narrowed down in Opinion 1/94 on the WTO agreements. The Court did not dispute the existence of external implied powers as an automatic consequence of the existing internal powers, but it nevertheless stated that the test of necessity is met where the internal powers were already exercised, save where the internal powers could have been effectively exercised only at the same time as the external powers.[25] In case of the WTO, the concept of an external implied Community power based on the necessity to attain a Community objective was rejected by the Court.[26]

Additional Powers

The third possible source for Community external powers is art. 235.[27] The Article is an instrument to create new internal as well as external powers if it is 'in the course of the operation of the common market'. It can be employed when an action is necessary for the attainment of a Treaty objective, but no specific powers are provided for it.

In the opinion on OECD,[28] the Court made clear that it will accept measures based on art. 235 only as long as there is no specific alternative provision in the Treaty granting the necessary legal base. It also declared that art. 235, which enables the Community to cope with any insufficiency in the powers conferred in it, expressly or by implication, for the achievement of its objectives, cannot in itself vest exclusive competence in the Community at international level.[29]

THE COURT'S ROLE IN DETERMINING EXTERNAL COMPETENCIES

Regarding the common commercial policy, the issues are more effectively regulated at Community level than through actions by each member state. The member states have therefore transferred their national sovereign competencies to the supranational Community. When it comes to the external field, however, the member states are very reluctant to accept this transfer of sovereignty, because once the Community is exclusively competent they are no longer competent. Amendments and new measures may be adopted only if express authorization is given by the Community.

Exclusive Competencies

Already in the ERTA case the Court touched upon the exclusivity of Community external power: 'concurrent powers exercised by the member states would be incompatible with the unity of the Common Market and the uniform application of Community law.'[30] It also stated that 'when Common Rules have entered into force the Community alone is in a position to assume and carry out contractual obligations towards third countries affecting the whole sphere of application of the Community legal system.'[31]

In an opinion on the International Labour Organization,[32] the Court declared the exclusive competence dependent on the degree of Community internal action. If more than minimum norms have been established internally then it is necessary to see whether the international convention might affect those rules. 'The Community's tasks and the objectives of the Treaty would be compromised if member states were able to enter into international commitments containing rules capable of affecting rules already adopted in areas falling outside common policies or of altering their scope.'[33] Nevertheless, the Court has declared that until common rules exist the member states retain their right to enter into obligations with non-member countries.[34]

The Court rejected the Commission's claims in the Opinion on WTO that the external powers were of an exclusive nature by noting that 'the Community's exclusive external competence does not automatically flow from its power to lay down rules at internal level.'[35] The Court set the preconditions for the Community's exclusive external competence; 'only in so far as common rules have been established at internal level does the external competence of the Community become exclusive.'[36]

In the Opinion on the OECD[37] the Court confirmed the previous conditions for exclusive competence for the Community. The request for an opinion concerned the legal base for Community action and whether Community competence excluded member states from participating in a mixed agreement. It was argued by the Commission that the agreement fell under art. 113, but this argument was rejected by the Court on the grounds that Community internal measures did not cover all fields of activity to which the agreement related. The Court confirmed the principle that internal competence can give rise to exclusive external competence only if it is exercised, save where internal powers can only be effectively exercised at the same time as external powers.[38]

In the recent opinions on the WTO and the OECD it appears that the Court favours a stricter application of the requirements for exclusive Community competence. The consequence of this is that recourse to joint participation for external action is needed.

Joint Competencies

'Joint competence' means that neither the Community nor the member states have the power to cover the issues dealt with on their own. A disadvantage with the joint participation is that it is complicated and time-consuming. Decisions are often taken by unanimity instead of by qualified majority and ratification is needed by all the national parliaments and by the Community. An advantage of joint participation can be the avoidance of conflict over division of powers between the Community and the member states.

THE COURT'S ROLE IN ASSOCIATION AGREEMENTS

Article 238 provides the Community with the legal base to conclude, with one or more States or international organizations, agreements establishing an association involving reciprocal rights and obligations, common action and special procedures. An Association Council is normally established to manage the association, and this body has the right to adopt decisions that are binding on the contracting parties. The Council is composed of representatives of the Third countries and of the Community.

An association agreement may also provide for a system of Courts, including a court with jurisdiction to interpret the agreement as long as it is compatible with the Treaty and with the jurisdiction of the European Court of Justice.[39] The latter has jurisdiction to interpret the decisions taken by the association Council because they form part of Community law.[40]

If association or cooperation agreements with third countries contain development aid then, it is normally the member states who take on the responsibility for financial contributions. Therefore, the Court has declared that the member states have the right to participate as parties in the negotiations and that the mixed procedure for concluding the agreement should be followed.[41]

In 1991, the European Parliament sought a declaration that the expenditure provided for as development aid in the fourth Lomé

Convention was Community expenditure and must be governed by the Community budget provisions.[42] The Court held that since the Community's competence in the field of development aid is not exclusive, the member states can take actions individually or collectively.[43] Here, the expenditure was assumed directly by the member states and distributed by a fund administered by the Community institutions. The Court ruled the expenditure not to be Community expenditure[44] that must be entered into the Community budget and dismissed the application.

This solution had already been adopted in the opinion on the International Agreement on Natural Rubber. The fund was intended to stabilize prices and therefore needed contributions from the Community budget or directly from the member states, a matter not decided upon at this stage. Since the question of financing remained undecided, the member states could remain as parties to the negotiations.

CONCLUSION

The Court's role in development cooperation is crucial, especially with regard to the interpretation and the determining of the scope of the Treaty provisions, since the Treaty itself does not provide necessary regulation in the field of external relations.

When the Court has interpreted certain provisions to be directly effective, it has allowed nationals of Third World countries to directly invoke agreements concluded between their home states and the Community. This means an immensely improved control of the rights conferred upon the nationals of Thirld World countries and as such forms part of development cooperation.

By determining the scope and the nature of the Treaty provisions regarding the external relations, the Court has very much influenced the structure of development cooperation. In extending the scope of art. 113 to cover also development aid, the Court has enhanced the Community's ability to operate in an effective manner towards Third World countries. Also, in cases where the external powers of the Community fall outside the exclusive competence, the Court has stressed the duty of cooperation[45] that exists when the member states and the Community take joint actions. This seems to be an emanation of the principle of good faith in art. 5 and of coherence, which has been stressed as a fundamental principle relevant to all activities under the umbrella of the European Union.[46] When the Court raises the requirements of unity in international representation of the Community, this lies in the interest of Third World countries because they are then entitled to address any claim either to the Community or to a member state.

It follows from the above reasoning that the Court has played an important role in defining the possibilities for the Community to establish real development cooperation.

Bibliography

Barents, R., 'The Internal Market Unlimited: Some Observations on the Legal Basis of Community Legislation,' *Common Market Law Review* (1993) pp. 85–109.

Bourgeois, J.H.J, 'The European Community in the WTO and Advisory Opinion 1/94: An Echternach Procession', *Common Market Law Review* (1995) pp. 763–87.

Brown and Jacobs, *The Court of Justice of the European Communities*, 3rd edn (Lasa, Butterworths, 1989).

Eckhout, P., *The External Dimension of the Completion of the European Community's Internal Market in Services and Goods – a Legal Analysis*, 1993.

Hartley, T. C., *The Foundations of European Community Law*, 3rd edn (Oxford University Press, Oxford, 1994).

Hilf, M., 'The ECJ's Opinion 1/94 on the WTO – No Surprise but Wise?', *European Journal of International Law* (1995), pp. 246–59.

Pescatore, P., *Relations Extérieurs des CE*, RCADI II (Paris 1961) pp. 1–242

Steenbergen, J., 'Legal Instruments and External Policies of the European Communities', in de Vree, J. K., Coffee, P. and Lauwaars, R.H. (eds), *Towards a European Foreign Policy* (1987), p. 113.

Völker, E. L. M, 'The Common Commercial Policy – Scope and Nature of its Powers', in *Protectionism and the European Community* (1987).

Cases and Opinions from the European Court of Justice

Case 22/70 *Commission* v. *Council* 'ERTA' (1971) *ECR* 263.

Case 181/73 *Haegeman* v. *Belgium* (1974) *ECR* 449.

Opinion 1/75 *Local Cost Standard* (1975) *ECR* 1355.

Case 87/75 *Bresciani* v. *Italian Finance Administration* (1976) *ECR* 129.

Opinion 1/76 *Draft Agreement Establishing a European Laying-up Fund for Inland Waterway Vessels* (1977) *ECR* 741.

Case 65/77 *Razanatsimba* (1977) *ECR* 2229.

Opinion 1/78 *International Agreement on Natural Rubber* (1979) *ECR* 2909.

Case 45/86 *Commission v. Council* (1987) *ECR* 1517.

Case 12/86 *Demirel* v. *Stadt Schwäbisch Gmünd* (1987) *ECR* 3719, 3750–51.

Case 192/89 *Sevince* v. *Staatsecretaris van Justitie* (1990) *ECR* I-3461.

Opinion 1/91 *Agreement between the Community and the EFTA on an European Economic Area* (1991) *ECR* I–6079.

Opinion 2/91 *Convention No. 170 of the ILO concerning Safety in the Use of Chemicals at Work* (1993) *ECR* I-1061.
Case 316/91 *European Parliament v. Council* (1994) *ECR* I-625.
Opinion 1/92 *Agreement between the Community and the EFTA on an European Economic Area* (1992) *ECR* I-2821.
Opinion 2/92 *On the Competence of the Community or One of its Institutions to Participate in the Third Revised Decision of the OECD on National Treatment* (1995) *ECR* I-525.
Opinion 1/94 *WTO* (1994) *ECR* I-5267.

Notes

1. Brown and Jacobs (1989).
2. For example Case 181/73 *Haegeman* v. *Belgium* (1974) *ECR* 449, 459, Case 12/86 *Demirel* v. *Stadt Schwäbisch Gmünd* (1987) *ECR* 3719, 3750–51.
3. Opinion 1/91 *Agreement between the Community and the EFTA on an European Economic Area* (1991) *ECR* I-6079 and Opinion 1/92 *Agreement between the Community and the EFTA on an European Economic Area* (1992) *ECR* I-2821.
4. Opinion 1/78 *International Agreement on Natural Rubber* (1979) *ECR* 2909.
5. Case 181/73 (1974) *ECR* 449, 459.
6. Case 87/75 (1976) *ECR* 129.
7. Case 65/77 (1977) *ECR* 2229.
8. Opinion 1/91 *The European Economic Area* (1991) *ECR* I-6079.
9. Hartley (1994).
10. The Court laid down in Opinion 1/75 *Understanding on a Local Costs Standard* (1975) *ECR* 1361 that the Community's powers under art. 113 are of an exclusive nature.
11. Opinion 1/78 *International Agreement on Natural Rubber* (1979) *ECR* 2909.
12. For an explanation of the views see for example Völker (1987) Barents (1993); Eeckhout (1993).
13. For example Steenbergen (1987) p. 113.
14. Opinion 1/78, para. 44.
15. Case 45/86 *Commission* v. *Council* (1987) *ECR* 1517.
16. Case 45/86, para. 17.
17. ibid., para. 19.
18. Opinion 1/94, *WTO Agreements* (1994) *ECR* I-5267.
19. For analysis, see Bourgeois (1995).
20. Case 22/70 *Commission v. Council* (1971) *ECR* 263.
21. Ibid., para 16.
22. Opinion 1/76 *Draft Agreement Establishing a European Laying-up Fund for Inland Waterway Vessels* (1977) *ECR* 741, p. 755.
23. The doctrine of 'necessity' was confirmed by the Court in Opinion 2/92 OECD (1995) *ECR* I-525.
24. Ibid., paras 4 and 5.

25. Opinion 1/94, para. 89.
26. Opinion 1/94, paras 82–86.
27. See Pescatore (1961).
28. Opinion 2/92 *on the competence of the Community or one of Its Institutions to participate in the Third Revised Decision of the OECD on National Treatment* (1995) *ECR* I-525.
29. Ibid., para. 37.
30. Case 22/70 *Commission v. Council* (1971) *ECR* 263, p. 276, para. 31.
31. Ibid., p. 274, para. 18.
32. Opinion 2/91 *Convention No. 170 of the ILO Concerning Safety in the Use of Chemicals at Work* (1993) *ECR* I-1061.
33. Ibid., paras 10 and 11.
34. Opinion 2/92 *OECD* (1995) *ECR* I-525, para. 31 referring back to the ERTA case.
35. Opinion 1/94 *WTO* para. 77.
36. Ibid., see also paras 79, 80 and 90.
37. Opinion 2/92 *On the competence of the Community*.
38. Ibid., para. 37.
39. Opinion 1/91 *The European Economic Area* (1991) *ECR* I-6079, paras 40, 69–72.
40. Case 181/73 *Haegeman* (1974) *ECR* 499 and Case 192/89 *Sevince* (1990) *ECR* I-3461.
41. Opinion 1/78 *International Agreement on Natural Rubber* (1979) *ECR* 2909.
42. Case 316/91 *European Parliament v. Council* (1994) *ECR* I-625.
43. Ibid., para 34.
44. Ibid., paras 38–9.
45. For example in Opinion 1/94 *WTO*.
46. Hilf (1995).

4 The Role of France in the Lomé IV Convention

Janick Rajoharison

'Je m'en appelle à ceux qui auront après moi la charge des affaires du pays. La France ne serait plus tout à fait elle-même aux yeux du monde si elle renonçait à être présente en Afrique aux cotés des Africains pour contribuer à construire un cadre de paix, de démocratie, de développement, pour réussir ensemble une grande aventure humaine.' (President Mitterrand at the Franco-African summit in Biarritz, November 1994[1])

INTRODUCTION

In the general context of reduction of development aid towards Third World countries, France seems to be an exception, particularly with regard to the countries of the Lomé Convention. France's attitude can easily be explained by its long-standing relations with those countries. Do we need reminding that the Lomé Convention was born at France's initiative?

Right from the beginning of the European Economic Community (EEC), General de Gaulle insisted on the inclusion of the Overseas Countries and Territories (OCT) in the customs union. Thus under arts 131 to 136, which formed Part IV of the Treaty of Rome, there was provision for an 'association' status for non-European countries having special relations with Community members. In reality, the association system was imposed on them unilaterally. France strongly sought the support of its European partners and encouraged its former colonies to diversify their relations with other EEC member states. It wanted to ensure free access to the EEC for the exports of those countries and to share with its European partners the cost of providing economic assistance to overseas territories it then shouldered. The association system was to last five years under the Rome Treaty.

For these countries the European construction was not only an economic or aid agreement, nor simply the development of old alliances but also the hope that Europe would definitely not see any war again on its soil and drag the African countries into this plague. Originally this was the most solid basis of Europe–Africa cooperation. Africa was part of France's universal identity. The notion of a natural partnership between the EEC and Africa was unmistakably French.

After the OCT gained independence and expressed their willingness to remain in an association led by France, the successor African states plus Madagascar and Mauritius became associated with the EEC under the two Yaoundé Conventions in 1963 and 1969. These conventions mainly benefited the former French colonies.

The Lomé Convention was a response to the United Kingdom's accession to the EEC in 1973 and to the problem of preserving trade preferences of the developing Commonwealth countries in Africa, the Caribbean and Pacific Ocean. The Lomé Convention became the general structure for EEC policies; Lomé I was signed in 1975 between 9 EEC countries and 46 African, Caribbean and Pacific (ACP) States, while Lomé II, III and IV were signed in 1979, 1984 and 1989, respectively. There are now 70 associated states. Lomé IV was signed for a 10-year period starting on 1 March 1990, with a mid-term review. Its financial protocol, the Eighth European Development Fund (EDF VIII), was adopted for 5 years.

Undoubtedly the Lomé Convention is strongly identified with France. The fact that all European commissioners from 1958 (Robert Lemaignen) to 1985 (Edgar Pisani) were French nationals is symbolic of the prominence of the French tradition of development cooperation. Today France still maintains an undisputed leadership in Community policies towards ACP states. Nevertheless, the Lomé Convention, considered as being a unique example of partnership between North and South, has been going through a difficult period since the mid 1990s. This chapter examines French priorities for the mid-term review of Lomé IV.

First, the Community and its member states must reinforce their support and maintain their priority towards ACP countries that currently undergo serious economic difficulties. To this effect, France sought the support of its partners through adequate finance and an institutional framework.

Second, in view of the economic deterioration of the ACP countries, France stressed the need for improved efficiency in European Community cooperation. Aid would be conditional upon institutional and economic development. The political and economic reforms which are under process in ACP states should definitely be encouraged.

It is significant that the following synopsis basically reflects the French government's official position.

MAINTAINING ACP PRIORITIES VIA FINANCE AND A EUROPEAN FRAMEWORK

France has always maintained an active African policy, and naturally seeks to give priority to ACP states in the distribution of the EC financial effort of development aid.

An Active African Policy

Traditionally, African policy has always been an important part of French foreign policy. All French presidents from de Gaulle to Chirac have displayed a clear commitment to the ACP states. De Gaulle instituted a paternalist policy, which was carried on by his successors. Development aid in France has become the preserve of the President and of his special African 'cell' at the Elysée palace (made notorious by Mr Foccart) despite the existence of a Ministry of Cooperation. The first European commissioner, Robert Lemaignen, also shared the feeling that the success or failure of Europe–Africa cooperation was more dependent upon emotional elements than intellectual perfection. Clearly, personal contacts were of crucial importance for cooperation to succeed. De Gaulle believed that France had a particular role to play in the world towards the least developed countries (LDCs) because of French history and the values France has always defended. Mitterrand also cultivated a relationship based on paternalism, although he condemned it from the onset. The effort to create a more institutional, less personalized approach to Africa, exemplified by the cooperation minister Jean-Pierre Cot, collapsed when the latter was forced out of office. Worse still, when the President brought his son Jean-Christophe to lead the cell, the family relationship reasserted itself. President Mitterrand was certainly Africa's advocate. At the Franco-African summit in Biarritz in November 1994, he called on his would-be successor to champion Africa's cause.

As for President Chirac, he is seen in Africa and France as the heir of President de Gaulle. According to Mr Soubestre, deputy Director-General of DG VIII, the African dossier is important symbolically for him. Just after his election, President Chirac toured West Africa and firmly denounced any thought of pessimism about Africa. The visit, said Amara Essy, Côte d'Ivoire's foreign minister, proves that he loves Africa and that France continues to care, though Africa is not the exotic protégé it once was. At the G7 summit in Halifax in June 1995, President Chirac declared that he was a determined advocate of the Thirld World and promised the invited African leaders a real commitment in Africa. More recently, on the eve of the francophone summit in Benin in December 1995, he reaffirmed that France had no intention either to withdraw its development aid or to modify its privileged relationship with a number of African countries. France's African policy is therefore characterized by its remarkable continuity throughout successive presidencies. This does not mean that there are no plans for change in the future. Clearly many authors and politicians have pleaded for a profound reform of the current policy, especially in a context of budgetary constraints.

Indeed, personalized relationships have led to a drift in Franco-African relations. Patronage is flourishing. Moreover, the implementation of development aid can be criticized for being inefficient and lacking transparency; ten different ministerial departments are involved. Only the aid managed by the Ministry of Cooperation (less than 15 per cent of total development aid) is really scrutinized by Parliament. The biggest contribution, more than 50 per cent from the Ministry of Economy and Finance, is never discussed. Despite criticisms, substantial reform is still not on the agenda. The Ministry of Cooperation still remains independent from the Ministry of Foreign Affairs.[2] Recent institutional reform only resulted in the creation in January 1996 of an Interministerial Committee for Development Public Aid, in charge of the general coordination.[3]

France's involvement in Africa can be justified on several grounds. Historically France had the strongest colonial past and the widest African interests of EEC member countries. Today French interests still lie in the vast oil reserves of Gabon and Congo and in the presence of numerous French firms. The franc zone also remains an area of stability and a preferred market.

France's influence on Africa gives it an international stature. From a cultural point of view, ACP states are allies of France and the French language. Following a proposal made in 1995 by the Senate, a debate is currently running on whether there should be an amendment to the French Constitution mentioning the francophone world and France's responsibility towards it.

Furthermore, France has a tradition of helping the LDCs – undoubtedly many ACP states belong to the category of the most deprived people of the world. Mr Balladur, the former Prime Minister, declared in 1993 that in the context of general reduction of development aid the African continent needed more than ever a supportive aid policy. It is France's moral duty to support ACP states. Worldwide, only Denmark, Norway, Sweden, and the Netherlands contribute more than 0.7 per cent of their GNP to development aid.[4] France also wants to concentrate aid on countries where the current European Union (EU) is active. Many African countries observe that France is the only country with a real African policy; this determination gives it a positive image. According to the 1995 first annual report of the of the French watchdog on cooperation, 23.8 per cent of development aid is devoted to multilateral aid and 76.2 per cent to bilateral aid.[5]

Lastly, negative feedback also plays a role in relations between the ACP States and France. Thus, during the much-contested French nuclear tests early in 1996, African countries supported France in the name of solidarity, even if they were not in favour of the tests.

In short, France still carries a great deal of clout in Africa, which is a major supporter of its role in the world. It is understandable that France sought financial backing from its EU partners during the mid-term review of the Lomé IV Convention.

THE NEGOTIATIONS FOR EDF VIII

EDF VIII (1996–2000) was the real test of whether priority for ACP states should be maintained. Negotiations took place during the French presidency of the EU and they clearly showed the differing alignments of the member states. France strove to maintain the level of EU aid under EDF VII, which expired on 1 March 1995.

A compromise was found on an amount of 13 307 billion ecu (EDF VII amounted to 10.9 billion ecu, which meant a nominal increase of 21.5 per cent in line with inflation). The figure also includes outstanding balances from the preceding EDF (450 million ecu). Loans from the European Investment Bank are to be added (1 683 billion ecu), which makes a total of about 15 billion ecu. At this figure, the enlarged, fifteen-nation EU maintains its efforts in real terms only by taking account of inflation and contributions from the three new member states. Initially the Commission asked for 14.3 billion ecu and the French presidency for 14.6 billion ecu, while the ACP states wanted 15.8 billion ecu.[6] This amount revealed a shift in the EU's approach to foreign policy as well as to trade and aid. In fact no agreement was reached at the Council of Ministers of Foreign Affairs in February 1995. France and the Commission could not accept a compromise inferior to EDF VII in real terms. Supporting France, the President of the European Parliament declared that it would not ratify a decision entailing a reduction of European aid. As a last resort, the issue had to be resolved at heads of state and government level by the European Council summit in Cannes in June 1995.

The commissioner for development, João de Deus Pinheiro, praised the French presidency for its determination and declared that the agreement was a compromise between what was desirable and what was possible. For the French presidency, the dossier was crucially important: the EU had to remain credible to the ACP. France accepted an increase in its contribution of 2.6 to 3.1 billion ecu. Under French pressure, Germany and the United Kingdom also accepted an increase in their contributions. France now replaces Germany as the main contributor to the EDF. Mr Juppé, presiding over the Council of Ministers, declared that Britain's wish to give priority to bilateral aid called into question the very concept of belonging to the EU. He also stated that the absence of historical links could not justify a lesser contribution, the policy being that of the whole EU and not one of certain member states. Belonging to the EU means accepting the multilateral discipline.

The outcome is certainly not generous, but it contrasts with the general downward trend affecting both bilateral and multilateral aid which has been seen in recent years. A range of factors explains the result. Many member states are under domestic pressure to curb deficits to meet the criteria of the European Monetary Union. Mediterranean and Eastern countries are becoming the new priorities for the EU. Throughout the world, donors have made drastic cuts to their aid programmes. Negotiations on the replenishment of the International Development Association (IDA – the soft loan arm of the World Bank) recently failed because the USA did not want to maintain its contributions. France is an exception, with 0.64 per cent of its GNP in 1994 allocated to development aid (i.e 45 billion french francs every year).[7] France ranks among the leading group of donor countries and stands in fifth position after Norway, Denmark, Sweden and the Netherlands.

From the ACP standpoint the result is reasonably satisfactory, although the new financial envelope did not really meet their expectations (they can in addition receive bilateral aid). The new financial protocol came into force in 1997 after the ratification process. Meanwhile transitional measures are applicable.

EUROPEAN POLICY AS A SUPPORT FOR FRENCH POLICY

In addition to financial support, France seeks complementarity and synergy with European policy through an adequate institutional framework. A multilateral approach has a greater impact on decisions about the ACP States or the Bretton Woods institutions (the World Bank and the International Monetary Fund) than has a bilateral approach, especially if they are unpopular (e.g. retaliation measures, or suspension of cooperation). Multilateralism is the only fair and effective way to implement relatively new aspects of development policy, such as good governance and human rights.

Other grounds militate in favour of a European cooperation policy. Neither the fights against immigration, drugs, insecurity based on fundamentalism, and aids nor the protection of the environment can find practicable solutions at national level. It is in Europeans' interest to contribute to the development of the ACP states to deal with all these problems and it is essential to find mutually satisfactory solutions.

France seeks a greater synergy between its projects and those of the EU. Its decision in June 1995 to extend the 'field of cooperation'[8] to the seventy signatory countries of the Lomé Convention, as well as to South Africa, will enable it to adopt a global view on development in Africa and to define development projects in a perspective of regional integration. France thus intends to contribute to the better development of the new countries without reducing its actions in francophone Africa. Such a decision was necessary because the opposition of francophone and English speaking areas is no longer relevant today in order to receive the international community's support in favour of a few emerging economic regions.

EU policies objectively support the interests or ambitions of France. However they do not only serve France's interests, otherwise they would not be successful in the long term. Relations between France and Africa are now entering a new stage of maturity. In view of the great risks that the ACP states will face in international competition, the most efficient way to express France's solidarity is to make aid conditional upon institutional and economic development.

MAKING AID CONDITIONAL UPON INSTITUTIONAL AND ECONOMIC DEVELOPMENT

In 1992 more than half of the aid to the ACP states was devoted to the payment of current expenses: these avoid the worst but do not invest for the future. Former Prime Minister Balladur stressed the need for tough solidarity, with the emphasis on long-term efficiency. Aid has to be provided in countries at peace with themselves and within a coherent economic policy. This reflects the modern consensus that genuine and sustainable development can take place only in a liberalized environment, both political and economic. Former Prime Minister Juppé underlined the need of a more transparent, efficient and simple development public aid.

Institutional Development

Rule of Law, Democracy and Human Rights

Respect for the rule of law, democracy and human rights are essential conditions of EC cooperation. France wishes the EU to provide political and financial support to democratic states, while imposing sanctions on serious infringements of those fundamental principles. France supported the addition of a suspension clause for such infringements in the revised Convention (see art. 366a). France itself suspended cooperation with several ACP states: with Togo in 1992 following the violent interruption of the democratic process by General Eyademe, president since 1967; with Zaire in 1991; France refused to protect 'old friend' dictators such as Hissène Habré in Chad in 1990 and Moussa Traoré in Mali in 1991; more recently, cooperation was suspended with Niger when Colonel Ibrahim Baré Mainassara forced out of office the democratically elected head of state (January 1996). France also seeks to reinforce the political dialogue in the ACP–EC Council of Ministers (ACP representatives will have to be elected politicians) and in other fora, e.g. at the regional level.

Political conditionality only surfaced after the end of the cold war. Before 1989, East–West logic prevailed and France had to support certain African regimes for political reasons, to prevent their countries becoming zones of confrontation between the USA and the USSR (as had happened in Angola). After the fall of the Berlin Wall and the end of bipolarity, emphasis was placed on universal values such as democracy. However, the democratic process had already been under way in several ACP countries since the end of 1980s (in Benin, Gabon, even in Zaïre). President Mitterrand's speech at the June 1990 Franco-African summit in La Baule accelerated the process. It heralded a new era. Mitterrand stated that France would hence forward link its aid to democratic reform and respect for human rights and be 'lukewarm' towards countries that did not strive towards institutions based on free elections, multiparty systems, the removal of censorship and an independent judiciary. The government subsequently promised debt reduction for middle-income countries on condition that they are engaged in a democratization process. However, the speech created a misunderstanding, because the President also advocated patience and that each country should set the terms and pace of its own reform. The speech even produced some negative effects: an increase in tribalism, threats to national unity, destabilization of states, and inadequate new constitutions in some countries. Consequently at the Franco-African summit in Biarritz in November 1994, Mitterrand stated that priority was not given to democracy over development but that the two of them had to be equated. Consolidation of the state is the primary objective. Mitterrand may have even thought that Africa was not ready for democracy; his philosophy was similar to that of his predecessors, but it was realistic. He underlined the dangers of the mechanistic implementation of democratic rules without popular commitment.

In practice, however, this doctrine was not always followed by France in certain African States. France clearly supported dictators as a result of patronage or in the sacrosanct name of stability. Zaïre and Togo were later considered 'decent' countries again and were therefore invited to the Biarritz summit. Rwanda's case was the most serious drift away from patronage and the most controversial issue of Mitterrand's presidency. Rwanda saw one of the worst cases of genocide in the twentieth century between April and June 1994. France was involved because of its close links with the racist regime of Kigali (General Habyarimana), and because of its military intervention, known as Operation Turquoise. The Ministry of Cooperation announced a radical change of its policy only in January 1995. France also failed to offer any obvious rewards to democratic reformers. It has been slow to impose, and quick to lift, penalties on reforms (e.g. in Gabon in 1993) where former autocrats have held on to or come back on power.

Democracy is certainly a long process, and a unique model of democratic society does not exist. However, a progressive resolution of these crises is to be hoped for. The Great Lake crisis (in Burundi, Rwanda, Tanzania, Zaïre, Uganda and Kenya) and other dramas should not conceal the few success stories in several African states. Mozambique, Zambia and Lesotho have adopted democratic rules. Swaziland, Malawi and Tanzania are implementing changes to their political system. Angola held elections in 1992 and Cape Verde saw the victory of the Movement for Democracy at the legislative elections of December 1995. France advocates EU support for the states themselves, but also for the protection of goods and citizens.

Institutional Support of States

France has from the outset supported pluralistic elections. Thus France contributed 8 million fr. for the Nigerian elections in 1993 and technical assistance for the organization of polls. The Ministry of Cooperation only intervenes at the request of a state itself. It also helps to elaborate constitutions and other fundamental texts that guarantee the protection of citizens against abuse by the administration.

Protection of Citizens and Property

Information and training in citizenship are fundamental to guaranteeing a lasting democracy. Access to justice for every citizen must be facilitated. France pays particular attention to the fight against corruption, criminality and drug trafficking. The Ministry of Cooperation contributes to the modernization of the Interpol network in Africa, helping to reinforce justice and police systems and financing a regional programme aimed at setting up uniform business law in fifteen states of sub-Saharan Africa and the Indian Ocean. France's military presence is important for security and contributes to limiting instability on the continent.

Media

France encourages a free and independent press through a legal environment adapted to each country, material (documentation) and technical support (satellites) and by training journalists. Indeed, the media reinforce the rule of law and bring the state closer to the citizen. French cooperation also aims at ensuring a French presence in the African audio-visual programme.

Decentralization

The present crisis shows the limits and failure of an economic model thath gives a prominent role to the state. Decentralization in rural and urban environment enables local development and democracy and is therefore encouraged. It helps to find solutions adapted to each country.

NGOs

Non-governmental organizations are essential partners and privileged actors in democracy; they and governments now have a more constructive partnership. Since the 1980s there has been a permanent dialogue between NGOs and French cooperation through the Development Cooperation Commission. In 1994 France initiated a fresh approach to its relations with NGOs; in future they will jointly define the broad lines of cooperation policy. NGOs will also be able to draw up contracts with the government and to receive global grants over a period of several years.

Decentralized Cooperation

Cooperation between French and African territories is encouraged, and favours decentralization and the emergence of a local management with power. It takes three forms: twinning, urban cooperation, and cooperation for the development of economic activities.

ECONOMIC DEVELOPMENT

In the 1990s new guidelines have been defined in French policy to support economic development.

Defining Adequate Trade Policies and the Need for Flexible Programming

In spite of a preferential trade regime for the ACP states, many African countries have seen their economic situation deteriorate. Their export share in the Community market has regularly decreased: from 3.5 per cent in 1980 to 1.8 per cent in 1992. Only 10 ACP products cover 60 per cent of the total exports to the Community and only

12 ACP countries provide more than 70 per cent of their exports. Trade between ACP states themselves is also weak, and several factors explain this situation: erosion of trade preferences, inadequate trade policies and low-added-value products.

France wants the EU to support policies promoting competitiveness, the diversification of exports and complementary specialization at regional level, and increasing ACP manufactured and processed products. Such a policy has been quite successful for Côte d'Ivoire and Mauritius. France's ambition found an application in the revised Lomé Convention with the insertion of a new article, art. 220p, according to which 'development financial cooperation shall provide support for the definition and implementation of trade policies and programmes to foster the harmonious and gradual integration of ACP states into the world economy.'

More flexible programming in the allocation of the funds is designed to render the aid more efficient. An agreement was reached with the two-tranche method in the mid-term review of the Lomé Convention: 70 per cent of the financial resources of the national indicative programmes will be distributed in an initial three-year period, with the remainder earmarked only after an assessment of how the first allocation has been deployed.

Structural Adjustment Policies

France has recently embraced International Monetary Fund (IMF) and World Bank policies, revealing a deep change in French cooperation since the late 1980s. At that time, France advocated the regional protection of African economies, whereas the World Bank favoured structural adjustment and the IMF stabilization programmes. Both recommended liberalizing exchange rates and opening new markets. Today, the development of Africa is perceived as possible only through its integration into the world economy. French politicians commend the need for sound public financial management and free market forces. In September 1993 Mr Balladur, the former Prime Minister, elaborated the Abidjan doctrine, according to which structural adjustment will be conditional upon the existence of negotiated programmes between African States and the Bretton Woods institutions. Structural adjustment means direct financing for countries whose convertibility and transferability of currency are guaranteed. This doctrine has been a real success and enables French aid to finance development projects, not just state deficits. Furthermore,

France wishes the use of STABEX as an instrument of structural adjustment to be fostered.

Structural adjustment has been joined by a new strategy known as 'good governance', a prescription for making economic austerity measures work by creating a supportive political environment.

The most significant expression of structural adjustment was the devaluation of the CFA franc on 14 January 1994 by 50 per cent (currently (1997) 1 fr=100 CFA fr.). The reasons lay in the worsening of the economic crisis of the 1980s, which thwarted development action in a number of African countries and heightened difficulties connected with the low level of competitiveness of ACP products (i.e. deterioration of the terms of changes and inadequate trade policies). At the end of 1993, the countries of the franc zone[9] faced large-scale economic difficulties: low or negative economic growth, increased public deficits, income decreased by 20 per cent, capital flight, fall in productive investment, and lack of external sources of financing. In these circumstances devaluation became unavoidable and it hit fourteen countries of the franc zone. It aimed to decrease imports and increase exports, enabling an increase in the recipient state's income and after a few years enabling the state to boost its economy through public spending. The only problem, a major one, is that devaluation affects the poorest first and foremost, and especially those in towns who depend on imports even for basic needs.

To reduce the negative effects of devaluation, the French government announced the cancellation of all franc zone public debt for the LDCs (cancellation of the debt of the poorest countries had already taken place at the Dakar francophone summit in December 1994) and half of this debt for the intermediate income countries. In January 1994 the French government set up a Special Fund for Development of 300 million fr. aimed at the population living on a precarious income. The Caisse Française de Développement (CFD) released the same amount for French firms working in the franc zone and suffering from cash shortages. The main problem with these measures is the lack of long-term commitment to the region; e.g. the FSD will not be renewed.

In hindsight, the CFA devaluation is seen on the whole as a success. On an economic level, devaluation was contemporaneous with favourable raw-material prices. Bretton Woods institutions have concluded agreements with most of the countries of the area, providing external financing. On a social level, urban incomes have been drastically reduced in favour of rural incomes, but there has not been the disaster some may have predicted. On the whole inflation is controlled (33 per cent in 1994, whereas the IMF forecast 40 per cent). In real terms, growth was positive again in most of the countries: 1.5 per cent for 1994 and probably 4 per cent for 1995. West Africa is, however, in a better situation than Central Africa. CFA devaluation particularly stimulated agricultural activities. Trade balances also improved (West Africa: 323 billion CFA francs; Central Africa: 1404 billion CFA francs in 1994) because of the reduction in imports and the increase of agricultural raw material prices since autumn 1993, rather than thanks to the increase of exports, with the exception of Côte d'Ivoire, Mali and Burkina Faso. Conditions of competitiveness have improved. On the other hand, public deficits remain significant, arrears of the internal and external debt are not completely absorbed, private investments are still slow to come and the industrial field has not been stimulated. Structural and sector-based political adjustments have to be made so as to create economic development favourable to GDP growth. Yet the debate for and against the devaluation does not address the real issue. What is called into question is the whole model of development. The franc zone is still dominated by France. To keep this zone does not encourage African states to take up their responsibilities and to work for their own regional integration.

Development of National Markets and the Organization of Agricultural Products

Today the main economic priority is not improvement in production but protecting market shares and exports.The action of the Ministry of Cooperation takes into account the regional dimension of markets. The agricultural sector is vital. Progressive disengagement of the state should be replaced by professionally organizing producers, while small farmers should be grouped into associations. French cooperation also aims at the pursuit of self-sufficiency in food and food security in the ACP states. France contributed 20 per cent of the European Union's aid programme. Food aid is only complementary to financial aid, which remains the essential part of development aid.

Development of the Private Sector and Private Investment

France's main mission is to encourage domestic and foreign private investment into the productive sectors in the ACP states, which alone can boost the African economy. France also intends to contribute to the development of private companies in Africa and to improve their legal, statutory and financial environment. It wants to take advantage of the presence of French enterprises on the continent. On 30 October 1995 a plan was presented to encourage private investment and private sector and should be applied by the CFD. This plan should enable exports to be diversified and advantage to be taken of the rules of origin of Lomé IVB.

Regional Cooperation

Regional cooperation develops intra-ACP trade, which is currently marginal, and France takes into account the regional dimension in its programmes. During the mid-term review it advocated that art. 159h of the Lomé Convention should be more explicit in its objective and should be written as follows: 'the scope of regional cooperation shall include development and expansion of trade *through the lifting of tariff and non tariff obstacles and the setting up of harmonized trade policies*'. But this was not introduced in the revised Convention. The extension in June 1995 of the French *champ* to the Lomé Convention states and South Africa is explained by the definition of development projects towards regional integration. Regional cooperation could be a solution after the expiry of the Lomé IV Convention.

Economic Development Respecting the Environment

Environment and development are indissolubly linked. Protection of the environment and natural resources are basic objectives. French cooperation policy consists of promoting forms of exploitation which associate local populations and take into account the need to renew resources and to guarantee their sustainability. The French government also supports the environmental policies of African states and has helped them to take part in conferences and international conventions since the Rio Conference of 1992 and Rio Plus Five in 1997. France elaborates and applies national action plans for the environment and to bring assistance to the various problems of urban growth; waste management, drinking water, conservation of biodiversity, rational exploitation of forests and desertification control. The objective is also to safeguard the living conditions of future generations.

HUMAN DEVELOPMENT

There is a strong correlation between the growth rate in a country and its human development.

Education

Improving primary school teaching is the principal objective. France provides assistance to improve human resource management, adapt-

cities and regional coopera-

es are also reinforced by

roblem. Today there are

ntries; by 2025 there will be

ties go to health structure

es (Aids) and family health.

en and children represent a

lopment.

embrace all areas of cooper-

on man himself and rooted in

nforce social cohesion and it

CONCLUSION: TOWARDS A NEW STRATEGY?

With the Lomé Convention, the EU is collectively involved in development aid to ACP States. This historical commitment is mainly a continuation of what happened in the past. France is aware that the EU's geopolitical and economic interests lie increasingly in other regions of the world, such as the Mediterranean and South-East Asian countries, and that French relations with the ACP states cannot return to the *status quo ante*. For the foreseeable future, however, there seems little prospect that France will switch its allegiance away from Africa. It seems unlikely that France (which has always advocated the cause of the ACP states since the birth of the EEC) will wish to jeopardize this one constant factor in its changing relations with the rest of the world. Mr João de Deus Pinheiro, the commissioner for development, declared just after his nomination in January 1995 that it would be a historical mistake if the European Union did not recognize Africa as an essential and natural partner in the future. France will therefore remain engaged in Africa, but on the basis of a new partnership which still remains to be defined. For the time being France has the duty of facilitating the progressive entry of the ACP states into the new liberalized economic world. The French ministry of cooperation believes in the future of Africa, which remains important for France for political, economic and cultural reasons. In the context of regionalization of world markets, the ACP states are also significant for the EU as a whole.

France has a moral and historical duty towards the ACP States. But development aid towards the Mediterranean and South-East Asian countries is becoming an unavoidable strategic necessity; the Euro-Mediterranean conference in Barcelona (27–28 November 1995) and the Euro-Asian conference in Bangkok (1–2 March 1996) testified to that. At the WTO Summit in Singapore in December 1996 President Chirac stated that France's future also lies in Asia.[10] The Socialist French government of Mr Jospin also appears to accept these new realities.

Given the dynamic Asian economies, this could seriously question the priority of development aid given to the ACP states despite France's official position. The possible extension of the Lomé Convention to other developing countries favoured by certain member states would definitely bring an end to this priority and would even marginalize them. It should be remembered that development aid is only a palliative measure. Ultimately the destinies of the ACP States are in their own hands.

Bibliography

Actionaid, *The Reality of Aid 1995* (Earthscan Publications, London, 1995)

Alibert J., 'La France et l'Afrique. L'observatoire permanent de la coopération française publie son premier rapport', *Revue des marchés tropicaux et méditerranéens*, no. 2843 (12 May 1995), pp. 968–70.

Courier International, no. 271 (11–17 January 1996).

Cumming, G., 'French development assistance to Africa: towards a new agenda?', *African Affairs*, vol. 94, no. 376 (July 1995) pp. 383–93.

Cyril, B. 'Quand le Nord perd le Sud – la politique française de coopération', *Projet,* no. 941 (printemps 1995), p. 43.

de Gaulle, J. 'Les Partis politiques français et l'Afrique', *Revue des marchés tropicaux et méditerranéens*, no. 2469 (5 March 1993) pp. 609–11.

Europe, hebdo sélection outre mer, no. 734 (26 June 1995).

Europe, no. 6422 (17 February 1995); no. 6508 (24 June 1995); no. 6514 (3 and 4 July 1995).

Gaulme F. 'Une année charnière', *Revue des marchés tropicaux et méditerranéens*, no. 2563 (23 December 1994) pp. 2698–2701.

Gaulme, F. 'La France et l'Afrique – De François Mitterrand à Jacques Chirac', *Revue des marchés tropicaux et méditerranéens*, no. 2845 (26 May 1995) p. 1122.

Griffon, M., 'L'Avenir européen de la coopération', *Projet*, Paris, no. 219 (September 1989) pp. 93–102.

Grilli, E. R., *The European Community and the Developing Countries* (Cambridge University Press, 1993).

Hargrove, C. 'L'Europe et l'Afrique – Le Conseil franco-britannique débat sur l'Afrique à Paris', *Revue des marchés tropicaux et méditerranéens* no. 2872 (17 November 1995) p. 2516.

Hoguet, P. 'La Convention de Lomé: un modèle en danger?', *Rapport d'information de l'Assemblée Nationale*, no. 2070 (1995).

Jalade M. 'La France et l'Afrique', *Revue des marchés tropicaux et méditerranéens*, no. 2872 (17 November 1995) p. 2519.

Jeune Afrique, 'Mitterrand – le jugement des Africains. Les Arabes et lui,' no. 1828 (18–24 janvier 1996) pp. 2–3.

Juppe', A. 'Quel horizon pour la politique étrangère de la France?', *Politique étrangère* no. 1 (Coll. Institut français des relations internationales, Paris, 1995) pp. 257–9.

Lemaignen R., *L'Europe au berceau. Souvenirs d'un technocrate* (Plon, Paris, 1964).

Libération 24 and 25 June 1995; 20 and 21 January 1996.

Le Monde 6 February 1995; 21 June 1995; 24 June 1995; 5 July 1995; 7 November 1995; 4 December 1995; 12 January 1996; 30 January 1996; 13 February 1996; 1, 3 and 4 March 1996.

Michel, J., 'Development Co-operation. Efforts and Policies of the Members of the Development Assistance Committee' *DAC 1995 Report* (OECD, Paris. 1996).

Percival, D. 'Successful Conclusion to the Lomé IV Mid-Term Review – Agreement Clinched at Eleventh Hour', *The Courier ACP-EU*, no. 153 (September–October 1995) p. 6.

Rapport d'activité du Ministère de la Coopération, 1994–1995 *West Africa*, no. 4082 (15–21 January 1996).

Notes

1. *Courier International* (1996).
2. *Le Monde*, 4 December 1995.
3. *Libération*, 20–21 January 1996.
4. *Le Monde*, 13 February 1996. The target for developed countries to allocate 0.7 per cent of their GNP to Overseas Development Assistance

(ODA) was recommended by the Pearson Commission in 1969 and adopted by the UN General Assembly in 1970.

5. Alibert (1995) p. 968.
6. Percival (1995); *Europe*, (24 June 1995); *Europe hebdo sélection outre-mer*, 26 June 1995.
7. *Le Monde*, 13 February 1996.
8. African countries with which France has preferential relations. These countries, most of them former French colonies, make up the French zone of influence.
9. The franc zone is a monetary system created in 1939 between France and the West Africa Monetary Union (WAMU), the Central Africa Monetary Union (CAMU) and the Comoros. WAMU includes Benin, Burkina Faso, Côte d'Ivoire, Mali, Niger, Senegal, and Togo. CAMU includes Cameroon, Central African Republic Congo, Equatorial Guinea, and Chad. The franc zone guaranteed money convertibility, making it possible to buy French francs with CFA francs in all situations and for any trade volumes, free movement of capital within the Franc zone, fixed exchange rate with French franc, the centralization of money reserves in an account of the French public revenue department. The franc zone is organized around three central banks. Monetary stability has thus been guaranteed for forty-six years.
10. *Le Monde*, 1, 3 and 4 March 1996.

5 Britain and the Lomé Convention

Philip Tod

INTRODUCTION

When Britain joined the European Community, the EC's development policy was based on the concept of association and was directed mainly at France's former colonies. In the years immediately after accession, the percentage of the British aid budget spent via the EC institutions was only 6 per cent. Yet by 1996 it had risen to 25 per cent, mainly via the Lomé Convention which had replaced the old association model.

Britain's priorities for the Lomé Convention and the EC's development policy have tended to reflect British bilateral aid priorities and, between 1979 and 1997, the New Right policies of the Thatcher and Major governments. Britain constantly stressed the need for greater effectiveness in EC development assistance, citing its own Overseas Development Administration (ODA) as an example. Other major priorities were the need for better evaluation of EC aid programmes and greater emphasis on structural adjustment and political conditionality. Britain's policy was also affected by the subordination of overseas development priorities to foreign policy and commercial considerations, which helps to explain the concern to halt the erosion of bilateral aid in favour of multilateral EC commitments.

This chapter provides an overview of Britain's role in the negotiations for the first Lomé Convention and assesses the increasingly important role of multilateral aid in Britain's overseas aid policy up to the end of the Conservative government in April 1997. The change in priorities in the 1980s following the election of a Conservative government in 1979 and its priorities for the 1990s are considered, including the elaboration of a new mission statement for the ODA and the reduction in Britain's contribution to the European Development Fund (EDF). The conclusion is that Britain's main priorities for the Lomé Convention and the wider development policy of the EC remained largely unchanged between 1979 and 1997. However, the election of a Labour government in April 1997 and the creation of a new Department for International Development heralds significant changes.

BRITAIN AND THE LOMÉ NEGOTIATIONS

Britain only joined the European Community in 1973 and therefore was not involved in framing the early development policies of the EC. These had been shaped essentially with the interests of France in mind, which meant that EC aid was directed mainly at France's former colonies. Britain faced an uphill battle in defending the interests of its former colonies and was forced to abandon the hope of EC ties with South Asia. However, Britain did manage to secure the widening of the EDF to include its former African colonies and several islands in the Caribbean and the Pacific that were members of the Commonwealth.

During the negotiations that culminated in the first Lomé Convention, there were two main areas of disagreement. Some countries, such as France, Belgium and Italy, favoured an association along the lines of the Yaoundé Agreement, whereas Britain, along with Germany and the Netherlands, supported a more open structure. Britain argued that the EC should see association as a transitionary stage only, leading to a more global policy. The intention was to secure more favourable treatment for the Commonwealth countries and the Asian countries who could not join an association with the EC. The EC's development model until British accession was essentially based on the French concept of 'Eurafrica' and there was no real attempt at a more global approach. During the renegotiation of British terms of membership of the EC in 1974–5, agreement was reached on a 50:50 division of aid between those countries associated with the EC and non-associates such as India and Pakistan. This adoption of a more global approach was to a large extent due to British influence.[1]

There was also disagreement on the question of reciprocity, which France favoured and Britain opposed. This was a controversial area, as the principle of reciprocity in trade relations with developing countries had been in place since the Treaty of Rome. It was eventually agreed that the Lomé convention would be based on non-reciprocity, which was a significant concession to the British and a victory for the ACP states, who had argued strongly for it.

Another achievement of the British in the early 1970s was the negotiation of a special Sugar Protocol. Sugar was a product in which the ACP countries competed against Community producers, yet Britain effectively secured the extension to selected Lomé countries of its Commonwealth Sugar Agreement. This agreement allowed ACP countries to export specified amounts of sugar to the EC at predetermined prices for an indefinite period.[2]

THE GROWING IMPORTANCE OF MULTILATERAL AID

The most remarkable aspect of Britain's overseas aid is the large and growing proportion channelled via the EC. This resulted from cuts in Britain's aid budget in the 1980s and 1990s, while Britain was less successful in holding down its contributions to the EDF and other EC development projects.

The UK's share of contributions to the EC's overseas aid nearly doubled between 1979 and 1989 and is set to rise further.[3] According to Adrian Hewitt, it was the agreement reached with the UK in 1973 'which dictated the pattern of a rapidly rising share of UK aid being channelled via Brussels from 1975 onwards'.[4] In 1978, 6 per cent of British aid was spent through the EC; this had increased to 12 per cent by 1979 and had reached 17 per cent to 19 per cent by 1989. In 1994, just under 25 per cent of British aid was channelled through the EC and this is set to rise to a third by 2000.[5]

This decrease in the size of Britain's bilateral aid programme in the face of increasing multilateral commitments has proved highly controversial. The British aid minister in the Major government, Baroness Chalker, said that she would have preferred the EU increase not to have gone ahead, arguing that it was a mistake because of the lack of expertise in the EU aid programme.[6] British policy was to halt the erosion of Britain's bilateral aid, which it perceived as more effective. According to Adrian Hewitt, the undeclared reason for this was that it could not 'allow its bilateral programme to run down too drastically and retain credibility, so long as a high foreign profile remains a plausible and declared national policy'.[7]

It could be argued that this reflects the subordination of British development policy to foreign and commercial interests. The ODA ceased to be an independent ministry under the Conservative government and became instead part of the Foreign Office. When the debate on incorporating ODA into the Foreign Office took place, the government argued that the aim was to facilitate the close co-ordination of foreign and Commonwealth policy and aid policy. According to Burnell, the former Overseas Development minister, John Patten, 'never tired of trying to convince anyone who would listen that Britain's political, commercial and industrial interests could be well served by the aid programme'.[8] In addition, there was also a desire to achieve other political goals by the maintenance of a significant bilateral aid programme, such as retaining close links with Commonwealth countries and promoting stability in developing countries.

The best example of the subordination of aid to political and commercial considerations was the Pergau Dam scandal, when the government was found to have linked funding for the building of a dam in Pergau, Malaysia, to arms sales. In November 1994, the British government was found guilty in the High Court of abusing the 1980 Overseas Development and Cooperation Act by approving the Pergau project, which was found to be economically unsound and not aimed at promoting development.[9] The scandal showed that the Foreign Office was prepared to overrule the ODA and fund a development project to further the interests of Britain's defence industry.

The government also faced pressure from commercial interests to reverse the trend towards the multilateralization of British aid and increase the percentage of bilateral aid, which was tied to the purchase of British goods, because they feared that their interests were not protected by EC aid programmes. There is some evidence for this: Britain was less successful in obtaining development contracts than France and Italy. For example, under the sixth EDF, the UK was awarded 10.07 per cent of total contracts, compared with 21.15 per cent for France and 16.54 per cent for Italy.[10]

An interest group representing major British overseas contractors, the Export Group for the Construction Industries (EGCI), argued that the UK should increase the amount of tied bilateral aid because multilateral aid has fewer commercial benefits for British companies.[11] Although the British government claims to favour 'untying' EU aid programmes, most British bilateral aid is tied to British products: 66.7 per cent of bilateral aid was tied in 1992, compared with an average of 40 per cent for countries in the Development Assistance Committee (DAC) of the OECD.[12] We will return to the British criticisms of the EC's multilateral programme later in the context of the debate over the eighth EDF (p. 69).

CHANGING PRIORITIES IN THE 1980s

The election of a Conservative government under Margaret Thatcher in 1979 had a significant impact on Britain's bilateral and multilateral aid programme. The Thatcher government placed much less emphasis on development than its predecessor and this is reflected in the decline of the British aid budget during the 1980s. According to OECD figures, Britain's overseas aid declined by an average of 2.8 per cent per year between 1981–2 and 1986–7.[13] British aid as a percentage of gross national product fell from 0.51 per cent in 1979 to 0.32 per cent in 1988.[14] Britain spent less on development aid as a percentage of GNP than many of its European partners: in 1994, Britain devoted only 0.31 per cent of GNP to aid, compared with Germany's 0.34 per cent, France's 0.64 per cent and Denmark's 1.03 per cent.[15] The comparatively low levels of British aid expenditure and their decline in the 1980s led to a greater emphasis on obtaining value for money from British and EC aid and to moves to contain the growth in multilateral commitments.

Increased Emphasis on Structural Adjustment as a Condition for Aid

Another characteristic of the 1980s was the emphasis laid on the need for developing countries to go through a process of structural adjustment in exchange for aid. This form of economic conditionality is illustrated by the shift in Britain from budgetary assistance to programme assistance, which represented £187 million of gross aid in 1989. According to Burnell, this kind of aid is usually conditional on the recipient country undertaking economic reforms.[16] The then minister for Overseas Development, John Patten, urged the European Community to shift its emphasis from what he regarded as complicated rural development projects to fast and effective support for structural adjustment, which would facilitate the introduction of market reforms in developing countries. The new priorities of the Conservative government were also seen in the technical and financial assistance to developing countries seeking to privatize public enterprises.

Adrian Hewitt argues that by the late 1980s the EC began to follow Britain's lead in supporting moves to a more liberal policy regime in developing countries. In the first Lomé IV period, the EC allocated 1150 million ecu in support for structural adjustment, which illustrates the importance the EC now attaches to this aspect of development policy.[17] The ODA also claims some success in bringing about changes in the EC's support for economic reform programmes by 'strategic secondments'.[18]

Concern for Greater Effectiveness of EC Help

Another priority for the British government during the 1980s was to increase the effectiveness of both British and European aid. The British argued that the European Commission was overstretched and could not effectively administer the considerable funds allocated to it by the European Parliament. Britain also claimed that the staff of the Commission lacked the professional qualifications and experience needed for the new priorities such as the environment and education. The British response was to send some of its own experts to work in the Commission on a temporary basis.[19]

The ODA sought to improve the effectiveness of British aid by increasingly concentrating on the poorest and low-income countries and called on the EC to do the same, instead of giving aid to countries which would raise finance from the private sector.[20] According to Actionaid, British aid is comparatively well focused on low-income countries and the least developed countries, but this aid does not necessarily reach the poorest within those countries. However, they also argue that 'EU aid is generally even weaker on poverty focus.'[21]

The ODA also set up mechanisms for the evaluation of British aid projects in order to improve the quality of future projects and urged the Community to do likewise. Lynda (now Baroness) Chalker, Britain's Overseas Development minister from 1989 to 1997, called for the EC and other multilateral aid organizations 'to ensure quality in the whole of their operations and a tight value for money approach to their own administration'.[22] The EC has taken steps to improve the evaluation of its aid programmes, with the introduction of the project cycle management method. This method has six distinct stages to improve the identification, implementation, monitoring and evaluation of aid, with the aim of improving the long-term effectiveness of aid. Evaluations have been carried out in a number of fields in 1994, including institutional development, trade and three structural adjustment programmes.[23]

Another British concern was that the EC should concentrate on ensuring that information was shared and the approaches of the various member states, the EC and other aid agencies were adequately coordinated. The Commission itself noted that there is a lack of coordination between the development policies of member states and the Community, and this is one of the main factors hindering EC aid. Actionaid argues that 'bilateral interests and different interpretations of subsidiarity mean that the Commission is still acting more as a sixteenth donor than the centre of coordination.'[24]

The EC sought to address this coordination deficit by setting up a pilot project for the coordination of member states development policies in Bangladesh, Côte d'Ivoire, Costa Rica, Ethiopia, Mozambique and Peru. At the November 1994 Development Council meeting, Baroness Chalker stressed the importance of the project and appealed for member states to share information before implementing projects.[25]

BRITISH PRIORITIES FOR THE 1990s

The New Mission Statement of the ODA

In 1994 the ODA set out its aims and priorities for both bilateral and multilateral aid in a 'mission statement', defining the purpose of ODA and the means by which it will be achieved.[26] The ODA's mission statement was 'to improve the quality of life of people in poorer countries by contributing to sustainable development and reducing poverty and suffering'.[27] The mission statement also set out the four aims of the ODA to achieve this goal, which were seen as interdependent and mutually reinforcing.

The first aim was 'to encourage sound development policies, efficient markets and good government'.[28] This aim reaffirmed the ODA's commitment to economic and political conditionality, which first appeared during the 1980s. The ODA saw this first aim as an essential condition for growth and sought to promote economic reforms by removing trade barriers, encouraging investment, and helping governments to stabilise public finances and control inflation.[29] Britain sought to pass on its experience directly and through multilateral institutions such as the EC.

The emphasis on good government is a recurring theme in recent British statements on development policy. The issue of governance was first raised by Douglas Hurd, the then Foreign Secretary, at a speech to the Overseas Development Institute in June 1990 and it has been a central plank of British policy ever since. In his speech, Hurd argued that there was a link between good government and development and therefore donors had to take into account the records of recipient countries on pluralism, public accountability, respect for the rule of law, human rights and market principles.[30]

The use of political conditionality has proved highly controversial. The British government argued that it was not seeking to impose its own model of democracy, or using governance as a justification for cuts in aid. Most importantly, the ODA insisted that its policy was not neocolonialist: the aim was to support the efforts of developing countries to set up appropriate systems of government that took into account their own social and political structures.

What the British government meant by good government was firstly that the governments of developing countries should 'promote the sound economic and social policies which are necessary for sustainable development', that is, they should introduce market reforms and increased competition as well as macroeconomic reforms. However, good government according to the ODA also involved measures to tackle poverty, illiteracy and disease and reductions in military spending. Britain sought to improve the competence of governments in developing countries by providing support for the training of officials. Finally, the ODA argued that democracy, human rights and the rule of law are essential to ensure the efficiency and sustainability of development.

Britain has taken a leading role in including good government criteria in aid policy and was successful in urging the EC to do the same. The fourth Lomé Convention included in art. 5 a commitment by the EC and the ACP states to uphold human rights, and in the mid-term review of Lomé in 1994 there was 'a broad consensus on political and institutional matters, as well as those linked to democracy and human rights'.[31]

The second aim in ODA's new mission statement was 'to help people achieve better education and health and to widen opportunities – especially for women'.[32] The purpose of this aim was to focus aid, both bilateral and multilateral, on the needs of people. ODA claimed considerable success in the fields of access to contraceptive services, coping with sexually transmitted diseases and maternal health care.

The ODA's third aim was 'to enhance productive capacity and to conserve the environment.'[33] This aim was intended to help developing countries to increase and sustain production, while reducing pollution and protecting the environment. The ODA sought to promote cleaner technologies and the better use of water resources. In its aim of promoting the sustainable management of forests, ODA seconded two forestry experts to the Commission to improve its expertise in this field.[34]

The fourth and final aim of the mission statement was 'to promote international policies for sustainable development and enhance the effectiveness of multilateral development institutions'.[35] A substantial part of Britain's development assistance programme was by 1995 spent through multilateral institutions and consequently the ODA was determined to pursue its aims through bodies such as the EC. Baroness Chalker restated her determination to improve the effectiveness of EC aid: the senior staff responsible for Britain's bilateral aid were also responsible for vetting decisions made in the EC context and representing Britain's point of view.[36] The Overseas Development minister also confirmed that Britain's priorities for EU development policy were sustainable development, poverty reduction, the debt burden and migration. However, there was another aim, which was not mentioned: halting the rise in multilateral commitments, which were eroding Britain's bilateral aid.

The Decision to Reduce the UK's Contribution to the Eighth EDF

The 1995 budget settlement in the UK reduced the ODA's budget, but this did not affect multilateral commitments to a great extent, as bilateral spending was protected. British policy was to 'ensure that multilateral contributions do not swallow up our bilateral aid'.[37] This followed on from the British government's controversial decision in February 1995 to reduce Britain's contribution to the eighth EDF. At the General Affairs Council of 16 February 1995, Baroness Chalker confirmed that Britain was determined to reduce its contribution to the EDF from 1790 billion ecu to 1270 billion ecu.[38] In a speech to the Royal Institute for International Affairs on 1 March 1995, she defended the decision, saying:

> What the UK is seeking to do is maintain as large and effective a bilateral programme for Africa as possible, as well as to get improved effectiveness from all EC spending...even with the reduction in our EDF contributions, our EC multilateral commitment will rise steeply over the next few years.[39]

Britain focused on the EDF because it could control the size of its contributions to it, whereas it had no control of the EC's budgetized aid programmes, which are the fastest-growing component of EC aid. British attitudes to the EDF as an effective aid instrument were ambivalent; in 1994, the ODA commissioned a study from the Overseas Development Institute on the effectiveness of EC aid. This concluded that EDF projects were evenly distributed between three categories: 'effective', 'partially effective' and 'ineffective'.[40] According to the ODA's 1995 Fundamental Expenditure Review, this equated with the performance of an average bilateral donor but was below that of Britain's bilateral aid. The report went on to argue that 'a greater degree of conditionality on EDF funds would increase the effectiveness of this channel'.[41] One of the report's central recommendations was to ensure that the EC budget ceilings were adhered to and to resist any attempt to budgetize the EDF.[42]

The British stance on the EDF was heavily criticized, and the dispute was only resolved at the Cannes European Council of 26 and 27 June 1995, with an increase in the French contribution. The dispute illustrated the British concern to maintain a significant bilateral aid programme and the continued priority that Britain attached to the increased effectiveness of a Community development programme which it regards as inferior to its own.

CONCLUSION

Britain's priorities for Lomé and the EC's other development programmes remained remarkably consistent between 1979 and 1997. The main aim was to improve their effectiveness and value for money, by seconding British experts to the Commission and seeking improvements in the evaluation of aid projects. A concern for encouraging structural adjustment became prominent during the 1980s, and in the early 1990s Britain led other donors in calling for political conditions to be attached to aid, such as human rights, democracy and good government. Most of all, as it became clear that Britain's contribution to the EDF was rising so fast that multilateral commitments would soon exceed bilateral British aid, Britain sought to curtail its contributions.

Britain had some success in seeing that its priorities were reflected in the EC's development programmes and the Lomé Convention. For example, the EC accepted the principle of linking some of its Lomé aid to structural adjustment. The EC also placed much more emphasis on political conditionality and the effective evaluation of EC programmes than in the past. However, British reductions in multilateral development aid spending suggests that Britain's main priority will be to maintain a large and significant bilateral aid programme, to promote its foreign policy and commercial interests. The Labour Government, elected in 1997, has given high priority to poverty alleviation in recipient countries. However, the new Department for International Development (with its Secretary of State in the Cabinet) has not shifted the emphasis of British aid towards multilateral institutions.

Bibliography

Actionaid, *The Reality of Aid 1995* (Earthscan Publications, London, 1995) p. 120.

Agence Europe, no. 6422 (February 17 1995) p. 4.

Agence Europe, no. 6432 (March 3 1995) p. 8.

Agence Europe, no. 6510 (June 28 1995) p. 2.

Burnell, P., 'Introduction to Britain's Overseas Aid: Between Idealism and Self-interest', Bose, A. and Burnell, P. (eds) *Britain's Overseas Aid since 1979: Between Idealism and Self-Interest* (Manchester University Press, 1991) pp. 1–30.

Chakrabarti, S., Wilson, R. and Rundell, P., 'ODA Fundamental Expenditure Review', *Overseas Development Administration* (July 1995) pp. 168–71.

Chalker, L., 'Britain's Role in the Multilateral Aid Agencies', *Development Policy Review*, vol. 8 (1990) pp. 355–64.

Chalker, L., 'Good Government and the Aid Programme', speech to the Overseas Development Institute at Chatham House, London, 25 June 1991.

Chalker, L., 'Britain's approach to Multilateral Aid', *Development Policy Review*, vol. 12, no. 3 (1994) pp. 243–50.

Chalker, L., 'ODA: New Aims and Priorities', speech to the Royal Institute for International Affairs, London, February 14 1996.

Christopoulos, S. '1995 – A Watershed Between Two Eras', *The Courier ACP-ELL* no. 154 (Commission of the European Communities, Brussels, 1995) p. 73.

European Commission, *Financial Co-operation under the Lomé Conventions: Review of Aid at the End of 1994* (Commission of the European Communities, Brussels, 1995) p. 136.

Grilli, E., *The European Community and the Developing Countries* (Cambridge University Press, 1993) p. 387.

Hewitt, A., 'Britain and the European Development Fund', in Bose, A. and Burnell, P. (eds), *Britain's Overseas Aid Since 1979: Between Idealism and Self-Interest* (Manchester University Press, 1991) pp. 86–96.

Hewitt, A., *UK Aid in the 1990s, Crisis or Transition in Foreign Aid* (Overseas Development Institute, London, 1995) pp. 72–9.

Michel, James H., *Development Cooperation Report 1995: Efforts and Policies of the Members of the Development Assistance Committee* (OECD, Paris, 1996) pp. 103–14.

Morrissey, Oliver, 'The Commercialization of Aid: Business Interests and the UK Aid Budget 1978–88', *Development Policy Review,* vol. 8, no. 3 (September 1990) pp. 301–22.

OECD, *Development Cooperation Report* (Paris, 1995) pp. 103–14

Overseas Development Administration, *Mission Statement* (ODA, London, 1996).

Oyowe, A., 'Enhancing efficiency and sustainability of aid', *The Courier,* no. 149 (Commission of the European Communities, Brussels, 1995) p. 48.

Vivekanandam, B., 'Britain, the EEC, and the Third World', in Lall, K. B. and Chopra, H. S., The EEC and the Third World (Humanities Press, London pp. 205–15.

Notes

1. Vivekanandan (1981) p. 211.
2. Grilli (1993) p. 31.
3. Hewitt (1991) p. 86.
4. Ibid., p. 86.
5. Actionaid (1995) p. 92.
6. Ibid., p. 93.
7. Hewitt (1995) p. 78.
8. Burnell (1991) p. 21.
9. Actionaid (1995) p. 93.
10. European Commission (1995) p. 129.
11. Morrissey (1990) p. 306.
12. Actionaid (1995) p. 94.
13. Burnell (1991) p. 10.
14. Ibid., p. 9.
15. OECD, *Development Co-operation Report* (1995) pp. 103–14.
16. Burnell (1991) p. 6.
17. Christopoulos (1995) p. 76.
18. Chakrabarti et al. (1995) p. 170.
19. Chalker (1990) p. 362.
20. Chalker (1990) p. 357.
21. Actionaid (1995) pp. 93–4.
22. Chalker (1990) p. 357.
23. European Commission (1995) p. 131.
24. Actionaid (1995) p. 101.
25. Oyowe (1995) p. 48.
26. Chalker (1996) p. 3.
27. Overseas Development Administration (1996).
28. Chalker (1996) p. 4.
29. Ibid., p. 4.
30. Speech by Douglas Hurd MP, Secretary of State for Foreign and Commonwealth Affairs, on June 6 1990 to a conference organized by the Overseas Development Institute on Prospects for Africa in the 1990s. Cited in Chalker (1990) p. 364.
31. European Commission (1995) p. 14.

32. Overseas Development Administration (1996).
33. Overseas Development Administration (1996).
34. Chalker (1990) p. 362.
35. Ibid.
36. Chalker (1996) p. 6.
37. Ibid, p. 6.
38. *Agence Europe*, February 17 1995, p. 5.
39. *Agence Europe*, March 3 1995, p. 8.
40. Chakrabarti *et al.* (1995) p. 169.
41. Ibid, p. 169.
42. Ibid, p. 171.

6 Italy, Spain and Portugal and the Lomé Convention

Annalisa Oddone

INTRODUCTION

Initiated particularly by France[1] and strengthened and expanded with the accession of the United Kingdom in the Community, the Lomé Agreements have been based on a compromise of interests between, *inter alia*, member states that formerly colonized territories in the African, Caribbean and Pacific (ACP) countries.

While Italy, except in of the Horn of Africa, cannot be considered a recent colonial power, Portugal and Spain only joined the European Community (EC) in 1986, which explains their initial reluctance towards and limited interest in the Lomé Agreements.

This chapter analyses the role of southern European states (Spain, Italy and Portugal) in development cooperation, particularly referring to their participation in the Lomé Conventions. The three countries are examined separately because each of them presents particular characteristics owing to their specific policy choices and historical links. Development policy is an integral part of all these countries' foreign policies; it serves the promotion of human rights and observes the principles of the United Nations as well as the Lomé agreements.

Each section shows how the interests and priorities of these member states clearly emerge in their activities within the ACP states, although multilateral aid inside the Community has been a framework for their bilateral programmes. This fact testifies how often commercial, strategic and cultural interests are the prevailing criteria when aid is distributed, while poverty only plays a marginal role.

Cooperation activity between these countries within the EU and the Lomé Agreements is analysed, taking into account the general framework of their development policy, including reference to their bilateral cooperation with the ACP states and other areas of the world.

After a specific analysis of the three countries, the conclusion will focus on a comparison between them and a general assessment of their bilateral and Community actions.

The three countries, while presenting many differences owing to their historical and social backgrounds, indeed demonstrate common features, mostly linked to their 'similar' current economic situation (agriculture producers, financial difficulties, efficient small and medium-sized enterprises) and their geographical position.

ITALY

Italian Development Cooperation

Italian development cooperation reached the level of other industrial countries only in the 1980s. Until then there was almost no bilateral cooperation[2] and the multilateral sector, dominated mostly by private export credits, accounted for more than 81 per cent of Italy's total transfers to the developing countries.

Since 1986, Italy has made several efforts to insert its development aid with the G7 countries. From 1985 to 1992, the Italian contribution to cooperation with the developing countries grew by more than 43 per cent. However, it started dropping sharply in 1993, affecting its bilateral commitments in particular.

The structural framework of modern Italian development cooperation, according to international standards, was established by Law no. 49 of 1987, which still applies today.

The most important features of this law include the guidelines of the Fondo Rotativo (fund for credit allocation) and the Fondo di Cooperazione, the central financing fund of Italy's development policy (for the allocation of subsidies). The Direzione Generale allo Sviluppo, the central office of the Ministry of Foreign Affairs (MAE), is responsible for the practical implementation of development cooperation.

Law no. 49/87 also identifies possible sectors for cooperation such as agriculture, education, trade, technology and information. These sectors are supported by implementing short and medium-term projects, selecting volunteers and organizing training activities involving local citizens in recipient countries. Factors driving Italy's development action can be summarized in five main categories: humanitarian decisions, commercial interests, strategic objectives, including security and the supply of minerals and raw materials, historical and cultural links and international prestige.

During the 1960s Italian cooperation was characterized by sporadic interventions without a clear, coherent and geopolitical strategy.

However, in the 1970s, policy focused mostly on multilateral aid. Throughout the last decade much importance was given to international prestige as a driving force, which explains the increase in official multilateral development assistance that still holds today.

Promoting economic returns represents another constant priority for Italy, guided by the interests of its business community (stimulating exports and protecting investments abroad), which sometimes override concern for social and economic conditions in the recipient countries.

Italy is very concerned about increased awareness of the value of peace, solidarity and democracy. It favours decentralized cooperation where society has a fundamental role to play in order to encourage local involvement and participation. In this context a major role is played by NGOs,[3] which sit on the Liaison Committee and have signed a contract with the EU Commission for the financing of cooperation activities during the last six years.

Italian Priorities in the Lomé Convention

As a founder member of the European Community, Italy joined the Lomé Agreements in 1975 (signing the first Lomé Convention), but, as in bilateral development cooperation, its aid started to be consistent only in the 1980s.

Among the ACP states, Italy has traditionally focused on African countries with which it has strong and longstanding geographical and historical ties.

Before the Lomé Conventions, Italy's development cooperation was already concentrated on the African continent; the aim was to encourage and support economic and social emancipation and to establish democratic and representative political institutions. Italy welcomed the Organization of African Unity, which was created in 1963 in order to achieve common goals based on unity, solidarity and cooperation.

Italian participation in the EU and in the Lomé Conventions increased Italian cooperation activity in Africa, so that nowadays more than a third of Italy's total multilateral aid payments are made through these channels. However, Italy's participation in these agreements reflects the influence of its political, economic and strategic motivations as well as its historical and humanitarian ones.

In particular, Italy's cooperation is characterized by a constant interest in a group of countries with which Italy has historical links, namely Somalia, Ethiopia and Eritrea, the Horn of Africa. These countries have enjoyed preferential treatment (*paesi prioritari*) in Italian development cooperation, which has been justified both by its colonial heritage and by the current financial constraints. They have received about 20 per cent of the total aid distributed by Italy during the last decade, which has mostly been destined for humanitarian assistance because of the devastating civil wars. In 1992 it was decided that these countries, with the addition of Mozambique and Tanzania, were to receive up to 75 per cent of total available funds.

Italian firms invest mainly in this area of Africa. However, concentration in only one sector, namely civil engineering, a lack of diversification and a weak training structure make Italian assistance in these countries often insufficient and sometimes even inefficient.

Italy also pursues its political interests by cooperating with the ACP countries, aiming to prevent instability that could degenerate and have repercussions on neighbour states. In Ethiopia, after the civil war and Mengistu's regime, Italy encouraged the adjustment process, while in Eritrea (Italy's first colony), Italy could find it easier to intervene and assist the consolidation of the new state.

During the revision of Lomé IV, Italy (together with the Ethiopian delegation) insisted on and was granted special assistance for Somalia (which had not ratified Lomé IV and was not able to use the funds of the seventh EDF), giving the country the possibility of benefiting from the instruments of the Convention and the possible renewal of its full membership.[4] Special treatment was also given to Mozambique and Angola, with which Italy has had close relations since their independence.

During the 1970s left-wing parties in Italy developed close links with Mozambican leaders who came to study in Italy, contributing to the creation of a series of personal links that influenced the direction of Italian development aid. Thereafter, Italy also played a very important role in the peace process, particularly after the visit of the Pope to the country. This interest in Mozambique was extended to Angola in order to support the democratization process in Southern Africa where Italy is trying to re-establish conditions and instruments already used in East Africa.

Apart from the above-mentioned countries, Italy has a 'second category' of ACP states with which it cooperates in key areas: Angola, Djibouti, Kenya, Senegal, Sudan, Zimbabwe, Jamaica and the Dominican Republic.

Italian development assistance in the ACP region is often destined to support productive sectors and economic, social (health and education) and administrative infrastructures. Commercial motivation is very strong if one considers the amount of Italian assistance that goes to countries having a higher level of trade with Italy; development cooperation is often considered the driving force behind Italy's economic policy towards developing countries.

While agriculture, including rural development and consequently food production, in developing countries is the most important sector for subsidies, energy is the priority sector for credit allocation. Other priority sectors, as already mentioned, include industrial projects to support infrastructure in public health and education. For example, financial and technical support were given for the construction of the University of Somalia in 1969. Other examples are the rehabilitation of the Kinkala–Boko road in Congo,[5] the construction of the M'Pack–St Vincente road in Guinea Bissau and the rehabilitation of the Amerigo Boavida Hospital in Angola, in cooperation with Portugal. Environmental protection and women's participation in development cooperation are among the more recent fields of Italian development policy.

The concern for the smallest states explains Italy's interest and participation in the Caribbean region, where Italian policy is mainly intended to avoid possible general extended crisis in small areas or island regions.

Although the main legal basis remains Law 49/87 and EC provisions, Italy also has a special agreement creating the possibility of cofinancing projects and programmes between Italy and the Commission in developing countries. This agreement, signed in 1985 and regularly renewed, represents the only written agreement of this kind that the EC has concluded according to provisions included in the same Lomé Convention.[6] The Community provides for this kind of agreement by which the EU implements cooperation using its own procedures but with funds from member states, third countries or international organizations. This agreement provides for the payment to the EU of a given amount by Italy (in the period 1985–90 it was 165 million), which is managed directly by the Commission and used for community projects involving Italian firms, offices, experts or infrastructures.[7]

Implementing the agreement has permitted the Italian economic operators to have a greater presence in many ACP markets and to participate more actively in the tendering procedure of the EDF for development contracts. Another important field in which the agreement applies is the creation of the programme to train young experts in the EU delegations in the ACP region.

The Current Situation and Possible Future Developments

Italian development cooperation is going through a period of transformation, indicating a different attitude compared with the 1980s, when aid flows increased. Within the Community framework, Italy has reduced its financial aid to the developing countries,[8] because of, on the one hand, competition from Central and Eastern Europe as recipients for the aid flows, and on the other hand its balance of payments difficulties. Furthermore, the Italian parliament has set up and approved an official inquiry commission to investigate Italian aid policy and officials in charge of development cooperation during the 1980s. At present, only emergency programmes and a few credits and grants are being implemented. The budgetary constraints imposed by the need to reduce public expenditure have had a marked impact on both the official aid programme and NGO activities. Considerable effort is being made to reorganize the operational and organizational structures. In June 1995 the Interministerial Committee for Economic Planning formally approved the guidelines for a new development cooperation policy.

Although Italy has developed somewhat into a leader in cooperation, making the country remarkably influential in international development policy, several criticisms have been raised, focusing on its highly tied aid and the duplication of administrative structures. Cooperation appears to lack a consistent and coherent line of foreign policy and is characterized by the fragility of the basic criteria, the inadequacy of economic expertise in assessing the profitability of individual projects and the lack of a clear framework.

During the Italian presidency of the Council, Italy launched the work of the intergovernmental conference on the review of the Maastricht Treaty. As far as development cooperation was concerned, it had to find an answer to problems such as the new regulation on security and food aid, the regulation on humanitarian aid, the resolution on migration and development and the regulation on the environment, the fight against drugs and Aids, and the question of demography.

Another element to consider is the importance that Italy gives to areas other than the ACP states; together with Spain it is one of the greatest supporters of closer cooperation between the EU and Latin

America. Cultural links and economic interests, represented by Italian firms and investments in South America in general, mean that Italy has promoted EU–South America relations. In the 1980s, before Spain's accession to the EC, Italy encouraged the Community to introduce a new political dimension to development cooperation with Latin America. Its overall aim was to facilitate recovery and productive growth, consolidate democratic institutions and support structural transformation. Recent agreements concluded between the EU and Latin America could represent a further incentive for Italy to devote greater attention to this area of the world.

Furthermore, strategic motives are becoming increasingly important, especially regarding the geographic proximity of the Mediterranean Basin and the Middle East. Italian cooperation in these areas has in fact increased rapidly and the security factor has gained in importance, as shown by the remarkable increase in aid to the countries that also generate large-scale immigration to Italy. The revision of geographic priorities currently under discussion will certainly attach considerable importance to these factors. Future Italian development cooperation will probably show an increased participation in multilateral actions, primarily concerning peacekeeping activities and conflict mediation, support for democratic processes and actions in support of human rights, demographic programmes and control of migration flows. Therefore, humanitarian aid will possibly increase within the multilateral framework and the Lomé Convention, but commercial and security interests could lead Italy to increase its bilateral aid towards other areas such as the Mediterranean Basin or the Central and Eastern European countries.

SPAIN

Accession to the EC and the 'Renewed' Spanish Development Cooperation

Before entering the EC in 1986, Spanish cooperation with developing countries was extremely weak. This was primarily due to economic and social conditions, which kept Spain as a recipient country until 1977, while it was not considered as a middle developed country until 1981.[9]

The rise of the Partido Socialista Obrero Espanol (PSOE) in 1982 brought great innovation in the alignment and consolidation of

Spanish foreign policy, which had an enormous impact on policy *vis-à-vis* official development cooperation. Activity in this area was stimulated and increased particularly after Spain's entry into the EC and its subsequent participation in the Third Lomé Convention (signed in 1984). Its active participation was also possible thanks to economic growth, the highest in the EU in the period 1985–7.

In 1985 Spain created the SECIP (Secretaria de Estado para la Cooperacion Internacional y Iberoamerica),[10] a department of the Ministry of Foreign Affairs, which now oversees the Spanish Agency for International Cooperation, founded in 1988. In 1987 the country also established the first Annual Plan for international cooperation.

Finally, in 1991, Spain entered the DAC (Development Assistance Committee) within the OECD, which produced a relevant increase in aid and led Spain to strengthen and expand institutional instruments of cooperation. Since the beginning of negotiations for EC membership, Spain has adopted a community policy in all fields, although maintaining a lower financial contribution in development aid than the other members of the Community (with the exception of Luxembourg).

An increase in Spanish participation and contribution to the development aid was the fundamental means of strengthening its role in the international scene. Since 1986 about 75 per cent of Spain's multilateral development aid has been channelled through the European Community, both in contributions to the EDF and in support of development cooperation programmes within the Union's ordinary budget.

The Multilateral Framework and Negotiations of Lomé IV

Although Spain's multilateral cooperation has been influenced by the EC and its inherent obligations within the framework of Lomé, Spanish interests remain unchanged since its accession to the EC. Geographical distribution of Spanish developing aid, like that of Portugal and Italy, is determined by commercial, strategic and cultural criteria. Most ACP states were already linked to Spain through bilateral trade agreements, but on the bilateral side Spain has always had special relations with Latin America (35 per cent of Spanish expenditure for development assistance goes to this area) and other countries that have historical, cultural, commercial and political links with Spain (North Africa, Equatorial Guinea, the Philippines and Portuguese-speaking African countries). Most of these states do not belong to the category of the least developed countries (LDC), which explains why

Spain is the DAC donor that dedicates the smallest percentage of aid to the LDCs.

Spain started its cooperation with Africa at the end of the 1970s, especially in those areas where it could offer support to the political regime and, at the same time, could benefit from strategic sectors vital to its economy (such as fisheries in the case of Equatorial Guinea). In the Caribbean, Spanish interests are limited to the Dominican Republic and Cuba (not included in the Lomé Convention), while in the Pacific zone Spain does not have any strategic interest.

Since the main priority areas have always been Latin America and the Mediterranean, one of the key objectives during negotiations for Lomé IV was the inclusion of the Dominican Republic and Haiti in the Convention itself. The introduction of these two Caribbean states faced many obstacles, especially from the United Kingdom, which initially argued that a possible inclusion of Haiti and the Dominican Republic in the Convention would constitute a precedent for any other request by other member states or ACP states.[11] The two Caribbean countries finally acceded to the Convention in 1990.

A second Spanish objective in the negotiation was the alignment of its contributions to the EDF with its real economic capabilities, its political priorities and its historical economic and trade links with the ACP states. The aid which Spain was initially supposed to contribute through the EDF was undermining the political and historical foundations of Spanish bilateral cooperation, mainly oriented towards Latin America.

Within the Lomé Convention (and relations with the ACP states), Spanish cooperation focuses on production sectors, technical assistance for agriculture, food supply, fishing, public building and financial support for the most indebted countries. Spain supports the basic principles of cooperation such as the respect of human rights and democracy, which represent an incentive to the institutional development and influence the evolution of social justice. The fight against poverty and the reform of economic systems and policies in the ACP are also prerequisites for further general development in these regions.

Spain has always stressed the necessity to have a greater transparency and better availability of information of all procedures and means by which the Community implements its development aid. Increasing communication and information can benefit not only the general implementation of EU development cooperation but also the ability of Spanish firms to tender for contracts financed by the EDF.

In recent ACP–EU meetings, Spain managed to obtain a greater transparency in the management of Community aids and a weighting in the voting system in the Committee of EDF, which reflects Spanish participation in and contribution to the programmes.

As expressed during its Council presidency, Spain considers that the Maastricht Treaty review must strengthen Title XVII, to ensure greater coherence in European policy towards developing countries. Aims relating to development policies should be taken into consideration in other policy areas, in order to reinforce transparency and democratic control of EU cooperation activities within the Lomé Convention.

Spain's Role in EU Cooperation with Latin America and the Mediterranean

Spain's long political isolation and relatively low level of development may account for its delayed participation in development cooperation. Its constant interest in Latin America explains and partly justifies the predominance of Spanish bilateral cooperation and the high shares of tied aid there. The tied nature of Spanish development cooperation has repercussions not only on the composition of the aid but also on its terms and distribution in specific geographic areas (also within the ACP countries) and in specific economic sectors, which influence the quality of the aid itself. Furthermore, the terms of aid credits for the least developed countries and low income countries are particularly vigorous. Some of the major problems Spain finds in development policy include a lack of qualified personnel and lack of agreement on goal criteria and priorities, while Spanish aid remains still closely linked to its political benefits for economic development and employment in Spain (particularly in SMEs).

Nevertheless, Spain is continuing its efforts to define and institutionalize a unified aid strategy, and, therefore, has created a Council for Cooperation to establish criteria and priorities in development cooperation and to facilitate participation by interested parties. The Council has representatives from various parts of the administration, NGOs, trade unions, business and professional experts. Spain also plays a significant role in the EU by insisting on the importance of improving and strengthening development cooperation in Latin America. Although this continent has not been among the EU's priorities until very recently, Spain has had and still has a huge role in the expansion and strengthening of EU relations with Latin America (the agreement with MERCOSUR is a recent example) and is now stressing the possibility of closer relations with Cuba, urging the Community to go beyond economic interests and favour political dialogue.

Moreover, Spain's net ODA expenditure in 1994 rose by 5 per cent in national currency terms; and, given the favourable attitude of the parliament and public opinion (in two polls in late 1994 over 60 per cent of those interviewed were in favour of reaching the target of 0.7 per cent of GNP), Spanish aid is likely to rise in future years.

PORTUGAL

The Multilateral Framework and the Lomé Convention

Portugal has always considered the multilateral framework fundamental to the efficient implementation of its cooperation. Therefore participation in Community activity and in the Lomé Convention is essential to maintaining its multilateral cooperation; it is not possible to cut down on the bilateral level because of the many financial constraints Portugal has to face compared with other European states.

Portugal plays an important role in Africa, having strong links with those countries whose national language is Portuguese (Angola, Mozambique, São Tomé and Principe, Cape Verde). Its relations with countries in this and other continents are longstanding and have left their mark on present-day relations. There is no contradiction between cooperation in this area within the Lomé Convention and existing cooperation between Portugal and its former African colonies. With them and within the Lomé Convention, Portugal and the Community, launched in 1992, have concluded the first Non-Geographical Regional Programme, which has become a *sui generis* model for regional cooperation in the framework of the Lomé Agreements. The main areas to be developed are: communications between the five countries, training programmes, coherence and complementarity between EU-funded and other national indicative programmes as well as with the activities of other donors.

Portugal supports economic adjustment in Angola and is actually intervening by providing funds for the reform of the agricultural sector. It gave 8.24 million ecu in order to help the school of agriculture in Angola, the Instituto Medio Agrario de Tchivinguifo (IMAT). The project envisages the Instituto becoming the major learning centre, a model for teaching agricultural techniques, contributing to the national policy of professional education and rural development. Although rich in oil, Angola needs to recover its agricultural sector because 75 per cent of its population is engaged in agricultural production. This policy is extremely important in the aftermath of the civil war, which has destroyed almost 90 per cent of the basic infrastructure.

Also, in Angola Portugal participates in the restructure of the Namibe–Lubango road and in humanitarian aid by increasing its financial support. Portugal can also play a very influential role in encouraging the Community to take a more generous line on ACP sugar imports, because Angola and Mozambique are potentially large sugar producers.

Portugal's close links with a number of African countries have given it great understanding of their problems and it always endeavours to facilitate the dialogue between the various states. Furthermore, Portugal strongly supports the establishment of closer relations with South Africa in the post-apartheid era with the aim of helping to consolidate the social and economic infrastructure and supporting South Africa's transition to a democratic society, free of racial discrimination.

In practical terms, to help implement cooperation, Portugal has highly qualified experts who can participate in most areas of development aid, particularly in tropical countries. Portuguese volunteers and officials adapt very well to the African environment and have expertise in tropical medicine, agriculture and geology. That is why Portugal has played a major role in running successful Community programmes such as the malaria control campaign, which it itself initiated and led.

Education and vocational training are in general a further concern: 'If you give a man a fish he will eat for one day; if you teach him how to fish he will eat every day.' In this field the role of women in development can become extremely important, especially in order to improve literacy, education and training programmes.

Furthermore, Portugal is active in restoring the cultural heritage of many of these countries (mainly Guinea Bissau, São Tomé and Principe, and Angola). For example, Cacheu in Guinea Bissau was apparently the first European-style town in Africa, displaying cultural influences derived from Portuguese navigators.

Community Development Cooperation: a Fundamental Policy

The latest Portuguese position is completely in line with the Community's action, as argued by the Portuguese commissioner for development cooperation, João de Deus Pinheiro. In a recent meeting he affirmed that 'the Community regards the fight against poverty as being one of the prime objectives of the European governments and supports this objective.' Cooperation with ACP countries at both Community and national level should try primarily to maximize the efficiency of aid (technical assistance), especially in those countries with fragile economies, massive debts, low manufacturing competitiveness, growing dependency and little coordination of aid at the domestic level. It is also very important to develop and stimulate the private sector, which can lead to dynamic and sustainable economic development and a fair distribution of growth in the ACP states, while also helping to solve the problems of poverty and unemployment.

Improving trade to combat further erosion of EU–ACP preferences is therefore extremely important. Portugal and the entire Community have to cooperate with the ACP states in trying to develop their financial sectors and to create the conditions for growth in private and foreign investment. Mr Pinheiro praised the reinforcement of political dialogue in the Lomé system with respect for democracy as an essential element and the reorientation of cooperation in the economic sphere towards the private sector and competitiveness in the ACP countries.

Another key element is the strengthening of decentralized cooperation (through the action of the NGOs and the involvement of subregional units), which can help to consolidate the rule of law, human rights and basic democratization and balance the interests of civil society, politics and economy in the running of public affairs.

Portuguese aid, which had fallen sharply in 1993, rose in 1994 to US $308 million, an increase of 23 per cent in real terms, reaching 0.35 per cent of GNP. The increase occurred primarily in multilateral aid, especially in Portugal's contributions to the EC aid. However, Portugal does not have an overall aid budget, so that many activities are carried out by different ministries largely financed from their own budgets, making Portuguese cooperation sometimes incoherent and unbalanced.

CONCLUSION

The need to maintain an equilibrium between bilateral and multilateral aid within all member states and with the contributions of the EDF has influenced the amount of aid in the framework of the Lomé Convention. Although within the Community the imposition of strict conditions on the part of the donor is hindered by the existence of a plurality of interests, these same interests often emerge when it comes to concrete development actions in the ACP countries. Actions taken by Italy, Spain and Portugal within the Lomé Convention reflect their instincts, traditions and history. The high concentration on specific geographical areas or specific sectors shows how cooperation is subordinated to other needs of internal policy, such as the Common Agricultural Policy (CAP) and the protection of industrial sectors.

Italy, Spain and Portugal have, of course, different attitudes towards development cooperation, and, as we have seen, concentrate on different regions or on different economic sectors. One of the main differences is characterized by high levels of tied aid in Spain and Italy[12] on the one hand, while Portugal on the other considers the multilateral framework as essential for greater efficiency and effectiveness.

However, these countries have a special interest in solving commercial problems with the ACP states such that their influence is particularly relevant when giving preferential treatment to developing countries. They are all concerned with preventing any substantial or deeper concessions to the trade sector that could risk causing them major difficulties. In recent negotiations they played a major role in excluding some agricultural products from preferential agreements such as olives, olive oil, wine and lemons from the reduction of 16 per cent in customs duties and the maintenance of the existing quotas for tomatoes and apples.

The three countries all agree to guarantee and strengthen respect for human rights and democratic principles as the basis for the general development in the ACP states, and recognize the importance that decentralized cooperation (and the role of the NGOs) has in consolidating the rule of law and in balancing different interests of civil society. They support a stronger dialogue with developing countries and greater involvement of local social actors in the formulation and implementation of programmes and plans. Their main concern is to contribute to peacekeeping activities and conflict-solving, to support the democratic process and actions in favour of human rights, democratic programmes and the control of migration flows. Nevertheless, although the needs of African people (food, health and education) have always been considered as a major objective of development policies, this is expressed more by public opinion and in national parliaments than in the EU institutions.

Italy, Spain and Portugal found many difficulties in maintaining their contributions to the EDF at the level agreed in 1989, when the Seventh EDF was negotiated. Because of the considerable depreciation of their currencies (especially those of Italy and Spain), these states will have to make a special effort to come up with their EU dues. That is why both Italy and Spain emphasise the need to reduce their public deficits and therefore lower expenditure.

Sometimes these countries face problems of coordination between bilateral and community aid with negative consequences not only for development cooperation itself but also for their own economies. Italy, Spain and Portugal, together with all the other member states, have managed through the Lomé system to build improving relations and to have a greater positive impact upon the economies of their ACP partners (to date seventy states). Community goals for the ACP states may be seen as part of a broader strategy for standardizing the relationship between the EC and LDCs and for promoting their development efforts of the latter.

Furthermore, the presence in the Community of three southern countries discussed in this chapter may catalyse limits, contradictions and possibilities of cooperation between North and South. Italy, Spain and Portugal together constitute a bridge for new areas of action for the Community in the Middle East, the Mediterranean and Latin America. This could lead to further openings for these regions, offering the European Union a major competitive edge in more developed economies than in the ACP. Therefore, the presence of Italy, Spain, Portugal and also Greece may have an increasing influence in moving the EC's attention to other areas which, especially in recent years, have gained in importance on the international scene and can have a growing impact on Community actions. Even the possible conclusion of a future Lomé V will be greatly dependent on the position and the decisions of these Southern European countries.

Bibliography

Agence d'Europe (Brussels from January to June 1995).
Albuquerque, F., 'La cooperacion oficial de España al desarrollo', *Informacion Comercial Española* (Madrid), no. 702 (February 1992).
Barbera, G., 'Presentation de la plate-forme italienne des ONGs', *Liaisons Info* (Brussels, December 1995).
Coordinadora de Ong Para el Desarrollo, 'Documento de posicionamento de la Coordinadora de ONGD ante la politica de cooperacion al desarrollo de la Union Europea' (Madrid, July 1995).
Deuchas, G., 'NGOs: Twelve Proposals for the Spanish EU Presidency', and 'Spain: Introduction to the end of 1994', *Liaisons Info* (Brussels, 1995).
European Commission, 'Communication de la Commission au Conseil et au Pe', *La Politique de coopération au Développement à l' horizon 2000* (Brussels, May 15 1992).
European Commission, *Financial Cooperation Under the Lomé Convention: Review of Aid at the end of 1994* (Brussels, 1995).
Giarra-Zimmermann, A., 'Colonial Legacy and Tied Aid', *Development and Cooperation* (Berlin, January 1996).
Leonard, Y., 'Dossier: le Portugal', *Notes et études documentaires*, no. 4991 (Paris, 1994).
Lima Araujo, G., 'As antiguàs colonias portuguesas e a convençao de Lomé', *Asuntos Europeus* (Lisbon, 1983).
Livi, G., 'Italia-CEE un impegno comune per lo sviluppo', *Cooperazione* (Rome, November 1995).
Lopez Moreno, 'El comité de ayuda al desarrollo de la OCDE: sus objectivos y prioridades para los años 90. La incorporacion de España', *Informacion Comercial Española* (Madrid), no. 702 (February 1992).
MFA-DGCS, *Programma per la ristrutturazione della cooperazione allo sviluppo* (MAE, Rome, 1993).
Ministero Affari Esteri, 'Dossier: L'aide multilaterale', *Cooperazione* (Rome, November 1993).
Ministerio dos Nogocios Estrangeiros (MNE), *Portugal: Dez años de politica de coperaçao* (Lisbon, 1995).
OECD, *Development cooperation*, DAC Report 1995 (Paris, 1996).
Ovi, A., 'La cooperazione allo sviluppo', in *Affari Esteri* (Rome, July 24 1992).
Pagni, L., 'The Quality of Cooperation depends on the degree of human contact,' Interview with Mr J. M. Barroso, *The Courier ACP*, no. 107 (Brussels, Jan/Feb 1988).
Rondot, P., 'Le monde et l' Afrique: le commmerce de l' Espagne avec l' Afrique en 1990,' *Marchés tropicaux et meditérranéens*, no. 2410 (Paris, January 1992).
Santoro, C. M., *I problemi della cooperazione allo sviluppo negli anni 90* (ISPI, Rome, 1993).
Tiberio, L., 'UE paga promesas a Angola', *Expresso* (Lisbon, February 1996).
XXI General Assembly of Development Organizations, NGOs, Extract from a speech by Commissioner Pinheiro, *Liaisons Info* (Brussels, May 1995).

Notes

1. Initially known as Yaoundé Conventions, they became the Lomé Convention in 1975.
2. In the 1950s and 1960s Somalia was the only case of bilateral cooperation with a systematic approach.
3. 127 NGOs are recognized by the Italian Foreign Ministry.
4. Somalia has to take all necessary measures in order to benefit from this clause, but many difficulties arise because of the absence of government.
5. At a cost of 13 million ecu.
6. Article 251, Title III, s. 4.
7. From 1985 to 1993, co-financing accounted for over 61 projects in the health sector, infrastructure, agriculture, energy and education. 75 per cent of these projects were carried out in ACP countries; the cost was 200 billion lire.
8. By 1994 Italy had reduced its funds by 55 per cent compared with 1992.
9. World Bank statistics.
10. State Secretariat for International and Latin American Cooperation.
11. He requested the accession of Namibia to the Lomé Convention.
12. Italy has indeed one of the highest shares of tied aid in the Community.

7 The Nordic Contribution to the Development Cooperation of the European Union

Audunn Arnórsson

This chapter introduces the priorities set out by the three Nordic member states with regard to development policy and their position concerning EU development cooperation, especially the Lomé convention. It focuses first on Denmark, the longest-standing EU member of the three, which is particularly committed to development cooperation. Sweden's position is examined next, then that of Finland. Finally the future prospects for Lomé cooperation are examined, as they are perceived by the Nordic countries. In conclusion, the 'Nordic contribution' to the EU's development cooperation is summarized.

INTRODUCTION

A Nordic Family Reunion

1 January 1995 was a momentous date for Nordic cooperation, when Sweden and Finland joined Denmark, the third Nordic member state, in the European Union (EU). Denmark welcomed this Nordic family reunion especially for EU development policy and cooperation with developing countries. Development assistance given by Denmark is significant and has earned wide respect. In spite of this, the limited size of the Danish economy in turn limits Denmark's influence on the EU's development policy and on the other member states. As the main principles and priorities of the development policy of the three Nordic member states are very similar, the Nordic enlargement has increased the possibility of influencing EU policy in this delicate field in a 'Nordic' sense.

The Nordic Council 'Europe' Conference, held on 4–5 March 1996 in Copenhagen, showed that there are not many issues or policies where Nordic member states can form a real bloc at the European level, despite the acknowledgedly broad scope of common values and principles shared by these closely related. However, development policy is one of those rare areas where a common and coordinated approach actually does exist. In their official strategies for development cooperation, all three governments refer to Nordic cooperation and stress its usefulness, especially in the context of multilateral development cooperation.[1]

For a long while, before Sweden and Finland acceded to the EU, the Nordic countries (Denmark, Finland, Iceland, Norway and Sweden) have been coordinating their policies in international fora (most significantly in reforming UN institutions), thereby creating a tradition and reputation for constructive influence. In recent years, the Nordic ministers for development cooperation have met regularly, normally twice a year.

The Nordics and the ACP Countries

Traditionally, the Nordic member states have few special interests in ACP countries: neither migration flows nor cultural ties have been significant, while economic and trade relations are relatively small. The seventy ACP countries together account for only 1 per cent of the three member states' trade, which is well below the EU average.[2] But as the bilateral aid programmes of the three have been concentrated to a great extent on some of the poorest ACP countries in sub-Saharan Africa, coordination of Community aid – via the Lomé Convention and the bilateral aid programmes – has not posed any major problems so far.

DENMARK'S AID RECORD

Denmark is committed to development aid. This small country has in recent years built up a reputation for being exceptionally devoted to the provision of assistance to Third World countries. In 1992, Denmark's aid contribution was 1 per cent of its GNP. This level, by far the highest in the EU, has been upheld since. Denmark has succeeded in virtually eliminating conditional aid; however, its political goal is that 50 per cent of aid should be spent in Denmark. Another political aim is that Danish aid funds should be evenly divided between bilateral and multilateral allocations. However, bilateral aid programmes enjoy a priority interest in Danish aid authorities; at the same time, Denmark is a major contributor to UN development agencies and other multilateral aid organizations (more than 40 per cent of total oda). In 1994, 6 per cent to 7 per cent of Danish aid was distributed through the EU, in contrast to the EU average of around 16 per cent.[3] The regional concentration of Danish aid in 1994 was approximately sub-Saharan Africa 60 per cent, Asia 21 per cent and Latin America 7 per cent.

Danish Aid Objectives

In 1994 the Danish government issued a plan entitled *A Developing World – Strategy for Danish Development Policy towards the Year 2000* (the 'Strategy'),[4] setting out the aims and priorities of all Danish development aid, including aid flowing through EU channels. The Strategy was built on the 1989 Plan of Action for Danish development cooperation and represents a continuation of earlier Danish development strategies. It aims to adjust Danish policies to the new global situation and to further improve coherence among these policies. It also confirms the main principle of poverty orientation, the 1 per cent of GNP and the 50 per cent division between multilateral and bilateral allocations, as the fundamental triangle of Danish development policy. While confirming fundamental and cross-cutting themes of Danish development cooperation, such as poverty alleviation, women in development, environment and good government, the Strategy introduces population, trade and debt relief as additional priority themes.

In sum, the Strategy aims to promote:

- economic growth and a more equal distribution of economic growth and social justice;
- development of human resources;
- pluralist societies and respect for the individual;
- protection of the global environment and a sustainable use of natural resources;
- global and regional cooperation;
- cultural cooperation.

In addition, the Strategy states that the consideration of the role of women, the environment and the promotion of democracy should become part of all activities on all levels. The Strategy also introduces a new form of bilateral assistance called sectoral programme assistance'. This combines various instruments such as training and education, investment, budget support and capacity-building in a given sector. The choice of sector will partly be dependent on Danish business interests.

To improve aid effectiveness, one of the common objectives of aid policy in all Nordic countries, the Strategy envisages concentrating official development assistance on a restricted number of recipient countries and on international aid organizations whose programmes correspond best to Danish aid priorities. There are now 20 countries, which benefit from Danish bilateral aid programmes, 12 of them less and least developed ACP countries in sub-Saharan Africa. The Strategy will be subject to a mid-term evaluation in 1997. The focus will be the implementation of the strategy's main components.

The 1995 DAC report on Denmark,[5] assessing the Danish development policy in practice, comes to the following conclusion:

> Danish development cooperation inspires confidence and optimism in the public mind, not only in Denmark, but elsewhere as well. The programme's achievements and efficiency could help to dispel confusion and cynicism regarding the role of aid and its effectiveness ... Above all, it is the care taken to maximize the effectiveness of the Danish contribution in terms of the specific development needs and institutional capacities of each programme country that is the fundamental strength of Danish development cooperation. This strength should be maintained and safeguarded.

The Impact of Danish Aid Policy on EU Development Cooperation

It was not until the Maastricht Treaty entered into force – thirty-five years after the original Rome Treaty – that provisions on development policy were given a treaty basis in the European Communities. Denmark succeeded in influencing the formulation of these new treaty provisions, especially the emphasis laid on the alleviation of poverty, and the prioritization of least developed countries in art. 130u TEU can be accredited to Danish engagement.[6]

A second aspect of EU development cooperation where Denmark has been able to make its mark is the system of evaluation and monitoring of Community aid programmes. In 1987 an 'evaluation expert group' was set up by the Commission as a result of a Danish initiative.

Further examples of Danish influence on Community policy in the field of development cooperation could be mentioned, but the two already given suffice to illustrate that the impact of Danish aid objectives on EU development cooperation has been considerable. The accession of Sweden and Finland has certainly reinforced Danish influence. There is reason to believe that the three Nordic member states from now on will pool their strength in order to continue influencing Community policies in a common 'Nordic' sense.

Danish Views on EU Aid Policy and Practice

Planning for Active Multilateralism – Organization Strategy: EU is the title of a document published by the development department of the Danish Foreign Ministry and DANIDA in November 1995. It contains a coherent overview of the state of EU development cooperation, as perceived by Copenhagen, as well as Danish points of criticism with suggestions for improvements. Some of these points are worth examining here; from a Danish perspective, the result of the negotiations on the new financial protocol for Lomé IVB were disappointing. The increase in the total volume of funding from 12 to 12.8 billion ecu failed to compensate for price development or enlargement of the Union from 12 to 15 member states. The Danish government would have liked to have seen the funding of the Lomé Convention increased by the review, because the aims and benefits of the Lomé Convention correspond with Danish aid objectives (more than 60 per cent of Danish bilateral aid is concentrated on poor ACP countries in sub-Saharan Africa) and the combination of aid and trade objectives in Lomé cooperation is interpreted very positively.[7]

In time, Denmark will, together with other like-minded EU member states, reconsider the future form of Lomé cooperation, especially whether to continue the current form of financing it (through the European Development Fund, EDF, separate from the Community budget) and the aid instruments which the cooperation encompasses. Regarding them, Copenhagen will particularly question the appropriateness of continuing instruments like STABEX and SYSMIN.[8]

The administration of Community aid is another area of interest for the Danes, especially the evaluation and monitoring of aid managed by the European Commission. Denmark wishes to submit Community aid to the same systematic monitoring of multilateral aid as that launched in 1994, where selected embassies in countries cooperating with the programme annually inspect the various multilateral organizations' efforts at field level. Moreover, Denmark, in cooperation with the Commission and other interested member states, wishes to see ongoing capacity analyses of the Commission's management in the recipient countries.[9]

As regards evaluation, Denmark wishes to strengthen the 'evaluation expert group' of the Commission (mentioned above), by giving it a more independent position, which will be necessary if it is to deliver effective results. The focus of the evaluation should be on the Commission's aid management, but in order to help coordination and complementarity of Community and national aid, the member states' bilateral aid activities should also be included in the evaluation, as far as this will be useful in illuminating the relevant aspects of the Commission's activities.[10] In accordance with the principle of increased openness and transparency in the EU, much favoured by Denmark and its Nordic allies, all evaluation reports should be made public. Generally, Denmark supports all efforts to increase transparency and improve accessibility to reliable information on the implementation of Community aid. To this end, the level of statistical information must be improved.[11]

Other points of interest regarding Denmark's position *vis-à-vis* the Lomé Convention dealt with in *Organization Strategy: EU* are:

(a) the developing countries in the global economy/trade policy and increased access to the Single European Market;
(b) the general system of preferences (GSP);
(c) the structural adjustment programmes (SAP);
(d) the debt problem;
(e) the coherence of the EU's external policies;
(f) the coherence of the EU's development policy.

In 1994–5 an upswing was observed in the global economy, even in much of the Third World; however, sub-Saharan Africa was a notable exception. This fact worries Denmark and focuses attention on the EU's external trade policy. In the name of the priority objective of the fight against poverty, Denmark proposes the liberalization of the EU import regime for agricultural goods from the ACP countries with the aim of offering better support to the poor countries of sub-Saharan Africa. Denmark sees this as a part of a necessary discussion about what should succeed Lomé IV.[12]

Denmark has a positive attitude towards the EU's GSP, which was reformed in 1994 (the new GSP is valid for the period 1995–8).

Similarly, Denmark welcomes the instrument of structural adjustment introduced in the Lomé IV Convention and wants it to be used to support economic growth, believing that it should be linked to the recipient countries' own priorities, in order to help build their own institutional and performance capacities.[13] As regards the debt problems of some of the poorest ACP countries in sub-Saharan Africa, Denmark is in favour of considering the possibility of fully or partly annulling the debts of the ACP countries to the EU on a case-by-case basis.[14] *Organization Strategy: EU* addresses some further aspects of EU development cooperation, but those described here are sufficient to give a comprehensive overview of Denmark's position.

SWEDEN

Sweden's Aid Record

Since the mid 1970s Sweden has been one of the few countries in the world committed to allocating 1 per cent of its GDP to development cooperation. Owing to the deep recession which struck the Swedish economy in the early 1990s, from which it still has not fully recovered, the aid budget has been frozen at the current level, thus abandoning the 1 per cent target. The current level, 0.92 per cent, is nevertheless the third highest aid-to-GNP ratio in the world. Only Sweden's neighbours Norway and Denmark give more. A small proportion (1993: 10.9 per cent) of Swedish aid is tied,[15] and it is Sweden's policy to keep tied aid to a minimum; consequently, Sweden will support the EU in a policy of untying aid.

In 1993 almost 75 per cent of Swedish development aid was spent on bilateral projects (including aid organised through non-governmental organizations (NGOs), the remaining 25 per cent going mainly through UN institutions and the World Bank group. Around 10 per cent of Sweden's aid between 1996 and 1999 will be spent through EU channels, thus increasing the allocation of multilateral aid in the Swedish aid budget. At the same time, as part of the Nordic–UN project (launched in 1988, it seeks to put pressure on UN agencies to reform and to strengthen their capacity), in 1994 Sweden decided to 'punish' the World Health Organization (WHO) for inefficiency by cutting support by 50 per cent. As regards regional concentration, some 45 per cent of bilateral Swedish aid goes to least developed countries (LDCs) in sub-Saharan Africa.[16]

Swedish Aid Objectives and the EU

The Swedish government considers the fourth Lomé Convention to be an important part of the Community's development cooperation, containing many elements in common with Swedish aid policy:[17]

'Precisely because the aims and priorities of EU's development cooperation largely coincides with Sweden's, Sweden has experiences and skills which can undoubtedly reinforce the Commission's efforts.'[18]

As the policy and engagement of the various member states in development cooperation differs considerably, Sweden has in this respect more in common with some member states than others. Here, Sweden considers Denmark, Finland and the Netherlands to be its primary natural allies and, in certain matters, also Germany and the United Kingdom.[19] The Swedish minister for development cooperation, Pierre Schori, had an optimistic view on EU membership.[20] In his opinion, Sweden now has now better opportunities for strengthening its solidarity with poor countries. EU membership enables it to have a direct influence on the allocation of development aid which is more than double the size of the Swedish aid budget and covers more than a hundred countries. Secondly, he stressed the need for coordinating the aid policy of donors, although not underestimating the difficulties. Many member states often seek to promote their own national aid programmes and in many cases they distrust the Commission's ability to manage development aid effectively. Such scepticism is noticeable in the Swedish aid administration.

Sweden's main priorities *vis-à-vis* EU development cooperation can be summarized as follows:

- Actions aimed at improving the effectiveness and quality of aid. This includes better planning, reinforced coordination and better evaluation of projects and programmes.[21] The Community should be able to benefit from the experiences of Swedish authorities.
- The environment must be taken into account in all aid projects.
- Support for democratization processes, legal order and respect for human rights.
- Support for social issues. Gender equality should be given greater weight in cooperation. Health care, education and population should also be given more attention; in these areas Sweden considers it has long experience, which can contribute to the reinforcement of the EU's development aid.

In view of these priorities, Sweden is not surprisingly pleased with the new emphasis in the revision of the Lomé Convention, where aid is now conditional on the recipient showing results in due course. Another trend Sweden sees in common with EU aid policy is an increased emphasis on human rights and democracy. The fact that environmental and gender equality issues have also been gaining more attention in the EU is seen as a positive development. An important common element of Swedish and EU development cooperation is that of the EU's 25 biggest aid recipients, 11 are countries which are also major recipients of Swedish aid. Hence, Sweden sees the impact of EU accession on its own development policy as being rather limited; the most important change is that around 10 per cent of total Swedish oda now flows through EU channels. The influence Sweden intends to exert on the EU's development policy is seen as an opportunity to increase the relevance of Swedish aid objectives at a global level.[22]

FINLAND

Finland's Aid Record

In 1991 Finnish oda reached 0.8 per cent of GDP, thus exceeding the 0.7 per cent goal recommended by the UN. Owing to the recession, which had a severe impact on Finland's economy since the beginning of the 1990s, the figure has declined drastically since then, reaching 0.31 per cent in 1994, the lowest level since 1982. It is however the declared aim of the Government to restore the level to 0.7 per cent by the year 2000.[23]

On 31 January 1996 a new report on Finland's development cooperation was presented. The author of the report, Mr Pertti Paasio, an MP, states in a summary:

> The main enabling factor in my accepting this commission [of the Government to prepare the report] was the Government's determined commitment to reattaining the UN recommendation of dedicating 0.7 per cent of GDP to development cooperation. In public debate, this aim has been regarded as unrealistic or even unattainable. I have become convinced in the course of my work that it is in fact a realistic goal: attaining it is a question of political will and the capacity for turning principle into practice.[24]

However, having regard to Finland's persistent economic difficulties, Mr Paasio's optimism may be overstated. More than a third of Finland's aid is tied, which corresponds to the view of its aid authorities, that 'purchasing the goods and services needed for development cooperation from Finland both increases contacts between Finland and developing countries and reduces the inevitable negative effects of development cooperation on our balance of payments.'[25] The bulk of Finnish aid has been allocated bilaterally, of which (in 1993) two-thirds flowed to least developed and low income countries (LDCs/LICs), mainly 'primary cooperation countries' in sub-Saharan Africa.

Finnish Aid Objectives and the EU

'Finland's membership of the European Union makes it necessary to consider development cooperation more as a part of the foreign policy. The EU introduces new duties and opens new possibilities.'[26] The main aims of development policy in Finland and the EU do not differ significantly. The Finnish government therefore sees no reason to change its development policy following membership.[27] Its major principles guiding aid policy are to reduce poverty, to combat global environmental threats and to promote social equality, democracy and human rights.[28] A declared aim of Finland, as a new member of the EU, together with Sweden and Denmark, is to try to influence the EU's record on funds allocated to basic needs and social development in developing countries.

Finland has pursued the first aid objective, namely the alleviation of poverty, through dialogue, influencing its multilateral partners, through design of specific projects and programmes and through its support of NGO activities.[29]

However, the 1995 DAC report on Finland's development cooperation points out that 'in sum, Finland's poverty alleviation objective is reflected in many parts of the programme but the actual pattern of resource allocation does not reflect the stated policy as strongly as that policy would lead one to expect.'[30] The report also points out that Finland 'has made tremendous strides in improving its own capability in assessing aid effectiveness. The number and quality of evaluation products and assessments produced in recent years is impressive.'[31] It is therefore expected that as an EU member state Finland will actively contribute to improving the quality of assessment and the effectiveness of EU development cooperation. The principle of complementarity of Community aid and coordination of the development cooperation of the member states are issues which Finland will promote in the EU.

FUTURE PROSPECTS

The Question of 'Communitarization'

With the financial framework laid down at the European Council meeting in Edinburgh (December 1992: the 'Delors II' package) and the decisions made at the Cannes Summit in June 1995, the EU has defined the priorities and distribution of Community aid to the end of the century. As for the financial protocol of Lomé IVB, the Nordic contributions to the EDF will amount in total to 815 million ecu, or about 6,3 per cent of the total 12,85 billion ecu new funds to the EDF VIII.

All questions concerning future external relations of the EU, including the volume and distribution of its development cooperation, will be decided in the framework of the Council of Ministers (for Foreign Affairs and Finance) and the European Council. In this context, the Danish Government attaches great importance to the question of eventual integration of the EDF into the Community budget.

The background lies in the two separate procedures for Community aid appropriations by member states. On the one hand the Lomé Convention is financed through 'principally voluntary contributions' via the EDF, 'even though they are based on the GNP key.'[32] On the other hand, all other Community aid is financed through the official budget, where the GDP key for 'Category 4' expenditure is applied. It is the view of the Danish aid authorities that this division of financing of Community aid will be increasingly challenged:

> The 'voluntary' character of EDF contributions in particular is likely to lead to problems. Enlargement of the Union's membership is envisaged in the coming years ... to comprise more than 20 countries, including a number of Central and Eastern European countries with very limited experience (and tradition) of development cooperation. Some of these countries will in the coming years change from being recipient countries (of PHARE funds) to become donors. The possibility of maintaining in this situation a

> special 'voluntary' financing of the EDF seems unlikely. The considerable problems which accompanied the decision concerning the size of EDF VIII will be negligible in comparison with the corresponding problems in connection with an eventual EDF IX.[33]

As expected, Sweden and Finland share this Danish view. Moreover, the European Parliament will be increasingly unhappy that such a substantial part of development policy – the Lomé Convention – is based on intergovernmental cooperation, where its influence is very limited. These circumstances would lead one to expect an intense debate among EU member states in the coming years on the question of the 'post-2000' form of EC–ACP cooperation. In this debate, the Nordic states will stand on the side of those in favour of 'communitarization' of EU development cooperation with the ACP states.

CONCLUSION

The Nordic Contribution to EU Development Cooperation

The participation of the three Nordic member states in the Lomé Convention only forms a small part of their (multilateral) development aid engagement and does not enjoy any special priority interest. However, the Community's involvement in development aid – of which the Lomé Convention forms the substantial part – is unanimously welcomed as complementary to the bilateral national aid programmes. Hence, policy coordination between the Community and the member states (and between the member states themselves) is one priority issue supported collectively by the Nordic member states.

Denmark and its Nordic partners see a high correlation between their own aims in development cooperation and the aims of EC–ACP cooperation through the Lomé Convention. However, as they all attach great value to key principles which they have applied to their own development cooperation programmes, they will try to exert influence on the EU's policy of development cooperation and try to reform it to reflect their views. This includes objectives like improved efficiency and accountability in the use of public funds and reduction of tied aid. The commitment of the Nordic member states should contribute to a better quality of development assistance from the EU through the Lomé Convention. The Nordic countries have been at the forefront of support for 'good governance' and for human rights and democracy issues in developing countries. They are also particularly sensitive to income distribution and other social agenda issues. Finally, they make strong use of and offer substantial support to NGOs in development cooperation.

In sum, it is a justified argument that the Nordic contribution to EU development cooperation is positive and is likely to improve the efficiency of EU development assistance and its timely adaption to new challenges.

Bibliography

Actionaid, *The Reality of Aid 1995* (Earthscan Publications, London, 1995).

Danish Ministry for Foreign Affairs, *A Developing World – Strategy for Danish Development Policy Towards the Year 2000* (Copenhagen 1994).

European Commission, *General Report on the Activities of the European Union 1995* (Brussels, February 1996) section 14, pp. 367–77).

Finnida/The Finnish Ministry for Foreign Affairs, *Finland's Development Cooperation in the 1990s. Strategic Goals and Means* (Helsinki, 1993).

Finnish Government, *Official Report to the Finnish Parliament Regeringens berättelse till riksdagen om utvecklingssamarbetet 1994 Finnish Development cooperation 1994* Helsinki, 1995 B 14/1995 rd).

Granell, Francisco, 'The Enlargement of the European Union and the ACP Countries', *The Courier*, No. 146 (July–August 1994) pp. 6–8.

OECD, *DAC Report: Denmark 1995*, Development Cooperation Review Series no. 10 (Paris, 1995a).

OECD, *DAC Report: Finland 1995*, Development Cooperation Review Series no. 11 (Paris 1995b).

Paasio, Pertti, *Report on Finland's Development Cooperation*, Summary. (Helsinki, 31 January 1996).

Swedish Government Official Document, Gvt-prop. 1995/96: 36 (Stockholm, 1996).

Udenrigsministeriet [Danish Foreign Ministry] / DANIDA, *Handlingsplan for Aktiv Multilateralisme: Organizationsstrategi Den Europæiske Union (EU)* (Copenhagen, November 1995).

Utrikesdepartementet (the Swedish Foreign Ministry), *Aktuellt i Biståndspolitiken. EU, Sverige och biståndet* (Stockholm, 1995).

Notes

1. See e.g. Finnish Government (1995) p. 29 (author's translation): In international organizations the Nordic dimension has been a part of

Finland's foreign policy profile ...Today, regard is given first and foremost to EU membership. EU membership does not, however, change in any significant manner the fact that, for Finland, the Nordic countries constitute a natural reference group. European integration has taken on a Nordic dimension which is a positive resource for the EU in the framework of development aid. It remains to be seen which needs and possibilities EU development cooperation inspires continued Nordic cooperation in its firm commitment to strengthen Nordic perceptions inside the EU.

2. Granell (1994) p. 8.
3. This big difference illustrates the unusually high level of the total Danish aid. Denmark contributes to the EU aid funds in relation to the size of its economy no less than the other EU member states, but, as the total volume of Danish aid is relatively much bigger, this forms a much smaller part of the total.
4. Udenrigsministeriet DANIDA (1994).

4a. DANIDA is the Danish International Development Agency, the central aid management authority.

5. OECD (Paris 1995a) p. 9.
6. Udenrigsministeriet (1995) p. 3.
7. Ibid., p. 22.
8. Ibid., p. 24.
9. Ibid., p. 25.
10. Ibid., p. 27.
11. Ibid., p. 28.
12. Ibid., pp. 32–3.
13. Ibid., pp. 34–5.
14. Ibid., p. 35.
15. This is tied completely to purchases from Sweden.
16. Actionaid (1995) p. 86.
17. Views expressed in the parliamentary debate in the Riksdag on the ratification of the revised Fourth Lomé Convention and attached Financial Protocol, 29 February 1996. Swedish Government Official Document, Gvt.-prop. 1995/96:36.
18. Utrikesdepartementet (1995). Author's translation.
19. Ibid., p. 44.
20. Ibid., s. 45–6.
21. For example, in March 1996, Swedish aid authorities decided to cut aid to Mozambique, after having confirmed that much of Swedish aid funding had not reached its destination but that large sums had gone to individuals.
22. Ibid., p. 47.
23. Finnida (1993) p. 21.
24. Paasio (996) p. 1.
25. Finnida (1993) p. 32.
26. Finnish Government (1995) p. 25.
27. Ibid., p. 26.
28. Ibid., p. 15.

29. OECD (1995b) p. 11.
30. Ibid., p. 12.
31. Ibid., p. 11.
32. Udenrigsministeriet/DANIDA (1995) p. 23.
33. Ibid., pp. 23ff.

Part 2
The Lomé Convention

8 EU–ACP Relations in the 1990s

Gioia Scappucci

INTRODUCTION

Over the past twenty years, the Lomé Conventions have been the main framework for European Union (EU)[1]–ACP relations. The characteristics of the Lomé framework – 'partnership, dialogue, contractuality and predictability'[2] – have gained EU–ACP relations the label of a 'unique model of North–South cooperation'. Since 1975 this model has been adapted to changing political trends and economic thinking while building on previous achievements. How have the end of the cold war and the new World Trade Organization (WTO) rules influenced this model?

Unlike its predecessors, the Lomé IV Convention, signed on 15 December 1989, was concluded for a ten-year period, taking effect on 1 March 1990. The financial protocol attached to it was nevertheless limited to half of that period and provision was made for it to be reviewed after five years. Article 366 of the Convention was flexible enough to set a procedure allowing a review of the text, should negotiations for the new financial protocol take place. Such a review did not have to constitute a renegotiation of the Convention, but only an amendment of those points on which mutual agreement of the partners was possible. Nonetheless, the mid-term review (MTR) of the Lomé IV Convention[3] turned out to be an occasion to consider the future of EU–ACP relations. Some important innovations were adopted. This chapter studies the MTR as a mirror of the main elements characterizing EU–ACP relations in the mid 1990s.

A brief outline of the course of the MTR negotiations may help to understand the main factors influencing the agreement reached. The core of the chapter analyses the major innovations agreed upon during the MTR, grouped under three main headings: political and institutional changes, trade cooperation, and finance development issues. This perspective looks at the innovations as indications of possible new trends in EU–ACP relations. The objective is to enquire whether such trends build on previous achievements or whether they put in question basic principles of EU–ACP relations to date. The chapter concludes by referring to the debate on the future of the relations between the EU and the ACP countries.[4]

THE NEGOTIATIONS

The MTR negotiations had to strike a balance between the maintenance of the 'Lomé culture'[5] and the need to adapt to a radically transformed global economic, political and commercial context. The end of the East–West confrontation, the extension of democratization processes to ACP countries, the worsening of the economic crisis, altered regional priorities as well as new development policy principles for the European Union,[6] all contributed to make the negotiation process a challenge.

The ACP states and the Community informed each other of their requests for modification of the Lomé IV convention on 28 February 1994. The MTR negotiations opened on 20 May 1994 in Swaziland. The negotiations were long and complex. In order to progress, three working groups were created: one on institutional and policy matters, a second on trade, and a third on development finance cooperation. During the negotiations three EU–ACP ministerial meetings took place in Brussels. Considerable results were achieved during the first and third of these meetings. The second was hindered by disagreement on financial issues. Indeed, the funding of the second financial protocol for the Lomé IV convention was indisputably the most arduous matter to resolve. The ACP states requested a package of 15.8 million ecu. Since Lomé IV came into operation the EU has been enlarged by the accession of three other countries: Austria, Finland and Sweden. The ACP states expected the funding of the second financial protocol to increase compared to the first one. This was not the widespread opinion among the European leaders.

The member states' priorities were considerably divergent.[7] An agreement was reached during the last minutes of the French presidency on 30 June 1995 in Brussels. The compromise was 14.625 million ecu.[8] Since this amount includes the inflation rate within the EU member states, it does not entail a 'real' increase of the funds allocated.

The financial protocol deal was possible thanks to agreement on other issues such as decisions on EU development assistance packages for six Eastern and Central European countries in line for accession to the EU and twelve Mediterranean nations with whom the EU foresees a free trade zone. The financial deal also led to a special one-day meeting of the EU and ACP ministers on June 30 1995 to tackle

> more open access to EC market, tariff concessions, a declaration on the protection of tropical forests, another on the alleviation of ACP debt, a compromise on methods of allocating development funds and finally, a breakdown of the financial package for the next five years among the different instruments of the Convention.[9]

The results of the MTR negotiations were formalized in an agreement on the revision of Lomé IV signed in Mauritius on 4 November 1995.[10] How far-reaching were the modifications adopted? To what extent are the changes introduced with regard to human rights and democracy commitments that may be concretely implemented? Do the trade concessions achieved in the MTR correspond to the trade strategy followed up to date? What does 'tranched programming' of resources entail? Answers to these questions will help in understanding whether Lomé IVB may be considered 'a milestone'[11] in EU–ACP relations.

POLITICAL AND INSTITUTIONAL CHANGES

The most significant political changes concerned human rights, democracy and the rule of law. The strengthening of political dialogue was fostered also by a few new provisions concerning the functioning of the joint institutions. The MTR negotiations were characterized by long discussions on innovations concerning procedures, but no satisfactory agreement was found. Among the political and institutional changes one might also class the innovations concerning 'decentralized cooperation'. By strengthening the so-called 'grassroots' initiatives the new provisions on 'decentralized cooperation' contribute to the democratization process fostered in the ACP countries.

Strengthening Human Rights, Democracy and the Rule of Law

The preamble of Lomé III (1985) timidly affirmed the Parties' 'belief in the fundamental human rights'. The Convention stressed the importance of economic, cultural and social rights. No link between human rights and EU aid was foreseen, however. In 1990, when Lomé

IV was signed, the protection of human rights became one of the objectives of the Convention. Article 5 of the Convention strengthened the importance of the protection of human rights for development. Indeed, 'respect for human rights is recognised as a basic factor of development and ... cooperation is conceived as a contribution to the promotion of these rights.'[12]

During the MTR negotiations, at the request of the Commission of the EU, the above-mentioned 'human rights clause' was supplemented by a 'democracy clause'. Article 5 was in fact amended, and now foresees that 'development policy and cooperation shall be closely linked to respect for and enjoyment of fundamental human rights and the recognition and application of democratic principles, the consolidation of the rule of law and good governance'. An ECDPM Working Paper, *Perspectives on Lomé Cooperation*[13] explains that 'under the modified agreement, measures to promote human rights, support democratization processes and to strengthen the rule of law and good governance, can and should be financed within the framework of the national indicative programmes.'

Another fundamental innovation in this domain is the fact that according to art. 5 of Lomé IVB, the 'respect for human rights, democratic principles and the rule of law, which underpins relations between the ACP states and the Community and all the provisions of the Convention, ... shall constitute an essential element' of the Convention.[14] According to the Vienna convention on treaties,[15] the violation of an essential element of the treaty by one contracting party is a reason for the other to invoke the suspension of its application. Within the framework of Lomé IV B, it means that the violation of human rights, democratic principles and the rule of law[16] may lead to the suspension of development cooperation. Such a radical consequence is mitigated by art. 366a, which sets the procedure for the suspension of aid. Suspension is seen as a last resort. When a party

> considers that the other has failed to fulfil an obligation in respect of one of the essential elements referred to in [a]rticle 5, it shall invite the [p]arty concerned, unless there is special urgency to hold consultations in view to assessing the situation in detail and, if necessary in remedying it.

If these consultations are unsuccessful, then 'the [P]arty which invoked the failure to fulfil an obligation may take appropriate steps, including the partial or full suspension of application' of the Lomé convention.[17]

The strengthening of human rights, democracy and the rule of law may be interpreted as the affirmation of an underlying trend in the previous Conventions, namely Lomé III and IV. To what extent might these innovations be qualified as a 'turning point' in EU–ACP relations? According to the former director-general for development at the European Commission, the 'conditionality' in Lomé IVB is a step backwards. He bluntly remarks that 'for the sake of efficiency, the tendency is to take on the tasks and responsibilities of the other partner ... Dialogue has taken a back seat to greater conditionality – in the sense of externally imposed conditions.'[18]

Certainly the increased 'conditionality' of aid granting may be seen by the ACP partners as a change in the traditional interpretation of the partnership principle. This implied a blind trust in the partner's administration of the aid allocated and no interference at all in its domestic affairs. This is probably true, and indeed may influence future relations between the EU and the ACP states. On the EU's side it displays the need to integrate the new provisions on development cooperation contained in the TEU in the EU's relations with the developing countries. As a recent judgement of the European Court of Justice highlights, the contents of art. 130u, paragraph 2, TEU, demonstrates the importance one should attribute to the respect of human rights and democratic principles and the fact that the EU's development cooperation activities are committed to integrate the latter in its concrete engagements with the developing countries.[19] Finally, the increased focus on 'conditionality' might also simply manifest the fruit of a widely spread recognition, by the international community as a whole, of the paramount importance of the respect of human rights and democratic principles.

Reinforced Political Dialogue and Institutional Innovations

According to Lignau, one of the positive achievements on Lomé's balance sheet is its 'institutionalised dialogue', namely the fact that 'cooperation is negotiated, planned, programmed and supervised in bodies in which the partners are equally represented'.[20] The joint institutions are commonly referred to as the ideal forum for dialogue. The MTR negotiations attached to these institutions the competence for 'political' dialogue. The agreement signed in Mauritius in fact 'makes express provision for political dialogue with the ACP partners, i.e. a dialogue about political issues in the true sense, not to be confused with development policy dialogue, which existed beforehand.'[21] The amendment adopted concerns art. 30, which falls under the chapter on the joint institutions and deals with the Council of Ministers. It was agreed that the 'Council of Ministers shall conduct an enlarged political dialogue' and that 'to this end, the Contracting Parties shall organize themselves to ensure an effective dialogue.'[22] Furthermore, it is foreseen that such dialogue may also develop in regional discussion circles.

As regards the common institutions, according to the head of the Commission's Coordination Group for the revision of Lomé, 'an important compromise was reached on the subject of the Joint Assembly's composition'. As he explains,

> after several months of discussion on the EU's proposal that Article 32 of the Convention refers exclusively to parliamentary membership, the negotiators finally agreed to leave the way open for ACP representatives from other sources, provided that these are appointed by the parliament of the country in question.[23]

Even if the above-mentioned innovations might appear as marginal, they should not be underestimated. On the contrary, they exemplify a substantial change in EU–ACP relations. This change is the result of a slow transformation that was already taking place at the beginning of the 1990s but that seems to have been brought to light with the MTR. Indeed, as Frisch explains, 'one of the features of Lomé used to be its political neutrality.'[24] Lomé could not have existed if the Europeans had awarded political and ideological marks to its partners. With the Single European Act[25] and especially since the entry into force of the Maastricht Treaty,[26] things have changed; the EU can no longer be politically neutral in its relations with third countries because it has to attain specific common foreign policy objectives.

DECENTRALIZED COOPERATION

The head of the Commission's Coordination Group for the Lomé IV Review reveals that 'from the outset there was general agreement on the advantages of developing decentralized cooperation ... however, differences of opinion arose during the negotiations over the conditions necessary to give substance to this new impetus.'[27] The main obstacles encountered were due to the difficulties in agreeing on the question of direct access of the various actors involved in decentralized cooperation to Community financing and 'to the inspection by national authorities of the recipient countries'.[28] The outcome of the negotiations was, in the event, interesting.

It should be noted that the Lomé IV articles dedicated to 'widening participation in cooperation activities' were deleted and replaced by an entirely new section entitled 'decentralized cooperation'. This section has a new placing in the Convention: while the Lomé IV provisions on 'widening participation in cooperation activities' were located in Part I of the Convention regarding the general provisions of cooperation, by contrast the Lomé IVB provisions on 'decentralized cooperation' are situated in Part III of the Convention, which concerns the instruments of cooperation. This choice demonstrates the contracting parties' will to define more precisely the possibilities offered by this new instrument for the development of the ACP states.

The stated objective of increased emphasis on decentralized cooperation is to strengthen and diversify the basis for long-term development of the ACP states. For this purpose all agents from the Community and the ACP states are encouraged 'to put forward and implement initiatives ... within the framework of decentralized cooperation'.[29] The 'agents' in question are defined by para. 2 of art. 251a as

> decentralized public authorities, rural and village groups, cooperatives, trade unions, teaching and research institutions, non-governmental development organizations, other associations, groups and agents which are able and wish to contribute to the development of the ACP states on their own initiative, provided that the agents and the operators are non-profit-making.

In the Lomé IVB framework, 'decentralized cooperation' is characterized by the combination of efforts and resources of organizations in ACP countries and their counterparts in the Community. Decentralized cooperation may be supported by resources from the indicative programmes or counterpart funds.[30] A ceiling on EDF contributions to these operations was also fixed at 300 000 ecu per project or programme.[31]

The intent of the MTR negotiators was to highlight the potential of decentralized cooperation as a newly defined instrument in EU–ACP cooperation. The fact that particular attention was dedicated to clearly define its use and facilitate its implementation is indicative of an attempt of the EU and the ACP countries to explore untravelled roads in their relation.

TRADE COOPERATION

From the start, the Lomé conventions have been based on a mix of aid and trade, the latter's characteristic being preferential treatment and non-reciprocity in favour of ACP exports.[32] As Frisch explains:

> unilateral free access to the European market was agreed by treaty, though preferences were not set down contractually. The obligations of the Lomé partners towards the Community did not go beyond the principle of the most-favoured-nation treatment ... and non discrimination between the EU member states.[33]

The accordance of special preferences was tolerated by GATT.

Innovations in trade cooperation had to cope with a series of obstacles and constraints of different kinds. There is the necessity to adapt to the new WTO rules, which emphasize more the creation of free trade areas (FTAs) rather than the accordance of special preferences. The WTO seems likely to be more strict in the granting of waivers to global liberalization principles than the GATT rules of 1947. Also, the MTR negotiations had to face an increasing lack of support by European public opinion for the Lomé framework. The latter has been losing momentum because of negative performance by ACP economies and the widespread perception that 'European' money is spent and invested without any positive outcome. Figures demonstrate that the ACP countries have lost market shares despite the preferences. Frisch inquires whether 'since many people consider the preferences to have achieved nothing, we should perhaps ask whether such acrobatics can be justified at all.'[34]

How much did these problems and constraints influence the decisions taken by the MTR negotiators in evaluating how to improve the provisions on trade cooperation? How far-reaching are the innovations concerning trade cooperation adopted in Mauritius? There are two fundamental categories: the importance of trade in the context of EU–ACP relations and the concrete measures that will lead to practical consequences.

Trade as an Energizing Factor in Development

The MTR negotiations shed a new light on trade as a means to energize the development process. According to *The Courier*, negotiations on the commercial section were marked by a radical, new approach: for the first time since Lomé I the main focus of debate was not preferential access which previously constituted the main way of ensuring trade flows from ACP states.[35] Talks were much more wide ranging. There was a general determination to analyse all the factors behind commercial success and the necessary means to ensure such success through a sectorial integrated approach.

This approach is disclosed in the new provisions introduced by the Mauritius agreement describing the aim of trade cooperation.[36] Art. 6 of Lomé IVB underlines in fact that 'The Community and the ACP states agree to give high priority to the development of trade with a view to accelerating the growth of the ACP states' economies and to integrate them in the world economy in a harmonious and gradual manner.'[37] General consensus was therefore reached that trade 'must be at the heart of future EU–ACP cooperation and that all the instruments provided for by the Convention must be employed to improve the trading performance of the ACP states.'[38] How was this renewed attention for trade translated into concrete engagements? Do these correspond to the ambitious objectives set for trade cooperation?

Not surprisingly, it was far more easy to reach consensus on the enunciation of principles than to strike a similarly ambitious agreement on the way to implement those principles. It must be underlined that the concrete changes envisaged to make trade cooperation truly an 'energizer' of development failed to be as far-reaching as the enunciation of the aims of trade. The main changes concern access of ACP products to the EU market and rules of origin.

Access of ACP Products to the EU Market

The EU made some concessions with regard to market access for certain agricultural products which were previously subject to custom duties and levies, tariff quotas or marketing calendar. Special protocols were signed to deal with the always 'hot' topics of beef/veal and bananas. The EU easily accepted a bigger reduction in beef and veal import duties from specific ACP countries to satisfy an ACP request, while banana negotiations were slightly more arduous. As the head of the Commission's Coordination Group for the revision of Lomé explained, 'the debate was finally concluded with a joint declaration on bananas (Annexe LXXXVIII of Lomé IVB) which makes provision for dealing with the specific problems of the Community's ACP banana suppliers in the context of programmable aid.'[39] A new protocol on the sustainable management of forestry resources saw the light of the day at the insistence of the ACP countries. As far as trade is concerned, some provisions of the protocol are dedicated to the question of trade in tropical timber.

Rules of Origin

The ACP states successfully negotiated new provisions concerning 'rules of origin'. Indeed,

> countries may and do, for a variety of purposes, distinguish products according to their origin. The application of certain domestic commercial policy rules may require either to distinguish imported from national products or to differentiate between imported products.[40]

According to the agreement signed in Marrakesh, these rules should not be designated as a protectionist device, therefore the criteria used to determine the origin of a product must *inter alia* be the country of last substantial transformation.[41] These principles were already embodied in articles 3 and 6 of Protocol 1 of the Lomé IV convention.[42] During the MTR negotiations 'rules of origin' were highly debated, however, with particular emphasis on the subject of cumulation. The ACP countries wanted to extend the list of countries with which they are allowed to 'cumulate' to all the countries to which the EU grants preferential treatment. The compromise reached is contained in art. 6 of Protocol 1. According to the new provision, it is now possible to consider a product as originating in the ACP states, even if it actually originates in a neighbouring country belonging to 'a coherent geographical entity', provided certain conditions are fulfilled. This list of countries with which the ACP countries may 'cumulate' has been extended, but falls far short of ACP hopes, particularly with regard to the Pacific. Moreover, some products are excluded from art. 6: canned tuna, rice and certain textile products.

The amendments concerning rules of origin seem to reflect the desire to promote regional economic integration between ACP and non-ACP neighbouring countries. Notwithstanding the limits of the aforementioned compromise, the new provisions constitute a positive step forward.

FINANCIAL COOPERATION

Probably the most innovative changes adopted during the MTR negotiations are those concerning financial cooperation. In fact, as Europe Information[43] effectively points out, 'apart from the question of the amount of funds to be available under the new financial protocol, there was a shared concern to make aid more effective.'[44] This common endeavour was pursued in three ways, first, by introducing the concept of 'programmable aid', secondly, by envisaging the possibility of direct budgetary aid and other structural adjustment measures and, thirdly, by relaxing the financial conditions attached to the European Investment Bank (EIB) operations and by foreseeing for the latter a greater role in private sector promotion.[45] The EU and the ACP also discussed possible reforms concerning the procedures for implementing financial and technical cooperation.

Programmable Aid

In the past the Commission prided itself on the fact that 'governments of countries receiving Community aid have the sovereign right to determine their priorities; they decide on how to use their own resources and those which the Community places contractually at their disposal.'[46] These claims were mitigated in practice by specific provisions in the various Lomé conventions which obliged the Community to programme country aid at the beginning of each convention period in order 'to permit the beneficiary country to have the clearest possible idea of the aid that it could expect over this period and specifically of the amount of aid, modalities and objectives to which it should be applied.'[47] As Grilli explains, 'programming of aid was intended, on the one hand, to provide foreseeability and, on the other, to be the vehicle for clearly identifying country development priorities and making them compatible with EC priorities.'[48] What did the MTR negotiations change in this concept of 'programmable aid?'

As was the case previously, also according to Lomé IVB, 'each ACP state shall obtain from the Community a clear indication of the total indicative programmable financial allocation from which it may benefit during that period as well as any other relevant information ...'[49] The fundamental difference, compared to the past, is that the resources shall be allocated in two 'tranches'. As soon as an agreement is reached on the volume of the national indicative programme (NIP) and after the ACP state has drafted a timetable showing how the NIP shall be implemented,[50] and how the first 70 per cent of the NIP shall be allocated. Provision is made to allow a revision of the NIP 'when the ACP state has achieved a high level of commitments in the implementation of the programme and in any case no later than three years after the entry into force of the Second Financial Protocol.'[51] Only then, may the 'second tranche' of funds be released. This is not automatic. On the contrary, art. 282 clearly lists various conditions to be taken into consideration. The scrutiny covers both the progress made in the implementation of the NIP's objectives[52] and the 'state of preparation of the activities the ACP state intends to undertake within the second phase of the indicative programme'.[53] If the conditions are not fulfilled then the second 'tranche' is not allocated. Provision is made, in art. 282, para. 5, that 'any unallocated resources remaining from the programmable resources shall be used for financing operations falling within the scope of development finance cooperation, notably those relating to programmable assistance.'

The two-tranche method has at the same time gathered both positive reactions and criticisms. One of the arguments brought forward to support its introduction is the fact that it has introduced a performance criterion. This seems to be a response to the general sense of frustration caused by the overall balance sheet of the Lomé record. Indeed the new method seems to encourage a planned use of the aid and therefore a probably more effective, one. Nonetheless, as Lignau remarks:

> the measure is insufficient since it takes into consideration only the disbursement of funds. In other words, additional criteria ... have yet to be put in place. Criteria of particular relevance are: country needs, government reform orientation, progress and success in implementing development programmes and reform measures.[54]

More strongly, Bossuyt brings into relief that phasing of aid represents a 'donor driven approach that is not compatible with realities and the existing managing capacities. The important thing is to find country-specific, realistic and non bureaucratic procedures.'[55]

Whatever the merits or the limits of this new method of aid programming, it again is a symptom of a new trend in EU–ACP relations. The ambition seems to be that of structuring the granting of aid in order to try and obtain specific results. The ideal is pursued by putting pressure on the counterpart to encourage it to use the resources allocated in the most effective way. The unveiled strategy on the EU side might be a need to be able to justify the survival of a privileged relation with the ACP countries in the context of its altered regional priorities. It also gives evidence of the decreasing amount of funds that the member states of the EU are willing to invest for development cooperation purposes.

Direct Budgetary Aid and Other Structural Adjustment Measures

The major innovations relating to structural adjustment are the possibility of granting direct budgetary support to improve the implementation of ACP budgets[56] and the introduction of the regional dimension of structural adjustment programmes. Article 243 has been modified to stress that

> the ACP states and the Community recognise also the necessity to encourage reform programmes at regional level ensuring that, in the preparation of execution of the national programmes, due consideration is given to the regional activities which have an influence on national development.

To foster this goal structural adjustment should incorporate, from the start, measures to encourage regional integration. In order to fulfil the dual aim of regional integration and of structural reform at the national level, harmonization and coordination of macroeconomic and sectoral policies should be supported. Sectoral reforms as well as the liberalization of trade and payments and transborder investments should be encouraged.[57]

These innovations were adopted at the request of the ACP countries. They reflect the desire of these countries to encourage intra-regional economic liberalization as well as the need to make procedures more flexible.

Procedures

According to the head of the Commission's coordination group for the Lomé Review, 'the question of procedures for implementing cooperation in development financing constituted one of the most difficult points under discussion.'[58] No substantial change was agreed upon. It was decided, in a joint declaration annexed to the Lomé IVB convention, that the ACP–EC Council of Ministers should deepen its examination of the procedures relating to the award of contracts and to the role of executing agents. The Council of Ministers' work should have to be carried out through the development finance committee instituted by art. 325 of Lomé IVB.

The fact that no substantial change was possible in this domain is understandable given the complexity of the issue, and especially because it would probably have implied amendments exceeding the mere modification of certain provisions of the Convention.

LOMÉ IVB: A MILESTONE IN EU–ACP RELATIONS?

The analysis of the major innovations introduced by the MTR has tried to cast some light on the state of the relations between the EU and the ACP countries in the mid 1990s. One conclusion might be that the first serious thoughts of re-evaluating the Lomé cooperation model became evident during the MTR. While the MTR negotiations were not concluded yet, the development commissioner, Mr Pinheiro claimed: 'This is the last Convention as we have come to know them.' If this statement is a promise, indeed Lomé IVB may be qualified as a 'milestone'. As explained in this chapter, the MTR could not lead to a new convention. The scope of the negotiation was, therefore, limited and consequently the innovations adopted could not put into question in the overall general framework of the relations. Nevertheless, some of the amendments agreed upon are indicative of possible evolution in the relation. Innovations such as the increased focus on human rights, democracy, rule of law and good governance are likely to influence future debates on what kind of partnership should be devised for the year 2000 when the Lomé IV Convention comes to an end. The debate on the future[59] of the Lomé cooperation model will also be inclined to deepen the potentialities of trade as an energizer of development. The two-tranche method of aid allocation has certainly launched reflection on the usefulness of introducing a *merits* criterion in the allocation of aid. These are vitally important issues which will strongly influence the future of Europe's relations with the ACP states.

Bibliography

Berrod, F., 'The Evolution of the Rules Affecting Trade in Goods: an Introductory Note', in Bourgeois, Berrod, Gippini, Fournier (eds), *The Uruguay Round Results, The Bruges Conferences no. 8* (European Interuniversity Press, Brussels, 1995) pp. 143–50.

ECJ Judgement, 3/12/1996–Case C-268/94.

European Commission, 'Financial Cooperation Under the Lomé Convention–Review of Aid at the End of 1994', *Europe Information–Development* (March 1995) pp. 14–15.

European Commission, 'Financial Cooperation Under the Lomé Conventions – Review of the Aid at the End of 1995,' *Europe Information – Development* (September 1996) p. 11.

European Commission, Directorate-General VIII Development, Study Group – Partnership 2000, Green Paper on the relations between the EU and the ACP countries on the eve of the 21st century: *Challenges and Options for a New Partnership* (Brussels, 20 November 1996).

Frisch, D., *The Future of the Lomé Convention – Initial Reflections on Europe's Africa Policy after the Year 2000*, ECDPM Working Paper no. 11 (Maastricht 1996).

Grilli, E., *The European Communities and the Developing Countries* (Cambridge University Press, 1993).

Koulaimah-Gabriel, A; 'Beyond Lomé IV: Main Issues at Stake for EU–African relations', *Review of European Community and International Environmental Law,* Special Issue on Africa (March 1997) pp. 90–104.

Lingnau, H., *Perspectives on Lomé Cooperation*, ECDPM Working Paper no. 12 (Maastricht 1996).

Percival, D., 'Agreement Clinched at the Eleventh Hour', *The Courier*, no. 153 (September–October 1995).

Vernier, G., 'The Lomé IV Mid-Term Review – Main Innovations', *The Courier*, no. 155, special issue on the revised Lomé Convention (January–February 1996) p. 13.

Notes

1. Strictly speaking the European Union has only existed since the Treaty on European Union (1992) came into force and therefore it cannot have on record a twenty-year-old relationship with the ACP countries. In this chapter 'European Union' or 'EU' has nonetheless been chosen in order to facilitate reference to the 'European' partner in the relationship, thus avoiding having to specify whether the actor is the EU (for political dialogue, for example), the EC (for the trade and aid provisions), the member states (MS) of the EC (for the allocation of funds to the European Development Fund) or the EC and its MS (for the conclusion of 'mixed agreements' such as the Lomé conventions).
2. These are the Lomé framework's specific characteristics (see Frisch, 1996). The commitment to partnership is clear in the preamble of the Lomé Convention, which stipulates 'complete equality between partners'. The right of each 'partner' to determine its own political, social and economic options is interpreted as a consequence of the partnership principle. The expression 'dialogue', recapitulates that 'cooperation is negotiated, planned, programmed and supervised in bodies where the partners are equally represented' (see Lingnau, 1996). The 'contractual' nature of the relationship stems from the fact that the objectives of the cooperation and the rights and obligations of the partners are set down in a binding form. The Lomé conventions have been

concluded for periods of five years (except the last one) and this long-term character places cooperation on a predictable footing.

3. The outcome of the mid-term review negotiations was an agreement signed in Mauritius on 4 November 1995 to revise certain provisions of the Lomé IV convention. This agreement is commonly referred to as 'Lomé IVB' or, more familiarly, 'the Mauritius agreement'. Both expressions are used in this chapter.
4. The debate on the future of the relations between the EU and the ACP countries has become an important issue since the MTR, during which the Joint EC–ACP Assembly engaged itself in drawing up a report on the future of the Lomé convention. The ACP countries planned to agree on a joint position of the future of Lomé before the end of 1997, but failed to do so. On the European side, the Commission presented the main topics and problems for discussion (see: European Commission, ... Green Paper).
5. 'Lomé culture' is the expression generally used to summarise the particularity of the cooperation framework created by the Lomé conventions. It implies reference to the principles characterizing the relationship (see note 2 and Frisch, 1996).
6. Treaty on the European Union, Title XVII, Development Cooperation: this sets out the objectives of the European Union's development cooperation, namely:
   - sustainable economic and social development of the developing countries and more particularly the most disadvantaged among the LDCs;
   - smooth and gradual integration of the developing countries into world economy; campaign against poverty in the developing countries (art. 130u, s.1);
   - consolidation of democracy in the developing countries within the framework of political stability (art. 130u, s.2);
   - consistency with objectives approved in UN context or within other International Organizations (art. 130u, s.3).
7. See Part I, Chapters 4–7, of this book for an analysis in depth of the different priorities of the Member States during the Lomé IV MTR negotiations. Chapter 10 on the European Development Fund also broadly covers the main controversies among the member states while negotiating the eighth EDF.
8. Agreement amending the IV ACP–EC Convention of Lomé, signed in Mauritius on 4 November 1995, Second Financial Protocol, art. 1.
9. Percival, (1995) p. 6.
10. The event brought together foreign and development ministers of the 15 EU member states and 69 of the 70 ACP countries The only absentee was Somalia, which had not ratified the Convention at the time. South Africa participated as an observer. Information about the course of the negotiations is taken from *The Courier*, no. 155 (see Vernier, 1996).
11. The development commissioner, Mr Pinheiro, defined the agreement as a 'milestone' during the signing ceremony of the Lomé IVB convention.

12. Article 5, para. 1, Lomé VI.
13. Lingnau (1996) p. 4.
14. A recent judgement of the European Court of Justice (Arret de la Cour de Justice des Communautés Européennes, 3/12/1996 – Affaire C-268/94) clearly interprets the fact of considering the respect of human rights and democratic principles as 'essential elements' of an agreement, as completely in accordance with the EU's development cooperation objectives.
15. Vienna Convention on Treaties, 1969, Art. 60.
16. It should be noted that 'the promotion of good governance' was not mentioned among the 'essential elements' of the Convention. The definition of 'good governance' is controversial. Moreover, setting parameters to qualify the concept might be interpreted as a non-respect of the right of each partner to determine its political options.
17. Article 366a, Lomé IVB.
18. Frisch (1996) p. 9.
19. ECJ Judgement, 3/12/1996 – Case C-268/94, point 24.
20. Lingnau (1996) p. 2.
21. Frisch (1996) p. 6.
22. Extracts of Art. 30, para. 3, Lomé IVB.
23. Vernier (1996) p. 9.
24. Frisch, (1996) p. 6.
25. Article 30 of the Single European Act legally bound the member states of the European Community to pursue 'European Political Cooperation.'
26. Article J, Title V of the TEU, establishes a 'Common Foreign and Security Policy' for the EU and its member states.
27. see Vernier (1996) p. 11.
28. Ibid.
29. Extract of Article 251a, s. 4a, 'Decentralised Cooperation', Lomé IVB.
30. Article 251c, Lomé IVB.
31. Article 251d, Lomé IVB.
32. An in-depth and critical analysis of the record of the trade provisions of the Lomé conventions is the specific object of another chapter of this book. The main focus here is on the different provisions concerning trade introduced in the Lomé IV convention by the MTR and their influence on the EU–ACP relationship.
33. See Frisch (1996) p. 11.
34. Ibid., p. 12.
35. Vernier (1996) p. 11.
36. The contents of the new art. 6 of the Lomé IVB convention reflects the EU's development cooperation objectives as enshrined in the TEU.
37. Lomé IVB, extract of art. 6 of the Objectives and Principles Chapter.
38. European Commission, *Financial Cooperation Under the Lomé Convention (1994)*, p. 14.
39. Vernier (1996) p. 10.
40. Berrod (1995).
41. Agreement on Rules of Origin of the Multilateral Trade in Goods Agreements, 1994.

42. Protocol 1 of Lomé IV is specifically dedicated to the definition of the term 'originating products and methods of administrative cooperation'.
43. European Commission, *Financial Cooperation Under the Lomé Conventions* (1995) 11.
44. The issue of the allocation of funds under the second financial protocol has been mentioned in describing the course of the MTR negotiations.
45. See Chapter 11 for a comprehensive panorama of the Bank's increased role in the private sector promotion.
46. Extract of the Pisani Memorandum, 1982; see Grilli (1993) p. 108.
47. Article 51, Lomé I; Grilli (1993) p. 111.
48. Grilli (1993) p. 111.
49. Article 281, para. 1, lett. (a), Lomé IVB.
50. Article 281, para. 2, lett. (j), Lomé IVB.
51. Article 282, para. 3, Lomé IVB.
52. Article 281, para. 2 of the Lomé IVB convention provides that the indicative programme should be consistent with development cooperation objectives and priorities. It also specifically refers to certain elements such as the support for poverty alleviation and sustainable development as well as proposals for private sector and/or industrial sector development for which the ACP state envisages that risk capital and other available resources could be used.
53. Article 282, para. 4, lett. (c), Lomé IVB.
54. Lingnau H. (1996) p. 5.
55. Basset's opinion is referred to by Lingnau (1996) footnote 14, p. 5.
56. Article 247, para. 4, lett. (b), Lomé IVB.
57. Article 243, para. 2, lett. (a) to (d), Lomé IVB.
58. See Vernier (1996) p. 13.
59. For an accurate analysis of the challenges facing EU–ACP relations in the future, see Koulaimah-Gabriel (1997).

9 The Record of the Trade Provisions of the Lomé Convention

Kai Radtke

LOMÉ IV – SHORTCOMINGS AND PROSPECTS AFTER THE MID-TERM REVIEW

The fourth Lomé Convention has further institutionalized the colonial heritage of association with the former colonies of the EU member states. Based on the notion of equity and partnership between the 15 European and 70 African, Caribbean and Pacific states (ACP), it provides for improved trade and aid provisions compared with its predecessors. It was negotiated in 1989 under the political and economic conditions of the Cold War. Since then the parameters of international cooperation have changed and only one ideology, that of the market economy, has survived the Cold War. Even the mid-term review of Lomé IV changed only marginally the Convention, but not the underlying idea of the natural relationship of 'EurAfrica'.[1]

This chapter questions the appropriateness of the current provisions of the Lomé Convention and its general approach. The record suggests that it has not helped the ACP states to diversify and increase their exports, and, taking into account the triumphant march of the market economy, the reasons for this failure and the general shortcomings of the Lomé approach are discussed. Neither the aid nor the trade preferences of the Lomé Convention enabled the ACP states to achieve economic development; instead they became poorer and poorer. Why is this so, and how could the underlying principles of the Lomé Convention be changed in order to improve the trade performances of the ACP states? Even more, could a possible renewed Lomé V still follow the same approach, i.e. can the provisions of any accord further be based on trade preferences and financial assistance towards a group of states as diversified as the ACP group?

In order to deal with these questions this chapter will first discuss the current trade provisions of Lomé IV and its results. It will show the relationship between aid and trade provisions in order to demonstrate that trade is far more important for the ACP states than aid. Second, it will analyse the main limiting factors for the efficiency of the trade provisions. Third, the question arises whether trade and aid should be managed within the same framework of a further Lomé Convention or whether they have different aims. Whereas trade provisions should enable the ACP states to profit better from the export economy, aid provisions should concentrate on the immediate needs of the peoples themselves. Against the folio of the new chapter on development cooperation in the Treaty on the European Union (TEU) that introduced its horizontal character, one has to ask whether or not development cooperation in general can be considered separately from other EU policies.

THE RECORD OF TRADE AND AID PROVISIONS OF THE LOMÉ CONVENTIONS

From its inception, the Lomé Convention was intended to 'promote and expedite the economic, cultural and social development of the ACP States'.[2] In the field of trade cooperation the object of the Lomé Conventions was to 'promote trade between the ACP states and the Community ... and also between the ACP states themselves'.[3] Did the trade provisions achieve this aim? What was the role of the aid provisions in relation to trade preferences?

In principle, the Lomé Conventions guarantee ACP states access to the European market free of any duties or quantitative restrictions, excluding products covered by the Common Agricultural Policy of the Union (CAP) or special protocols annexed to the Convention. However, despite these exceptions, under the Lomé Conventions the EU provided the ACP states with the most preferential treatment, compared with any other countries in the world. Whether or not the Lomé Conventions contributed to their objectives, as set out above, should be considered on two levels: the aggregate level of trade performance and the individual level of particular countries, as well as that of particular commodities.

Trade Performance of the ACP States at an Aggregated Level

At the aggregated level, ACP states performed unsatisfactorily, if not badly. Indeed, some say that 'at an aggregate level, the Lomé preferences in fact failed to improve the ACP trade performances.'[4] As Table 9.1 shows, this assertion seems to be correct. Though EU imports from ACP countries increased in absolute terms between 1976 and 1992 from 10.5 billion ecu to around 18 billion ecu, with a peak in 1985 of 26.8 billion ecu, the relative share of EU imports decreased from 6.7 per cent to 3.5 per cent during the same period. This is due to the fact that the trade between the EU and developing countries in general decreased.[5] But why is this so, if the ACP countries had the comparative advantage of receiving the most preferential treatment from Europe?

One explanation for this lies in the fact that the ACP group of states is extremely heterogeneous in terms of geography and the size of the individual countries. Consequently, they were extremely vulnerable to price changes of commodities on the world market. Figure 9.1 shows the dominance of single commodities like cocoa beans, coffee, bananas, diamonds, raw cane sugar, tropical wood and crude petroleum, which accounted for 53.2 per cent of the EC imports from the ACP states in 1994.

As for the dominance of individual countries, Figure 9.2 leads to the overwhelming significance of Nigerian exports for the ACP group. Nigeria is also an example of the extreme vulnerability of price fluctuations in the oil market, because 90 per cent of its 1993 exports were oil. The 12 countries of Figure 9.2 stand for 68 per cent of the EU imports from all ACP states.[6]

Furthermore, most of the ACP states have such a small domestic market and so merely marginal an industrial structure that the cost disadvantages of their production *vis-à-vis* other developing countries could not be outweighed by the trade preferences of the Lomé Convention. This can easily be shown by the example of bananas. Whereas in 1992 the ACP states received a considerable preferential treatment concerning the quantitative import of bananas, they accounted only for 16.6 per cent of the EU's banana imports. Other developing countries, most of them in Latin America, accounted for 67.4 per cent of total banana exports to the EU at 412 ecu per tonne as against 599 ecu per tonne for ACP bananas.[7]

A third reason why Lomé preferences were not so favourable for ACP exports may be explained by the fact that only 36.6 per cent of EU imports from ACP states received preferential treatment to a significant degree. The other two-thirds or so would have entered the European market duty-free in any case. The Lomé Convention offers higher preferential treatment, particularly for the export of manufactured

Table 9.1 EU imports, billion ecu (share of extra EU imports, %)*

	1976		1980		1985		1990		1992	
ACP	10.5	(6.7)	19.4	(7.2)	26.8	(6.7)	21.9	(4.7)	18.0	(3.7)
Asia†	6.7	(4.2)	16	(5.9)	26	(6.5)	50.9	(11.0)	66.4	(13.6)
Latin America††	8.3	(5.3)	13.7	(5.1)	25.8	(6.5)	25.7	(5.6)	24.8	(5.1)
Mediterranean§	9.6	(6.1)	16.4	(6.1)	32.3	(8.1)	29.8	(6.5)	30.3	(6.2)
All LDCs	70.7	(44.8)	114.3	(42.2)	128.9	(34.7)	143.8	(31.2)	145.6	(29.9)
Extra EC	157.7		518.9		828.2		1127.6		1207.8	

Source: Eurostat, compiled by ODI (1995a) p. 81.
Notes:
* These figures represent imports of the 69 states that were contracting parties to the Lomé Convention in 1992, although in earlier years some of them have not benefited from the Lomé trade provisions.
† *Asia*: Afghanistan, Bhutan, Brunei, Bangladesh, Burma, Cambodia, China, India, Indonesia, Kampuchea, Laos, Macao, Malaysia, Maldives, Mongolia, Nepal, North Korea, Pakistan, Philippines, Singapore, South Korea, Sri Lanka, Taiwan, Thailand, North Vietnam, Vietnam.
†† *Latin America*: Argentina, Bermuda, Bolivia, Brazil, Chile, Colombia, Costa Rica, Cuba, Ecuador, El Salvador, Guatemala, Honduras, Mexico, Nicaragua, Panama, Paraguay, Peru, Uruguay, Venezuela.
§ *Mediterranean*: Algeria, Egypt, Jordan, Lebanon, Libya, Morocco, Syria, Tunisia, Turkey.

Figure 9.1 Major ACP exports in 1994

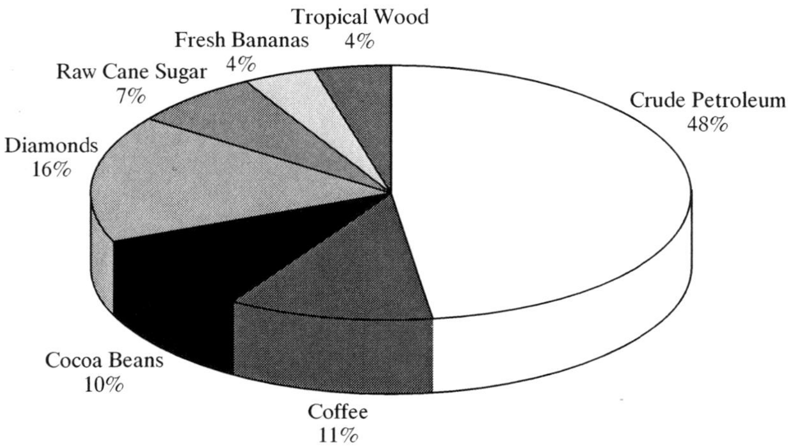

Figure 9.2 EU imports from major ACP countries in 1994

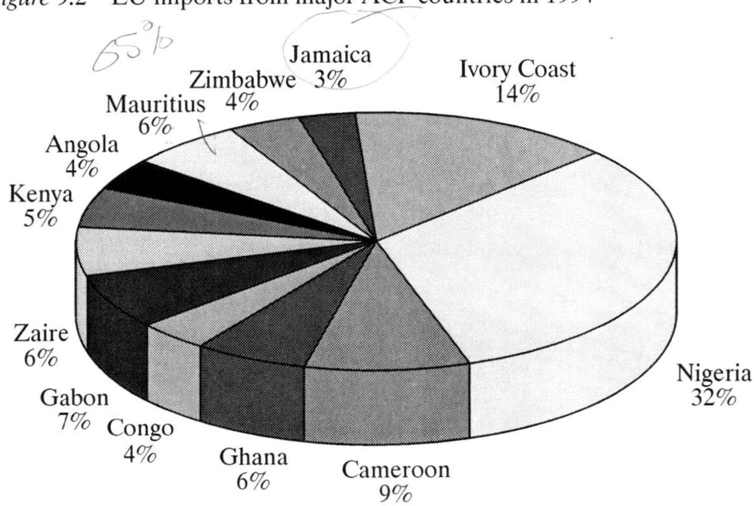

Sources: Eurostat, *Statistics in Focus. External Trade: The European Union (EU) Trade with African, Caribbean and Pacific Countries (ACP)*.

Table 9.2 Exports to EU of top 15 ACP exporting countries, 1976–94 (million ecu)

	1976	1980	1985	1990	1992	1994	1994 exports to EU %	Average annual growth rate 1976–94 %	Average annual growth rate 1992–4 %
Nigeria	3228	7872	10071	4430	3991	3911	21	1.1	–2.0
Côte d'Ivoire	1006	1412	2329	1660	1554	1739	9	3.2	11.9
Cameroon	367	710	2156	1380	1073	1126	6	6.8	4.9
Gabon	378	780	1060	1095	1049	854	6	4.9	–9.1
Mauritius	193	320	431	757	834	821	5	8.9	–1.6
Angola	68	214	569	1101	824	560	3	13.2	–32.0
Zaire	864	1316	1396	1142	716	758	4	–1.0	5.9
Congo	104	316	309	602	647	563	3	10.4	–13.0
Ghana	318	392	346	730	572	787	3	5.4	37.6
Kenya	269	455	709	520	526	594	4	4.8	12.9
Zimbabwe*	1	158	539	577	514	565	3	7.8	9.9
Liberia	334	453	608	702	462	370	2	0.6	–19.9
Jamaica	113	169	188	278	282	335	2	6.6	18.8
Guinea	82	100	296	306	270	318	2	8.2	17.8
Senegal	311	191	299	411	253	289	2	–0.4	14.2

Source: Eurostat, compiled by ODI (1995a) p. 8 and the author.
Note: Growth rate since 1980.

commodities, because the general structure of the Common External Tariff (CET) imposed higher taxes on processed goods.[8] But the share of ACP exports in manufactured goods as a percentage of the overall exports only increased from 20 per cent in 1976 to about 27 per cent in 1992. Other developing countries were much more successful in further diversification of their exports. Asia increased its share of value-added goods; its exports of manufactured goods to the EU increased from 65 per cent in 1976 to 91 per cent in 1992, those of the Mediterranean countries from 10 per cent to 37 per cent.[9] Individual cases of ACP countries indicate further evidence of their diversity as well as the factors on which future development policy should focus.

MAURITIUS AND ZIMBABWE: A CASE STUDY

Mauritius and Zimbabwe pursued different policy strategies to exploit their trade preferences, to increase their share in overall ACP exports to the Community and to diversify their exports.[10] All ACP states have individual characteristics, and moreover the volume of individual trade with the EU is rather unimportant for Zimbawbwe.

Between 1976 and 1992, Mauritius had an average annual growth rate of exports of 10.24 per cent.[11] It mainly exported clothing products – 68 per cent of its entire output. In total, however, Mauritius exported 833 million ecu worth of goods to the EU, representing only 4.64 per cent of all ACP exports to the EU.[12] The reasons for Mauritius's relative success in exporting processed textiles stems mainly from the active export policies of its government. For example, these policies generated an Export Processing Zone and an Export Promotion Authority, delivering wide-ranging services to exporters. Furthermore, Mauritius was able to attract foreign investment and its population is rather well educated compared with other LDCs.[13]

Between 1976 and 1992, Zimbabwe's growth rate was only 8.17 per cent, but it was able to increase its share of manufactured exports from 10 per cent (1986) to 18 per cent (1990/1), although tobacco remains its main export commodity. Zimbabwe's diversification in export markets from the EU and South Africa to Japan and the USA was supported by a change in government trade policy. The liberalization of the import regime as well as the removal of foreign exchange controls fostered both incentives for foreign investment in Zimbabwe as well as the necessary conditions for exporting manufactured goods, which are heavily dependent on foreign inputs.[14] Hence, the main reasons for the relative success of Mauritius and Zimbabwe are to be found in intelligent governmental policy towards liberalization and diversification of products and of markets, both of which make them less vulnerable to price fluctuations.[15] Considering individual commodities exported by ACP states, McQueen and Stevens found that the trade preferences of the Lomé Convention helped some countries to diversify their exports in manufactured goods such as leather, cut flowers and out-of-season vegetables. However, according to them, the 'new' products are no longer insignificant: 'the margin of tariff preference may be important in particular cases, [but] it does not appear in general to have been a critical determinant of export growth rates'.[16] The question then remains: what are the main limiting factors of the Lomé Convention?

THE MAIN LIMITING FACTORS OF THE LOMÉ CONVENTION

Several provisions of the Lomé Convention limit market access for sensitive products from ACP states. The most important are the restricting rules of origin and the constraining Common Agricultural Policy of the EU. Though the rules of origin[17] for ACP exports were less strict than under the General System of Preferences (GSP), their application has had a protectionist impact. 'The Community imposed lists of exceptions containing unilateral specification of cases where a change in tariff heading did not constitute sufficient evidence of substantial transformation.'[18] Rules of origin, owing to their very character, prevent the development of intra-industry trade between the ACP countries and other countries on the world market which might be best prepared to supply ACP producers with the necessary components. The cumulation rule applies only to ACP states and EU countries. Mauritius, for example, was not able to import the necessary components from Asia and had to import less competitive pieces from Europe because of the rules of origin.[19] The cumulative rule is particularly problematic for the Caribbean and Pacific states, not only because of their island character, but also because their natural trading partners are to be found on the American continent, Asia and Australia. One limited step towards defusing the rules of origins was made at the 1995 mid-term review, when the contracting parties introduced the notion of a 'coherent geographical entity' (Protocol 1, art. 6, para. 5). However, the rule is applicable only to some countries explicitly listed, and again excludes sensitive products.[20] The effects of these innovations remain to be seen. Nevertheless, this seems to be a positive step away from the 'nationalization' of trade policies inherent in the rules of origin in times of global trade and production. They could however be further defused by introducing a minimum size of ACP domestic markets before the rules of origin are applicable.

The rules of the Common Agricultural Policy of the EU are imposed upon the Lomé countries by art. 168. Because the Community shall 'ensure more favourable treatment than that granted to third countries benefiting from the most-favoured-nation clause for the same products' (art. 168, 2), the Lomé Convention contains some protocols for sugar, bananas, rum, beef and veal, extending certain duty-free quotas for these commodities to the ACP countries. The Lomé Convention protocols for sugar, bananas, rum, beef and veal stipulate either quotas (bananas, rum), specific quantities at guaranteed prices (sugar) or quotas for selected ACP countries (beef and veal). It is difficult to derive general rules from the protocols, but it does seem as if they assured sufficient conditions to enable them to export these products, at least for some of the small countries highly dependent on them.

The preferences for tropical agricultural products (coffee, cocoa, palm and coconut oil) compared with non-ACP suppliers are small, though exports of these commodities are extremely important for some of the ACP states. Though trade performances of ACP states are different, 'no simple relation is evident between exports and ACP affiliation.'[21] Substantial ACP exports of temperate agricultural products are restricted by the CAP. Exports of these goods are covered either by levies or by quotas, despite the fact that ACP countries may have comparative advantages, especially with regard to these commodities.

Summarizing trade performance at aggregated and individual levels, one can say that the trade preferences of the Lomé Convention were only of minor advantage for the ACP countries. More importantly, many of their possible exports were hampered by restricted market access for certain commodities like temperate tropical products which fall under the CAP; were these shortcomings compensated by financial aid from the EU?

Trade Versus Aid – Which Counts Most?

Traditionally the content of the Lomé Convention could be divided into trade and aid provisions. Trade development in the ACP states was supposed to be fostered by the concession of tariff preferences and quotas. The aid component was provided for in an extra financial protocol for the European Development Fund (EDF) and was never part of the budget.[22] The Lomé Convention refers to aid in Title II and III of Part Three: *Cooperation in the Field of Commodities* and *Development finance cooperation*. A long list of objectives comprise to

> support and promote the efforts of ACP States to achieve long-term, self-determined, self-reliant and self-sustained integrated social, cultural and economic development, help raise the standard of living, encourage intra-ACP co-operation and regional co-operation among ACP States. (art. 220)

The last financial protocol of the Convention, concluded in the framework of the mid-term review in November 1995, provides for 14.625 billion ecu during the period 1995 to 2000, of which only 9.592 billion ecu are grants.[23]

However, at an aggregated level, ACP states gain more from trade than from aid. Cosgrove reports that the export revenues of ACP countries amounted to about 18 billion ecu in the year 1992, whereas total EU aid to the ACP states was only about 12 billion ecu for the years 1991 to 1995, i.e. 2.4 billion ecu p.a.[24] Dearden shows that for the twelve largest recipients of EU aid, its value represented less than 10 per cent of the value of their exports to the EU.[25] This leads to the conclusion that the 'development impact of multilateral aid from the Community to the associated countries is uncertain at best.'[26] This is due to the effectiveness of aid being doubtful,[27] because Community and bilateral aid often run parallel to one another.[28] The prospects for an increase in the financial contributions from member states are small. In fact, there has already been a depreciation of funds in real terms, further exacerbated when considered at a per capita level. While the southern countries of the EU resist more trade preferences, Germany and the UK refused to provide the Eighth EDF with a real appreciation of funds. In 1996, for the first time since the inception of the Lomé Convention, France is the largest donor of funds to the Financial Protocol.[29]

It seems that neither the trade nor the aid provisions of the Lomé Convention has had a significant impact on the trade performances of the ACP states. Trade preferences existed only at the margins and did not help the ACP countries to diversify their export structures, although they might have prevented an even worse performance.[30] Aid was either too small or badly coordinated, and its effects were similarly negligible. Before questioning the Lomé Convention in its entirety, factors which limited the effect of the Convention have to be addressed, particularly in view of recent changes in world trade and with a focus on the internal factors in ACP countries.

Factors Limiting the Efficiency of the Trade Provisions

This section considers factors limiting the effects of the Lomé Convention provisions, the most important of which are the GATT agreement and the impact of the Single European Market (SEM) as well as factors within the ACP states themselves.

Factors External to the ACP

The SEM has two principal effects, trade diversfication and trade creation. Trade diversification, i.e. increased intra-EU trade at the expense of extra-EU trade, could bring a decrease in EU–ACP trade, but as yet there is no evidence to support this view. In contrast, Lomé countries hope to gain from the impact of the Single European Market on trade creation. Dearden estimated in 1990 that this may lead to an increase of 6 per cent (5.5 billion USD) in LDC exports to the EU, of which 75 per cent would be oil. However, the increased demands of harmonized EU standards on technical, environmental or health norms may prove difficult for the ACP states. The harmonization of excise duties on coffee, cocoa or tobacco might have positive or negative results, depending on the level of harmonization.[31]

The Uruguay agreement mainly brought about a general reduction of the most-favoured-nation clause (MFN) tariff to an average of 3.9 per cent. This reduced further the preferences of the Lomé countries at an aggregate level. The other main effects of the agreement are an increase in world prices for some commodities, particularly in temperate agricultural goods, and increased competition in textiles due to the phasing out of the Multifibre Arrangement (MFA), which might have a negative impact on some ACP countries. Estimates of the losses resulting from the innovations of the Uruguay Round agreement are believed to be up to 713 million USD for the ACP countries, 1.1 per cent of their world exports.[32]

Factors Arising from ACP Internal Policy Management

Since the Lomé Conventions did not ensure the diversification of and increase in ACP trade, many European politicians tend to claim that internal conditions in the ACP states are responsible for this failure. First, ACP governments give low priority to export policies. This is because ACP countries have had to cope with more immediate problems, and also because officials in ACP states have insufficient knowledge of trade possibilities with the EU. 'Many African decision makers are still unaware of the potential offered by Lomé IV to provide direct and practical assistance to the ACP export sector.'[33] In contrast, the example of Mauritius showed how an intelligent, export-oriented use of the 'human factor' might lead to a successful trade performance.

Second, there is a lack of financial skills and services in the ACP states. A World Bank report points out the lack of familiarity with financial institutions as a serious constraint to exports. Furthermore, 'ACP banks tend to have more expertise in import financing than in export-oriented payments and insurance.'[34] Further shortcomings such as the lack of an adequate infrastructure in the ACP states, an insufficient service sector or inadequate transportation systems are currently under scrutiny, e.g. by the Trade Development Project as introduced in Annexe XX of Lomé IV.

Aid and Trade Development, Human Rights and Democracy

This chapter has shown that despite the Lomé Conventions, the ACP states have not been able to improve their trading position in the world market, although in absolute terms ACP trade performance has increased and their relative share of EU imports has decreased. This is due to shortcomings in the Lomé provisions themselves as well as to external factors, and is also due to internal policy management. The facts are known, but the strategy for a future EU development policy is far from clear. The European Commission Green Paper represents a first step in revising EU–ACP relations. The emphasis of the mid-term review away from aid to sustainable development has to be pursued further. The European style of development cooperation is under attack, e.g. by the USA in view of the global rules of the World Trade Organization (WTO).

Considering global developments and the TEU requirement for a smooth and gradual integration of the LDCs into the world economy, it seems clear that non-reciprocal trade relations between the European Union and the ACP states will come to an end. Development cooperation should be conducted at a global level, guided by the economic rules of the World Trade Organization.

Furthermore, as introduced by the Lomé Convention mid-term review, support from the EU is bound by political conditions:

> Respect for human rights, democratic principles and the rule of law ... shall constitute an essential element of this Convention. [art. 5]. If one Party considers that another Party has failed to fulfil an obligation in respect of on of the essential elements referred to in Article 5 ... the partial or full suspension of application of this Convention to the Party concerned [can be envisaged]. (art. 366a) Today, the historical and regional approach of EurAfrica, the notion of a colonial heritage, has come to an end.

Two factors should be taken into account for future EU–ACP relations and EU development cooperation in general. First, the ACP states have to develop trade ties with their regional neighbours as a priority. Therefore, it might be useful to divide the ACP group geographically, instead of continuing the Lomé group approach. This would take heterogeneity into account and the different needs of the ACP states as shown above. Within the European Commission these countries could then be assigned to their respective geographical entity and stronger and more consistent trade ties could be developed, not only within the respective region but also between the region and the EU. As demanded by the Treaty on the European Union (art. 130y), the aims of development cooperation should be taken into account in Community-implemented policies which are likely to affect developing countries. This could also contribute to greater consistency in the Community's external actions in general, as required in the common provisions of the Treaty on the European Union (art. C).

Second, the focus of future development policy should be on trade and trade development rather than on aid, because trade revenues are far more important for ACP states than revenues from aid.[35] However, this argument should not be used for reducing aid, even in nominal terms. This shift of importance has already been introduced by the mid-term review of Lomé IV and takes into account the political realities of today's international politics, because European governments are less and less inclined to fund large aid programmes when their own unemployment schemes and budgetary deficits offer enough problems on the domestic front.

Measures in the field of trade and trade development should therefore be guided not only by the notion of a 'coherent geographical entity' but also by a differentiation of the poorest countries from the others, taking into account the United Nations human development index. A trade development policy following these lines would also be able to help those LDCs which are currently beyond the reach of the Lomé Convention. Community aid activities should therefore be divided into financial and technical assistance, plus humanitarian aid. The former aims at supporting the creation of favourable trade conditions in developing countries. This means in particular that LDCs should be supported in strengthening not only the 'human factor' but also the institutional and sectoral shortcomings of their political systems. The latter are more immediate and highly political in character.[36] Humanitarian catastrophes and refugee problems are particularly common to the African continent, and the EU has already taken care of these concerns through the foundation of ECHO, the EU's office for humanitarian aid. This is important, because not only do the 30 million refugees world wide need immediate and non-bureaucratic help and support, but also this area of development aid could become a major contribution to Europe's foreign policy activity.[37]

As for the provisions of the Treaty on the European Union and other regions, for example the Mediterranean, development cooperation cannot be disconnected from trade and economic measures; this chapter has made some suggestions.

Trade provisions for the ACP states have to be adjusted to the requirements of the global economic environment, but also need to reflect an obligation to help the poorest of them.

Bibliography

Bach, D., 'Un Ancrage à la dérive, la Convention de Lomé', *Revue Tiers Monde,* no. 136, vol. XXXIV (October–December 1993) pp. 749–58.

Bossuyt, J., *The Future of EU–Africa development co-operation. With or without the Lomé Convention?* Working Paper of the European Centre for Development Policy Management (Maastricht, 1995).

Bossuyt, J., Laporte, G., Brigaldino, G., *La Politique européenne de développement après le traité de Maastricht. La Revue à mi-parcours de Lomé IV et le débat sur la complémentarité,* (Maastricht, European Centre for Development Policy Management, 1994).

Christopoulos, S., The future of European Development. 1995 – a Watershed between Two Eras', *The Courier ACP–EU,* no. 154 (1995) pp. 73–7.

Cosgrove, C., 'Has the Lomé Convention Failed ACP Trade?', *Journal of International Affairs,* vol. 48, no. 1 (summer 1994) pp. 223–49.

Cosgrove Twitchett, C., *A Framework for Development: The EEC and the ACP* (George Allen & Unwin, London, 1981).

Cosgrove Twitchett, C., *Europe and Africa: From Association to Partnership* (Saxon House, Westmead/Farnborough, Hants, 1978).

Davenport, M. 'Africa and the Unimportance of Being Preferred', *Journal of Common Market Studies*, vol. XXX, no. 2 (June 1992) pp. 233–51.

Dearden, S., *The European Union and the Third World*, McDonald, F. and Dearden, S. (eds), *European Economic Integration*, 2nd edn (1994) pp. 253–70.

Grilli, E. R., *The European Community and the Developing Countries* (Cambridge University Press, 1993).

Kappel, R., 'Africa's Marginalisation in World Trade. A Result of the Uruguay Round Agreements', *Intereconomics* (January–February 1996) pp. 33–42.

McCarthy, S., 'Nations, Peoples and Donors in Africa', *European Investment Bank Papers*, no. 24 (February 1996) pp. 41–62.

McQueen, M., *ACP Export Diversification: The Case of Mauritius*, ODI Working Paper no. 41 (London, August 1990).

McQueen, M. and Stevens, C., 'Trade Preferences and Lomé IV: Non-traditional ACP Exports to the EC', *Development Policy Review* vol. 7, no. 3, (September 1989) pp. 239–60.

ODI, *Europe's Preferred Partners? The Lomé Countries in World Trade* (London, 1995a).

ODI, *EU Aid Post-Maastricht: Fifteen into One?* Briefing Paper no. 2 (London, April 1995b).

Peamen, H. 'The Significance of the Uruguay Round', Bourgeois, B. and Fournier, G. (eds), *The Uruguay Round Results, College of Europe, The Bruges Conferences Series* (European Inter-University Press, Brussels 1995) pp. 33–41.

Penketh, K. 'External Trade Policy', in McDonald, F. and Dearden, S. (eds), *European Economic Integration*, 2nd edn (1994) pp. 238–52.

Pérille, J. M. and Trutat, J. M. 'Institutional Cooperation in Development. Does Aid Have a Future?', *The Courier ACP–EU,* no. 152 (July–August 1995) pp. 6–8.

Riddell, R., *ACP Export Diversification: The Case of Zimbabwe*, ODI Working Paper no. 3, (London, June 1990).

Stevens, C. (ed.), *EEC and the Third World: A Survey. 4, Renegotiating Lomé* (Hodder & Stoughton, London, 1984).

World Bank, *Africa Can Compete! Export Opportunities and Challenges for Garments and Home Products in the US Market* (Washington, DC, 1994).

Notes

1. Grilli (1993) p. 332.
2. Lomé IV, Chapter I, art. 1, in *The Courier ACP–EC*, no. 120 (March–April 1990).
3. Ibid., art. 167.
4. ODI (1995a) p. 25
5. This also hints at a decreased dependency of the industrialized European countries on the developing world. It is clear that intra-industry trade rose instead.
6. Nigeria accounted for 21.14 per cent of the overall ACP exports to the EU in 1994.

7. Regulation 404/93 introduced quantitative restrictions for the import of non-ACP bananas. The non-ACP states were allowed to export bananas up to a limit of 2000 tonnes, with duty payable at 100 ecu per tonne. Each additional tonne was levied at 850 ecu. 170 per cent tariffs should have given ACP banana exporters a considerable advantage in the European market (Dearden, 1994, p. 266).
8. Cosgrove (1994) p. 225.
9. ODI (1995a) p. 7ff.
10. ODI (1995a) pp. 27 and 36.
11. ODI (1995a) pp. 82.
12. In 1992 the ACP countries represented only 3.7 per cent of all extra-EU imports, i.e. 0.17 per cent of EU imports came from Mauritius (see ODI, 1995a, p. 81, Table A2).
13. McQueen (1990).
14. Riddell (1990).
15. A further discussion of such factors appears later.
16. McQueen and Stevens (1989) p. 256.
17. Rules of origin specify the conditions under which the production of a good is considered as originating in an ACP state. Their analysis and application is extremely complicated and full of exceptions, for which they are criticized.
18. Grilli (1993) p. 167.
19. ODI (1995a) p. 33.
20. Furthermore the 'value tolerance' (the permissible amount, by value, of materials from third countries contained in ACP manufactures) was raised from 10 per cent to 15 per cent. (*The Courier* ACP–EU no. 155 1995 p. 10).
21. ODI (1995a) pp. 10ff.
22. Since tariffs represent the EU's own resources, tariff reduction and quota concessions for ACP export commodities to the Single European Market were, in principle financed by reduced budget revenues.
23. *The Courier ACP–EU* no. 153 (September–October 1995) p. 7.
24. Cosgrove (1994) p. 244.
25. Dearden (1994) p. 262, Table 15.6.
26. Grilli (1993) p. 122.
27. Pérille and Trutat (1995).
28. Although contributions to the EDF come from individual EU member states, the funds are managed by the Commission. Therefore it can be considered as a multilateral form of aid.
29. France contributes 3120 MECU, Germany 3000, the UK 1630 and Italy 1610; *The Courier ACP–EU*, no. 153 (September–October 1995) p. 7.
30. Michael Davenport (1992) claimed that ACP states could actually benefit from reducing the preferences for themselves because it would make them more aggressive on the world market.
31. Many ACP countries for example, fear a directive concerning an increase of vegetable fats in chocolate. However, the EU commissioner Mr Pinheiro explained to the ACP–EU Joint Assembly that no such official proposal for modifying the existing directive exists. See *Agence Europe,* no. 6693 (22 March 1996) p. 11.

32. ODI (1995a) p. 46. For further details of the results of the Uruguay Round see Peamen (1995).
33. Cosgrove (1994) p. 237.
34. Ibid., p. 239.
35. This is not applicable, however, to the smaller states. As McCarthy (1996, p. 6) showed, for many of the poorest countries, net development finance (sum of financial aid – excluding technical assistance grants – plus non-concessional loans from development agencies such as the IBRD) coming from external aid agencies was huge and often higher than government revenue raised domestically.
36. In March 1996 the Council of the European Union adopted three 'common positions'–rehabilitation and reconstruction in favour of LDCs (no. 10/96), the management of food aid (no. 11/96) and the adoption of a regulation on humanitarian aid (no. 12/96). Though based on art. 130w, the notion of 'common position' indicates the political character of the measures (see OJ, C 87, 29 March 1996).
37. See also the discussion during the meeting of the ACP–EU Joint Assembly in March 1996 in Namibia (*Agence Europe,* no. 6694, 23 March 1996, p. 10).

10 The European Development Fund

Emanuele Giaufret

INTRODUCTION

The European Development Fund (EDF) was established with the European Community itself. In 1957 the six founding members of the Community decided to create a fund (EDF I) in order to contribute to the economic and social development of a number of African countries that had special links with four member states.[1] Some of these African countries were still colonies of France and Belgium and the Netherlands, while others, such as Somalia, which was a trust territory of Italy, had a transition status. Thus the EDF is one of the oldest instruments of the European Community. It has proved to be quite flexible, because it has been able to survive for forty years, during which the concept and the actual implementation of development aid has changed radically. The first great change occurred with the independence of most of the African countries at the beginning of the 1960s. After the Yaoundé Convention was signed, the Fund (EDF II and III) became the instrument of cooperation between the EC and the États Africains et Malgaches Associés (EAMA). A second major change occurred with Great Britain's accession, which led to an increase in the number of recipient countries. The Lomé Convention was the framework in which the EDF (IV, V, VI, VII and VIII) was used as the principal instrument for financial cooperation with the African, Caribbean and Pacific countries (ACP).

The basic idea behind the Fund is that the member states collectively assume the responsibility of helping the ACP countries in their development process. In order to carry out this task the member states have created the EDF. It operates on a five-yearly basis and its operations are supposed to be complementary to efforts made by the recipient countries and other donors. The Fund, therefore, cannot be considered a self-sufficient instrument of development.

The actual functioning of the EDF, however, is more complicated than this simple logic would have us suppose. The large number of actors involved in its operations and the wide range of local situations make the system diverse and complex. This chapter will try to give a general overview of the EDF and how it works. The first section starts with a general definition, a description of its juridical sources and of its position in respect of the general budget. The next section focuses on the structure and the functioning of the EDF, and the one after the management of the Fund. After this we turn briefly to a description of the evolution of the EDF over forty years in terms of development priorities and with respect to the financial dimension. Subsequently there is a comment on the present fund (EDF VIII), which was set up in June 1995 at the Cannes European Council. Finally, general conclusions are drawn regarding the Fund and its future perspectives.

THE EDF, ITS JURIDICAL SOURCES AND ITS FINANCIAL AUTONOMY

The EDF is the main financial instrument of the European Union's cooperation policy towards the ACP countries.[2] It is a financial institution without juridical personality. The EDF derives from an Internal Financial Agreement signed among member states (and completed by a financial regulation which sets out the details).[3] One of the main features of the EDF, therefore, is that it is not negotiated with the beneficiary countries. The EDF is linked to the association convention through a financial protocol.[4] Because of its particular nature, the law applicable to the EDF derives from various sources; these are the Lomé Convention, the acts derived from the Convention itself (i.e. decisions of the ACP–EC Council and Convention acts between the Community and the recipient countries, e.g. the Financing Convention), autonomous juridical order, the Internal Financial Agreement, the financial regulation and, finally, the national laws of the ACP countries where the projects are eventually realized.[5]

A second fundamental aspect is that the EDF, although managed by the Commission, is not part of the general budget of the European Union, but is composed of national contributions by the member states. Each member state contributes according to its 'contributive capacity'. There are therefore no formal links between national contributions and trade with the recipient countries.[6]

In 1970 the Council decided to finance the general budget through the Community's own resources, which are essentially the earnings from the Common External Tariff, the agricultural drawings and part of the VAT earnings of the member states. These resources superseded the national contributions. However, an exception was made for the EDF, which was kept outside the Community budget and financed through the traditional system. Since then the member states have refused to 'budgetarize' the EDF, because they believe it necessary to review the financial cooperation conditions with their ACP partners every five years. Moreover, they want to keep the political control of the aid.[7] On the other hand, the European Parliament has pushed for the budgetization of the EDF, which would put the Fund under its control[8]

Since 1977 expenditure of the Commission Delegations to ACP countries has been paid by the general EC budget. When it was introduced, this procedure was seen as the first step of a progressive process of budgetization, but this interpretation proved to be wrong. However, during the constitution of the last Fund 160 million ecu were drawn from the Community budget.[9] The reluctance of member states to increase (or to maintain) their financial commitments towards ACP countries in the present world situation could finally bring about the long-awaited budgetization of the EDF. If this were to happen, an automatic consequence would be that the Fund would become part of a common budget line of subsection B-7 (cooperation).

At present, the financial autonomy of the EDF has other consequences. First, the principle of the budgetary year is not respected. Since commitments and payments are made as the projects evolve,[10] several Funds are in operation during that same year.[11] Second, the European Parliament has very limited power over it. The Parliament can only approve the Commission's management of the EDF on the basis of the Court of Auditors' report.

THE STRUCTURE AND FUNCTIONING OF THE EDF

The recipients of EDF aid are principally the governments of the ACP countries. The resources are distributed among them, taking into account the level of their needs and a number other factors. There are special provisions for least developed countries, landlocked countries and islands that enjoy a privileged status in aid distribution.[12] However, the aid allocation process is not very transparent. Not only specific ACP countries are entitled to receive aid through the EDF: regional projects are too,[13] and regional aid is used by the European

Union to encourage intra-ACP regional cooperation. Subnational actors, such as small and medium enterprises (SMEs)[14] and territorial cooperatives participating in micro-projects, can receive aid from the EDF,[15] though at subnational level the central government must agree to the projects.[16]

Almost all financial aid from the EDF to recipient countries takes the form of grants.[17] This has not always been the case; in fact, until EDF VI part of the aid was given as special loans which, theoretically, were supposed to be refunded.[18] With EDF VII, after the debt crisis made an impact on the liquidity of the less developed countries, the EC decided to abolish this type of finance.[19] This example shows the flexibility with which the Fund has been used by the EC.

Aid can be divided into two categories: programmable and non-programmable. The first category represents the main feature of EU–ACP cooperation, containing the National Indicative Programme (NIP), the Regional Indicative Programme (RIP) and the Structural Adjustment Facility (SAF).

The NIP indicates the amount of money designated to each country and agreed development priorities. The envelope for each country is decided by the Commission through criteria such as population, GNP per capita, geographical position and aid received from the EU member states on a bilateral basis.[20] The NIP is the backbone of the programming process, and allows each ACP country to know precisely how much money it can use from the Fund and for which goals it should be used. The revision of the Lomé IV Convention brought two main innovations into this system. Firstly, the new art. 283 invites the Community and the ACP countries to take all necessary measures to ensure that NIP is adopted within twelve months from the signing of the financial protocol, so the programming had to be completed by October 1996.[21] Second, the principle of 'two-tranche' (i.e. two-slice) programming has been introduced. This means that 70 per cent of a country's envelope is released initially, the remaining 30 per cent only after an assessment of the use made of the first tranche.[22] This innovation reduces the autonomy of the recipient countries in using EDF resources once allocated.

The RIP fulfils the same function as the NIP, but on a regional level. In EDF VII, 1250 mecu was assigned to regional cooperation.[23]

SAF was introduced with Lomé IV. To be eligible to receive aid under it, a country has to pursue a policy of macroeconomic reforms, generally under the supervision of the World Bank and the International Monetary Fund.[24]

Non-programmable aid consists of instruments whose use cannot be programmed but depends on unforeseen events. They are STABEX (a financing facility to stabilize the export revenues introduced by Lomé I), SYSMIN (System for the Mining Sector introduced by Lomé II, whose purpose is to maintain productive capacity levels in this sector in a period of temporary crisis),[25] the risk capital allocation, managed by the EIB, the interest rate subsidies (which are linked to the operations tied to the EIB's own resources) and emergency aid, which is supplied in the event of natural or man-made catastrophes.

THE MANAGEMENT OF THE EDF

The EDF is basically managed by the Commission through DG VIII (Development). The only exceptions are the capital risk and interest rates subsidies, which, because of their banking characteristics, are managed by the European Investment Bank (EIB).

Programming occupies a central place in the management of the EDF. It can be divided into three phases. In the first phase, the ACP country sets its development priorities and subsequently the programming mission of the Commission, with the cooperation of the national authority, produces a country dossier. In the second phase, the NIP is decided through a common agreement between the Community and the recipient country for five years (it can be revised once during this period). In the last phase the EU member states are informed.[26] Project implementation involves important key actors at both Community and national level. At the Community level the central figure is the principal authorizing officer, who has the power to commit the money and who is the director-general of DG VIII. The payments are made through the designated authorities. At the national level, the national authorizing officer (usually the minister of finance) commits the money, which is paid by the delegated payer, who is usually the national central bank. The Commission is represented by the head of delegation, who participates in all the local steps of the project as the interlocutor of the national authorizing officer.[27]

The recipient countries are responsible for running the projects and the national authorizing officer has to organize the tenders. He has to guarantee two principles: openness to international competition (i.e. the tenders are open to all ACP and EU countries) and equality of conditions (which means that all companies have to be able to participate in tendering on a equal footing). In order to facilitate the participation of companies from ACP countries and taking into account their lower competitiveness (as well as the low degree of interest in work contracts in Europe) a preferential system has been adopted[28] that forecasts an accelerated procedure.[29]

However, despite this preferential system, EU companies have proved to be more able to compete in this market. ACP companies won 30.1 per cent of the contracts during the EDF IV, but their share dropped to 24.1 per cent during EDF VI.[30]

It is important to note that the member states keep complete control of the decision making process through which individual projects are adopted. After the preparatory phase which has to set up the NIP and after the financing proposal made by the Commission on the basis of the dossier presented by the recipient country, the assent of the EDF Committee is needed. The EDF Committee, which is composed of member states' representatives and is chaired by the Commission, has to give its assent to the Commission financing proposal before the financing convention can be signed. The EDF Committee votes by qualified majority, but the weighting system is not the one generally used, because it is determined by the size of national contributions to the EDF. For this reason, during EDF VII Germany had the highest voting power with 52, France was second with 49 and Italy, which usually has as many, had only 26 votes.[31]

Only after the assent of the EDF Committee or of the Council (if the Commission appeals to it) can the Commission sign the Financing Convention with the recipient country, opening the execution phase of the project. The management of the EDF is controlled financially and politically. Financial control is assured by the financial controller and by the Court of Auditors as for the general EC budget. Political control is exercised at Community and association level. At Community level, the Commission has to make a report to the Council and has to answer questions from the European Parliament in the Development Committee. Furthermore, the European Parliament has to approve the Commission's management of the Fund on the basis of the Court of Auditors Report. At association level, control is assured by the ACP–EC Council of Ministers and by the Joint Assembly.[32]

THE EVOLUTION OF THE EDF

The first EDF (1958–63) was concerned primarily with financing economic and social infrastructures in associated countries. During the

1960s, more attention was paid to rural and agricultural development. Since the recipient countries' economies were mainly agricultural, and food security was a goal and not a reality, it was decided to concentrate EDF aid efforts in this sector. However, since the 1960s African countries have asked for more activity in the industrial sector. Lomé I took some measures in favour of industrial development, among which was the formation of the Centre for Development of Industry. Industrial cooperation has remained less significant (it covered 14.3 per cent of EDF IV, 20 per cent of EDF V and 11.9 per cent of EDF VI) than rural and agricultural cooperation (23.7 per cent of EDF IV, 24.5 per cent of EDF V and 36 per cent of EDF VI). With EDF VII there has been a decline in rural cooperation to the benefit of the social sector, probably as a consequence of social needs brought about by the debt crisis and the structural adjustment policies that followed.[33]

The first EDF amounted to 58,125 mecu. After the accession of the United Kingdom, Denmark and Ireland, EDF IV (Lomé I) amounted to 3,150 mecu.[34] EDF VIII consists of 13,307 mecu. The increase of the Fund has been impressive in nominal terms, and without any doubt its contribution to the development of the recipient countries has been significant. However, to understand the real extent of the resources channelled to ACP countries through the EDF, it is helpful to add two elements to the analysis. First, taking into account the increase in the number of recipient countries (from 18 to 70), as well as the number of donor countries (from 6 to 15), together with the rate of inflation, it can be shown that the Fund has not increased in real terms. Moreover, most of the ACP countries are suffering the consequences of the debt crisis and debt servicing is absorbing a substantial amount of their financial resources. This means that financial flows are actually directed from poor countries to Europe. Indeed the total size of EDF VIII amounts to only 65 per cent of the scheduled debt repayments by ACP states to EU countries between 1995 and 2000.[35]

EDF VIII

EDF VIII amounts to 13,307 mecu as compared with the ACP request for 15,800 mecu. Again, taking into account the inflation rate within the Union in the past five years (21.5 per cent) this means there has been no real increase in the amount received by the 70 ACP countries since Lomé IV came into operation, despite the accession of Austria, Finland and Sweden to the EU.

The negotiations for EDF VIII lasted for more than six months; the difficulty in finding agreement was probably due to the desire of some member states to renationalize development aid.[36] The United Kingdom wanted to reduce its contribution to the Fund in real and nominal terms (eventually the British contribution declined from 1,790 to 1,630 million mecu, which did not completely satisfy the British). At the same time Germany wanted to reorient its development priorities towards Eastern Europe. Agreement was finally reached at the European Council in Cannes on 26–27 June 1995; the role of the French presidency was fundamental. The French government proved once again to be the champion of European solidarity with Africa within the European Union, and agreement was reached through an overall compromise regarding aid policy. At the same time, it was agreed that 6,700 mecu over the period 1995–2000 would be allocated to CEECs to meet the Germans' requests and 4,700 mecu to the Mediterranean countries for the same period to meet the Spanish and Italian requests.[37] Moreover, France had to accept an increase in its contribution, from 2,665 to 3,120 mecu. For the first time since the first EDF, France's contribution is now more important than Germany's (which rose from 2,840 to 3,000 mecu).

CONCLUSION

The difficulties encountered in reaching an agreement on EDF VIII and the relatively disappointing results for the ACP countries clearly demonstrated that EU–ACP relations are going through a delicate phase. These events suggest that the special relationship between Europe and Africa has come to an end; changes in Eastern Europe and the renewed European focus on the Mediterranean basin are modifying the EU's development priorities. At the same time the negative results of African economic development are prompting scepticism about the possibilities of real success in Africa. The introduction of the 'two-tranche system' (as well as the political conditionality clause) has increased EU control over aid management in the ACP countries. The future of the Fund is tied to the future of the Lomé Convention, and the renewal of the Convention, its modification, the budgetization of the EDF and the locus of control are major issues likely to be debated in the next few years. The performance of EDF VIII and the development of the international economy will contribute to this debate on the future of EU relations with the ACP states.

Bibliography

Baron, F., and Vernier, G., *Le Fonds européen de développement* (Presse Universitaire de France, Paris, 1981).
European Commission, *Ten Years of Lomé* (Brussels, 1986).
European Commission, *Lomé III Mid-Term Review,* 1986–1988 (Brussels 1989).
European Commission, *La Coopération UE–ACP en 1993* (Brussels, 1994).
European Commission, *La Coopération UE–ACP en 1994* (Brussels, 1995).
European Commission, *La Coopération financière dans le cadre des Conventions de Lomé, bilan de l'aide à la fin de 1994* (Brussels, 1995).
European Commission, *Les Finances Publiques de l'Union Europèenne* (Brussels, 1995).
European Commission, *La Coopération financière et technique dans le cadre des Conventions de Lomé, bilan synthétique* (Brussels, 1996).
Ndoung, J. P., *L'Évolution du fonds européen de développement prévu par les conventions de Yaoundé et Lomé* (Bruylant, Brussels, 1994).
Percival, D., 'Agreement Clinched at the Eleventh Hour', *The Courier ACP–EU*, no. 153 (September–October 1995) pp. 6–8.
Vernier, G., 'Main Innovations', *The Courier ACP–EU*, no. 155 (January–February 1996) pp. 8–13.

Notes

1. The EDF was established under art. I of the Implementing Convention on the Association of the Overseas Countries and territories with the Community, signed at the same time as the Treaty of Rome on 25 March 1957.
2. The others are the European Investment Bank (EIB) and the European Community Humanitarian Office (ECHO).
3. Baron, F., and Vernier, G. (1981) pp. 19–23.
4. For the present financial protocol see *The Courier ACP*, no. 155 (January–February 1996) p. 103.
5. Baron, F., and Vernier (1981) pp. 19–23 and Ndoung, (1994) pp. 2–9.
6. Ndoung (1994) p. 11.
7. Ibid., p. 486.
8. *European Report*, no. 2058, July 15 1995, Section V, p. 3. According to the European Parliament the budgetization of the EDF would improve the efficiency, transparency and the overall coherence of the European development policy.
9. *The Courier ACP–EU*, no. 153 (September–October 1995).
10. Baron, F., and Vernier (1981) pp. 27–30.
11. Usually, three funds are operating in any one year; *Les Finances Publiques de l'Union Europèenne*, p. 64.
12. Ndoung (1994) pp. 75–7. This category – the most in need countries – encompasses the majority of the ACP countries.
13. Lomé IVB, Title XII, regional cooperation.
14. Lomé IVB, Title VIII, enterprise development.

15. Lomé VIB has stressed the importance of this decentralized cooperation, Lomé IV B, Title III, ch. 2, s. 4a, decentralized cooperation.
16. Under the VII EDF, 300,000 ecu have been destined to microprojects; Ndoung (1994), p. 105.
17. In the VIII EDF, 11,967 mecu out of a total of 12,967 mecu are given as grants and 1,000 mecu as capital risk which should return to the EDF; *The Courier ACP–EU*, no. 155, p. 12.
18. In reality a large amount of the special loans became grants because the recipient countries could not refund them.
19. Ndoung (1994) p. 145.
20. Baron, F., and Vernier (1981) pp. 52–3.
21. *The Courier ACP*, no. 155, p. 13.
22. Ibid., p. 3.
23. Ndoung (1994) pp. 87–8.
24. *The Courier ACP*, special issue, *EU–ACP Cooperation,* (1994).
25. For a more detailed analysis of STABEX and SYSMIN see Ndoung (1994) pp. 186–230.
26. Ndoung (1994) pp. 270–9.
27. Baron, F., and Vernier (1981) pp. 36–40.
28. See Ndoung (1994) p. 331.
29. Lomé IV B, Art 301, the accelerated procedure applies to work contracts whose estimate value is under 5 mecu, or in the case of emergency assistance.
30. European Commission (1989).
31. Ndoung (1994) pp. 296–8.
32. Ibid., pp. 419–78.
33. *The Courier ACP–EU*, special issue on EU–ACP cooperation in 1994, (1995) p. 29.
34. For the figures for the first EDF VII, see Ndoung (1994) p. 12.
35. *European Parliament*, PE 191–512, pp. 14–15.
36. *The Courier ACP–EU*, no. 154, November–December 1995, p. 76.
37. *The Courier ACP–EU*, no. 153, September–October 1995, p. 6.

11 The European Investment Bank

Ana de Castro

INTRODUCTION

The Nature and Funding of the EIB

The EIB was created by the Treaty of Rome (Part Three, Title IV, art. 130[1] to

> contribute to the Community's balanced development by providing loans or guarantees for capital investment projects which should help economic development of less favoured regions; improve communications between the member states; help the Community's energy objectives; involve protection of the environment, enhance the international competitiveness of the industry and its integration at Community level; support activities of the Small and Medium-sized Enterprises (SMEs).

The Bank stands among the Community institutions as autonomous;[2] in fact is financially independent, which means that it is not funded by the EC budget, and has its own decision-making bodies.[3] The idea of the negotiators of the Treaty of Rome was to create an international bank (following the pattern of the World Bank) to represent the interests of the then European Economic Community (EEC).

The EIB's financial structure is based first on the capital subscribed by the member states (who own it), second, on the capital that it obtains by borrowing in its own name and finally on its own credit on the capital markets of the world. The latter consists of new public bond issues floated on international markets, national markets or by public placement with a bank or a group of banks or directly by major institutional investors like insurance companies, pension funds and savings banks. The fact that those bonds have a creditworthiness rating of AAA[4] on the financial market permits the EIB to mobilize significant volumes of investors' savings every year.

It should be noted that the EIB operates on a nonprofit basis, though neither may it incur losses. It remains at all times a bank, and so repayment of loans is always mandatory. Its borrowing and lending activities must at least be sufficient to enable the bank to meet its obligations, cover expenses and build up the necessary reserves.

Structure of the EIB

The EIB is structured like a corporation. As mentioned above, it is endowed with its own decision-making bodies whose *modus operandi* is defined in its statute. The latter takes the form of a protocol annexed to the Treaty and forms an integral part of the Treaty, carrying the same legal authenticity.

The decision-making bodies are as follows:

- The board of governors, which, given the fact that the Bank is owned by the member states, usually has the same composition as the Ecofin Council of the European Union.[5] Its primary functions are the laying down of general directives on credit policy, and the approval of the annual report and balance sheet and any decisions on increases in the Bank's capital.
- The board of directors, whose members are nominated by the member states plus one by Commission. It has the highly relevant tasks of deciding on the granting of loans, the raising of funds and the fixing of interest rates.[6]
- There is also a management committee, which is responsible for day-to-day operations and for the implementation of the decisions of the board of directors.

The administrative structure comprises a secretariat-general, operational directorates-general, a technical council (formed by professionals, most of them engineers, able to rule on all technical aspects of a project before the decision to finance is taken) and finally a legal service.

THE EIB AND EU DEVELOPMENT COOPERATION POLICY

In accordance with the objectives set down in the Treaty, the EIB's main field of operation is within the territory of the EC;[7] nevertheless it has been called upon to participate in the implementation of the

Community's development policy. Within this policy's framework, the EIB operates outside the EC either on an *ad hoc* basis (through blanket authorizations to provide financing in these countries or groups of countries issued by the Board of Governors acting by majority voting)[8] or in a systematic way under the following arrangements:

- financial protocols attached to the cooperation agreements with 12 countries in the Mediterranean region and 30 countries in Asia and Latin America;
- successive conventions with the 70 ACP states, as well as with 11 Central and Eastern European countries.[9]

Consequently, EIB involvement in the preparation of those agreements is required. The financial component of these agreements is implemented in close cooperation with the European Commission, which is responsible for a different kind of financing: grant aid and technical cooperation.[10]

The criteria applied to the choice of the projects to be financed are technical viability and economic justification. This approach follows the existing constraints imposed by the need to raise funds on the money markets and above all by development aid imperatives (trying to make finance as productive as possible). Therefore a depth appraisal of the projects is made to asses the merit of projects and their contribution to the development of the country in question. Like financing inside the Community, it is generally limited to 50 per cent of the fixed investment cost of the project, so as to help mobilize other sources of finance from the promoters' own resources, from other development banks or from local funds.

Types of Loans

There are two major sources of loans: the bank's own resources and risk capital. The former are funded by the EIB's borrowings on the capital markets, mainly taking the form of public bond issues, but they can include also a part of the paid-in portion of its subscribed capital plus reserves. In this case the contract clauses are exactly the same as the contracts inside the EC. Interest rates are fixed according to the rates prevailing on the capital markets, the term of the loan and the currency in which it is made available. The term of the loan depends, of course, on the nature of the project, and it can run from 10 to 12 years or for 20 years. Generally, a guarantee is demanded from the state hosting the project; exceptionally, other first-class guarantees may be required. With risk capital loans, the funds are drawn from the member states' budgets through the European Development Fund;[11] Loans of this kind were developed by the EIB in the early 1970s and were first used under the second Yaoundé Convention.[12]

THE LOMÉ CONVENTION

This section examines the role of EIB funding in the context of the Lomé Conventions agreed with the ACP states, especially the Lomé IV Convention. The first financial protocol of this Convention (settled for the period between 1990 to 1995) previews a total aid of 12,000 billion ecu, whereas in Lomé III it did not exceed 8,500 billion ecu. Analysing the total aid managed by the EIB and by the Commission, only 1.2 billion ecu came from the EIB compared with 11.4 billion ecu from the EDF and from that total only 2,305 billion ecu are managed by the EIB. The conclusion is that the bank has a marginal role, although its areas of action are well defined in contrast to those of the Commission. As we will see, it plays an important role in private sector financing in general and in small and medium-sized enterprises in particular. A new financial protocol was adopted by the ACP–EC Council decision of December 1995.[13]

The Commission and the EIB – Areas of Competence

In any search to match the most suitable financial conditions to the needs of projects and borrowers, responsibilities between the two institutions are clearly defined. On the one hand, the EIB operates in those sectors where investment can be financed by means of loan aid, that is to say, reimbursable aid. It is suited for productive sectors which can generate sufficient revenue directly or indirectly so as to be able to service the debt (i.e. essential infrastructures, industry, energy, mining, tourism and agricultural development). On the other hand, the Commission takes a grant aid approach. The EDF takes those other areas that can only be financed by grant aid (e.g. social infrastructures like schools and hospitals, rural development programmes and technical assistance). Despite this clear separation of areas of competence within the framework of the Lomé Convention, both the European Commission and the EIB work side by side in establishing indicative programmes for each ACP country that specify the main sectors to be assisted. The Bank then uses this instrument to set its own list of priorities.

Finance

As mentioned above, special emphasis is given to conditions that may affect the soundness of the projects, but when it comes to imposing conditions relating to the economic policies of the countries involved there are no clauses in the contracts. EIB finance is untied and no condition is imposed that EC companies must be involved in the development of the projects financed. In this context the only condition usually put on the contracts applies to the need for a competitive call for tender relating to the supply of goods and services. In the case of international tendering it must be open at least to companies in the EC and ACP states.[14] Other rules include the following provisions:

- Any possible beneficiary including individuals and legal persons, seeking finance from the EIB, whether for private or public projects, must do so through the authorities of the country concerned or at least seek its approval. Private, public or semi-public enterprises as well as the state itself or a public authority can be the possible beneficiaries of the loans. Additionally, not only can EC-based enterprises wishing to undertake productive projects in an ACP state be considered; also, financial institutions which promote and finance private investment in the ACP states can obtain credit from the EIB.
- Co-financing has been current practice in development policy. By using bilateral financial agencies in EU member states, financial institutions in the ACP states and international development aid organisations (e.g. the World Bank) co-financing is possible and is, to some extent, normal EIB policy in the ACP states.
- Nature of the loans: in this field the distinction between loans from own resources[15] and loans from risk capital is worth repeating.[16] With loans from the Bank's own resources, interest rates benefit from an EDF subsidy of 4 per cent. Where necessary, adjustments will be made so that the interest rate supported by the beneficiary will be no more than 6 per cent, nor less than 3 per cent. In previous Lomé Conventions this interest rate subsidy was below 3 per cent, whereas the interest rate effectively borne by the borrower should not be more than 8 per cent nor less than 5 per cent. For this purpose the EDF VII previewed a total amount of 280 million ecu.[17]

For risk capital loans, the funds are drawn from the member states' budgets through the EDF, which the EIB manages under EDF mandate. The loans preferably serve to reinforce an enterprise's own resources in an ACP state and can take the form of an equity participation (*prises de participation directes*), i.e. subscriptions on behalf of the EC in enterprises or financial intermediaries (e.g. development banks) in ACP countries. Participation involves a temporary minority holding; this is intended to be disposed of in due time, preferably to nationals or institutions of the ACP state in which that enterprise is established. These holdings are usually combined with a loan from the Bank's own resources or with quasi capital assistance. There are two types of quasi capital loan; subordinated loans or conditional loans. Subordinated loans are only repaid or an interest is only paid after other claims relating to the project have been settled. Conditional loans require the interest and the repayment terms to be linked to the project's performance, technical and financial. In both cases conditions are predetermined in the contracts.

THE FOURTH LOMÉ CONVENTION

An Innovation: Private Sector Investment by Small and Medium Enterprises

Traditionally in operations outside of the EU, the EIB should only be able to finance specific projects, but for many years the Bank has used its own resources as well as risk capital assistance to act not only directly but also indirectly through global loans.

When directly financing, the Bank aims at projects above a certain size which are considered indispensable to the development of private enterprises. Global loans are contracted with appropriate national or regional financial institutions or development banks in ACP states. The preferred strategy is to consider whether intermediaries enjoy close contacts with private sector and government authorities, and to assess their knowledge of local markets and of economic development priorities. In view of criticism of their actions in the 1960s and 1970s, an essential condition now holds: the independence of that body from the state.[18] These institutions then serve as kind of a channel for funding selected small and medium-sized undertakings.[19] Thanks to the cooperation of those institutions the EIB has a substantial influence over capital amounts invested in SMEs within the framework of the Lomé Convention.

Within the Fourth Lomé Convention, an even greater emphasis is given to the promotion of the private sector than in previous conventions.[20] In fact, the broad range of financing facilities available to the EIB has been enlarged; moreover, the Bank has been authorized to work with new intermediaries. Accordingly, the EIB now has powers to provide partial funding for EC promoters who wish to acquire a stake in a joint venture in an ACP country with a local partner; to make funds available to EC financial intermediaries;[21] to help them assist SMEs in ACP states; in certain circumstances, to assist long-term lending institutions within the ACP states to restructure or rebuild their capital base; and, finally, to finance certain pre-investment costs.

Sectoral Breakdown of EIB Financing[22]

Regarding the division of financing among various sectors of the economy, according to the first financial protocol of the fourth Lomé Convention (1991–5), the main sector of the Bank's operations was the industrial sector (including small and medium-sized enterprises) with more than 600 million ecu, i.e. 50 per cent of its total financing in ACP countries, mainly for mining, chemicals, food processing, textiles, leather and metal production (some examples: projects to expand cotton spinning facilities in Zambia and to manufacture plastics in the Côte d'Ivoire). It is interesting to note that in support of investment schemes for SMEs up to 360 million ecu were made available in the form of global loans to local financial institutions.

Energy projects amounted to 417 million ecu, corresponding to approximately 35 per cent, a substantial growth compared to 264 million ecu, just 20 per cent of the total financing under Lomé III. Most of the investment was designed to build up and modernize power stations, to develop oil and natural gas deposits and to expand transmission and supply capacity. Examples of projects financed are the high-voltage lines interconnecting Cabora Bassa hydroelectric power station on the Zambezi River in Mozambique with the Zimbabwe grids, the construction of a hydroelectric power station on Muela, Lesotho, and the development of a gold mine in Mali.

In the infrastructure sector a fall, as compared with the previous convention, was recorded.[23] It constitutes only 14 per cent of the total financing and priority is given to the development of telecommunications[24] (60 million ecu) and transport (44 million ecu). Over the years of the first financial protocol, the EIB devoted 84 million ecu to drinking water supply, sewerage and sewage treatment schemes, like the drinking water supply networks on islands in the Bahamas or the water supply system in Dakar, Senegal. Interestingly, a relevant amount is provided for financing tourism projects, especially hotels.

The New Financial Protocol

Lomé IV was signed to cover a period of a ten years, but a mid-term review took place in 1995. This mid-term review was signed in Mauritius on 4 November 1995; it aimed to 'increase the effectiveness of Community support for the development of the ACP states by modernizing and adapting the instruments of the convention without calling into question the fundamental principles underlying the ACP–EC cooperation.'[25] The agreement also contains the new financial protocol (eighth EDF) for the second period of the application of the Convention in accordance with what had been agreed to at the European Council of Cannes in June.[26] The total aid granted via EDF is now settled at 12 967 million ecu and the EIB's own loan resources are 1,658 million ecu.

Following this new financial protocol a more flexible programming has been introduced, thanks to the new two-slice system. (Under this, the first slice, or tranche, representing 70 per cent of the total indicative national programme, is paid initially, and the second slice, i.e. the remainder, follows only if good use has been made of the first). The financial conditions of reimbursable aid, that is to say the ones for which the EIB is responsible, have been rendered more flexible,[27] notably when it comes to the risk capital. Art. 284.2 provides for 50 per cent of the overall figure under this heading to be allocated to the least developed countries. Other innovations concerning the EIB relate to the programming procedure and its improvement. The EIB will give each ACP country an overall indication of the resources and risk capital it can expect to receive during the five-year period (art. 281.1.b of the Lomé IV Convention). The new agreement will enter into force only at the end of the ratification procedure.[28] Interim measures will ensure that the programme of European financial assistance is not interrupted.

CONCLUSION

The amount of financial aid provided by the European Investment Bank is not substantial when compared with that managed by the

Commission. However, it is of a different nature. As noted, the EIB has a different approach to aid policy from that of the Commission, given its nature as a credit institution: all the financing has to be repaid, albeit under more favourable conditions, namely interest rate subsidies or reimbursement provisions that are inserted in the contracts. Therefore its financing instruments are better suited for projects that can then generate sufficient revenue to repay the capital and interest.

A comparison of financing provided for in this area with other activities of the EIB outside of the European Union would show that finance provided under Lomé is exceeded by that loaned to Central and Eastern European and to Mediterranean countries. This can be explained by the EU's political priorities in the rest of the European continent, namely the preparation for the future accession by such countries.

In conclusion to this analysis of the Bank's activities in the field of the Lomé Convention, we can say that although the most relevant role of cooperation policy in this area is played by the Commission, the EIB has its own area of influence, and within it the EIB has an important role. What is more, it will probably increase in importance; in fact the more the ACP economies evolve, the more they can initiate viable projects suited to the EIB's type of financial aid.

ANNEXE 11.1

The Lomé IV Convention – Financial Protocol 1991–5 (million ecu)

Managed by the European Commission from EDF resources				
Grants	7,715		4,645	
STABEX *	1,500		925	
SYSMIN †	480	9,695	415	6,585
Managed by the EIB				
Loans from own resources	1,200		1,100	
Risk capital from EDF resources	825		600	
Interest subsidies form EDF resources	280	2,305	215	1,915
Grand Total		12,000		8,500

Source: EIB.
* Transfers for the stabilization of export earnings.
† Special financing facility for mineral products.

ANNEXE 11.2

Financing available under the four Lomé Conventions (million ecu)

Convention	Lomé I	Lomé II	Lomé III	Lomé IV (first half)	Lomé IV (second half)
Total	3,393	5,329	9,001	12,600	14,625
EDF	3,003	4,644	7,901	10,800	12,967
Grants	2,096	2,945	4,999	7,995*	9,592
Special loans	412	525	600	—	—
Risk capital	96	275	600	825	1,000
STABEX	390	669	1,449	1,500	1,800
SYSMIN	—	230	253	480	575
Emergency aid	—	—	—	250	—
Refugee aid	—	—	—	100	—
EIB Loans from own resources	390	685	1,100	1,200	1,658

Source: European Commission.
* Includes 1150 million ecu of Structural Adjustment Facility.

Bibliography

Bulletin of the European Union, no. 11 (Brussels, 1995) p. 103.

Carter, P., 'Aid policy and small economies of the ACP', *EIB Papers*, (Luxembourg, September 87) pp. 39–54.

Carter, P., Innamorati, M., and MacCarthy, S., 'A Review of the EIB Operations through Financial Intermediaries in the ACP', *EIB papers* (Luxembourg, June 1989) pp. 54–77.

European Commission, 'De Lomé III à Lomé IV Bilan de l'aide des Conventions de Lomé a la fin de 1990', *Europe Information – Development* (April 1992) p. 67.

European Commission, *Financial Cooperation under the Lomé Convention – Review of the Aid at the End of 1994* (Brussels, August 1995) p. 135.

European Investment Bank, *Annual Reports* (Luxembourg, 1985–1994).

European Investment Bank, 'From Lomé II to Lomé III; the EIB and the Aid Granted to the ACP States', *EIB Information,* no. 47 (January 1986) p. 1–4.

European Investment Bank, *Financing Facilities Under the Fourth Lomé Convention* (Luxembourg, January 1991) p. 19

European Investment Bank, 'From Lomé III to Lomé IV; the Role of the EIB in the ACP Countries', *EIB Information,* no. 70 (November 1991) pp. 1–10.

European Investment Bank, '100 Questions and Answers', *EIB – General Information,* (Luxembourg, 1995) p. 52.
European Investment Bank, 'EIB operations outside the EU', *EIB Information,* no. 83 (October 1995) pp. 1–6.
European Investment Bank, '*The EIB – the European Community's Investment Bank* (Luxembourg, 1993) p. 25.
Ingram, V., *Guide to European Community Grants and Loans* (Eurofi, Edinburgh, 1995).
Logli, P., 'New Approaches to SME Projects – the Role of the Intermediate Organisations', *The Courier ACP-EU* no. 123 (September/October 1991), pp. 6–8.
Vaillant, M. (ed.), 'Prêts et subventions CE', *Dictionnaire Permanent–Droit Européen des Affaires, feuillets 23* (*Éditions Legislatives,* Paris, December 1994) pp. 2135–48.
The Courier ACP–EU, no. 120 (March–April 1990) and no. 155 (January–February 1996).

Notes

1. With the Maastricht Treaty it has changed and is now art. 198d.
2. However, it is not an institution in the sense of art. 4 of the EU Treaty.
3. See the section on the structure of the EIB (pp. 155–156).
4. Best banking rate.
5. That is, the economy and/or finance ministers of the member states.
6. See below on financing provided by the Lomé Convention.
7. Where it finances projects alone or in parallel with the structural funds.
8. Article 18.1 of the Statute.
9. In 1994 EIB financing outside the EU amounted to 2246 million ecu, comprising 1 978.5 million ecu from its own resources and 267 million ecu from EDF. 462 million ecu went to ACP and OCT countries, 607 million ecu to the Mediterranean countries, 957 million ecu to Central and Eastern Europe and 220 million ecu to Asia and Latin America.
10. On the division of competencies between the EIB and the Commission, see below, pp. 196–197.
11. A special financial instrument of the EU's cooperation policy towards ACP countries, drawn from member states' contributions and managed by the European Commission (DG VIII) and by the EIB when it comes to risk capital and interest rate subsidies.
12. For developments see below, pp. 159–160.
13. ACP–EC Council Decision 95/556.
14. The EIB ensures that the tender notice is published in the *Official Journal* of the European Community.
15. The Lomé IV financial protocol for 1991–5 sets aside 1200 million ecu; this is not such a surprising increase compared with Lomé III's 1100 million ecu.
16. They have increased in value: by 825 million ecu in Lomé IV compared with a 600 million ecu increase in Lomé III.

17. In Lomé III it was 215 million ecu.
18. To ensure that projects will be chosen without political interference. In fact, in recent years it has been noted that support has being channelled more towards social than economic ends.
19. Conditions for granting these loans are usually fixed or at least controlled by the EIB.
20. See art. 258 to 280 of the Convention.
21. And not just to ACP-based institutions.
22. Sources of information for this section are EIB's annual reports.
23. 330 million ecu, corresponding to 25 per cent in Lomé III.
24. Including optical fibre connections in urban areas and microwave radio links.
25. *Bulletin of the EU*, no. 11-1995; 1.4.102.
26. *Agence Europe*, no. 6510, 28 June 1995.
27. Articles 234 to 236, Lomé IV Convention.
28. *Agence Europe*, no. 6599, 6/7 November 1995.

12 South African Membership of the Lomé Convention

Cybèle Haupert

INTRODUCTION

This chapter deals with South Africa and accession to the Lomé IV Convention, which is the most preferential trade agreement the European Union (EU) grants to seventy African–Caribbean–Pacific (ACP) countries. For more than twenty years, South Africa was set aside from the international relations because of its apartheid regime. Since April 1994, when free elections took place and put an end to apartheid, the democratic government has sought to play a new role in international relations. In August 1994, the Republic of South Africa became a full party to the Southern African Development Community (SADC) and to the Southern African Customs Union (SACU). Besides, in Autumn 1994, South Africa was granted observer status at the ACP institutions.

During the apartheid regime the European Union dealt with South Africa through the European Community's Special Programme on South Africa, which, notably, consisted of the granting of aid by European Non-Governmental Organizations (NGOs). This programme was improved and renamed as the European Programme for Reconstruction and Development in May 1994.[1] The European Union members committed themselves on several occasions to help South Africa set up a democratic regime and to foster its trade. An Interim Agreement was signed between South Africa and the European Union on 10 October 1994. This agreement combines a package of initial measures with an offer to negotiate a comprehensive long-term arrangement (human rights clause, provisions for specific co-operation and development activities, access to the funding of the European Investment Bank, etc.).

Since all Southern African countries benefit from the Lomé Convention, the South African government applied to be a full member of Lomé. Although the accession to the Convention for most countries does not raise any substantial difficulty, South Africa's membership of the Convention is very controversial because of the distorted structures of its economy and society and its political dominance over the Southern African region. In the first part of this chapter, we will examine the pros and the cons of South Africa's full accession to the Lomé Convention according to the three main actors involved, i.e. the European Union, the ACP countries and South Africa. We will then examine the current solution agreed upon, which denied South Africa's plea. The current agreement, still under negotiation at this time, foresees South Africa's qualified membership of the Lomé Convention and the signing of a Trade and Cooperation Agreement between the European Community and South Africa and the conclusion of Development Cooperation. In this chapter, in order not to confuse the reader, we will always refer to the European Union and not the European Community, because the agreement with South Africa refers not only to trade aspects but also to aid and cooperation aspects. We will also make mention of the EU–ACP countries or group of institutions as the European Commission does.

Before beginning with the analysis of the different interests at stake for the different actors, the dualistic social and economic framework of South Africa must be stressed. The legacy of apartheid at the social and economic level still remains: although in per capita income terms South Africa is classified as a middle income country, the life circumstances of the majority of its black population are such as to give it many of the characteristics of a developing country (for instance in terms of life expectancy). All the contradictions of its economic and social structures lies in the fact that South Africa would be one of the richest signatories of Lomé but would not qualify for membership because of the huge disparities in wealth in the population.

THE CONTROVERSY OVER SOUTH AFRICA'S ACCESSION TO THE LOMÉ CONVENTION

The European Union Point of View

European Union–South Africa Trade Options

As the European Union committed itself to help the new democratic South Africa, different trade preferences schemes were offered to it consistent to the long trade tradition of the European Union with third countries. The Commission characterized its choice as between a reciprocal and a non-reciprocal agreement.[2] The type of reciprocal agreement included: most-favoured-nation status; a reciprocal trade and cooperation agreement (such as the one concluded with the former USSR in 1989); a free trade or customs union arrangement (as was negotiated with Israel, Turkey, Cyprus, etc.); and some form of an association agreement. The preferential or non-reciprocal options covered: the General System of Preferences (GSP); full membership of the Lomé Convention; and 'qualified membership' of Lomé, a form of associated status invented for the first time for South Africa.

In the end, the European Union decided to deny South Africa's application for full membership of the Lomé Convention; we will now analyse some of the reasons put forward by the European countries for this refusal.

Reasons for Denying South Africa Full Lomé Membership

From the legal point of view, South African membership could arguably be denied because of its economic structure. The criteria and procedures for accepting a new party to the Convention are dealt with in art. 356–363. Art. 363, s.1, points out that a request for accession to the Convention must be submitted by a state whose economic structure and production are comparable with those of the ACP states. Even if the South African economy can be compared to the average of ACP countries, some of its sectors are highly developed in comparison with corresponding levels within the ACP. Moreover, its trade structure with the European Union is atypical of ACP economies (see the figures in the next paragraph). At this stage, we can add that a new membership must be approved by the EU–ACP Council of Ministers. Art. 363 also stresses that the rights and obligations derived from the Convention foresee some exceptions. As a matter of fact, the possibility of creating a so-called qualified membership is legally feasible by the text of the Convention itself, even if it has never been used before the South African case.

The sheer size of the relationship between South Africa and the European Union ruled out full Lomé membership. The value of South Africa's exports to the Union would exceed 50 per cent of all exports from the 70 Lomé partners. The European Union accounts for 50 per cent of foreign direct investment in South Africa, for 40 per cent of South African exports and for 33 per cent of imports. In 1993, Pretoria ran a trade surplus of 3 billion ecu with the European Union.

Moreover, the GATT refused to grant South Africa developing country status, and only developing countries can be part of Lomé. South Africa has instead the status of a country-in-transition, enjoying only some of the privileges accorded to developing countries. Moreover, if South Africa had become a full member of Lomé, then it would probably have been impossible to get a waiver from the GATT free trade rules. Indeed, the South African economy is too large to be accommodated within the special dispensation allowed by GATT for the Convention. Full membership of Lomé would have implied that South Africa had a 50 per cent trade weighting, which would encourage GATT members to withdraw their support for the Convention, so threatening its future. So it was decided that South Africa's particular economic structure and development needs called for a 'special arrangement' to be negotiated. This hybrid arrangement was called 'minus Lomé' or 'qualified membership of Lomé'.

The European Union is allegedly willing to help the South African economy and society to recover fast from the apartheid regime and its consequences and to build democracy, granting South Africa the best trade conditions. Because 72 per cent of South Africa exports already enter the European Union markets either duty-free or under GSP, the benefits of full Lomé were not expected to be large, so another solution had to be found.

Full Lomé membership would have ensured that South Africa's agricultural goods, like fresh and processed fruits and vegetables, would have captured a significant amount of the European Union market. This fear apparently prompted Spain and Italy, in particular, to object to South African membership, even if the South African government reassured the European countries that it is a country with limited agricultural potential and that their products will not compete because they have different seasons. South Africa could buy European apples in winter. Moreover, some countries expressed their concern over the implications of extending the Lomé trade provisions to South Africa in terms of its impact on European Union producers such as those in clothing or papermaking.

On the other hand, some European Union member states (in particular Holland, Germany and the United Kingdom) strongly supported South Africa's plea, because they share strong investment and trade links with South Africa. All these contradictory positions may explain the difficulty entailed in negotiations for an economic agreement between the European Union and South Africa.

The ACP Point of View

Negative Factors

Even if the ACP countries eventually agreed on South Africa's accession to Lomé, many countries' first reaction was to fear that South Africa would undermine their own current benefits from their Lomé status. However, South Africa committed itself to accept to be a party of the Convention only on the condition that it will not be to the detriment of current beneficiaries.

For instance, some ACP countries were concerned that South Africa's access to the European market would seriously compete with their own exports to the European market, at least for the Southern African countries whose production structure is similar to the one of South Africa. In fact, they were afraid of South Africa's potential domination of the ACP countries. For instance, they were concerned about aid diversion, because National and Regional Indicative Programmes under the Lomé cooperation are drawn from a common fund. At the same time, the ACP countries accepted South Africa's accession to the Convention because of various reasons explained below.

Positive Factors

As has been mentioned, a new accession to the Lomé Convention must be approved by the EU–ACP Council of Ministers. Thus, all ACP countries would be *de jure* parties to the negotiations, while any other type of agreement would not allow for it.

It was collectively agreed that South Africa's accession to the Lomé Convention would also benefit the ACP countries, notably in Southern Africa, since it would obviously create an impetus to regional cooperation. First, regional cooperation would gain support from the European Development Fund, which is designed to foster regional cooperation. Second, ACP countries could benefit from the cumulation under the Lomé Rules of Origin with South Africa, which would obviously open up a range of new intra-regional trade and investment flows between South Africa and ACP countries. Indeed, the Convention provides the rule of origin which is designed to establish where a good was produced and therefore whether it is eligible or not under the Convention's trade preferences. The Convention's provisions on regional cumulation allow two or more EU–ACP states to undertake different parts of the production process and then to enjoy the trade preferences when entering the European Union market. An example is provided by woven clothing,[3] the Lomé rule of origin for which allows trade preferences only if articles originate from cloth produced entirely within the EU–ACP group. As a matter of fact, this rule of origin restrained ACP woven clothing exports. With South Africa integrated in the Lomé beneficiaries, its textile industry could provide inputs to ACP clothing companies. Third, the Convention would foster regional trade, because all ACP states can tender for aid contracts financed under the Convention. Finally, the Convention provides for regional political cooperation through regular meeting of the various EU–ACP institutions.

The South African Point of View

Negative Factors

When Lomé accession was refused, the government of South Africa believed that the European Union had failed to keep its promises. South Africa continued to lobby sympathetic countries (the United Kingdom, the Netherlands, Germany) in order to avoid signing a bilateral agreement leading to the setting up of a free trade area (FTA). South Africa conducted tough negotiations.

The economic reasons defended by South Africa prevailed. Obviously, the creation of an FTA means that there will be a product-by-product negotiation whose outcome is not yet known, while market access facilities under Lomé is an existing package. It was considered that full membership of Lomé would have greatly enhanced South Africa's share of the European Union agricultural market.

The Lomé Convention offers better coverage of duty-free access of industrial products than a FTA. The Lomé solution better suits the rapidly evolving state of South Africa's economy. Indeed, those areas which would benefit from the Lomé provisions are precisely those which South Africa is seeking to expand, especially over a range of industrial products like textiles and clothing, whose Lomé provisions allow substantial preferences. Not only are the ACP states exempted from formal controls on exports of originating clothing or textiles, but the Convention also rules out control under the Multifibre Arrangement (MFA). Mineral products (like coal), which represent important income for South Africa, are equally well covered by the Convention.

Labour-intensive areas like farm production carry high tariffs. Table grapes are one of the most labour-intensive farm products; they have to be picked by hand and enter the Single European Market at an 18 per cent tariff. Under the Lomé Convention most agricultural products would benefit from free access. However, we must keep in mind that even if art. 169, s.1, states unequivocally that 'The Community shall not apply to imports of products originating in the ACP states any quantitative restrictions or measures having equivalent effect,' the sole exception being the Common Agriculture Policy (CAP), products are still submitted to specific rules, which could be extended to grapes.

The changing economy of South Africa calls for a flexible agreement to allow future competitive sectors of its economy to be covered by preferential conditions. As noted in the analysis of Stevens *et al.*:

> Only the Lomé Convention has complete flexibility, at least for manufactured goods, with its commitment to offer unrestricted access to all industrial products meeting the rules of origin. None of the agreements provides major flexibility for sensitive agricultural products, although here again the Lomé Convention tends to be the most flexible.[4]

Since the end of the apartheid regime South Africa has embarked on a path of trade diversification, and the setting up of an FTA was expected to lock South Africa into the Single European Market. At the same time, South Africa's government believed an FTA could jeopardize South African efforts to restructure uncompetitive industries and to develop an integrated regional trade regime.

On the other hand, South Africa accepted the European Union proposal on the qualified membership of Lomé and on the setting up of an FTA, because it was obvious that South Africa needed a special agreement with the European Union, even if its form and content were different from what was expected.

Positive Factors

Liberal proponents argued that if South Africa is to prosper in the long run then it needs to open up its own markets to competition right now, rather than concentrate its efforts on gaining concessionary access to other markets. Indeed, South Africa has made commitments under the Uruguay Round, and the creation of an FTA would be the opportunity to foster the implementation of these.

Another major disadvantage linked to granting the Lomé trade provisions is that South Africa would have been classified among developing countries, which certainly would have frightened away foreign investments; the Lomé Convention is commonly perceived as the poor man's club. South Africa also admitted that many products important to its economy were not well protected or not covered by the Convention's provisions. Rather, there are some specific quotas or other restrictions which would have had to be renegotiated if South Africa membership had been accepted. As an example, apples and pears are constrained by a small quota of 1000 tonnes each. In 1990, ACP apple exports exceeded the quota (at 1751 tonnes), while pear exports nearly reached the quota. If South Africa had entered the Convention, these quotas would have had to be revised, as allowed by some provisions of the text, because South African production of apples is important. However, the issue of the negotiations could not be known in advance, notably because of the reluctance of Southern European states, and could have led to disadvantages for the other ACP exports. Even if the Lomé Convention covers the bulk of South Africa's most important exports, only a small proportion of its products faces a serious tariff entering the European Union market.

Finally, both parties agreed that Lomé did not provide the best solution to the specific social and economic situation of South Africa. It seems that those who were inclined to full Lomé membership, like the African National Congress (ANC), were more influenced by political considerations of solidarity with the Southern Africa neighbours, than by the business of trade. Mr Van Heerden, South Africa's ambassador to the European Union, claimed that 'we can help our region better if we are stronger'.[5] The ambassador inclines towards associate membership, where solidarity is signalled by association but where market access is tailor-made to suit South Africa's own situation.

THE CURRENT AGREEMENT

A twin-track approach for the new agreement has been agreed.

Qualified Membership of the Lomé Convention for South Africa

South Africa will participate in all the institutions of the ACP–EU cooperation as identified in Part II of the Convention. Given the strength of certain sectors of South Africa's economy, the parties agreed to suspend South Africa's eligibility to certain articles of the Convention.

A special article, no. 364[6] in Part V on the Final Provisions, on South Africa's accession to the Convention, with reference to the future protocol (describing the terms and conditions of South Africa's admission to the Lomé Convention) has been included in the text of the Lomé IVB Convention during its mid-term review.

South Africa is eligible to tender for EDF financial contracts on the same terms as European companies, i.e. excluding the 10 per cent to 15 per cent preference margin granted to ACP countries in order to make them more competitive. Plainly, South Africa's accession to Lomé has been mostly limited to the political aspects of the Convention, promoting regional integration, since South Africa belongs to the Southern African Customs Union (SACU) and the Southern African Development Community (SADC), all of whose members are ACP countries.

South Africa will *not* benefit from certain facilities covered by Lomé, namely trade concessions for exports, STABEX or SYSMIN funds and aid under the EDF (it would only benefit from the aid designed for the refugees).

The European Union–South Africa Trade and Cooperation Agreement

The Agreement will govern all economic and trade relations between the European Union and South Africa (in so far as they are not addressed by the protocol to the Lomé Convention). In line with WTO regulations, any free trade area must cover substantially all trade. The Agreement will therefore cover trade in commodities as well as services and financial transactions.[7] It appears that for South Africa this will mean around 90 per cent. The other 10 per cent will be on the list of sensitive products such as textiles, wine, farm produce and paper-making, needing protection from European Union competitors in the South African market. The Agreement will include a clause stating that EU–SA relations and the Agreement itself are to be based on respect of human rights and democratic principles.

For the constitution of a free trade area it has been envisaged that it would include an asymmetric time-frame of ten years (the WTO allows only for asymmetrical reduction of ten years). However, for certain sensitive products longer transitional periods may be necessary for both parties (around twelve years). It must be added that agreement was reached only on 28 February 1996 on the 'global architecture' for a complementary mandate to the Commission for negotiating with South Africa on the trade aspect of the agreement, i.e. the setting up of a free trade area. Indeed, negotiations had been blocked by France on the compatibility of an FTA with WTO rules, on its consequences for European Union common policies (the CAP in particular), on the relations with the other European Union African partners and on the overall impact the FTA will have on the European Union and its economic partners.

Development Cooperation – a Special Budget Line

South Africa is eligible to have the provisions of financial cooperation under the Lomé Convention suspended for a certain period of time (except as regards regional projects and emergency assistance), in favour of a special financial facility to support its development. This facility, the European Programme for Reconstruction and Development, which is financed by a special budget line (different from the EDF facilities under the Lomé Convention), aims at improving the living standards of its population, in particular the poorest sectors of the population, during the first period of transition. For the period 1996–9, the amount allocated to this programme will reach 500 million ecu.

This facility will also provide financial resources for South Africa's participation in regional cooperation under the Lomé Convention. In each of the individual programmes financed through the EPRD, the South African government and the European Union will encourage the appropriate involvement of NGOs, so as to contribute to a healthy and diverse civic society.

CONCLUSION

To assess the benefit of this specific solution will take time, because it is already known that the problems which arose during the debate on South Africa's full membership of Lomé will reappear when the bilateral agreement's is negotiated. Besides, it is worth stressing that the South African government feels disappointed at the reluctance of some individual European Union member states to grant the Commission its mandate to open negotiations on trade issues. Finally, we may ponder whether this very particular agreement that the European Union has conceded to a country in which it has many economic interests is to be interpreted as the beginning of the end of the Lomé Convention.

ANNEXE 12.1

Lomé – History of Relations Between the European Union and South Africa

April 1994 – Democratic elections, end of the apartheid regime.

May 1994 – The last of the remaining European Union sanctions against South Africa – a ban on trade and on military cooperation – lifted.

10 May 1994 – Help from the European Programme for Reconstruction and Development.

August 1994 – South Africa entered the Southern African Development Community (SADC) and the Southern African Customs Union (SACU).

10 October 1994 – An interim agreement signed by Executive Deputy President Thabo Mbeki and European Union External Economic Affairs Commissioner Sir Leon Brittan: combines a package of initial measures with an offer to negotiate a comprehensive long-term arrangement. This framework agreement provides, with a human rights clause, provisions for specific cooperation and development activities, access to the funding of the EIB.

Autumn 1994 – South Africa included among the GSP beneficiaries. The current GSP system came into operation on 1 January 1995 and will run until the end of 1998, unless a new trade agreement is found before this deadline. This scheme, valued at 1.7 billion rand, replaced the previous GSP system of which South Africa had been a beneficiary on an interim basis since September 1994. Initially the GSP only affected 7.7 per cent of South Africa exports to the European Union, but in July 1995 the list of South Africa agricultural products eligible to benefit from preferences expanded from 26 per cent to 59 per cent, although South Africa asked to benefit from 100 per cent of agricultural GSP.

Autumn 1994 – South Africa granted observer status at the EU/ACP institutions.

November 1994 – The European Community Investment Partners programme was launched in South Africa. It amounts to 4 million rand and provides support to direct investment projects in which the European Union and local companies cooperate either in joint ventures or through licence agreements.

Late October 1994 – Deputy President Mbeki asked for a special relationship with Lomé and a parallel agreement on matters not covered by Lomé.

30 November 1994 – Mr Manuel, the South African trade and industry minister, asked for full Lomé membership at the ACP–EU Joint Council on condition that the current beneficiaries accept it, which proved to be the case.

January 1995 – At the request of the French delegation, the Commission created a task force to study the possible consequences of South Africa entry into the ACP group while the ACP countries also created a similar study group. Consequently, the Commission has decided to establish an interdepartmental working group involving the different directorates general with authority in this connection (development, trade and external relations) as well as the legal service.

February 1995 – European Union denied South Africa full Lomé membership.

March 1995 – The European Union proposed a twin-track approach: qualified membership of Lomé for nontrade aspect and a bilateral trade and co-operation agreement dealing with trade and other issues.

30 June 1995 – Talks began on a bilateral agreement and on a protocol for partial entry into the Fourth Lomé Convention by South Africa.

4 November 1995 – Mid-term review of the Lomé IV Convention by the agreement signed in Mauritius. Inclusion of art. 364 in the part of the final provisions, which foresees the signing of a protocol to be added to the Convention when an agreement on the form of South Africa's accession to the Convention is reached.

[End 1998 – Still no agreement concluded.]

ANNEXE 12.2

Text of Article 364 of the Lomé Convention as Revised by the Agreement Signed in Mauritius on 4 November 1995

If before the entry into force of the provisions amending this Convention in accordance with Article 366(2), the negotiations with South Africa lead to an agreement on its accession to this Convention, then, notwithstanding the conditions for accession referred to in Article 363, the Council of Ministers shall act on the outcome of such negotiations and take a decision on the terms and conditions of the accession of that State, having regard to the specific characteristics of South Africa.

These terms and conditions shall be set out in a special Protocol which shall be an integral part of this Convention.

In case of positive decision, South Africa shall be added to the States signatory to this Convention without further ratification needed by the signatories of this Convention. The decision by the Council of Ministers shall indicate the date of entry into force of such accession.

Bibliography

'Développement et Coopération, Dossier de l'avenir du partenariat de Lomé', (Berlin, September–October 1995.

Holland, M., *Plus ça change … ? The European Union 'Joint Action' and South Africa.* Centre for European Policy Studies Paper no. 57 (Brussels 1994).

Kibble, S., Goodison, P. and Tsie, B., 'The Future of Lomé', *International Relations*, vol. XII, no. 4 (London, April 1994).

Page, S. and Stevens, C., *Trading with South Africa: the Policy Options for the European Community* (Overseas Development Institute Special Report, London, 1992).

Representation Permanente de la France Auprès de L'union Européenne, Note: *Les Relations entre l'Union Européenne et l'Afrique du Sud* (Brussels August 1994).

Stevens, C., Kennan, J. and Ketley R., 'EC Trade Preferences and a Post-apartheid South Africa', *International Affairs*, vol. 69, no. 1 (January 1993).

Stiftung, F. E. *South Africa and the Lomé Convention* (European Research Office, Trade Policy Monitoring Project, Johannesburg 1994).

South Africa, *Official Yearbook, Republic of South Africa* (Johannesburg, 1995).

Notes

1. See Annexe 1 for the History of EU–South Africa relations concerning Lomé.
2. See Holland (1994).
3. Stevens *et al.* (1993) p. 98.
4. Ibid.
5. In the South African newspaper the *Star*, Johannesburg 11 November 1994, p. 13.
6. See Annexe 2 (text of art. 364 of the Lomé Convention, as revised by the agreement signed in Mauritius on 4 November 1995).
7. The Agreement will precisely govern: economic and trade relations between the European Union and South Africa; financial and technical cooperation; economic cooperation; cooperation over a wide range of areas of mutual interest (technology, environment…); political dialogue and institutional arrangements; promotion of regional co-operation and integration.

13 ECHO – Humanitarian Aid

Emma Ascroft

INTRODUCTION

The European Community (EC),[1] its member states and institutions have played a key role in the evolution of humanitarian aid in recent years. The geopolitical impact of the end of the Cold War era and the proliferation of humanitarian disasters that has ensued since (both natural and man-made) have made the role played by humanitarian actors in international relations very important. It was in response to this evolution that the EC, together with its member states, began to rethink the Community's humanitarian activities and to examine the shortcomings of the existing policy. The result of this re-examination was the creation of a new, specialist administration within the European Commission dealing specifically with humanitarian aid. This was the European Community Humanitarian Office (ECHO), officially established in April 1992 with its first full year of operation in 1993.

This chapter examines ECHO's mandate and its position in relation to the other internal services of the Commission. It also examines practical aspects of ECHO's activities as a donor and coordinator in the broader context of international humanitarian assistance and its relationship with partner organizations, examining the strengths and weaknesses of its position. The study will conclude with a brief look ahead to highlight some of the potential challenges ECHO may face in the future.

A MANDATE FOR HUMANITARIAN RESPONSIBILITY

The primary aim in creating ECHO was to improve the efficiency and effectiveness of Community action, increase the visibility of the EC as a humanitarian donor and facilitate a better coordination of member states' own, national, response to humanitarian disasters. The mandate received by ECHO from the Commission was to take full responsibility for Community humanitarian aid, emergency food aid and prevention and disaster preparedness activities – in other words, the administration of humanitarian tasks previously carried out by a plethora of Commission services scattered within several directorates-general (DGs) were brought under a single administrative roof. It was hoped that this radical restructuring would give ECHO the degree of flexibility necessary to ensure the effective provision of immediate, appropriate and better coordinated help to countries and people who needed it.

At this stage it is worth noting that although by their very nature humanitarian disasters, whether natural or man-made, occur with little or no warning in terms of both timing and geographic location, a certain amount of 'planning' has been possible. In addition to sudden humanitarian assistance (e.g. earthquakes or floods), ECHO currently draws up so-called 'global plans' which set out a longer-term strategy (six months each) for areas experiencing chronic humanitarian upheaval. The former Yugoslavia and the ex-Soviet Republics in the Caucasus are prime examples. Furthermore, ECHO finances disaster preparedness projects in areas prone to natural disasters such as floods, typhoons or earthquakes. Projects of this kind are designed to reinforce the infrastructure of an endangered area so that it can better cope with an emergency. These may include the construction of flood barriers, typhoon shelters or the storage of emergency food supplies and equipment.

A FLEXIBLE AND AUTONOMOUS STRUCTURE

Flexibility in Decision-Making

In order to improve the effectiveness of Community policy, ECHO has been endowed with a special status within the Commission, that of an 'office' rather than that of a directorate-general. This innovation has several significant advantages. For example, ECHO is not bound by the internal procedures of DG I (external relations), DG VIII (development policy) and DG VI (agriculture), which previously handled urgent humanitarian aid. This allows ECHO to use a unique and simplified decision-making procedure, well suited to the rapidly changing environment in which it has to function. Indeed, a typical decision on a long-term development project in DGI or DG VIII can take up to six months, because the budgetary details of the accompanying financing have to be decided before the contract for the project in question can be signed. ECHO, on the other hand, can allocate the funds, sign the contract and fill in the details once the relief effort is under way. In this way, emergency decisions can be made in a matter of days, or in 24 to 48 hours in the case of sudden emergencies.

Flexibility in Budgeting

As a result, ECHO also enjoys a high degree of freedom to allocate funds to humanitarian projects not enjoyed by other DGs on quite the same scale. Within certain limits,[2] ECHO is free to allocate considerable sums of money from its operational budget[3] to humanitarian disasters that even large international aid agencies are unable to match. For example, ECHO gave 200 000 ecu for relief efforts in Zaire during the ebola epidemic without recourse to the usual decision-making procedures of the Commission or member states, while a typical UN agency is in a position to mobilize perhaps only half this amount. Moreover, ECHO project budgets themselves are more flexible. Unlike DG I and DG VIII project budgets, ECHO budgets allow transfers between different lines so that more money can be spent on medicine rather than transport if need be. Similarly, a contract can be extended if not all the available financing has been spent, even though the overall amount cannot be increased. Such a degree of flexibility is not permitted in DG I or DG VIII development contracts.

Autonomy of Decision-Making

Perhaps the most significant advantage of ECHO's privileged status within the Commission structure is its political autonomy. ECHO has the freedom to allocate money where there is an acute need rather than having to fit in with the rather more 'political' agendas of DG I and DG VIII. Of course, a certain amount of coordination is necessary and these mechanisms will be examined in the next section.

AN OPERATIONAL PARTNERSHIP

As indicated in the previous section, the EC's humanitarian activities take the form of contracts financed by ECHO, but because it does not have a direct operational capability *per se*, these contracts are implemented by so-called partners. These are usually non-governmental organizations (NGOs) or international agencies such as the United Nations High Commission for Refugees (UNHCR), which either submit their own proposals to ECHO or respond to requests for help received and drawn up by ECHO itself. Since the 1970s the Community has been using NGOs to undertake aid projects, in recognition of their high level of expertise and their sophisticated infrastructure, which allows them to react quickly, to adapt to rapidly changing circumstances and to distribute large quantities of humanitarian aid efficiently and effectively.

Relations between NGOs and ECHO are formalized by a framework partnership agreement (FPA) which forms the basis of the partnership. Rather like a 'gentleman's agreement', an FPA constitutes an administrative contract between the two sides, setting out what is expected from the NGO by ECHO and vice versa.[4] In other words, it keeps administrative procedures to a minimum so that it is not necessary to repeat the negotiations for each contract.[5] As a result, each operational contract is concerned only with the details such as the duration of the project and overall size of the budget, which are decided first with the details being finalized between ECHO and the NGO a few weeks later once the project is under way.[6]

For very practical reasons, ECHO deals mainly with large NGOs such as the International Committee of the Red Cross (ICRC). This has several advantages, the most significant being that they generally have the necessary funds and stores together with the capacity to mobilize them within a very short period of time. In other words, once ECHO has given the green light for the ICRC, for example, to implement a project, then work can begin before the first tranche[7] is released by ECHO and so help arrives where it is needed faster.

This works particularly well with the FPAs, because not only are the partner NGOs confident that they will be paid by ECHO but also proposals can even be submitted once a relief effort is in operation, and in this case any financing granted by ECHO is retroactive. The partnership therefore benefits both sides if an NGO has the necessary cash-flow to act first, but at the same time it does disadvantage smaller NGOs that cannot put an operation into practice until the funds have been received for the purchase of supplies and transport facilities. Thus the nature of the relationship between ECHO and its partners varies greatly from one NGO to another.

COORDINATION FUNCTION

Non-Governmental Organizations

As explained above, NGOs are vital to ECHO's work and give humanitarian relief operations the flexibility they require. However, ECHO's ability to coordinate the activities of several NGOs working in an area is limited by several factors. NGOs are after all independent by definition and ECHO is only one of numerous donors for many NGOs. Moreover, NGOs also have their own agenda in terms of 'visibility' and they need to be seen to carry out effective humanitarian work in order to secure funding for the future. NGOs often have individual areas of expertise and 'favourite' geographic areas of operation perhaps endowed with a higher profile. For this reason, ECHO can have difficulty in finding NGOs interested in carrying out projects proposed by ECHO in so-called 'forgotten crisis' areas or areas where NGOs have not previously worked (eg. the Caucasus), and thus ECHO finds its own agenda to a certain extent in competition with those of its partner organizations.

This is not to say that coordination cannot be effective in some situations. As mentioned above, the relationship between ECHO and its NGOs can vary greatly, and it depends to a large extent on the mix of organizations and personnel on the ground and the nature of the area of operation. Thus flexibility on both sides of the partnership and the ability to adapt to each individual situation is imperative to the success of an ECHO operation. In Cuba, for example, ECHO operations are extensively coordinated such that fifty NGOs are each responsible for the initial supply of one particular product to the island and for the distribution of all products within a specific geographic area of the country. Conversely, in Rwanda, ECHO engaged only one NGO, ICRC, to carry out the Community's humanitarian response.

The Commission

The appointment of a Commissioner with sole responsibility for humanitarian aid[8] has made a great impact on the internal co-ordination of the Community's actions in this field. This has had the effect of increasing the profile of the Community's humanitarian role and has meant that more 'care' has been taken in its administration and in its relations with other services of the Commission. By its very nature, humanitarian aid must be coordinated with the work of other directorates-general for several reasons. First, ECHO and all the DGs involved in a geographic area must ensure that their respective projects do not overlap in terms of content or interfere operationally. Secondly, in some cases projects can be rationalized through co-ordination. This is especially true of longer-term aid. Finally, co-ordination prevents cases of fraud whereby NGOs try to obtain funds from more than one DG. In this way, ECHO can consult other services on one of its own proposals and vice versa.

Coordination on a preparatory, practical level is carried out through inter-service groups[9] established by the Commission, bringing together officials from all the DGs on an *ad hoc* basis to exchange information on the proposal in question and to iron out any problems. On a more formal level, ECHO consults the 'geographic' Commissioners.[10] This may sound as if it could slow down decision-making considerably, but, in a sudden emergency, consultation is more often than not carried out between ECHO and the cabinets by telephone and the details transferred in writing afterwards. This close cooperation between the different services of the Commission is reflected in the recent internal restructuring of ECHO to facilitate operational coordination with DG I and DG VIII. As a result, ECHO is now divided into six units,[11] three of which correspond with the three main geographic regions of the Commission, with the remaining three dealing with finance, planning and relations with NGOs.[12]

However, the relationship between ECHO and other directorates-general can be fraught with difficulties. As mentioned above, the staff of ECHO are sometimes grateful for their independent status, because it can give aid regardless of the political agendas of other services. However, there are occasions when coordination is far from smooth. On the one hand, ECHO's mandate makes the connection between humanitarian aid and disaster preparedness, both of which fall within its competencies; on the other hand, however, the connection between humanitarian aid and development and rehabilitation policy has proved harder to make in practice. This is partly because long-term development policy falls within the mandate of DGVIII (and in some cases DGI), but also because the relatively slow decision-making and budgetary and political problems in other services cause expensive delays when ECHO is seeking to transfer responsibility for an area where it believes a longer-term programme would be more appropriate. This has occurred in southern Sudan, for instance.

Member States

Another responsibility handed down to ECHO with its mandate was to ensure 'closer relations between member states'[13] in the field of humanitarian aid. The intellectual basis of all coordination is the exchange of information. Mechanisms in place to facilitate this include a telex reporting system through which member state permanent representations and ECHO keep each other regularly informed of their respective humanitarian actions. There are also quarterly meetings between ECHO and member state officials to discuss the information received. However, the supply of information can sometimes seem to go in one direction only, with member states often unwilling to cooperate. Moreover, ECHO has no mandate to influence the coordination of bilateral actions. In this respect, ECHO simply acts as another donor, or a sixteenth member state, which must 'fit in' and avoid duplication.

CHALLENGES FOR THE FUTURE

The role of ECHO in international humanitarian aid has evolved rapidly in the few years it has been in operation. Since its inception, ECHO has seen its budget more than double from just 353 million ecu in 1992 to 840 million ecu in 1995.[14] This is significant at a time when governments throughout the world and other organizations are cutting back on aid expenditure and is reflected in the fact that ECHO is now the biggest single donor for many organizations, UNHCR among them. This fact, together with the recent proliferation of world-wide humanitarian disasters, begs the question as to what ECHO will look like in the future. This chapter has aimed to show the flexibility of ECHO as an aid donor and its adaptability, whether it is to local needs and circumstances, the nature of its partner NGOs or the internal functioning of the Commission and its relations with EC member states. The evolution of these complex interrelationships has led to speculation that ECHO may seek to develop a direct operational capacity of its own.

ECHO has been directly involved in humanitarian relief efforts in the past such as in the former Yugoslavia,[15] when it took responsibility for the programming, purchase and delivery of food aid for the whole region. ECHO set up two teams based in Zagreb and Belgrade with responsibility for the administration and follow-up of the operation assisted by NGO personnel and integrated into the European Community Task Force (ECTF) deployed in the area. ECHO's action was effective in so far as food aid was purchased in enormous quantities (often at auction) at a lower unit price rather than money being donated to NGOs to make smaller, individual purchases. Savings were also made on transport costs and ECHO also increased the visibility of Community aid to the region. ECHO still had to rely heavily on NGO structures for the distribution of aid on the ground, but its direct contribution to the relief effort made a positive impact. Not only did it make efficient use of budgetary resources, but ECHO also ensured that all sides involved in the conflict received equal long-term assistance, independent of any political agenda of NGOs or other donors.

Thus, direct Community action in the field of humanitarian relief can bring genuine benefits to areas of conflict and disaster but it is not appropriate in all cases. The situation in the former Yugoslav republics required large-scale humanitarian assistance over a prolonged period which allowed ECHO to make significant budgetary savings by acting directly. However, ECHO did not provide the aid significantly more effectively than an NGO and its action was complementary to operations already under way. Direct intervention on the part of ECHO is therefore limited to areas where it is appropriate, such as the creation of 'ECHO Flight'[16] in Northeastern Africa, which provides transport for NGO personnel in the region. ECHO structures are seen as inappropriate for the direct provision of sudden emergency relief by the Community, because it does not have the expertise, the capability or the stocks to implement an operation in the field. By its own admittance, ECHO is not seeking to transform itself into another global humanitarian agency. Besides, it has no mandate to do so. ECHO is still a bureaucracy and for this reason alone it will remain reliant upon NGOs in urgent situations.

The future for ECHO will indeed be a challenge. The Madrid Humanitarian Summit on 14 December 1995[17] concluded with a declaration to the international community. This declaration contained three appeals of particular relevance to the work of ECHO. All delegations called for the 'development of a global system of proactive crisis prevention'. A second appeal was made to bring support to the many 'forgotten crises' currently out of the public eye, and a third called for the link between relief and development to be strengthened. All three form part of the ECHO mandate and, as argued above,

ECHO faces a multitude of obstacles in its bid to carry out these tasks assigned to it. The Summit declaration is recognition that a genuine problem exists which needs a global solution, but as the delegations rightly point out, 'determination and political will' on an international scale will be needed to address these questions.

CONCLUSION

ECHO was created as a Community response to the multitude of humanitarian disasters that have befallen the world in recent years. The establishment of a separate administration for the European Community has meant that humanitarian aid is no longer a mere appendage of development policy and gives expression to the EC's commitment to the growing role of humanitarian assistance in international relations. In partnership with NGOs and other international agencies, ECHO has proved itself flexible and adaptable to a broad range of international disasters around the globe. Its unique internal structure and administrative autonomy have allowed it to evolve with the changing shape of other parts of the Commission.

Its mandate gives ECHO responsibility for all aspects of EC humanitarian assistance, be it sudden or chronic relief or disaster preparedness. ECHO is charged with coordination of Community humanitarian activities both internally within the Commission and externally between the member state governments and among partner NGOs. The day-to-day coordination of Community activities is facilitated by the creation of inter-service groups and consultation between the Cabinets, but the link between emergency relief and rehabilitation has proved hard to reinforce. In the same way, an effective coordination of autonomous actors such as national governments and of NGOs is similarly dependent on goodwill and the personalities of the organizations and actors concerned.

The future for ECHO remains uncertain in terms of the changing face of development policy in general. With many EC member states and other organizations such as USAID cutting back rather than strengthening their aid budgets, it remains to be seen what effect if any this will have on the level of financial support and the degree of control on programming for Community humanitarian operations. There are already moves in process to increase the degree of member states' control[18] of ECHO's programming and, if adopted, the regulation in question has the potential to place obstacles in the way of decisions on which many NGOs depend. The conclusions of the Madrid Humanitarian Summit constitute a declaration of intent, but only time will tell if the political will to answer its call will be forthcoming.

Bibliography

Aptel, C., *La Politique d'aide humanitaire de l'Union Européenne: la création d'ECHO et ses enjeux*, Collège d'Europe Documents de Travail, no. 13 (1995).

Conclusions of the Madrid Humanitarian Summit, 14 December 1995 (Brussels, 1996).

Council of Ministers, Common Position of 29 January 1996 with a view to adopting a Council Regulation Concerning Humanitarian Aid. (Internal document, Brussels, 1996)

Dumon, G., 'How NGOs see European development policy', *The Courier*, no. 141 (October 1993).

European Commission, *Annual Report on Humanitarian Aid 1993*, COM(94)40 Final (16 February 1994).

European Commission, *Annual Report on Humanitarian Aid 1994*, COM(95)47 Final, (22 February 1995).

European Commission, *General Report on the Activities of the European Community* (Brussels, 1992 and 1995).

Notes

1. For the purposes of this chapter, the term 'European Community' or simply 'Community' will be used. However, the reader should note that the European Union (EU) officially came into being in 1993 as a result of the Treaty revisions undertaken at Maastricht in 1992 and is used to describe the new three-pillar structure, comprising the EEC, Common Foreign and Security Policy (CFSP),' and Justice and Home Affairs Co-operation (JHA). Since the majority of the policies, legal bases and procedures referred to in this study relate to the first pillar, reference will mostly be made to the European Community.
2. There is a draft regulation concerning humanitarian aid under discussion in Council which envisages the introduction of 'committology' [standard rules of conduct for EU decision-making committees] for approving ECHO finance for projects above a certain threshold value. This could potentially delay decision making if proposals are referred to Council and increase administration costs if documents have to be translated into all working languages (ECHO works in French and English only).
3. Mainly budget lines B7-51, B7-5000 and B7-6000 and a proportion of the European Development Fund (EDF) for actions in ACP countries.
4. Such as labelling aid deliveries and follow-up procedures and submitting final accounts after completing a project.

5. This is the case for NGOs that have not signed FPAs.
6. This includes the breakdown of the budget into the various areas of expenditure.
7. ECHO releases a percentage of the budget in advance; the remainder comes once the NGO has produced detailed accounts after completion of the project. This undertaking is explicit in the FPA.
8. At its establishment in 1992, ECHO was placed under the joint responsibility of two of the then DGI Commissioners, Andriessen and Matutes, together with Commissioner Marin of DGVIII, before being transferred to the portfolio of Marin only as Commissioner for Co-operation and Development in January 1993 with the appointment of the last Delors Commission. It was not until January 1995 and the approval of the first Santer Commission that Commissioner Emma Bonino was given responsibility for the ECHO portfolio independent of the DGI Commissioners.
9. For example, the inter-service group on refugees, internally displaced persons and returnees in third countries (established in December 1993) which aims to define a common, coherent strategy for EC refugee aid and to establish ways of working closer with international agencies such as the UNHCR. It was transformed into the Permanent Inter-Service Group (PISG) in November 1994.
10. Currently [End 1998] they are: Sir Leon Brittan – OECD Countries and GATT/WTO questions; Mr Manuel Marin – Asia, Mediterranean and Latin America; Mr Hans van den Broek–Central and Eastern Europe, the former USSR, CFSP and enlargement; and Mr João de Deus Pinheiro – ACP and South Africa.
11. The new *organigramme* was adopted by ECHO on 28 February 1996.
12. This compares with the old structure of only three units, two geographic and one dealing with general administration, budgetary matters and disaster preparedness activities. Disaster preparedness now falls within the responsibilities of the geographic units.
13. European Commission (1994) p. 3.
14. *General Report of the European Community* (1992 and 1995).
15. Aptel (1995) ch. 3, p. 61.
16. European Commission (1995) p. 26.
17. Organizations represented were: USAID, World Food Programme (WPA), UNICEF, UNHCR, ICRC, Médecins sans Frontières, InterAction. Emma Bonino attended on behalf of the European Commission.
18. See note 2 above.

Part 3

The Mediterranean Challenge

14 A Review of the Barcelona Conference and a Summary of EU Policy Objectives

Francisco Javier Raya

'La Mediterranée ... elle est trop étroite pour séparer, elle est trop large pour confondre.'

Bichara Khader, *Le Grand Maghreb et l'Europe*

INTRODUCTION

The Mediterranean, an area where different cultures and religions coexist and where national and religious minorities may clash, is a perfect stage for the so-called 'New Order' and its contradictions. The gap between North and South can be physically measured. Only 14 kilometres separate Gibraltar from Africa.

After the raising of the Iron Curtain, the EC committed itself financially to assist its poorer cousins in the Central and Eastern European countries (CEECs). These countries are thus competing with the ACP states and Mediterranean non-member countries (MNMCs) to obtain EU financial and commercial cooperation. It seems therefore that EU policy towards the Maghreb and Mashrak countries is somehow linked to that towards its eastern neighbours, which is reflected in a different hierarchy of interests among member states in the field of EU external relations.[1] However, the EU has begun to recognize that stability in its broad southern flank is as important as in Eastern Europe.[2] This is the main purpose of establishing a new and more far-reaching EU policy towards this region that envisages the establishment of a Mediterranean Free Trade Area by 2010.

This chapter examines the evolution of the so-called Mediterranean Partnership. First, the main problems in that region will be reviewed, then former EC Mediterranean policies will be described (Part III) and finally the new EU policy officially launched at the Barcelona Conference in November 1995 (Part IV) will be discussed.

THE MEDITERRANEAN: A BRIEF DESCRIPTION

The Mediterranean is 'a cultural melting-pot, a symbol of the fruitful cross-exchange of civilizations'[3] where three different religions and numerous cultures coexist. This cultural diversity leads logically to the existence of heterogeneous political regimes.

The most striking difference, however, is the economic gap between the northern and southern shores. France, Italy, Spain and Greece have 88 per cent of the basin's total GDP. The southern shore's total GDP represents only 4 per cent of EU total GDP. Furthermore, accumulated external debt is an acute problem. In 1990, about a quarter of total exports were used to cover debt servicing on public debt in several southern Mediterranean countries. Except for oil-producing countries such as Algeria and Libya, the MNMCs' trade balance is negative. The consequences of such an economic imbalance cause grave concern, in particular if they are seen in the light of the demographic profile and the social and political situation in the area.

In 1950, two-thirds of the Mediterranean's population lived on the northern shore, but by the year 2020 the situation will be reversed. Most of the southern population will be concentrated in overcrowded metropolitan areas on the coast lacking basic infrastructure.[4]

Another perturbing factor is the average unemployment rate of 20 per cent and a proportion of the active population of only 28.3 per cent in 1990, due to the marginal participation of women in economic activities.[5] The social unrest created by these figures is reflected in an unstable political situation, ranging from terrorist attacks in Morocco, Egypt and Turkey to serious civil conflicts in Algeria. Diverse factors such as poverty, the lack of effective democracy and the ideological vacuum left by the collapse of the Arab approach to socialism have fostered the appeal of Islamic fundamentalism in important sectors of the population.[6]

The consequences of these economic, social and political trends are an increase in migration flows towards Europe. During the European economic boom years this migration was welcomed by EC member states because of the need for manpower.[7]

The situation has nevertheless changed during the last decade and the EU has to face now its own economic and social problems such as unemployment and increasing xenophobia. However, this exodus from the South to the North cannot be prevented by establishing a 'Fortress Europe' mentality through police measures alone. It is necessary to address the ultimate cause for this migratory flow, the economic situation in the southern shore countries of the Mediterranean.

THE EU AND THE MEDITERRANEAN

EU Interests

As mentioned, Europe has strong historical and cultural ties with North Africa, particularly in the case of former colonial powers in the area such as France, the United Kingdom, Italy and Spain. Other countries have privileged relationships, such as Germany and Turkey. The area has also an important strategic interest for Europe. Much of the petroleum consumed in the EU comes from either North Africa or the Middle East. The Mediterranean includes some militarily and commercially important strategic points such as the Suez Canal and the Straits of Gibraltar.

Moreover, the economic importance of the area cannot be underestimated. The region is both an important outlet for EC exports and a supplier of basic products such as petroleum and natural gas. Its countries represent 8 per cent to 8.5 per cent of total EU exports and 6.7 per cent to 6.8 per cent of imports, while the EU's share of MNMC exports ranged between 28 per cent and 83 per cent. This relationship displays a strongly asymmetric trade interdependence. In 1996, about 45 per cent of southern Mediterranean countries' exports were to the EU, compared with 26 per cent of exports from Central and Eastern European countries (CEECs). The EU imported 27 per cent of its primary products from MNMC, whereas only 0.5 per cent came from CEECs in 1996. A further factor to be considered is that the MNMCs are a permanent manpower stock for a Europe, whose population is steadily ageing.

Finally, the security dimension should be given special consideration. The EU must provide for stability on its eastern and southern flanks.[8] The aim of security in the Mediterranean basin cannot be exclusively achieved through military means (NATO and WEU), because the origin of political turmoil in MNMCs is mostly caused by the economic and social conditions in those countries and by religious fundamentalism.

EC Mediterranean Policies

The Treaty of Rome in 1957 envisaged the establishment of special relations with former French colonies in North Africa. The EC then concluded a number of agreements with some Mediterranean countries during the 1960.[9] This patchwork of agreements was regarded with dissatisfaction by the EC institutions, as indicated by the Rossi Report to the European Parliament in 1971.[10] By then, many bilateral agreements were about to be renegotiated and the first enlargement was on the EC agenda. Furthermore, the Mediterranean's importance as a strategic area for Europe increased as the producers of strategic commodities, mainly petroleum, were becoming more confident in their claims over the control of their natural resources. In the meantime, the Soviet Union extended its military presence in the area. The heads of states and governments of the member states asserted the EC's strong commitment towards the Mediterranean in their October 1972 summit in Paris. This was followed by a declaration of the foreign ministers in Copenhagen in 1972, immediately after the membership agreements with the United Kingdom, Ireland and Denmark were signed, where they confirmed that the EC should 'reinforce its long-standing links with these countries ... and cooperate over the establishment and maintenance of peace, stability and progress in the region'.[11]

The Global Mediterranean Policy (GMP) was thus launched in the early 1970s, which sought both more coherence and a broader scope. As such, it envisaged not only trade links but also social and financial cooperation. However, the Community seemed incapable of systematizing its global policy, so bilateral agreements were signed again. In contrast, the First Lomé Convention, concluded at the same time, was multilateral. Although these agreements allowed almost free tariff entry to the EC for MNMCs' manufactured products, the outcome of these agreements can be placed at a lower level than the Lomé Convention, in the so-called 'EC pyramid of preferences'. Most ACP agricultural products do not compete with those protected by the EC Common Agricultural Policy (CAP), whereas the MNMCs' agricultural and textile products do compete with that of the EC member states.

The historical and economic context explains the partial failure of this new approach. The first enlargement of the EC extended the Yaoundé convention to the former British colonies in the ACP area. Subsequent political changes in Southern Europe introduced pressing challenges to the Community, as a possible second enlargement was envisaged.[12] It was realized in two stages: 1980 for Greece and 1986 for the two Iberian countries. After these enlargements, not only had the MNMCs to compete with ACP countries for development aid but they also suffered from competition from the new Mediterranean member states of the EC, whose traditional Mediterranean crops of fruit, vegetables, cotton, tobacco and rice were now protected by the CAP. Further, the Community's southern neighbours cannot take full advantage of an EC system of general preferences (GSP), because their economies have a reduced tendency to export due to their traditional protectionist policies. Moreover, the European GSP has been extended to almost every country in the Third World.

A Redirected Mediterranean Policy (RMP) was initiated in 1992 and substantially increased the amount of development aid and extended EC trade preferences. It also encompassed environmental policy, the protection of human rights and the promotion of democratic principles while encouraging inter-MNMC trade, which by 1992 was only 5 per cent. Notwithstanding these improvements, this new policy again lacked a global and coherent vision of the region. It is highly significant that no new agreements were concluded, although they were amended by the Fourth Financial Protocol (1992–6).

The MED decentralized cooperation programmes are some of the RMP's most original instruments, which try to involve the private sector in the task of developing MNMC. They provide a framework where individuals, groups and organizations from the EU and MNMC form direct links, i.e. networks, to undertake different projects. If the project is chosen by the Community, the European Commission will cover it up to a maximum of 80 per cent of the total cost. The funds are allocated and administered by the Transmediterranean Networks Agency (ARTM). Currently several MED programmes are operating:

- MED-MEDIA aims to increase trans-Mediterranean cooperation between professionals in the mass media by encouraging an exchange of experience and know-how in order to better understand the political, cultural and everyday conditions of their counterparts. In 1995, 35 projects were selected.

- MED-URBS is intended to improve the quality of life of Mediterranean cities including the strengthening of local democracy and decentralized cooperation among local authorities in the two shores. A total of 48 networks were selected.
- MED-CAMPUS aims to foster cooperation in higher education; universities and other institutions are encouraged to pool both information and know-how. In the academic year 1994–5 103, networks were chosen.
- MED-INVEST is a response to the need to encourage the creation of small and medium-sized enterprises (SMEs), arguably the real engine of the EU economy, in the MNMC. After a pilot phase from 1992 to 1995, the consolidated stage of this programme was launched in 1996.

New programmes, such as MED-TECHNO and MED-MIGRATION, were set up in 1996; those named aim respectively to improve the application of efficient technologies and to facilitate co-operation among local communities and organizations involving migrants.

THE EURO-MEDITERRANEAN PARTNERSHIP

Towards a Euro-Mediterranean Partnership, 1990–5

Why was it felt that there was a need for a new approach towards the area? Many member states alleged the failure of previous Mediterranean policies, citing several factors. In 1970, MNMCs represented 14.7 per cent of EC imports, whereas this declined to only 6.8 per cent in 1994. During 1980 alone, EU–MNMC commercial exchanges fell by 13 per cent. It seems that EC policies in the area during the last three decades have favoured the export diversification of these countries more than they have helped them to penetrate EC markets, mainly because of difficulties in exporting MNMC agricultural products. The total EC expenditure provided by both the global and redirected policies from 1978 to 1996 is not more than 5 billion ecu. From 1979 to 1987, public financial aid in the area, from both the EC and its member states, represented only 17 per cent of the total received, compared with 31 per cent from the USA and 28 per cent from the OPEC countries.

Second, new political circumstances in the area after the end of the Cold War, despite reviving traditional conflicts in the Balkans, have nevertheless favoured Arab–Israeli dialogue, initiated in Madrid in November, 1991. It is now possible for the EU to consider the Mediterranean's southern and eastern rim as a whole.

Third, there are also new economic circumstances. The world economy is undergoing a process of both globalization and regionalization. The first process results from the conclusion of the Uruguay Round in 1994 and the creation of the World Trade Organization the following year, while the second is reflected by the development of free trade areas and organizations of economic integration such as NAFTA, MERCOSUR and ASEAN. After the end of the bipolar world it seems that special trade relations are being established not on historical or ideological considerations but on geographical ones. In that sense, one should take into consideration that the southern Mediterranean rim will constitute a potential market of 300 million consumers by the year 2010, located on the EU's doorstep. A further factor is the intensification of specific problems of stability, such as terrorism, illegal immigrants and Islamic integrity.

By 1990, the Spanish and Italian Foreign Ministers had already launched the idea of a Conference on Security and Cooperation in the Mediterranean, following the example of the Conference on Security and Cooperation in Europe (CSCE). Although this idea was not successful, the Spanish intention of creating a Euro-Maghreb partnership was supported by the European Council in Lisbon in June 1992. The European Council meeting in Corfu two years later considered extending this plan to third Mediterranean countries. Following these proposals, the Commission issued the two communications of 19 October 1994 and 8 March 1995, in which a Euro-Mediterranean partnership was defined.

The Euro-Mediterranean project was finally endorsed by the European Council at its meetings in Essen and Cannes in December 1994 and June 1995. It was also decided to hold a Euro-Mediterranean Conference in Barcelona on 27 and 28 November 1995 and to increase substantially the budget resources devoted to MNMC to 4685 million ecu[13] in the form of grants for the period 1995–9, to be topped up from the EIB's own resources. Instruments of this policy are the Euro-Mediterranean Association agreements[14] and a unified financial tool named MEDA similar to that used for the CEECs, the PHARE programme, which replaces the former Financial Protocols.

The Barcelona Conference

The 15 foreign ministers of the EU met with their counterparts of the 12 MNMCs[15] in Barcelona, where they endorsed a declaration pledging the promotion of peace and stability in the region, respect for the right to self-determination, the settlement of their disputes by peaceful means and the strengthening of their cooperation in preventing terrorism. They also concluded a work programme to translate the declaration into concrete actions.

The Barcelona Declaration, following a three-basket structure which resembles the CSCE's Helsinki Final Act, encompasses three main dimensions:

- Political and security partnership, aimed at defining a common area of peace and stability.
- Economic and financial partnership, aimed at building a zone of shared prosperity by progressively establishing a free trade area by the year 2010.
- Social, cultural and human partnership, aimed at encouraging exchanges between civil societies. The decentralized cooperation MED programmes already set up by the RMP will be further improved.

Subsequently, the Conference will hold meetings of the 27 partners at three levels:

- Frequent high-level meetings of foreign ministers.
- Intermediate senior-official level meetings, the 'Euro-Mediterranean Committee for the Barcelona Process', known as the Barcelona Committee, will be held regularly to prepare the high-level meetings and to take stock of and evaluate the follow-up to the Barcelona process.
- At a lower level, the various services of the Commission will undertake the necessary technical assistance and follow-up.

The Euro-Mediterranean partnership will encourage parliamentary dialogue in which the European Parliament is intended to play a major role, as well as regular contacts among European organs and their counterparts in the Mediterranean countries, in particular the Economic and Social Committees.[16]

CONCLUSION

We have seen how the southern Mediterranean countries have been steadily climbing the Community's 'pyramid of preferences'. The EU is thus willing to partially overcome some of the previous Mediterranean policy mistakes, such as the lack of a global vision and insufficient financial aid. However, the Barcelona Declaration could remain an ineffective goodwill paper if its objectives are not properly matched with genuine political and financial commitment. This implies the involvement not only of the southern but also the northern European states, allowing MNMC agricultural products to enter the EC market and increasing their financial aid.

The MFTA, the most ambitious project of the partnership, cannot succeed if the economic gap between the two shores continues. Paradoxically, the main adjustment effort required by the year 2010 has to be faced by the poorest area, and strong foreign investment in the area will be needed. The private financial market, nevertheless, has not yet displayed much interest in the region but has focused on CEECs and other emerging markets in Latin America and Asia. In this regard, the MFTA could be the only way to attract private capital provided that it is accompanied by generous public aid to improve MNMC's infrastructures.[17] Otherwise, this project could provoke a devastating impact on MNMC's economies.

Furthermore, it is essential that the EU completely liberalizes trade in agricultural and textile goods, which form the bulk of Mediterranean exports (owing to their comparative advantage on these sectors). Only then can these countries face the competition of the EU's manufactured products. This would necessitate a radical reform of the CAP at a moment when future EU enlargement towards the East seems to require it to be strengthened.[18] We see again how the MNMCs' fate is inextricably linked to the CEECs and the interaction of EU policies to the south and east.

The EU, which had to choose between aid or trade in its Mediterranean policy, has decided to apply 'shock therapy' to revive the flailing economies of this region, namely through the creation of the MFTA. Accepting such relatively open competition with its northern partners is a risk for Europe's southern neighbours, because it can either foster their development or inflict the ultimate coup de grace on their economies. However, the potential effects of a total collapse of the southern rim economies would be felt dramatically in Europe.

The EU should therefore take this into account when it comes to fulfilling, or eventually increasing, its future commitments towards this region.

ANNEXE 14.1

First Phase of Mediterranean Policy

Special Association Agreements under art. 238 (Limited duration except Greece and Turkey)

Greece	(1961)
Turkey	(1963) (additional protocol 1980)
Tunisia	(1969)
Morocco	(1969)
Malta	(1970)
Cyprus	(1972)

Trade Agreements under art. 113 and art. 114 (Limited duration)

Preferential		*Non-preferential*	
Spain	(1970)	Israel I	(1964)
Israel II	(1970)	Lebanon I	(1965)
Lebanon II	(1972)	Yugoslavia I	(1970)
Egypt I	(1972)	Yugoslavia II	(1973)
Portugal	(1972)		

Second Phase of Mediterranean Policy

Cooperation Agreements under art. 238 (Unlimited duration)

Israel III	(1975)
Algeria	(1976)
Morocco	(1976)
Tunisia	(1976)
Egypt II	(1977)
Lebanon III	(1977)

Jordan	(1977)
Syria	(1977)
Yugoslavia III	(1980)

The Euro-Mediterranean Association Agreements

In Force January 1997		*Negotiations in 1995*	*Negotiations in 1995–6*
Tunisia	(July 1995)	Jordan	Algeria
Israel	(November 1995)	Egypt	Syria
Morocco	(February 1996)	Lebanon	Palestinian Authority

Bibliography

Bichara, K. and Nuñez Villaverde, J. A., 'La Asociación Euro-mediterránea: promesas y sombras', *Politica Exterior* no. 48 Madrid, 1995–6 pp. 59–74.

Bistolfi, R., 'Euro-Méditeranée: pour un projet régional', in Bistolfi, R. (ed.), *Euro-Méditerranée: une région à construire, Collection Espaces Méditerranées* (Publisud, Paris, 1995) pp. 9–20.

Clairet, P., 'EC-Middle East Relations: The Peace Process and Revisions to the Community´s Mediterranean Policy', in Ludlow, P. (ed.), *Europe and the Mediterranean* (Brassey, London, 1994).

Council of the European Communities, Copenhagen Declaration, reprinted in *Bulletin of the European Communities*, 12/73, Annexe 1 (1973).

Granell, F., 'El Espacio Mediterráneo después del Consejo Europeo de Cannes 2', *Política Exterior* no. 47, Madrid, October–November 1995, pp. 91–103.

Grilli, E. R., *The European Community and the Developing Countries* (Cambridge University Press, 1994).

Khader, B., *Le Grand Maghreb et l'Europe, Collection Espaces Méditerranées* (Publisud, Paris, 1992).

Lopez Garcia, B. and Nuñez Villaverde, J. A., 'Europe and the Maghreb: Towards a Common Space', in Ludlow, P. (ed.), *Europe and the Mediterranean* (Brassey, London, 1994).

Mortimer, E., 'Europe and the Mediterranean: The Security Dimension', in Ludlow, P. (ed.), *Europe and the Mediterranean* (Brassey, London, 1994).

Naïr, S., 'Un dispositif insuffisant pour un projet incontournable', in Bistolfi, R. (ed.), *Euro-Méditerranée: une région à construire, Collection Espaces Méditerranées* (Publisud, Paris, 1995) pp. 101–5.

Parlament Européen, *Rapport sur la Politique Commerciale de la Communauté dans le Bassin Méditerranéen,* Documents de Séance no 246 (February 1971).

Ravenel, B. (ed), *Méditerranée: l'ímpossible mur, Collection Les Cahiers de Confluences*, (L'Harmattan, Paris, 1995).

Regnault, H., 'Logique economique et impulsion politique', in Bistolfi, R. (ed.), *Euro-Méditerranée: une région à construire, Collection Espaces Méditerranées* (Publisud, Paris, 1995) pp. 107-11.

Rhein, E., 'Le pari Euro-Méditerranéen', in Bistolfi, R. (ed.), *Euro-Méditerranée: une région à construire, Collection Espaces méditerranées* (Publisud, Paris, 1995) p. 23–36.

Tovias, A., 'The Mediterranean Economy', in Ludlow, P. (ed.), *Europe and the Mediterranean*, (Brassey, London, 1994).

Tovias, A., 'The EU's Mediterranean Policies under Pressure', in Gillespie, R. (ed.), *Mediterranean Policies*, vol. 2 (Pinter, London, 1996).

Notes

1. During European Council meetings in Essen and Cannes, Spain, Italy and France's special interests in the area had to be appreciated and negotiated with Britain and Germany, in the light of their similar interests in the CEECs. The balance was found; the EU will devote financial aid to the MNMCs equivalent to two-thirds of that to the CEECs.
2. Since the TEU came into force in 1993, those policies have come under the scope of both the EC action and inter-governmental coordination of the member states under the second pillar. Therefore, since then the expression EU is preferred unless otherwise mentioned.
3. Commissioner Manuel Marin at the opening ceremony of the Barcelona Conference on 27 November 1995.
4. The most important one could be the scarcity of water. Countries in the southern rim usually only receive 15 per cent of the region's rainfall, while its population will outgrow the northern one. Pressure is again higher in the coastal areas where population and tourism concentrate.
5. Only 10 per cent of women participate in the labour market, compared to 32 per cent in Italy, 38 per cent in Germany or 45 per cent in Denmark.
6. When fundamentalist groups are allowed to participate in democratic elections they poll, on average, 14 per cent of the vote.
7. At the close of the century, the Maghreb countries will have lost some 2.4 million inhabitants, circa. 4 per cent of their population, because of this migratory flow.
8. This is particularly valid when the USA is reluctant to intervene in those areas. Although its leadership in the area is decreasing, it is not likely that the EU can take its place in the short term, as has been proven by late but effective intervention in former Yugoslavia by the USA.
9. Every agreement has been accompanied by a financial protocol, establishing the amount of financial aid to be received by the country concerned. This protocol has been substituted three times.
10. Parlament Européen (1971).
11. Council of the European Communities (1973).

12. Those events were the end of the Generals' dictatorship in Greece in 1974, the Portuguese revolution in 1974 and the end of Franco's era in Spain in 1975.
13. The Commission proposed 5.5 billion ecu, but this figure had to be renegotiated down to 4685 million ecu at the Essen European Council.
14. These agreements have been already signed by Israel, Tunisia and Morocco. They will be expanded to the other MNMCs and possibly to the Palestinian Authority with the only exceptions being Turkey, Cyprus and Malta. A customs union has been established with Turkey since January 1996; Malta and Cyprus started negotiations on their future membership in 1996.
15. In addition to the Palestinian Authority, the Med 12 include Algeria, Morocco, Tunisia, Egypt, Israel, Jordan, Lebanon, Syria, Turkey, Cyprus and Malta. The only excluded Mediterranean country is Libya. Special guests included the United States, Mauritania, the Arab League and the Maghreb Union (UMA).
16. An Inter-Parliamentary Conference on Security and Cooperation in the Mediterranean was held in Valletta in November 1995. The Economic and Social Committees and the equivalent bodies of the EU and the MNMC met in December in Madrid.
17. However, as early as January 1996 London vetoed the implementation of the financial mechanism (MEDA) due to differences in voting. Greece, on the other hand, also poses some problems regarding Cyprus and Turkey.
18. In 1992 the CAP was reformed to adapt itself to the agreements on this matter within the GATT's Uruguay Round. Once they were agreed in 1994 and after the transitional periods thereby envisaged, difficulties for MNMC products in entering the Single European Market will be eased.

15 Turkey, Cyprus, Malta – Potential EU Members?

Maria Pia Pace

INTRODUCTION

Turkey, Cyprus and Malta all demonstrate a close and long-standing relationship with the European Union (EU) that has culminated in each applying for full EU membership, mostly so as to gain improved access to EU's export and labour markets, which, with possible financial assistance, could accelerate their economic development. The Mediterranean region not only has political and strategic interest for the EU; it also provides privileged access (especially in the case of Turkey, with a market of 62 million people) to protected markets.

This chapter assesses separately the record of EU's cooperation with Turkey, Cyprus and Malta, in each case with regard to three main points: history, recent developments, and the key issues in any negotiations on accession.

EU–CYPRUS RELATIONS

History[1]

An EU–Cyprus Association Agreement was signed in December 1972. The purpose of the agreement was to create a customs union between both parties after a ten-year transition period. The customs union consisted of two stages; the first came into effect in June 1973 and was meant to run until June 1977. No details of the second stage were discussed at the time.

As a result of the Turkish invasion of Northern Cyprus in 1974 and the subsequent *de facto* division of the country, EU–Cyprus relations were blocked. Consequently the implementation and further development of the Association Agreement was out of the question for political reasons. Moreover, the severe economic dislocation caused by the division of the island made a customs union with the EU impractical, even on the Greek side. The only feasible way forward was an extension of the first stage of the agreement. This extension was carried out until 1987, although financial protocols continued to be agreed and implemented in the meantime, when the EU moved to a revised version of the second stage of association. The second stage involved the gradual implementation of a customs union. Once again, the process would occur over two phases, with the first entering into force in January 1988 and lasting for a period of ten years.[2,3]

The (Greek) Cypriot decision to apply for EU membership in July 1990 was essentially a natural step towards an 'ever-closer relationship with the EU'. More generally, there has been a growing realization that a customs union places Cyprus in a position whereby it must comply to EU rules (without having a say in their formulation) and open its markets to EU competition with no possibility to 'exploit' the EU's structural funds, agricultural subsidies and other benefits that accrue to full members. The security guarantee provided by EU membership is also attractive, as is the belief that EU membership for Cyprus would boost the chances of reuniting the island.[4]

The Commission opinion on the Cypriot application was issued in June 1993. The *avis* was overall positive, although no proposal for the initiation of accession negotiations was made. In the opinion, the Commission recognizes that the adoption of the *acquis communautaire* should pose few problems, although the division of the country implies that the four freedoms of the European Single Market (particularly the free movement of people) could not be exercised over the entire island. The economic situation of Cyprus is essentially positive. Concern is, however, expressed about the Greek-speaking South's dependency on tourism and its level of industrial competitiveness as well as the Turkish-speaking North's economic decline – mainly due to its isolation.[5] Nevertheless, neither of these problems is considered insurmountable; rather, accession is seen as potentially beneficial, especially in helping the North bridge the economic gap. Moreover, the opinion questions Cyprus' ability to participate fully in the day-to-day running of the Community's institutions due to practical difficulties and the lack of a sufficient number of experienced public officials. Another question raised is whether Cyprus would be able to handle the wide-ranging responsibilities and obligations entailed by the presidency of the Council.[6]

The key passages were contained in the concluding paragraphs of the *avis*, which made Cypriot accession conditional on an internal political settlement whilst offering a caveat, i.e. the stated intention of reviewing the Cypriot application in January 1995 if there was no internal political settlement by that date.[7] At that point, the Commission did not propose accession negotiations, but 'talks ... to familiarise the Cypriot authorities with all the elements that constitute the *acquis communautaire.*'[8]

The Council of Ministers endorsed the Commission's opinion on 4 October 1993 and the Commission has thus been mandated to explain the *acquis communautaire* to the Cypriots in order to identify areas where the EU might help Cyprus adjust and to facilitate the Cypriots' preparation of their negotiating position.

Subsequent Developments

At the European Council meeting of Corfu in June 1994, although no specific dates for the initiation of accession negotiations were specified, the Council made a concrete commitment wherein 'the next phase of enlargement of the Union [would] involve Cyprus and Malta.'[9] The Council's position was confirmed at the European Council of Essen the following December.[10]

March 1995 marked a significant development in the relations between the EU and Cyprus; the General Affairs Council agreed on a general policy framework for the development of relations with Cyprus, involving:

- the implementing of a structured dialogue between Cyprus and the EU with a view to
- opening membership negotiations on the basis of a Commission proposal six months after the conclusion of the 1996 Intergovernmental Conference (IGC).[11]

This breakthrough in EU–Cyprus relations could be defined as the result of a deal between the EU and Greece. In return for Greece's agreement to lift its fourteen-year-long veto on the customs union with Turkey, the EU offered a more definite timetable for Cyprus' accession to the Union.[12]

In June 1995, the European Council Meeting of Cannes reaffirmed that negotiations on the accession of Cyprus and Malta to the Union would commence six months after the conclusions of IGC 96.[13]

Moreover, during the same month, a draft fourth Financial Protocol between the European Community and Cyprus was signed in Luxembourg providing for a total budget of 74 million ecu.[14] See also *EU Bulletin* 4/95, p. 65 (para 1.4.70). The Protocol provided for a total budget of 74 million ecu; 24 million ecu from the Community budget and 50 million ecu in the form of EIB loans. These funds were allocated to finance economic and social development projects with a view to Cyprus' accession to the EU and to promote a settlement of the Cypriot question.

A council decision adopted in July 1995 stipulated the detailed procedures for the structured dialogue between the EU and Cyprus. Briefly, the dialogue will take the form of an annual meeting of heads of state or government on the fringe of a European Council, and six-monthly meetings of Foreign Ministers on matters of common interest, particularly foreign policy and accession-related issues. Similar meetings will be held for justice and home affairs ministers, which could be held jointly with Malta, as well as meetings with the Permanent Representatives Committee and the K.4 Committee on Justice and Home Affairs.[15] During 1995 at least two structured dialogue meetings were held in Brussels.[16]

Accession Issues[17]

The political situation in Cyprus creates a difficult position for the EU, and there is no doubt that the division of the island is the greatest obstacle to the Cypriot application for membership. The partition also has an economic impact which takes the shape of a regional imbalance whereby the Turkish-speaking North registers a gross domestic product equivalent to a quarter of that of the Greek-speaking South. Inevitably a significant injection of EU funds into Northern Cyprus would be required if the island were to accede to the Union. On a wider European scale this would be a manageable problem. A more fundamental question relates to the practical impossibility of having both Greek-speaking and Turkish-speaking Cyprus belonging to the same single market. This is impossible to envisage in the present circumstances, particularly with regard to the free movement of people.

Beyond political and economic concerns, the relationship between Cyprus and the EU also has a security and strategic dimension. The North is supported (both politically and economically) by Turkey, a full NATO member as well as an associate member of the EU. The

South is supported by Greece, which is also a full NATO member, and a full EU member, and which maintained a fourteen-year-long veto on Turkey's customs union with the EU. The non-aligned status of Cyprus poses a question of a different kind. Although it is a major cause of the only Greek Cypriot political opposition to a closer relationship with the EU, the accession of the EFTA 'neutrals' has reduced this problem. Finally, the small size of Cyprus raises a variety of institutional concerns, which also apply to Malta and which will be taken up at greater length in the next section.

EU–MALTA RELATIONS

History[18]

Malta's relations with the Community are governed by an association agreement signed in December 1970. The association agreement provides for the creation of a customs union over two five-year stages: customs union being defined as the total elimination of obstacles to trade between the two parties and the adoption of the Community Customs Tariff by Malta.

Following the election of the Labour government in June 1971, the second stage of the customs union never got under way – mainly as a result of the Labour administration's ambivalent attitude towards the West in general and the EU in particular.[19] Thus the association agreement has remained stuck in an extended first stage since 1977. Three financial protocols have been signed since 1978, under which Malta has received a total of 93.5 million ecu in financial assistance. These funds have been used to finance infrastructure and economic cooperation projects.

When the (Christian Democrat) Nationalist Party returned to power in 1987, EU–Malta relations thawed and were able to begin to develop once more. Nevertheless, the government declined to relaunch the customs union process envisaged in the 1970 association agreement, arguing that, after this long interim period (sixteen years), accession to the Community had become the only practical objective. Meanwhile, the Labour Party's opposition to EU accession persisted.

Malta applied for EU membership in July 1990. This marked formally the end of a difficult phase in EU–Malta relations, which had begun after the election of the Labour government. The Commission opinion on Malta, as with Cyprus, appeared in 1993. The *avis* was overall positive, although no proposal for the initiation of accession negotiations was made. The *avis's* review of the situation in Malta focused on two difficulties: firstly, the opposition of the Labour Party to EU accession and, secondly, the introduction of the status of neutrality into the Maltese constitution.

In sharp contrast to the opinion on Cyprus, when examining the economic implications of Malta's membership, specific economic issues were singled out, such as the dichotomy of local industry and extremely stringent trade-protection measures.[20] Moreover, the *avis* was clear that 'a root and branch overhaul of the entire regulatory and operational framework of the Maltese economy' was necessary in order for Malta to comply with the Community's *acquis communautaire*. The discussion on Malta's participation in the EU's institutions was similar to that raised by the Cypriot application; shortage of skilled personnel and the ability to manage the presidency were seriously questioned by the Commission.

In conclusion, the Commission was '[only] willing to open accession negotiations with Malta when conditions allow', i.e. once the necessary' priority reforms are implemented and the global reform programme has been adopted'. In order to achieve this objective the Commission proposed starting an immediate 'intense dialogue with a view to establishing jointly the nature and timetable of the priority reforms needed to equip the Maltese economy to cope with international competition and to prepare the ground for integration with the Community.'[21] The Council of Ministers endorsed the Commission's opinion in October 1993; discussions began later that same month with a view to identifying the areas of the Maltese economy needing reform so that the Commission could be given the appropriate instruments to assist in this restructuring process.

Subsequent Developments

In June 1994, the European Council meeting in Corfu made a concrete commitment to include Cyprus and Malta in the next phase of enlargement, though no specific dates for the initiation of accession negotiations were given. The Council's position was reconfirmed at the European Council of Essen held the following December.

As with Cyprus, March 1995 marked a significant step forward in the development of EU–Malta relations. In fact, as a result of a report from the Commission to the Council on the implementation of economic reforms in Malta, the Council similarly decided that membership negotiations with Malta could begin on the basis of Commission proposals six months after the conclusion of the 1996 IGC, taking account of the outcome of that conference. In this report the Commission took into account the Maltese government's efforts in implementing the economic reform programme agreed with the Commission in March 1994. The Commission also noted that the programme had largely been accomplished within the agreed time limit. It viewed this as an important step towards aligning Malta's economic structures to those of the Community and stated that it would continue to monitor implementation of the reforms.[22]

In June 1995, the European Council Meeting of Cannes reaffirmed that negotiations on the accession of Cyprus and Malta to the Union would commence six months after the conclusions of IGC 96. Moreover, the same month, a draft fourth Financial Protocol between the European Community and Malta was signed in Luxembourg providing for a total budget of 45 million ecu.[23] A council decision adopted in July 1995 stipulated the detailed procedures for the structured dialogue between the EU and Malta. The terms of the dialogue are equivalent to those offered to Cyprus.[24]

Accession Issues

The primary issue raised by Malta's (and Cyprus's) application relates to the problems that arise from incorporating such a small country into the EU. For Malta, the basic question is whether it would be able to offer sufficient human resources to cope with the appropriate representation required within Community bodies. Small countries have to negotiate, agree, implement and monitor the same number of EU rules and regulations as does every other member state. Furthermore, acceptable programmes have to be worked out, monies claimed and expenditure justified.

For the EU, Malta's (and Cyprus's) accession opens up the controversial issue of the role of small states in the Union. Under the current institutional framework, this would imply an additional Commissioner and another voice in the Council (problems also posed by other applicants) as well as the prospect of EU initiatives being blocked by a country with a population of only a third of a million, either by tipping the balance during majority voting or by a veto when unanimity is required. The final question concerns whether a small country like Malta (or Cyprus) could really take its turn at running the EU Council

presidency – i.e. doubts arise on the grounds of expe
availability of administrative and technical supp
whether such a presidency would command credibil

The prospect of accession also raises the questi
neutrality, which was incorporated into its Constitution in 198
amendment which states that 'Malta is a neutral state actively pursuing peace ... by adhering to a policy of non-alignment and refusing to participate in any military alliance.'[25]

The (Christian Democrat) Nationalist Party government took the view that neutrality did not prevent Malta from aligning itself with common EU foreign policy positions; rather it relates to military neutrality and simply prohibits the use or deployment of military bases, facilities or personnel in Malta. However, the election of a Labour government at the end of 1996 fundamentally changed the situation. The Labour Party claimed that although the Cold War may have rendered the traditional concept of neutrality obsolete, the turbulent situation in the Mediterranean gave Maltese neutrality a new significance. Moreover, the Labour government was much less convinced of the economic benefits of EU membership.

However, elections in September 1998 returned a Nationalist government which immediately confirmed Malta's wish to join the EU.

EU–TURKEY RELATIONS[26]

History

Turkey signed an association agreement with the European Economic Community in September 1963. The agreement outlined a three stage process, leading to an eventual customs union, together with the progressive alignment of economic and social policies; an Association Council was to oversee this process and settle mutual disputes. In November 1970 an Additional Protocol, providing for a series of staged tariff reductions and the abolition of import quotas, was also signed. Between 1973 and 1976 both parties proceeded smoothly with the implementation of the agreement; however, as a result of the EU's decision to impose quotas on Turkish yarn and textile products, and, more seriously, Turkey's relapse into political anarchy, the implementation of the customs union was interrupted.

Despite the fact that the EU was reluctant to draw closer to a country that was without democratic government (a military regime took power from 1980), the EU ratified a 600 million ecu package of grants and loans to Turkey, the fourth Financial Protocol. This package was later frozen following the ruling military's decision to outlaw all political parties. Moreover, as a result of a Greek veto, the financial package remained frozen until March 1995.

EU–Turkey relations resumed after the re-establishment of an elected civilian government in December 1983. The new Prime Minister, Mr Turgut Ozal, was committed to the deregulation of both foreign trade and the domestic economy. The planned reduction of import duties on industrial products was restarted and a formal application for accession to the EU submitted in April 1987.

In response, the Commission prepared an official Opinion on the application. This was issued in December 1989 and endorsed by the EU Council of Ministers in February 1990. The Opinion concluded that:

> it could not recommend starting accession negotiations with any country before 1993 ... As far as Turkey is concerned, the Commission, having reviewed in depth the economic and social situation in that country, concluded that Turkey would find it hard to cope with the adjustment constraints with which it would be confronted in the medium term if it acceded to the Community. There was also the need to bear in mind certain substantial political problems ... Nevertheless, the Community wished to strengthen its relations with Turkey ... [and thus] ... it proposed a set of measures aimed at helping the country to modernise politically and economically.[27] In September 1991, a process of normalizing relations between the Community and Turkey was launched with the organization of the first Association Council meeting since 1986.

By the end of 1992, the most immediate item on the agenda was the implementation of the customs union, to which both sides repeated their commitment. For the EU, the customs union would offer improved access to Turkish markets, without raising the huge problems of free movement of labour as well as participation in the Common Agricultural Policy, the allocation of regional and structural funds and the EU's decision-making framework – rights entitled by full EU membership. For Turkey, the customs union would aid the modernization and expansion of its industry.

On the other hand, implementation of the customs union would not be an easy task, particularly for the Turkish authorities. Whilst successive Turkish governments were reducing customs duties during the 1980s, they were simultaneously increasing other charges on imports. Moreover, although Turkish industrialists now seem to be more confident of withstanding the challenges posed by EU competition, further developments are necessary. The *Financial Times* (14 December 1995) reports that '[w]ith few exceptions, Turkish companies suffer from weak management, outdated technology, poor quality, low productivity, unimaginative marketing and insufficient investment.'[28] Particular problems are the nationalized industries, or 'state economic enterprises', which, although dominating heavy industry, have a reputation for inefficiency and regularly register large losses which are shouldered by the public treasury.

Politically, the principal objection in Turkey to a customs union was mainly related to the risk that such a relationship would become permanent rather than act as a stepping stone towards eventual membership. A customs union would leave Turkey shouldering most of the burdens of accession, in the form of low tariff barriers, without the political advantages of membership.

Subsequent Developments

At the EC–Turkey Association Council meeting of 19 December 1994, most of the negotiating points on the customs union were settled, including those related to the free movement of industrial products and non-tariff barriers. Turkey would agree to adopt both the *acquis communautaire* in this area and the Community rules on competition, intellectual property, trade and the system of generalized preferences, particularly for textiles.[29]

Despite the fact that both parties had reached an agreement on most points, immediate signature was not possible due to:

- The European Parliament's (EP) concern about the human rights situation in Turkey (the Treaty of the EU requires the EP's assent for such international agreements).
- Greece's fourteen-year-long veto on the agreement.

The Association Council meeting of March 1995 marked a landmark deal. In fact, the participants reached agreement on finalizing the customs union. The parties agreed that the decision on the customs union would enter into force on 31 December 1995, with the possibility of postponement until 1 July 1996 if Turkey did not fulfil the necessary conditions by the end of the year.[30]

Politically the agreement was made possible by a compromise between the EU and Greece *vis-à-vis* the Cyprus question. 'Greece broke its stranglehold on closer economic and political ties between Ankara and the EU' in exchange for a more definite timetable for Cyprus's accession to the Union.[31] In addition, the Commission also agreed to examine the consequences of the customs union on the Greek textile industry as a result of opening its textile markets to Turkey.[32]

The customs union will, in effect, remove tariffs and establish a common external tariff for products from countries outside the region. On the other hand, some Turkish industries will remain protected from EU competition and Turkish agricultural products will not enjoy free movement into EU markets.[33] Moreover, the deal involves the transfer of 2.5 billion ecu in loans, investment and subsidies for Turkey's economic and social restructuring.[34]

The European Parliament's concern about Turkey's human rights record is particularly reflected by the publication of a number of resolutions during 1995.[35] Parliament gave its assent to the signature of the customs union between the EU and Turkey on 13 December 1995. 'After much sighing and arm-twisting,' the European Parliament voted by 343 to 149 to allow Turkey to join Europe's customs union.[36]

Accession Issues [37]

Both economic and political issues come into play when discussing the question of Turkey's accession to the Union. In the economic sphere, apart from the significant economic gap existing between EU member states and Turkey, two specific issues will hang over whatever accession negotiations are handled in the future: the EU's Common Agricultural Policy and the free movement of labour. Since Turkey is an important agricultural producer and normally registers a surplus of around 1.5 billion USD per annum[38] in its agricultural trade, Turkish accession could lead to the further growth of European crop surpluses, particularly if the current price regime continues to encourage over-production. As for the free movement of labour, art. 36 of the Additional Protocol of November 1970 stipulated that unrestricted movement would be established in progressive stages between 1976 and 1986. However, when the first of these two targets was reached in 1976, the EU limited itself to improving the free movement of Turkish workers already resident in Europe and undertook to accord priority to Turkish workers if a member state's manpower needs could not be met by other EU members. Given the current wave of xenophobia in Germany and France and the relatively high unemployment rates recorded in the EU, it seems unlikely that member states would be willing to support free movement of labour at least until the disparity between Turkish and western European wage rates is reduced.

Politically, major obstacles come into play when discussing Turkey's accession. First there are persistent disputes with Greece over offshore rights and territorial waters in the Aegean Sea, the treatment of Greek Christian and Turkish Muslim minorities in the two countries and the failure to reach a new constitutional settlement in Cyprus. Then there is Turkey's poor record in human rights, a problem constantly highlighted by the European Parliament. The main causes of complaint include the improvement of Turkey's civil rights and democratic institutions,[39] as well as abolition of art. 8 of Turkey's anti-terrorist law, which makes illegal anything that 'damages the unity of the state' and has been used to suppress demands for freer use of the Kurdish language, of regional self-government and even the peaceful espousal of Kurdish cultural rights.[40] Also see 'Turkey facing Europe', in *The Economist*, 21 October 1995, p. 20.

Another objection to Turkish membership of the EU rests on the assumption that the EU should be limited to countries with a European, or perhaps Christian, cultural and geographic identity and that Turkey does not fit into either of these categories. These arguments are probably most serious when discussing Turkey's accession, since it is impossible to know how they could be overcome, even if the economic and other political obstacles were to be eliminated.

CONCLUSION

Cyprus's and Malta's applications for membership have a tendency to be 'twinned' together by the EU. Moreover, whilst the processing of both applications has been strongly dependent on the outcome of the IGC,[41] for Cyprus the settlement of the internal political situation still remains a vital issue that will have a serious bearing on its application to join the EU.

Conversely, this could have the negative effect of slowing down the progress of Malta's application by making 'Malta's entry a hostage to Cyprus's.'[42]

Turkey's accession still remains very much dependent upon the accession issues discussed in the last section on EU–Turkey relations.

Finally, be it Turkey, Cyprus or Malta, each of the three applicant countries has to face the problems of stiff competition from the 'bigger fish of Central and Eastern Europe,'[43] as well as from current EU internal matters such as the European Monetary Union, the reform of the Common Agricultural Policy (as required by the World Trade Organization) and the reduction of high and persistent unemployment rates registered in most member states.

ANNEXES 15.1 AND 15.2

1. EU imports from the Mediterranean Countries

In 1994,Turkey was the most important Mediterranean supplier, with ecu 7.6 billion (21 per cent of total EU imports from these countries), followed by Libya and Algeria with 16 per cent each. Israel and the four Mashreq countries (Egypt, Jordan, Syria and Lebanon) together accounted for 24 per cent of EU imports from the region, while Malta and Cyprus, together represented 3.5 per cent (ecu 1.6 billion).

BY MEDITERRANEAN COUNTRIES
1994

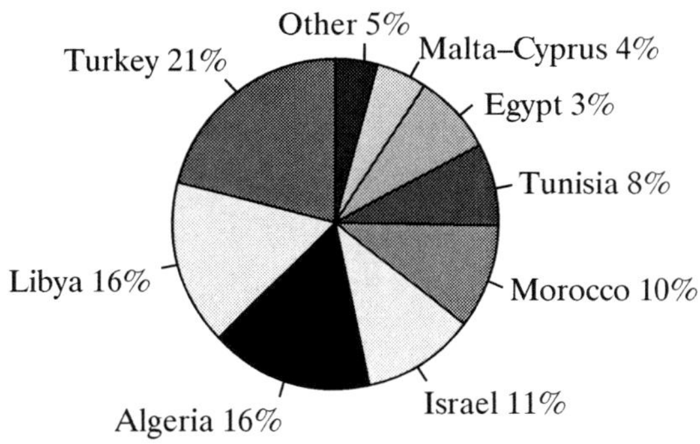

Germany and Italy were the main outlets for Mediterranean exports to the EU, each accounting for 23–24 per cent of the EU's total imports (ecu 8.5 billion) for 1994, followed by France (19 %).

BY EU COUNTRIES
1994

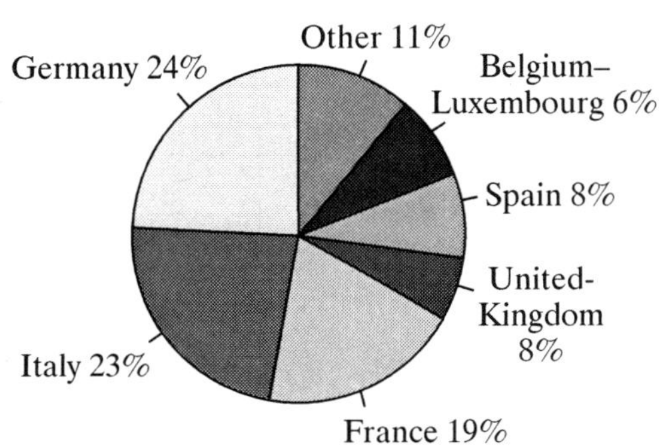

Source: Eurostat, *Statistics in Focus – External Trade*, No. 9, 1995.

2. EU exports to the Mediterranean Countries

Israel and Turkey were the two main destinations for European products in 1994, with around ecu 9 billion each (corresponding to almost 20 per cent of total EU exports to the Mediterranean). The Maghreb countries (Morocco, Algeria and Tunisia) and Libya together absorbed one third of EU sales in the Mediterranean region (ecu 14.7 billion), while Malta and Cyprus took about 4 per cent of EU exports.

BY MEDITERRANEAN COUNTRIES
1994

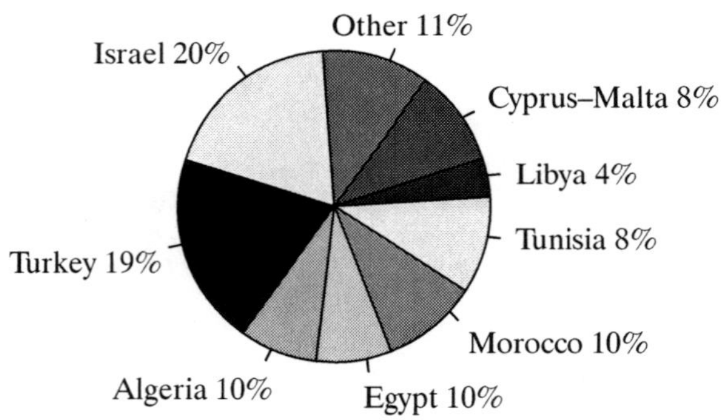

The breakdown of EU exports to the Mediterranean Basin by member state, like that of imports, is highly concentrated: 22.5 per cent of the 1994 value of EU exports to the Mediterranean countries came from Germany (ecu 10.3 billion), while France and Italy followed with 21.8 per cent and 20.5 per cent respectively.

BY EU COUNTRIES
1994

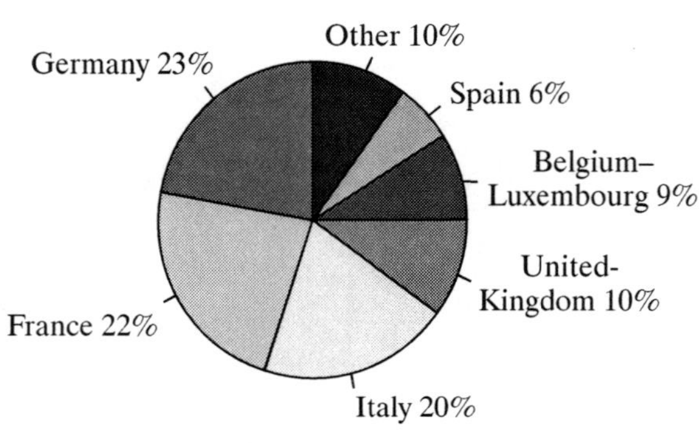

Source: Eurostat, *Statistics in Focus – External Trade*, No. 9, 1995.

Bibliography

Barber, L. and Barham, J., 'EU and Turkey Seal Customs Pact: Treaty Intended to Strengthen Ankara's Role as NATO Member', *Financial Times*, 7 March 1995, p. 4.

Barham, J., 'Prospects Open as Income Gap Closes – Customs Union with the EU May Not Eliminate the Problems of Trading with the Country but It Will Open a Potentially Lucrative Market – Turkey and the EU', *Financial Times*, 14 December 1995, p. II.

Commission of the EC, 'The challenge of enlargement, Commission opinion on Malta's application for membership', in *Bulletin of the European Communities*, Supplement 4 (1993a).

Commission of the EC, 'The challenge of enlargement – Commission opinion on the application by the Republic of Cyprus for membership', in *Bulletin of the European Communities*, Supplement 5 (1993b).

EC/EU Bulletin:
12/89, p. 88.
06/94, pp. 13–14.
12/94, pp. 26–7, 114–15.
1/2 – 95, p. 99.
03/95, pp. 71–3.
04/95, pp. 65–6.
06/95, pp. 13, 115–16.
7/8–95, pp. 85–7.
09/95, pp. 55–56.
11/95, p. 79.
Bulletin UE (French version) 12/95, p. 146.

The Economist, 1995:
'... And the Malta One'? 9 March, p. 40.
'Ciller's Killer', 23 September, p. 37.
'Full Circle', 21 October, p. 36.
'Turkey Facing Europe', 21 October, p. 20.
'Turkey – Double or Quits', 16 December, p. 32.

Eurostat, *Statistics in Focus – External Trade*, no. 9 (1995).

Hale, W., 'Turkey: A Critical but Problematic Applicant', in Redmond (1994) pp. 118–25.

Redmond, J., (ed.), *The European Initiative – Prospective Europeans, New members for the EU* (London Harvester-Wheatsheaf, 1994) ch. 6 and 7.

Reflection Group Report, *Intergovernmental Conference*, Council of the European Union Brussels (December 1995).

Southey, C., 'France makes Progress on EU–Turkey Pact', *Financial Times*, 1 March 1995, p. 4.

Southey, C. and Barham, J., 'Greeks Veto EU–Turkish Customs Deal', *Financial Times*, 10 February 1995, p. 2.

Notes

1. Redmond (1994) ch. 7.
2. Commission of the European Communities (1993) p. 13 (para. 23); the second phase was scheduled to take place between 1997 and 2002.
3. Redmond (1994) p. 135; progression to the second phase is not automatic but requires a decision from the Association Council (The Association Council is the institution provided for by the Association Agreement).
4. Ibid.
5. Commission of the European Communities (1993) p. 15 (para. 35); the economy in the northern part of the Island is closely linked to the economy of Turkey, from where it receives a substantial amount of budgetary support and which provides 40 per cent of its imports as well as being the second export market after the Community.
6. Ibid., p. 16 (paras 39–43).
7. Ibid., p. 17 (para. 48). 'The Community considers Cyprus as eligible for membership and that as soon as the prospect of a settlement is surer, the Community is ready to start the process with Cyprus that should eventually lead to accession.'
8. Ibid., pp. 17–18 (paras. 48–51).
9. *EU Bulletin* 6/94, pp. 13–14 (para. 1.11).
10. *EU Bulletin* 12/94, pp. 26–7 (para. 1.55).
11. *EU Bulletin* 3/95, p. 71 (para. 1.4.60a).
12. Barber and Barham (1995) p. 4; also Southey and Barham (1995), who report that in order to accept the EU customs deal with Turkey, Athens required concessions on four points:

    (i) a definite undertaking that negotiations on Cyprus' accession would begin six months after the completion of the EU's IGC;
    (ii) a structured procedure for accession similar to the enlargement arrangements for eastern and central European countries;
    (iii) mention of specific sums of money to be excluded from an ecu 1 billion EU financial package agreed for Turkey;
    (iv) financial assistance to help restructure Greece's textile industry.

13. *EU Bulletin* 6/95, p. 13 (para. 1.12).
14. Ibid., pp. 115–16 (paras 1.4.70–1.4.71). Also *EU Bulletin* 4/95, p. 65 (para. 1.4.70). The Protocol provided for a total budget of 74 million ecu: 24 million ecu from the Community budget and 50 million ecu in the form of EIB loans. These funds were allocated to finance economic and social development projects with a view to Cyprus' accession to the EU and to promote a settlement of the Cypriot question.
15. *EU Bulletin* 7/8–95, pp. 85–6 (paras 1.4.72).
16. *EU Bulletin* 9/95, pp. 55–6 (para. 1.4.39). Also *EU Bulletin* 11/95, p. 79 (para. 1.4.59).
17. Redmond (1994) pp. 136–7.
18. Commission of the EC (1993a).
19. Redmond, p. 138.

20. Commission of the European Communities (1993a) p. 11 (paras 25–33) on the dichotomy of Malta's industry; the great majority of Malta's industrial companies (more than 75 per cent) employ fewer than five people. Of the 2300 companies registered, under 3 per cent employ more than 100 staff and only 12 employ more than 300. The larger companies are primarily involved in electronics and textiles, whilst the smaller companies are engaged in sectors such as construction, machinery repairs, food and furniture and primarily target the domestic market.
21. Commission of the European Communities (1993a) pp. 14–15 (paras 44, 47 and 48 respectively).
22. *EU Bulletin* 3/95, p. 72 (para. 1.4.63).
23. *EU Bulletin* 4/95, pp. 65–6 (para. 1.4.71).
24. *EU Bulletin* 7/8–95, pp. 86–87 (para. 1.4.75).
25. Commission of the European Communities (1993a) p. 10 (paras 17–19).
26. Hale (1994) in Redmond ch. 6,
27. *EU Bulletin* 12/89, p. 88.
28. Barham, 14 December 1995.
29. *EU Bulletin* 12/94, pp. 114–15 (para. 1.3.62).
30. *EU Bulletin* 3/95, p. 73 (paras 1.4.65 and 1.4.66).
31. Barber and Barham (1995) p. 4.
32. *EU Bulletin* 3/95 p. 73 para. (1.4.65); Southey (1995). Also, *The Economist*, 16 December 1995. Turkish manufactured goods (excluding textiles and clothing) already enjoyed free access to the EU under the 1963 agreement.
33. Barber and Barham (1995) p. 4.
34. *The Economist*, 16 December 1995.
35. *EU Bulletin* 1/2–95, p. 99 (para. 1.4.87). *Bulletin UE* (French version) 12/95, p. 146 (para. 1.4.70).
36. *The Economist*, 16 December 1995.
37. Hale (1994).
38. Ibid., p. 119.
39. *The Economist*, 23 September 1995.
40. *The Economist*, 20 October 1995, p. 36 and p. 20.
41. Particularly those aspects concerning the participation of small states in the EU's institutional framework. Cyprus and Malta will be regularly informed of progress in the IGC discussions and will be able to express their points of view in meetings with the Presidency of the EU. This procedure has been equally offered to Central and Eastern European countries, the European Economic Area and Switzerland. The Reflection group report (December 1995) makes no mention of Turkey.
42. *The Economist*, 9 March 1995.
43. Ibid.

16 EU–Israeli Relations*

Andrzej Kosnikowski

INTRODUCTION

Relations between the European Union and Israel have for many reasons been of growing importance. The attention that has been given to the elaboration of the New Mediterranean Policy and the Union's significant involvement in the peace process in the Middle East call for reconsideration of Israel's role in the EU policy in the region.

This chapter aims at discussing the place Israel occupies and has occupied in the EU pyramid of preferences, the role of the Community's diplomacy in solving the Palestinian question, and also EU trade and aid policies targeted at Israel and the Occupied Territories. To this end political, legal and economic analyses are applied.

ISRAEL: GENERAL CHARACTERISTICS

Israel has a special place among developing countries. Indeed, it is arguable whether this term should still be used in Israel's case. Israel is a mature industrialized economy combining elements characteristic of emerging as well as developed markets. The country has a varied industrial base, a small, highly capitalized agricultural sector and a growing service sector. Foreign trade accounts already for more than 75 per cent of Israeli GDP.[1] Israel represents the second highest degree of urbanization among OECD countries after Belgium. Its per capita GDP reached 13 000 USD in 1995, on a par with that of Spain and 170 per cent of Greece's, whereas Israel's neighbours

---

Editor's note: Since this book was written, events in the Middle East have moved on. Nevertheless, this chapter offers valuable insights into the present situation.

Table 16.1 Selected economic indices 1993 – an international comparison

Country	Per capita GDP USD	GDP growth %	Inflation %	Unemployment %
Israel	**12 365**	**5.4**	**11.2**	**10.0**
Spain	12 225	1.4	4.5	17.9
Greece	7 130	0.8	14.5	9.8
Syria	2 615	8.7	11.8	7.0
Jordan	1 338	4.6	4.5	n.a.
Egypt	725	3.4	12.1	9.2

Source: Bank Hapoalim, *The Israeli Economy: Re-inventing Israel*, Tel Aviv 1995, p. 24.
n.a. = not available.

(the Mashrak countries) record much lower levels of GDP per capita, reflecting a substantial development gap between them (Table 16.1).[2]

Immigration plays and has always played an important role in Israel. When the state was founded in 1948 it had only 800 000 citizens. In 1995 the number exceeded 5 million. In the 1990s alone, the Israeli population has grown by 18 per cent, basically because of immigration from the Commonwealth of Independent States.[3]

The geopolitical situation of Israel is clearly unfavourable. Surrounded by hostile Arab states, the country has already seen more than six wars and military conflicts. So far Israel has managed to normalize relations with Egypt and Jordan, but those with Syria and especially Lebanon are far from being neighbourly and peaceful. This is why defence spending constitutes 15 per cent to 18 per cent of Israel's budget, compared with 3 per cent in the EU.[4] The country will still have to wait to take full advantage of the peace dividend in the Middle East.[5]

THE CONTRACTUAL FRAMEWORK OF EU–ISRAELI RELATIONS

There is a special character to relations between the European Union and the state of Israel and the basis for their cooperation has roots in the past. Initially four main reasons were recognized:[6]

- the Arab countries' blocking of Israel and the boycott of Israeli products in their markets;[7]
- climatic differences that did not make Israeli agricultural produce competitive in European markets;[8]
- the high standards of Israeli manufactured goods comparable to those of European industry; and
- special linkages between the Jewish people and European nations.

Israel was one of the first countries to recognize the European Economic Community and to establish diplomatic relations with the new entity. In 1958 the Israeli government had already submitted a memorandum to the Commission calling for negotiations so as to conclude a trade agreement.[9] Yet the first Trade Agreement between the EEC and Israel, based on art. 113 of the Rome Treaty, was signed only in 1964 and was non-preferential in character.[10] Tariff reductions offered to Israel were negligible, the only substantial one being that applied to grapefruit. The agreement expired in 1967 and Israel did not even ask for a renewal. The EEC kept applying the provisions of the 1964 agreement, but then they were worth even less because of the Kennedy Round of the GATT. Conclusion of a new agreement proved impossible, because as such attempts met with constant French vetoes, which had their origin in special Franco-Arab relations. It was only at the end of the 1960s that the French position softened and a new agreement with Israel became feasible.

The first preferential Trade Agreement between the EEC and Israel was signed in 1970.[11] It was concluded for a period of five years and offered a 50 per cent cut in the Community's Common External Tariff for Israeli manufactured exports and smaller tariff reductions for 'sensitive' goods and agricultural produce from Israel. The 1970 agreement also contained a negative list of items which were not subject to any tariff reductions (textiles, chemicals, glass).

Advantages offered by the EEC in 1970 were soon offset by the introduction of GSP[12] in 1971 and by the 1973 EEC enlargement.[13] Hence renegotiation of the agreement became one of the most crucial policy goals for Israel. The United Kingdom, as a member of the EEC, also advocated progress on renegotiations. Yet, concluding a new accord, already within the framework of the EEC's Global Mediterranean Policy, was deferred to 1975.

On 11 May 1975, Israel and the EEC signed a new agreement, which is still the contractual base for their relations. The agreement, based on art. 113 of the Rome Treaty, was concluded for an unlimited period.[14] According to its provisions, the Common External Tariff for Israeli manufactured goods and certain processed agricultural products was to be phased out over two years. However, quotas and other restrictions for 'sensitive' industrial imports from Israel remained in place until the end of 1979. Tariffs on agricultural exports were maintained, although 85 per cent of Israeli exports enjoyed reductions and 70 per cent of those enjoyed reductions of more than 50 per cent.

In Israel's case, tariff dismantlement was slower thanks to the asymmetry of the agreement. According to the agreement, 60 per cent of EC exports entered the Israeli market duty-free as of 1 January 1980 and the remainder, i.e. 'sensitive' goods, in 1987.[15]

The contracting parties included also an 'infant industry' clause allowing Israel to reintroduce customs duties by up to 20 per cent for manufactured goods originating from such industries but covering not more than 10 per cent of manufactured imports.[16]

The agreement envisaged technical cooperation in fields such as exchange of know-how and made it possible for Israel to participate in scientific and technological activities between the EEC and third countries. Financial cooperation was not stipulated in the accord and was included only later in the form of financial protocols.[17]

The Joint Committee was provided for in the Agreement to administer its proper implementation. In 1977 it was replaced with the Cooperation Council on the basis of the Additional Protocol to the EEC–Israel Agreement.[18] The protocol became an integral part of the 1975 agreement and extended cooperation to the following areas:

- industrialization,
- export promotion,
- achievement of agricultural complementarity,
- promotion of private investment,
- environmental issues,
- scientific cooperation.

Between 1977 and 1991 there have also been numerous amendments and protocols to the 1975 agreement.[19]

In general the agreement helped towards developing EU–Israeli relations and entailed actions aimed at fighting the Arab boycott against Israeli trade. Over time, however, it was felt that there was a need to conclude a new and more forward-looking agreement.

As a result, following a two-year period of negotiation, a new trade agreement between the European Union (EU) and Israel was signed on November 1995.[20] It was due to be ratified by the end of 1997, when it will replace the 1975 agreement still in force. The purpose of the new agreement is to provide a framework for political dialogue and to strengthen economic relations between the two parties. Based on the principle of reciprocity, it was termed a Treaty of Association. Politically, it envisages a regular dialogue at different levels; to this end, *inter alia*, the Association Council which will convene once a year at a ministerial level, was provided for.

Economically the treaty expands the parameters of the existing free trade area by updating the rules of origin, granting easier access to public and government procurement markets and simplifying terms of trade. The agreement includes possibilities for phased freedom of movement in financial services and provisions related to the right of establishment and supplying services. It also contains measures regarding competition, forbidding the creation of cartels and other associations preventing competition. It provides for free movement of capital and for protection of scientific, intellectual, industrial and commercial property. The treaty also aims at closer scientific, technical and economic cooperation.[21]

As regards agriculture, the EU and Israel will progressively establish greater trade liberalization. Five years after it came into force both parties will examine progress made and determine new measures to be applied from 1 January 2001 in view of a full free trade area in conformity with the new Mediterranean Policy.

At Israel's request, the Treaty includes new areas of cooperation in the promotion of culture, education and audio-visual production. A full section is also devoted to social issues.

A dialogue in all spheres of mutual interest will thereby be established, primarily in questions such as unemployment, equality of the sexes, working relations and professional training. Moreover, agreement was reached on social rights for Israelis within the EU. Overall, the new Treaty of Association is a very ambitious document and a great deal will depend on its full and proper implementation. It may help towards solving the problem of the constant trade deficit that Israel has witnessed since 1948.

In 1994 alone, Israeli exports to the EU totalled 4.9 billion USD, while EU imports stood at 12.7 billion USD, creating an Israeli trade deficit of 7.8 billion USD with the EU. Israel's trade deficit with the EU is larger than that with the rest of the world. It is noteworthy that, in the same year, Israel recorded a surplus of 928 million USD in trade with the USA, with which it signed a preferential trade agreement in 1985.

In recognition of Israel's progress in research and development,[22] in 1995 Israel was admitted as a full member of the EU's Fourth Framework R&D Programme. In the same year an R&D agreement between the two parties was signed, allowing Israel to take part in the Union's R&D committees (without voting privileges). It also makes it possible for Israel to participate in EU R&D tenders.

THE PALESTINIANS AND THE COMMUNITY'S DIPLOMACY

The Community's involvement with the Middle East peace process dates back already to the 1960s and 1970s, although member states have often had diverging interests in the region and hence different priorities. On the eve of the Six Day War, at the 1967 Rome Summit, the EEC failed to work out a common position. The first common declaration was possible only in 1973, in which the then EEC adopted four UN principles:

- inadmissibility of gaining territory by force;
- a need for Israel to end territorial disputes maintained since 1967;
- respect for the sovereignty, territorial integrity and independence of every state in the area; and
- the establishment of a lasting peace taking into account the legitimate rights of the Palestinians.[23]

In the wake of the Camp David peace agreement, the Venice Declaration (considered to still be the cornerstone of the EU's foreign policy in the area) was signed in June 1980.[24] The declaration is still relevant for three elements:[25]

- for the first time, the right to self-determination of the Palestinian people was explicitly stated;
- also for the first time, explicit reference was made to the 'association' of the Palestine Liberation Organization in any future peace negotiations;
- the European Community announced a more active foreign policy.

This commitment to the Middle East problem was not consistently reflected in the EEC's foreign policy, at least not for the first half of the 1980s. At that time actions were limited to supporting other initiatives: the Fahed Plan of 1981 and the Reagan Plan of 1982. The first serious involvement, although indirect, was in 1988. The European Parliament refused at that time to give the assent required for accepting three additional protocols to the 1975 EEC–Israeli agreement signed in 1987 and made it conditional on lifting Israel's barriers on Palestinian trade. Amazingly, this political conditionality did work, and trade conditions for the Occupied Territories were improved. Another step in the EEC policy in the area was signing the Madrid Declaration of 1989, which contains five elements worthy of mention.[26] The Twelve were then in favour of:

- convening an international peace conference under UN auspices;
- the participation of the PLO in the peace process;
- a negotiated solution to the conflict in which the EEC pledged to cooperate, basing the final negotiation on the principle of 'land for peace';
- elections in the Occupied Territories.

Two years later, in 1991, the Madrid International Peace Conference was convened at the initiative of the USA and the USSR. The EC was accorded only an observer status, which can be explained by its lack of a coherent foreign policy. The negotiations took place on a two-track basis. The first consisted of bilateral talks between the protagonists in the Middle East, and the EEC had no formal role in this track. The other track comprised multilateral negotiations in which the EEC took an active part. The multilateral negotiations were inaugurated in Moscow in 1992 and a framework for talks was adopted. The EC fully took part in two out of six working groups: the Arms Control and Regional Security Working Group and the Regional Economic Development Working Group in which the Community has the chair. Furthermore, the relative importance of what is now the EU has grown over time, because the Treaty on European Union was then being finalized with a chapter on the Common Foreign and Security Policy (CFSP). In 1993 the EU became a member of the newly created Ad Hoc Liaison Committee aimed at coordination of international assistance to Palestine.

The first tangible result of the Regional Economic Development Working Group was the Action Plan approved at the Copenhagen Summit in 1993, then extended at the next round of talks in Rabat. The EU itself offered Palestine 1 million ecu for nine projects in industrial development, waste management, urban planning, tourism and ecologically acceptable pesticides.[27] Within the framework of the Ad Hoc Liaison Committee, a Coordinating Committee for International Assistance to a Palestinian Police Force was formed and the EU automatically became its member. It subsequently contributed to the preparation of the Declaration of Principles signed in 1993, the Gaza–Jericho Agreement, the agreement providing for the transfer of powers, both signed in 1994, and the Interim Agreement signed in 1995. The EU was also present at the Economic Summits of Casablanca and Tangier in 1994 and 1995 for Northern Africa and the Middle East. There, the Twelve advocated opening a regional bank as a powerful agent for regional cooperation.

AID POLICIES TO ISRAEL AND THE OCCUPIED TERRITORIES

Apart from the financial protocols with Israel mentioned above, the Community granted more financial aid to Israel as well as to the Occupied Territories. The European Union is nowadays the most important donor to those countries. 1971 marked the beginning of EEC aid to Palestine; this was channelled through UNRWA, because the Palestinian population was then perceived as consisting of refugees, and thus, until 1981 assistance was limited. In 1992, this overall aid granted to the Occupied Territories totalled 550 million ecu and was targeted at education, health and food.[28]

From 1981 onwards the EEC granted direct aid to the Occupied Territories and from 1986 a gradual increase in the amount could be observed. To this end, a special line in the Community budget was envisaged. In October 1986 the Council agreed to allocate 3 million ecu of financial aid to projects for vocational training, job creation and improving the functioning of new local Palestinian institutions.[29] On the basis of this decision, the Commission released 10 million ecu in 1991. Priority was then given to farming, industrial and services sectors and institutions.[30] For the period 1990–2 a doubling of this aid was envisaged at the Strasbourg European Council in 1989.[31]

In 1991 the Council decided to grant, as part of the 'symmetrical assistance' to Israel and the Occupied Territories, 160 million ecu of a medium-term loan plus an interest rate subsidy of 27.7 million ecu to Israel and a grant of 60 million ecu for Palestine, these to be administered solely by non-governmental organizations. In 1993 the Commission adopted a Communication to the Council on 'EC support to the Middle East peace process',[32] with a 500 million ecu budget to be spent between 1994 and 1998 which was subsequently approved. The support is being used for two sets of operations, short-term ones comprised projects already under way in housing, the renovation of sewage systems, the construction of hospitals and credits for small and medium-sized enterprises, while medium and long-term operations include contributions to the creation of modern private sector and development of the economic and social infrastructure

The Community has also granted emergency aid both to the Occupied Territories and to Israel.[33]

CONCLUSIONS

The EU's New Mediterranean Policy calls for closer cooperation in the region and aims at creating a multilateral free trade area. The Treaty of Association with Israel could be a means of fully incorporating Israel. There is currently no discussion about future EU membership for Israel. The country is considered not to be European, but Cyprus is situated about 200 km away from the Israeli coast and Israel is by far the only country in the region to share European values and ideas. Moreover, Israel is an active member of the United Nations Economic Commission for Europe (based in Geneva) and in that forum works very closely with Cyprus, Malta and Turkey to promote more effective cooperation in the Mediterranean region. Will EU membership therefore really be out of the question in the future if sustained peace in the Middle East is achieved?

Bibliography

Bank Hapoalim, *The Israeli Economy: Re-inventing Israel* (Tel Aviv, 1995).

Brightman, I., 'Implications of the Agreement with the PLO for the Israeli economy', *Leumi Review,* no. 123 (1995a).

Brightman, I., *Manual for the Investor in Israel* (Bank Leumi, New York, 1995b).

Cogen, M. and François, A., 'Realizing the Right to Self-determination of the Palestinian People: the European Union and the Peaceful Settlement of the Israeli/Palestinian Conflict', in *Liber Amicorum Frans De Pauw* (Brussels, Free University of Brussels Press, 1995).

Commission of the European Communities, *Disbursement Status of the Exceptional Aid Programme for the Occupied Territories* (Brussels, 1993).

Commission of the European Communities, *Annotated Summary of Agreements Linking the Community with Non-member Countries* (Brussels, 1994).
EC Bulletin 10, [1973].
EC Bulletin 10, [1986].
EC Bulletin 10, [1986].
EC Bulletin 5, [1991].
EC Bulletin 6, [1980].
Greilsammer, I., *Israel et l'Europe* (Foundation Jean Monnet pour l'Europe, Lausanne, 1981) p. 6.
Greilsammer, I. and Weiler, J. H. H., *Europe and Israel: Troubled Neighbours* (Walter Gruyter, Berlin, 1988).
OJ, L 102/81, Second Additional Protocol to the Agreement between the European Economic Community and the State of Israel.
OJ, L 270/78, Additional Protocol to the EEC–Israel Agreement.

Notes

1. Bank Hapoalim (1995) p. 2.
2. Ibid., p. 5.
3. Brightman (1995b) p. 7.
4. Bank Hapoalim (1995) p. 2.
5. Brightman (1995a).
6. Greilsammer and Weiler (1998) p. 17.
7. This question was partially solved after signing agreements between Israel, Egypt and Jordan.
8. This has not been entirely the case since the 1981 and 1986 enlargements and since the Generalized System of Preferences (GSP) was granted to ACP countries.
9. Greilsammer (1981) p. 46.
10. Brightman (1995a).
11. Ibid.
12. Israel was not included in the list of GSP recipients. Its competitive advantages *vis-à-vis* other developing countries therefore worsened.
13. At the time, the United Kingdom was the second biggest market for Israeli exports and the UK's tariffs before the accession were lower that the CET.
14. Commission of the European Communities (1994).
15. OJ, L 102/81, p. 1. The timetable for the creation of a free trade area between Israel and the EEC was initially envisaged until 1985, but was subsequently deferred to 1987, according to the Second Additional Protocol of 1981.
16. Ibid. The timetable for phasing this provision out was originally 1988 but later was deferred to 1990.
17. Between 1977 and 1991, four financial protocols were concluded between the two parties: in 1977, 1981, 1987 and 1991. The last one expired in October 1996. They were all signed for five year periods and altogether

offered 215 million ecu of non-preferential loans from the European Investment Bank; Commission of the European Communities (1994).

18. OJ, L 270/78, p. 1.
19. Commission of the European Communities (1994).
20. SEC (95) 1719 final, *Proposal for a Decision of the Council and the Commission on the Conclusion of a Euro Mediterranean Agreement Establishing an Association Between the European Communities and their Member States on the One Part and the State of Israel on the Other Part.*
21. The primary spheres of envisaged economic cooperation are: regional and industrial cooperation, agriculture, standards, financial services, duties/customs, environment, energy, information infrastructure, tourism, correlation of laws, transportation, fighting drugs, money laundering and immigration.
22. Israel spends a relatively high percentage of its government budget on R&D (part of which is also devoted to military R&D). In the 1990s R&D spending as an Israeli budget percentage amounted to between 3.5 per cent and 4 per cent as compared with 3 per cent in Japan, the USA and Germany.
23. *EC Bulletin* EC10 [1973], point 2502, pp. 105–6.
24. *EC Bulletin* 6 [1980], point 1.1.6, pp. 10–11.
25. Cogen, M. and Francois (1995) p. 4.
26. Ibid.
27. Ibid.
28. Commission of the European Communities,(1993).
29. *EC Bulletin* 10 [1986], point 2.2.49 bis, p.76.
30. *EC Bulletin* 5 [1991] point 1.3.38, p. 67.
31. Within the three years the EEC released 33 million ecu.
32. *COM* (93) 458 final.
33. Cogen, M. and Francois (1995) p. 13.

Part 4

The Periphery – EU Cooperation with Asia and Latin America

17 EC Investment Partners Programme

Sarah Lamigeon

INTRODUCTION

The creation of the EC Investment Partners Programme (ECIP) arose from the need to promote economic and industrial dynamism in developing countries that were already benefiting from the established EC aid. An additional trade and economic cooperation scheme was set up to stimulate economy and industry by promoting Euro-South investments. This new strategy was adopted in 1988, in the context of the substitution of official assistance (which used to represent 56.4 per cent of capital flows) by private foreign direct investment flows (now representing more than 55 per cent of capital flows).

This chapter provides a global overview of this instrument used to promote the private sector, presenting the principles and mechanisms of the programme and an assessment of its implementation. It will assess the European Commission view that the success of ECIP has shown that it responds to a need of both the developing countries and of European operators and that business appreciates the decentralized character of the instrument, its scope, its flexibility and its rapidity of operation.

PRINCIPLES OF THE SCHEME

The legal basis of ECIP defines it as an instrument that was set up on an experimental basis in the framework of the appropriate trade and economic cooperation dispositions to be strengthened by the proposed following regulation.

The former framework of ECIP had EEC Regulation No 319/92 as a legal basis. The new framework has incorporated this regulation which was founded on art. 130 of the Maastricht Treaty where cooperation is the procedure in the decision-making process.

Origins and Aims of ECIP

ECIP had three general objectives:[1]

- to contribute to the development of developing countries through the creation of jobs and the transfer of risk capital and technology generated by joint ventures;
- to stimulate the private sector to improve its efficiency in the development of developing countries;
- to mobilize European public and private economic sectors.

This strategy is based on the assumption that the private sector is now a key stimulus in the development process, because ongoing liberalization of developing countries takes place and mainly aims at the creation of joint ventures, with EC support provided by four facilities, each taking place at a different stage in the creation of the joint venture.

The strategy was initially based on the promotion of joint ventures as the main financial mechanism. A joint venture is a foreign direct investment taking the form of an industrial agreement between two companies that decide to create an association of enterprises or branches in different countries to overcome protectionist attitudes.

Two sets of factors can influence joint venture decision-making. The joint venture's own profit-maximizing opportunities such as location (it is in general easier in a market economy), environment and resources (raw materials or manpower) available. The evaluation of local market conditions is thus made easier. This type of operation allows the company to conquer market shares in emerging markets such as NAFTA, ASEAN and MERCOSUR;[2] this produces a kind of fade effect and thus affects prices and other factors associated with the activities of parent firms and interdependence of profis. Costs and risks of R&D activities are also shared.

This kind of agreement is based on the principle of the mutual interest of the two partners. For developing countries, additional advantages may be drawn from the joint venture: managerial skills, training of manpower techniques, new technology are made available at lower cost for the companies of the host countries. Besides, as argued by Abel Matutes, former commissioner, in the 1990 presentation booklet: 'Developing countries that have a market economy and substantial development potential seek for joint ventures with European partners. This should stimulate foreign direct investment, encourage technology and know-how transfers and facilitate access to the European market.'[3] Additional problems may occur however as the agreement links a company in a developed country with one from a developing company. Conflicts may occur during negotiations and in the decision-making process.

HOW JOINT VENTURES CAN BENEFIT DEVELOPMENT

Foreign direct investment is usually seen as the tool for developing countries to use to integrate into the world market economy. Foreign direct investment allows countries to lighten the burden of their debt and compensate outward financial flows. As a form of foreign direct investment, joint ventures will convey these aspects but will also act as a catalyst.

Method and Procedures

Eligible Partners

ALAMEDSA countries: see the list in the Annexe (April 1995). Article 7 of the 1994 EEC regulation on ECIP states: 'Eligible countries are those that have concluded a cooperation agreement or association agreement with the Community.'

The first experimental programme addressed ALAMED, i.e. Asia, Latin America and the Mediterranean countries only. However, South Africa was included in 1994 following the conclusion of the Council of General Affairs on 19 April 1994.[4]

Examining the list of eligible countries calls for some comment. The geographical allocation seems quite balanced; nineteen Latin American countries, i.e. almost all, are eligible regardless of differences of economic development.

Nineteen Asian countries are also eligible, but Myanmar, Afghanistan and North Korea are excluded. Myanmar[5] is still experiencing a civil war and is recovering slowly following twenty-eight years of socialism. The economic reconstruction will depend on international aid. However, the state has not signed any agreement with the EU. France, the USA, Japan and Singapore are the only main investors. The non-respect of human rights seems to be one of the reasons North Korea is still not recognized internationally and Afghanistan is still in a state of war and has not signed any agreement with the EU. However, one may wonder why Bosnia and Croatia are still included. Seventeen Mediterranean and Middle East countries are involved in the scheme. Macroeconomic considerations are taken into account in selecting the countries, which explains why the scheme does not address sub-Saharan African countries.

There is thus a wide range of political and economic contexts. The evaluation of the scheme should take into account the allocation of the projects, because these different economic and political environments should affect the choice of the country where the joint venture could take place.

Small and Medium-Sized Enterprises (SMEs) as Main Targets

The ECIP scheme mainly benefits SMEs, although larger companies can also participate 'if their projects are particularly interesting for the development of the host countries.'[6] However, it strictly excludes multinationals. The Commission's presentation booklet specifies that any enterprise whose headquarters is in the EC or in an eligible country can apply for the scheme. It is also possible for two or more European enterprises to apply as long as a third of them is in one of the eligible countries. Special additional characteristics are required: five years' experience in the sector and adequate finance may also be asked for. The scheme not only addresses industrial companies; service and agricultural companies are also eligible.

J. Lebullenger[7] explains why SMEs are privileged in this programme. On the one hand, SMEs are assumed to have innovative potential, because they constantly have to adapt to market requirements to sustain competitiveness. They are also supposed to be better able to adapt their technology to local conditions, because they need to have dynamic changes in their production patterns. On the other hand, SMEs are sometimes unwilling to take risks because of their lower bargaining power on foreign markets, which is due to of their limited size and capacities. Their risk aversion being higher than multinationals', they thus need incentives and support to invest abroad. In this context joint ventures were found out to be the most effective instrument.[8]

A DECENTRALIZED APPROACH

The decentralized approach chosen at the launching of the scheme allows smoother management rules and everyday contact of the enterprises and financial institutions.

Financial institutions (FIs) have a key role because the scheme is 'managed from Brussels by the European Commission in a decentralized way through its network of ECIP financial institutions (FIs) and investment promotion agencies.'[9] The Commission insists on the following, which characterizes the ECIP: 'Its decentralized mode of operation ... emphasizes subsidiarity. They were involved in the scheme as soon as the programme was launched. They reinforce the ongoing commercial and financial viability of the projects.'[10]

Applications can only be made through these institutions for facilities 2, 3 and 4 (see below). The Commission does not thus interfere in the management of the project but has only a financial support role.

THE FINANCIAL INSTITUTIONS (FIS)

There are 55 institutions in the European Union, 21 in Asia, 22 in Latin America, 12 in the Mediterranean, 3 in South Africa and 4 are multilateral. The institutions are mainly commercial, merchant and development banks. Membership is open to any bank, subject to the approval of the Commission and committees located in the EC or eligible countries. All these financial institutions signed a Framework Agreement with the Commission. The institutions of the eligible countries are required to help local business seeking to attract foreign investors to access the ECIP through an institution close to their business place. Applicants are allowed to use any FI in the network regardless of its nationality, hence approval by an FI in one country may often involve a beneficiary from another. The Commission takes a position on each financial request on the basis of an opinion delivered by the ECIP steering committee, an interdepartmental Commission working committee.[11]

SELECTING PROJECTS

These are selected by the Commission following art. 6 of the EEC regulation[12] and four sets of criteria have to be fulfilled:

1. Feasibility: each projected investment must be viable and feasible. The quality of its promoters is also essential.
2. Contribution to development: the projected investment must contribute to development through the creation of added value, the creation of jobs in the host country and the promotion of local

entrepreneurs; i.e. it should have a large impact on the local economy. It is interesting to note that the proposal of the Commission to the Council included further details to the former art. 6. For example, more stress was given to the socio-economic impact of the projects. The consequences for women are mentioned, as well as the creation of 'local jobs in working conditions that do not imply the exploitation of employed people'. Transferring technology and know-how are also key items, because they promote further innovation and development. Another significant element is the necessity to develop employment among less favoured groups such as women. The impact on the balance of payments must be positive, because it is assumed to compensate for the lack of domestic savings. Respecting the environment is also important. Finally, producing and supplying goods which were not available or of a lower quality is necessary; it is part of a strategy which aims at substituting imports. Some of these criteria appear to be difficult to evaluate especially when one bears in mind that the effect of the benefits of the joint venture may occur within a relatively long time-span.

3. Compatibility with Community policy: some projects are thus automatically excluded, such as those that concern defence equipment and casinos.
4. Fulfilment of access requirements to each facility.

INSTRUMENTS: A RANGE OF FACILITIES ENSURING THE SCHEME'S COHERENCE

Annexe A provides an overview of the facilities offered by the scheme. The first and second facilities are supposed to prepare the field for the setting up of a joint venture, whereas the third facility finances the setting up itself. Within the first facility, conferences and seminars are organized to enable a better knowledge of the local market; it is addressed mainly to chambers of commerce or institutions representing a group of companies but not to individual companies. For example, a meeting between European, Egyptian and Maghrebian entrepreneurs was organized by a French regional chamber of commerce to examine the possibility of setting up joint ventures in agriculture. The Commission mainly emphasized facility 1 and facility 2, the objective of ECIP being to promote and prepare joint ventures. Applications for the first facility can be made directly to the

Commission by groups of enterprises or chambers of commerce. The financial institutions prefer the Commission to deal directly with this facility, because there is little scope for them to develop their relations with their clients, owing to the fact that it takes the form of a grant of up to 50 per cent of the eligible costs with a maximum amount available of 100 000 ecu.

The third facility is designed to finance the creation of joint ventures. Because only a limited number of joint ventures are actually being set up, the third facility takes the form of an equity holding or an equity loan up to 20 per cent of the incremental capital of the joint venture and must be cofinanced by the responsible financial institution. An example would be a participating loan of the Community to finance a joint venture designed for the production and conservation of asparagus exported from Peru, cofinanced by the Industrialization Fund for Developing Countries in Copenhagen.

Facility 4 aims at post-joint-venture assistance in human resources development and consists of an interest-free loan or a grant for SMEs of up to 50 per cent of the total costs of the project cofinanced by the financial institution. Until now it has been used rarely, but there has been a change in the financial conditions whereby it is allocated, which may make it more attractive to enterprises. Within this facility the elaboration of handbooks on methods of housing construction were financed in Pakistan with the participation of the Commonwealth Development Corporation of London.

Facility 1B was integrated in the scheme in the second experimental period, and concerns the preparation of privatization, or a build-operate-transfer (BOT) or a build-operate-own (BOO) scheme for private infrastructure, utilities or environmental services.

APPRAISAL AND PROSPECTS

Results of the Two Experimental Periods 1988–91 and 1992–5

The Commission accounts for 173 million ecu allocated within the framework of ECIP between 1988 and 1995 for a total of 1542 projects approved. The increase compared with the experimental period seems significant, because 9 out of 11 projects were accepted in 1988, representing 1 million ecu, compared with the 22.2 million ecu reached in 1992, when 215 out of 254 were approved. In 1995, 458 projects out of 648 were approved, representing an amount of

52 million ecu. The Commission thus asserts the success of the two experimental periods, but it is necessary to go beyond these figures to evaluate the scheme and its efficiency.

In 1996, the Kredietbank in Brussels accounted for six projects, reporting that the favourite geographical region is Asia, especially China and the Philippines, that is to say the more dynamic markets. Their clients show little interest in Latin America, which is considered too uncertain. Yet, the coordinator explains that their international network of agencies is particularly developed in Asia and not in Latin America. Until recently, they did not get any applications for South Africa. At the macro level, 44 per cent of approvals for the period 1988–95 concerned Asia (with 675 projects). South Africa had little weight, because it represented 0.23 per cent of approvals for its first year in the scheme and represented 1 per cent with 23 projects for 1995. The efficiency of these projects cannot be assessed yet because the scheme has only been in operation since 1994.

As mentioned above, the first two facilities have been emphasized by the Commission during the whole period, because they represent respectively 506 actions and 26.9 million ecu and 892 actions representing 94.4 million ecu. The second facility is the main priority, collecting 55 per cent of the total allocation. It seems to be efficient, with a multiplicative effect of 33, which means that for every ecu loaned it generates investments of 33 ecu. When the joint venture is completed, the interest-free loan must be refunded within 2 years unless the company negotiates for 3 further years. The third facility accounts for a high drop-out rate, showing that only 25 per cent of the projects were completed. Its multiplier effect is however 22, and it represents the second largest amount of money provided by the Community. Out of 52 projects approved in the period 1988–93 only 25 joint ventures were created. This facility may raise some problems for certain financial institutions. Belgium, for example, imposes additional fiscal levies on the company because of specific taxation on equity holdings and equity loans. In addition, the FI has to cofinance the projects, which represents an additional financial burden. Facility 4 is not yet well developed, but it seems efficient with an 82 per cent success rate in implementation. The independent audit by the SEMA Group for the Commission recommended that the loan should be transformed to a subsidy to become more attractive to private investors.

ECIP's main economic sectors are industrial sectors; manufacturing and construction, followed by primary processing and high tech. It seems to concentrate on the countries' comparative advantages.

The Commission has been very optimistic about the scheme, deciding to refinance it, within a new legal framework, and extending its activities with the introduction of facility 1B. The independent audit recognized that it has both an indirect (through the first two facilities) and a direct effect (through the third facility) on the development of the private sector in the eligible regions. Obstacles still remain, having been identified by both the Court of Auditors and the SEMA group.

OBSTACLES TO ECIP EFFICIENCY

The Court of Auditors provides a useful assessment of the scheme in terms of its efficiency, and an independent evaluation[13] was initiated in 1994. However, five broad sets of obstacles can be identified at the level of the institutions dealing with the setting up of the programme.

According to the Court of Auditors there are legal shortcomings linked to the place of ECIP financing in the Community budget. Anomalies seem to appear between the data given by the Commission and those given by the financial institutions. Projects abandoned were still on the list. ECIP was initially managed on the legal basis of budget lines B7-3005, B7-3015 and B7-4085. Article 5 of the ECIP Regulation specifies: 'The refunding of loans and other participations will generate renewable funds that will be held on the bank account of the Community in the Financial Institutions'.

Because of increased allocations, this would need to be placed in a special regulatory framework which was made in EEC 319/92. But it is not yet legally perfect and it is possible that art. 5(4) of the regulation infringes the budgetary principles and creates an opportunity for extra-budgetary management of Community funds.

Technical shortcomings seem to be the bigger obstacles. They occur at many levels. The form of financing does not appeal to certain clients, especially in the case of interest-free loans, because it must be refunded in case of success and the costs of the application to ECIP would not be covered by the benefit of the free interest. Delays between the signature of the contract of the FI with the Commission, the signature of the 'back-to-back' agreement with the receiver and the implementation of the joint venture do not allow an efficient evaluation of the impact on development. The difficulty in implementing certain facilities, as mentioned above, is also a problem.

The network itself also represents an obstacle. The Commission may not be selective enough when choosing its partners, because since some financial institutions are not really active, especially in Europe, and remain in the scheme to keep good relations with the Commission. The Commission has also failed to renew framework agreements with some of the FIs visited by the experts of the Court. The network also appears to be too extensive and thus difficult to manage. Since the network has been developed locally in the developing countries, the applications could tend to be made directly to the local financial institutions. It is noticeable that the more dynamic institutions are those with local agencies or correspondents in the eligible countries. It also affects the geographical preferences of the applications. When one considers facility 4, which is undertaken after creating a joint venture, it seems more likely to be implemented directly by an institution of an eligible country.

The selection of projects is also a problematic issue. A high dropout rate has been identified for certain facilities; moreover, even if the projects are achieved they might not fulfil the theoretical requirements established initially. The Court of Auditors made a sample study of 21 projects within the third facility; among them, 15 were commented on. For instance, a joint venture set up in Bolivia (date of contract 22 January 1990) disappeared at the end of the first financial year. Another illustration is a facility granted to build up an investment fund. It appeared that the local partner held only 6.9 per cent of the capital. The Commission replied that the impact on development was significant and that the application fulfilled the requirements. The question is whether the Commission wants to take a financial risk in allowing grants for projects that may not be feasible or if it wants to avoid any chance of success with projects that have an impact on the development but may not comply with the initial requirements. The Court recommended a 10 per cent threshold for participation of local partners in the capital.

Bureaucratic obstacles also seem difficult to overcome. Delays may be longer than in theory (twenty working days for each step of the procedure) between the application to ECIP, the decision of the Steering Committee, then the signature of the contract at two levels and the first allocation of funds. In the worst case the time-lap could reach fourteen months,[14] which represents a real burden for a company wishing to invest in the business as soon as possible. The financial institutions, however, recognize that in the last year of the experimental period delays have been shortened and more projects have been conducted. The money is usually given in two payments, 50 per cent on signature of the contract and the remainder when investments start. The Commission now makes a deposit of the full amount in its account in the FI, thus gaining time but leaving the responsibility of the payment to the FI. However there is a real problem in the information flow process at the level of the Commission, the FIs and the economic operators.

CURRENT ISSUES

The enlargement of the EU and its relations with Eastern and Central Europe calls into question the possible competition of ECIP with the 'Joint Venture PHARE Programme' (JOPP), which was modelled on ECIP. In general, the European banks in the ECIP network are also partners in the JOPP network. Since Eastern Europe has emergent markets that appear to be less risky and more attractive, there could be a shift in the geographical allocation of investment. According to some financial institutions, it seems that SMEs are more attracted by JOPP, which is also more appealing in terms of financial conditions (subsidies) whereas ECIP interests medium or bigger enterprises. The enlargement of the scheme in South Africa could create a possible diversion of investment flows to the detriment of eligible Mediterranean countries.

The Court of Auditors has tackled the issue of ECIP's relations with the European Investment Bank and with other European schemes for ALAMED. On the one hand, relations with the EIB and the BC-Net, which provides information about companies, are apparently useful because the ECIP unit in DG IB cooperates with the EIB, which grants loans for investment in ACP countries. The EIB has set up a new financial scheme called 'Euro Partnership' in order to facilitate the creation of joint ventures, so that some countries are eligible for several mechanisms. The question of extending ECIP to the most developed ACP states is also to be tackled, bearing in mind that they could benefit from ECIP's experience.

On the other hand, the Court argued that there might be too many financial instruments for ALAMED countries, referring particularly to the programmes ALINVEST for Latin America and MEDINVEST for Mediterranean countries, which are initiatives to connect economic cooperators to promote foreign investment. For example, Asia-Invest is a framework programme for industrial cooperation and promotion of investments encountering a set of measures and instruments in order to facilitate EU–Asia cooperation. There are three kind of initiatives, the Business Priming Fund, Asia-Enterprise and Asia-Partnership in order to cofinance business meetings, and the Asia Investment Facility to exploit investment opportunities. This programme excludes China, South Korea, Hong Kong and Macao, but closer cooperation between ECIP and these instruments is nevertheless recommended to avoid overlapping in the case of other Asian countries.

CONCLUSION

The growth in the implementation of ECIP, and in the amounts allocated, show the success of ECIP. However improvement in its management could make it more attractive. The analysis conducted by the SEMA group recommended as follows:

> While the Commission's management to date, with very limited resources has been effective ... the implementation in the future of an efficient system of information and follow-up of projects implies a total and permanent availability of management ... So it is necessary to implement an external technical assistance support service for ECIP so that the Commission can solve its management crisis.[15]

Yet, according to the manager of the scheme for a Belgian bank, the reorganization of the programme within DG IB in 1996 was accompanied by management changes in the scheme which made it more difficult for financial institutions and their partners in terms of delays.

ANNEXES 17.1 AND 17.2

1. ECIP: facilities

	Facility 1	Facility 2	Facility 3	Facility 4	Facility 1B
Type of operation	Identification of potential joint venture projects and partners	Feasibility studies or pilot projects	Joint Venture capital requirements	Training, technical or management assistance	Preparation of a privatisation or a Build Operate Transfer (BOT) or a Build Operate Own (BOO) scheme in private infrastructure, utilities or environmental services
Beneficiaries	Chambers of commerce, professional associations and ECIP Financial Institutions representing a group of companies. Individual companies may not benefit from this facility	Companies wishing to undertake a Joint Venture, a privatisation or a private infrastructure project	Joint Ventures established in the ALAMEDSA countries with locals by EU partners, or local companies which operate under a licensing and technical assistance agreement with an EU company		ALAMEDSA governments and public agencies

	Facility 1	Facility 2	Facility 3	Facility 4	Facility 1B
Type of ECIP finance	Grant of up to 50% of the eligible costs	Interest-free advance of up to 50% of the eligible costs	Equity holding or equity loan of up to 20% of the incremental capital of the joint venture	Interest-free loan for large companies, or a grant for small and medium-sized companies, of up to 50% of the eligible costs	Grant of up to 100% of the eligible costs
			The Financial Institution must cofinance the project		
Maximum amount available	100 000 ecu	250 000 ecu (within this amount 50% of pre-feasibility travel costs may be financed up to ecu 10 000)	1 000 000 ecu	250 000 ecu	200 000 ecu
Access	The beneficiary may apply directly to the EC or through an ECIP Financial Institution	The maximum total support per project is 1 000 000 ecu Application must be made through an ECIP Financial Institution			The beneficiary may apply either directly to the EC or through an ECIP Financial Institution

2. Figures on projects extracted from the 1995 Commission's, Report and 1994 Process Report

Number of projects each year

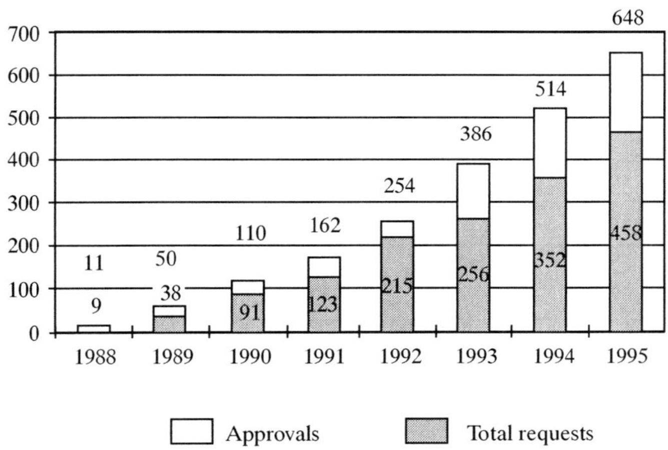

Amounts approved each year 1988–95

ecu millions

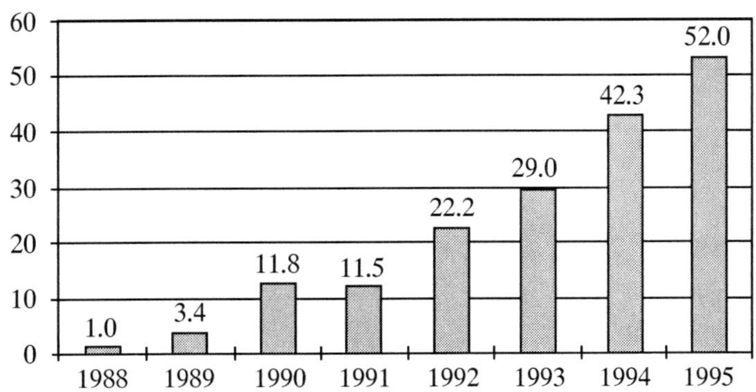

Amounts approved cumulative 1988–95

ecu millions

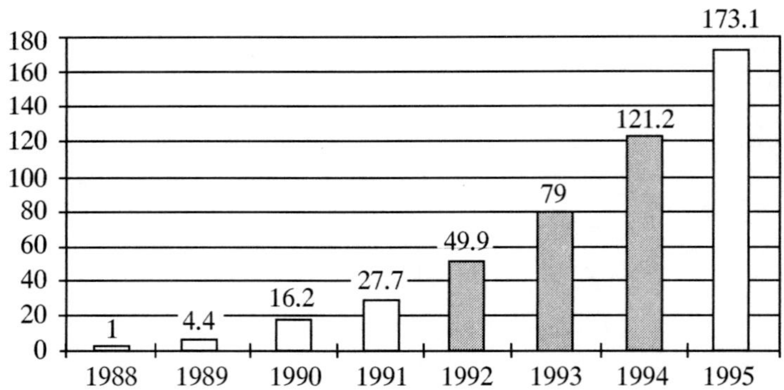

Bibliography

Bayerie, C., 'Que Sais-je?', in: *L'Investissement international* (PUF, Paris, 1993) pp. 43–60.
European Commission, Document *COM* (90) 575 Final (Brussels, 1990).
European Commission, Document *COM* (93) 200 Final (Brussels, 1993).
European Commission, Document *COM* (94) 632 Final (Brussels, 1994).
European Commission, Document *COM* (95) 603 Final (Brussels, 1995).
Court of Auditors, Report Luxemburg (1993).
ECIP, *Rapport d'activité* (Brussels, 1992).
ECIP, *Le guide de l'usager* (Brussels, 1992).
ECIP, *Progress Report* (Brussels, 1994).
ECIP, *Presentation Booklet*, European Commission (Brussels, 1995).
European Parliament, PE DOC A4-36/94, opinion of the Committee of the Budget (Luxemburg, November 1994).
Lebullenger, M. *L'Investissement international* (PUF, Paris, 1993).
SEMA Group, conclusions on ECIP, independent evaluation Brussels (1994) (not published).

Notes

1. See ECIP, *Progress Report* (Brussels, 1994) p. 2.
2. See Lebullenger (1993) p. 25.
3. ECIP *Presentation Booklet* (1995).
4. Considérant que le Conseil a conclu le 19 avril 1994 que pour encourager les investissments de l'union dans les PME d'Afrique du Sud, des avantages équivalents à l'instrument ECIP ou son instrument de suivi pouvaient être accordés à l'Afrique du Sud, et qu'un fancement spécifique de cet instrument serait assuré à cette fin, in *COM* (94) 358 Final.
5. *Le Monde*, 28 April 1995.
6. ECIP (1995).
7. Lebullenger (p. 26).
8. *COM* 94 (358) Final.
9. ECIP (1995).
10. ECIP (1995).
11. ECIP *Progress Report* (1994).
12. *COM* 94 (358) Final.
13. SEMA Group (1994).
14. Ibid.
15. SEMA (1994).

18 EU–ASEAN Relations

Mercedes Bonet

The aim of this paper is to analyze the changing relationship between the EU[1] and ASEAN in order to show its evolution from a donor–recipient relationship, following the signing of the EC–ASEAN Cooperation Agreement in 1980, up to the current intended partnership. The first section deals with introductory remarks on the history and present situation of ASEAN countries. The second section comments on the legal basis of EU–ASEAN relations. The third section is based on the different areas of cooperation between both regional groupings. Finally, the fourth section highlights future opportunities for strengthening the relationship.

ASEAN: A HETEROGENEOUS GROUPING

The Association of South-east Asian Nations (ASEAN) was established in 1967 by Indonesia, Malaysia, the Philippines, Singapore and Thailand. Brunei joined in 1984, after obtaining its independence from Great Britain, and was followed by Vietnam in 1995, and Myanmar (Burma) and Laos in 1977. ASEAN succeeded in creating stability and security in a region of high potential conflicts. It has been considered a rather successful example of regional cooperation, although the latter has been limited in the economic field. The explanation could be found in the Association's founding objectives. Originally, ASEAN[2] was designed to counteract the communist threat during the Cold War.[3] Therefore, geopolitical and security issues still play a dominant role in it, given the remaining territorial claims in the region. However, it has also been argued that the lack of readiness of these countries to participate in regional economic cooperation is due to their non-complementary productive structures and disparities in industrial performance.

Economic cooperation was considered relevant as a means to ensure stability rather than an end in itself. The ASEAN Preferential Trading Arrangement was signed in 1977 to promote intra-regional trade and investment. Nonetheless, it did not lead to the intensification of regional trade. In 1990, a common effective tariff on several industrial products was introduced, followed by the launching of the ASEAN Free Trade Area (AFTA)[4] after the fourth ASEAN Summit in Singapore in 1992. It was supported by the increasing readiness to liberalize trade within ASEAN following the area's fast economic growth and by greater regional interdependence based on the activity of foreign multinational companies (e.g. electronics or machinery manufacturers), which highly encouraged intra-industry specialization. Thus AFTA's aims were to increase ASEAN's competitive power in industrial production, to attract more foreign capital and to enhance intra-regional trade. It was triggered by ASEAN's fears that it could lose relevance at the international level because of the strengthening of economic integration in Western Europe (with the completion of the European Single Market), the establishing of the North American Free Trade Area (NAFTA) and the regionalism in Latin America. Nevertheless, it has been argued that AFTA's impact has been fairly limited up to now as regards the increase in intra-ASEAN trade.

ASEAN members have always followed a development strategy based on the maintenance of strong relations with Western industrial countries and Japan. Regardless of their common development pattern,[5] ASEAN countries, which comprise some of the world's fastest-growing economies, constitute a heterogeneous group regarding their size, resource endowments and level of development. Thus, whereas Singapore and Brunei are considered high-income countries, there are also middle-income countries like Malaysia and even low-income ones, such as the Philippines, Indonesia or Vietnam.[6] Moreover, they all present marked ethnic, political, ideological and religious discrepancies.

EU–ASEAN RELATIONS

The EU's interest in ASEAN began in 1972, after the entry of Great Britain to the EC. The latter has always tried to strengthen the EU–ASEAN relations in order to compensate those members losing their Commonwealth preferences. From the outset, relations were first established on an individual basis with ASEAN countries in the mid 1970s, and trade[7] has always been the cornerstone.[8] Additional factors contributed to trigger cooperation between both blocs. First, ASEAN directed its attention to the EU for security reasons after the withdrawal of US military forces from Indo-China. Second, the EU had economic interests in the region, namely with regard to imports of raw materials.[9]

Another reason for the EU's interest in the region can be found in ASEAN's membership in the APEC[10] (Asia–Pacific Economic Cooperation Forum), a multilateral forum through which the countries of the Pacific region cooperate to encourage regional trade and to develop key economic sectors. It is through ASEAN that the EU intends to gain access to the Asia–Pacific region. The first EU–Asia summit on 1–2 March 1996 can be considered a step forward in the EU's strategy. It provided both regions with the opportunity to confront opinions and is expected to lay the foundations for a strengthened EU–Asia relationship.

The Legal Framework

EU–ASEAN relations were established on the basis of both the 1980 EC–ASEAN Cooperation Agreement and the EC's 1992 Regulation on Financial Aid and Economic Cooperation. The former Agreement was concluded between the EC and the then five-nation ASEAN, and has been progressively enlarged to embrace new members, from both the EU and ASEAN. The objectives of the Agreement regarding commercial, economic and development cooperation were: (1) to strengthen regional organizations committed to economic growth, social progress and cultural development, (2) to develop EC–ASEAN trade and economic relations on the basis of comparative advantage and mutual benefit, (3) to contribute to the expansion of international trade and (4) to facilitate the development of the human and material resources of both parties. Concerning commercial cooperation, the reciprocal obligations taken were limited[11] to facilitate market access and consult with each other regarding the promotion of mutual trade. The Agreement included the GATT's most-favoured-nation (MFN) treatment and set up the ultimate goal of expanding and diversifying EC–ASEAN trade through cooperation rather than tariff preferences.

The economic provisions related to industrial and technical cooperation. Thus, they encouraged closer links between firms from both regions, which were to be enhanced through investment, technological and scientific progress, the opening of new markets and increasing employment opportunities. Similarly, it has also been normal practice that individual EU countries set up bilateral cooperation programmes with ASEAN, and the European Commission has complemented these programmes with those organized at the EU level. Cooperation has been intensified in such areas as science and technology, energy, environment, transport, communications and agriculture.

Regarding development aid, the EC is committed to supporting programmes in food production, rural development, education and training. The overall objective is to satisfy basic human needs and reduce economic and social disparities.

As far as the EC's 1992 regulation is concerned, it was concluded by the EC Council concerning Asian and Latin American developing countries and referred to financial and technical assistance as well as to economic cooperation.

EC's relations with ASEAN are also covered by the above-mentioned regulation. The financial and technical assistance gives priority to the development of the rural sector and the guaranteeing of food security. In the long term, it emphasizes the protection of the environment and natural resources as a basis for sustainable development. Similarly, it includes cooperation in the fight against drugs and regional cooperation in communications, research, training and energy. The economic cooperation is oriented to create an environment more favourable to investment, to take advantage of international trade and to enhance the role of businessmen, technology and know-how from the private sector. It therefore operates in such areas as the improvement of scientific and technological potential, the creation of institutions to facilitate trade and development and the support of undertakings, including human resource development.

AREAS OF COOPERATION

Development Aid

Given the different level of development between the ASEAN countries, it is obvious that the EU's cooperation needs to be oriented to the different economies; accordingly, EU development aid to ASEAN has averaged 60 million ecu since 1991. Nevertheless, rapid economic growth in the area soon contributed to turn the donor–recipient relationship into a cooperative one.[12] Development aid focuses now on Indonesia, Philippines, Vietnam and Laos.

ASEAN ECONOMIES (1995)

Brunei

0.3 million inhabitants
Land area: 577 000 hectares
GDP per capita: 10 908 USD
Exports: oil and natural gas resources (99 per cent of its exports).

Indonesia

197.5 million inhabitants
Land area: 181 157 000 hectares
GDP per capita: 720 USD
Exports: textiles and garments (16 per cent of export revenue).

Laos

4.9 million inhabitants
Land area: 23 080 000 hectares
GDP per capita: 363 USD
Exports: wood products (more than 1/3 of value of exports).

Malaysia

20.1 million inhabitants
Land area: 32 855 000 hectares
GDP per capita: 3108 USD
Exports: raw materials and manufactured products.

Myanmar

45.1 million inhabitants
Land area: 65 755 000 hectares
GDP per capita: 1372 USD
Exports: food and agricultural products.

Philippines

67.8 million inhabitants
Land area: 29 817 000 hectares
GDP per capita: 630 USD
Exports: more than 40 per cent manufactured products.

Singapore

3.3 million inhabitants
Land area: 61 000 hectares
GDP per capita: 13 451 USD
Exports: more than 80 per cent manufactured products.

Thailand

58.2 million inhabitants
Land area: 51 089 000 hectares
GDP per capita: 1843 USD
Exports: mainly manufactures and some raw materials.

Vietnam

73.8 million inhabitants
Land area: 32 549 000 hectares
GDP per capita: 816 USD
Exports: agricultural products and fuels.

The main objective is poverty alleviation, as well as the improvement in health and education; the EU has also agreed to help Vietnam, Laos, Cambodia and Myanmar in their transition from centrally planned to market-oriented economies. In 1994, the EU provided Vietnam with 30 million ecu of aid to assist the economic and social reintegration of refugees from Indo-China. Similarly, the EU and ASEAN's commitment to fight against drugs has led to the creation of a subcommittee on narcotics and the financing of ten cooperation projects by the EU.

The increase in the EU's Structural Funds in 1992 and the envisaged enlargement to the East have made ASEAN fear possible reductions in the aid they may receive in the future.[13]

Trade Relations

The most relevant feature of trade with ASEAN is the fact that the EU has continuously run a trade deficit with it since 1985 (see Figure 18.1). In 1994, the EU's trade deficit accounted for 2.2 billion ecu. Nevertheless, this is likely to be reduced in the future, as ASEAN's demand for both capital and consumer goods increases. The former will be led by the development of the economic infrastructure, while the latter will be the result of higher living standards in the region.[14] Regardless of EU's concern, ASEAN has always complained about restrictions on trade imposed by the EU, since they would prefer free access to the European market. Subhan[15] has highlighted ASEAN's concern about the introduction of Community quotas for bonito and tuna. They have also complained with regard to the duty-free entry of canned tuna from Latin American countries. In this respect, the EU has stated that these measures are only temporary. Pelkmans[16] has

Figure 18.1 EU–ASEAN trade balance

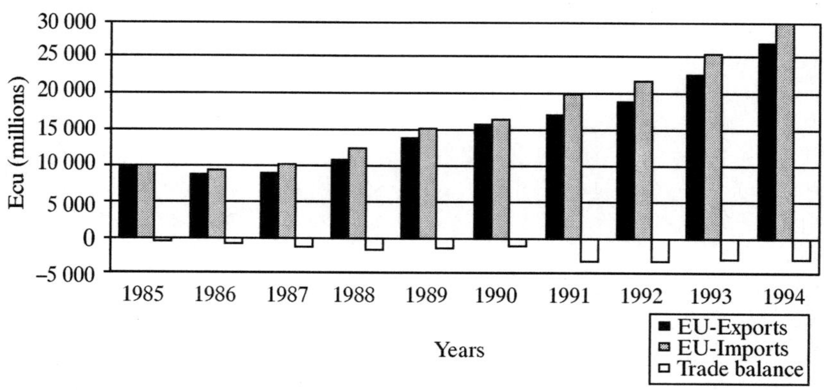

Source: OECD.

recognized that 'several trade policy issues strain the relationship of ASEAN with the Community.' He refers to the CAP, the complexity and exceptions regarding the GSP and the MFA.

ASEAN accounts only for 4.75 per cent of the EU's total exports, but the EU constitutes its third largest trading partner. In 1994 the EU's trade with ASEAN amounted to almost 58 billion ecu, the figure having quadrupled since the signing of the Cooperation Agreement in 1980. Moreover, EU trade with the region is higher than with the LDCs of the Lomé Convention.[17] After the USA, the EU is now ASEAN's second largest export market for manufacturers, which represents 75 per cent of their total exports to the EU. Though the EU's exports have always concentrated on manufactured products, ASEAN's exports have shifted from primary products, i.e. food and raw materials such as wood, rubber or palm oil, to manufactures, which include electrical and electronic products, textiles and clothing. Nonetheless, ASEAN still seems to be interested in developing its traditional trade of palm oil and wood. In 1993, imports from ASEAN represented a share of 22 per cent over the total of EU's imports of manufactures from LDCs. As far as the leading export sectors of textiles and clothing are concerned, ASEAN's products accounted for 13 per cent of the total EU imports from MFA[18] countries during the same year. However, there is a degree of anxiety in ASEAN in relation to specific restrictions imposed by the EU in this sector,[19] in which the EU has traditionally preferred to trade with the CEECs and non-EU Mediterranean countries.

In 1992 ASEAN accounted for almost 17 per cent of the EC's imports under the GSP[20] scheme. Hence, it has been argued that the scheme has contributed to the growth in ASEAN's exports to the EU. However, its impact should not be overestimated. It was only after ASEAN had shifted from exports of primary products to manufactures that it started to profit from the GSP. However, the growth of exports cannot be attributed entirely to the system, since the latter was only used up to 50 per cent of its potential in the four largest ASEAN members. First, the excessive formalities to apply for the scheme discouraged its use. Second, on many occasions ASEAN countries found more advantages under the MFN treatment. Moreover, textile exports were subject to the MFA to protect the EU industry. Here, quantitative restrictions imposed by the EU further reduced ASEAN's potential export benefits. Similarly, the latter was discriminated against in agricultural trade (cocoa, palm oil) by tariff preferences enjoyed by the ACP states, or by access to the European market being limited for products competing with European grains and feeds. Liberalization of international trade and the implementation of the Uruguay Round agreement are likely to benefit trade between the EU and ASEAN. Hence, the new GSP is bound to trigger export diversification in the region.

SCIENTIFIC AND TECHNICAL COOPERATION

The EU has been financing the transfer of both know-how and training and research activities in ASEAN. To improve ASEAN's technological potential regional technology centres are being set up, such as the ASEAN Timber Technology Centre (ATTC), the EU–ASEAN Energy Management Training and Research Centre (AEEMTRC) or the Europe–Singapore Regional Institute of Environmental Technology (RIET). ASEAN has always shown great interest in creating links between scientists and research centres from both regions. Nevertheless, the EU, which aims at establishing a partnership with ASEAN, has stated that the latter should aim at self-financing the regional centres for training and research that the EU contributes to create. There is a recent EU–ASEAN university cooperation network comprising five academic institutions from each region focused on applied research for industrial uses of new technologies. The EU also organizes sector-related technical assistance programmes regarding activities such as training in production or marketing.

Investment and Industrial Cooperation

Since it has been argued that EU–ASEAN trade and investment depend to a great extent on businessmen's and investors' initiatives, the EU has encouraged collaboration[21] through the European Community Investment Partners (ECIP) scheme and the European Business Information Centres (EBICs). To foster growth ASEAN has always favoured foreign direct investment (FDI), which has been mainly undertaken by multinationals. As a result, a relatively important share of the ASEAN's exports constitutes internal trade flows between their plants. ASEAN has not been a priority area for EU investment, although this trend has started to reverse in the last years. In 1992 European investment increased by 87 per cent, while Japanese investment grew by only 12 per cent, according to *The Economist*.[22] Japan's interest in the region was not only to exploit its comparative advantage for labour-intensive products but also to have access to raw materials and fuels.[23] Three countries, UK, the Netherlands and to a lesser extent Germany, represent 90 per cent of the total European investment. Japan and the USA, also major investors, are now being overtaken by Singapore, Taiwan and Hong Kong.

ASEAN opposed a proposal by EU Trade Commissioner Sir Leon Brittan on an international treaty to liberalize cross-border investments.[24] The region's authorities expressed their preferences for dealing with foreign investments on a bilateral basis in order to retain some discretionary power. They argued that acceptance of the proposal would be conditional upon an agreement to rule out restrictions in business activities imposed by Western multinationals.

To avoid commercial conflicts and reduce risk for EU investors in ASEAN there is a need for an effective regulatory framework as regards the protection of investment, industrial standards and intellectual property rights (IPR). In this respect, the TRIPS[25] agreement will be implemented, together with the 1993 EU–ASEAN industrial standards programme[26] relating to patents and trademarks to modernize the IPR. This is likely to contribute to improve the transfer of technology and cultural development.

FUTURE OPPORTUNITIES FOR THE DEVELOPMENT OF A REAL PARTNERSHIP

In 1978, after the first EU–ASEAN ministerial conference in Brussels, the EU, which had maintained a mainly commercial relationship with the grouping, recognized the latter's political importance for the very first time. Hence, political dialogue between the regions gained progressive importance, underpinned by ASEAN's growing interest in international affairs and EU's aim to access the Asia–Pacific region through ASEAN.

In 1993 it was proposed to strengthen the EU–ASEAN relationship on the basis of increasing equality to be developed into a real partnership.[27] Economic relations were to be enhanced and political dialogue as well as scientific and cultural exchanges intensified. An informal Eminent Persons Group (EPG)[28] was to design the way forward.

In March 1996, the first Europe–Asia meeting[29] was held in Bangkok, where the heads of state and government of ASEAN, the EU, China, Japan and South Korea met for the very first time with the final objective of creating a new partnership between Europe and Asia to contribute to the overall development of society in these regions. Prior to the summit an 'EU–Asia Forum on Culture, Values and Technology' was held in Venice in January, arranged to strengthen mutual understanding between both regions. The forum was held in the framework of the new EU strategy towards Asia, stated by the European Council in Essen in December 1994.

Both the EU and ASEAN are now going through the important process of creating strong regional groups while strengthening their external relations. The EU is laying the foundations for enlargement eastward to include CEECs. At the same time, its existing preferential relations with the southern Mediterranean countries are being enhanced. Similarly, ASEAN has also experienced an enlargement programme that first included Vietnam in 1995 and then the accession of Laos and Myanmar. In addition, ASEAN countries have expanded their trade with East Asian countries. Provided that the Chinese economy continues to grow, Chaponnière[30] has envisaged a 'virtuous circle' of growth in the region by the year 2000. Since 1994 there has been a commitment to promote the disarmament process as well as human rights and fundamental freedoms. Conflicting issues still remain, because the EU has always expressed its concern that in the ASEAN countries collective values are given priority over individual rights and economic development over civil and political rights.[31] The political conflict concerning East Timor, a former Portuguese colony annexed by Indonesia in 1975, cannot be ignored. The claim of Indonesia to the territory is not recognized by the UN, and the repeated episodes of human rights violations have been used by Portugal as an obstacle to prevent the conclusion of a third-generation agreement with ASEAN, which would substitute the 1980 Cooperation Agreement.

CONCLUSION

As has already been argued, there is a need for a wider-ranging agreement to support the intended EU–ASEAN partnership. However, political disputes will have to be solved first. The outcome in commercial and economic cooperation should be regarded with a certain degree of pessimism, since intentions to enhance market access for ASEAN exports and increase investment in the region have not sufficiently materialized. ASEAN considers Europe as being inward-looking and excessively protectionist. Likewise, the EU has always complained that the ASEAN market is too protectionist regarding services, the field in which the EU could exploit its comparative advantage. Thus, a level playing field on which real partnership can be based is still lacking.

The assessment of the evolution of trade flows has shown that Europe has been a more important market for ASEAN than vice versa. Nevertheless, considering the potential market that ASEAN represents, the EU should reconsider its position and take advantage of the possibilities offered for European SMEs. ASEAN is not only attractive on the basis of low labour costs, but also because of the increasing demand for capital and consumer goods in the region despite the financial crisis of 1997. Obviously, Europe has not yet solved the dichotomy of 'cooperation versus competition' regarding its relations with ASEAN, and continues to give with one hand and take away with the other.

Bibliography

Ariff, M., 'The Prospects for an ASEAN Free Trade Area', in Arndt, S. and Milner, C. (eds) *Global Trade Policy, The World Economy* (Blackwell, Oxford, 1995).

Cedar, S. 'The Economic Relations of China and Asia–Pacific with Europe', *Development Policy Review*, vol. 13, no. 3 (September, 1995) pp. 10–17.

Chaponnière, J., *L'Asie de l'Est et du Sud-Est à l'horizon 2020* (Paris, Les Futuribles, June 1993).

European Commission, COM(94) 314 final, *Towards a New Asia Strategy* (Brussels).

European Parliament, *Rapport sur les relations économiques et commerciales entre la Communauté Européenne et l'Association des Nations du Sud-Est Asiatique* (Luxembourg (reporter: Wisser, M.) 1992).

European Parliament, *APEC: The Asia-Pacific Economic Cooperation Forum*, in: Working Paper W-10, External Economic Relations Series (July 1995).

Fukasaku, K. *et al.* (eds), *OECD and ASEAN Economies: The Challenge of Policy Coherence* (OECD Development Centre, 1995).

Grilli, E., *The European Community and the Developing Countries* (Cambridge University Press, 1993).

Pelkmans, J., 'ASEAN and the EC – 1992', in Mayes, D. G. (ed.) *The External Implications of European Integration* (Harvester-Wheatsheaf, 1993).

Réglement Du Conseil no. 1440/80 du 30 mai 1980, *Conclusion d'un accord de coopération entre les pays de la Communauté Européenne et de l'Association des Nations du Sud-Est Asiatique* (Brussels, EU).

Subhan, M., *EU–ASEAN Relations: A Growing Partnership* (Brussels, European Commission, 1995).

Subhan, M., *EU–ASEAN Relations: The Facts* (Brussels European Commission, 1995).

Notes

1. The EU was established in 1993 with the Treaty on European Union (TEU). The cooperation agreement was legally concluded by the EC. Nevertheless, the term EU will be generally used in this chapter, even when referring to years prior to 1993.
2. The three overall objectives of the organization were:

   (i) to promote the economic, social and cultural development of the region through cooperation;
   (ii) to safeguard the region's political and economic stability;
   (iii) to serve as a forum for the resolution of intra-regional differences.

3. Ariff (1995).
4. Tariff and non-tariff barriers were to be dismantled (AFTA's original timetable called for a reduction of tariffs to between 0 and 5 per cent within 15 years and the dismantling of all NTBs among ASEAN countries within 8 years beginning on 1 January 1993. However, at the fifth meeting of the AFTA Council in 1994, the timetable was shortened to 10 years. Thus, the process should be completed by January 2003). Similarly, there was a need to harmonize the tariff nomenclature, customs valuation and standards. In addition, areas such as transport, telecommunications or banking were to be improved in order to enhance trade and investment.
5. ASEAN countries are trade-dependent market economies with a global orientation, their intra-regional trade accounting only for a fifth of their total trade. Their model of export-based industrialization allowed them to create employment opportunities and to improve their living standards. Moreover, the rapid economic growth has been coupled with rapid structural change and increasing specialization, given the different levels of development among the countries of the region.
6. To contribute to the understanding of the differences among countries, their consumption patterns could also be considered. Whereas the demand for food represents 30 per cent of consumption expenditures in Singapore or Thailand, the respective figure for Indonesia is 50 per cent.
7. There is no doubt that ASEAN, with a total population of 400 million and a GDP of more than 450 billion ecu, constitutes an important market for European goods and services. Likewise, the Single European Market with its 370 million consumers has also been considered a relevant market for ASEAN's exports, which have grown faster than to other markets since 1984.
8. Subhan (1995).
9. Grilli (1993).
10. Other members of APEC are Australia, Canada, Chile, China, Hong Kong, Japan, Korea, Mexico, New Zealand, Papua New Guinea, Taiwan and the USA.
11. Grilli (1993).
12. Subhan (1995).
13. Pelkmans (1993).

14. Subhan (1995).
15. Ibid.
16. Pelkmans (1993).
17. Subhan (1995).
18. The MFA was replaced on 1 January, 1995 by a new agreement whereby textiles and clothing are to be reintroduced into the GATT-WTO over a ten-year period. Hence, import quotas under the MFA are being ruled out and import duties reduced further in industrialized countries, while developing countries are to improve market access.
19. Pelkmans (1993).
20. The General System of Preferences came into force in 1971 and allows imports from LDCs to enter the EC at preferential tariffs or even duty-free.
21. By mid-1994 more than 150 projects were approved in the ASEAN countries under the EU scheme to foster joint ventures and other forms of collaboration.
22. *The Economist*, 2 March 1996.
23. Pelkmans (1993).
24. *Business Focus*, 18–24 April 1996.
25. Uruguay Round Agreement on Trade Related Intellectual Property Systems.
26. Thailand's Industrial Standards Institute coordinated the corresponding EU's programme for upgrading institutional capacity and testing facilities in the ASEAN countries.
27. The Communication from the European Commission to the Council in July 1994, *Towards a New Asia Strategy*, already proposed 'a partnership of equals'.
28. It comprises 19 members, nominated from both the private and public sector, 9 by the EU and 7 by ASEAN.
29. The UK has stated its intention to organize a second EU–Asia summit during the British presidency of the Council in 1998.
30. Chaponnière (1993).
31. Subhan (1995).

19 India and the EU

Joost Vandenborre

INTRODUCTION

The ties between the EU and India have been strengthened during the 1990s. On an institutional level, a 'third-generation' agreement has been concluded. Trade with India, although still of minor importance to the EU, has increased significantly, whereas the Indian trade deficit has decreased. Development aid is still a major component of the EU's activities when dealing with New Delhi. In general, the EU grants more attention to Asia, whereas India follows in the slipstream of East and South-East Asia. However, this implies that the Union considers India more and more as a potential competitor.

The importance of India on a global level simply cannot be underestimated. It is the second most populous country in the world, which will have an estimated population of more than 1 billion by the year 2000 and it is therefore the largest democracy. It is the fifth largest economy in the world after the USA, China, Japan and Germany, with an estimated gross domestic product of over 193 billion ecu.[1] However, the average annual per capita income using purchasing power parity is only 960 ecu, rather small compared with the EU average of 15 956 ecu. Needless to say, there exists a tremendous potential for growth. Hence, substantial policy changes were undertaken from 1991 onwards by the government of Narasimha Rao, aimed at making India an outward-looking market economy, which should make it possible to tackle the ever existing problem of poverty and demographic growth.

India has felt the need to review its traditional foreign policies following the collapse of the Soviet Union, the end of the Cold War and its need for international investment. However, India's military know-how and strength, its dominant position in the region and its traditional role as a leader of the Non-Aligned Movement make it inevitable that third countries listen to what New Delhi has to say.

The EU itself has changed considerably in recent years, with the completion of the internal market, the enlargement to new member states and the adoption of the Maastricht Treaty. Furthermore, the

EU finally seems to have realized that its approach towards the Asian region has been inadequate in the past and it has taken some initiative to readjust its policy in this matter. In the light of these facts it is interesting to assess the relations between the EU and India, both past and present.

INSTITUTIONAL FRAMEWORK

Neither India nor South Asia was mentioned in the Treaty of Rome. In fact, only developing countries with colonial links with EU countries were mentioned. The 'regionalistic approach' of France became the initial guideline of the EU's development policy, by which Germany in particular as well as the Netherlands had to abide. Since the United Kingdom was not a member of the early Community, it was in no position to defend the interests of its old colonies in general and India in particular – not that the Indian government itself showed a lot of attention to what happened among the Six at this initial stage.[2]

Nevertheless, India was one of the first countries to establish diplomatic relations with the EU. Until the early 1970s, Delhi's relations with Brussels were mostly dominated by the continuing influence of ties with the UK, for historical and economic reasons and because Britain had been the major trading partner since independence in 1947. The opening of a diplomatic mission was nothing more than the logical reaction of the first British application to join the Community in 1961, because India did not want to lose its preferential access to the UK market through the Commonwealth regime. The failure of the British accession negotiations in 1963 prevented the establishment of a working relationship and the possible conclusion of a general trade agreement, but it did put the country on the map. In 1964, the Commission suspended its tariff at zero level on major Indian export goods such as tea in bulk, certain spices and skins. This was followed by a bilateral trade agreement on jute and coconut fibres. Furthermore, India was granted duty-free quotas for silk, and some hand-loom fabrics and handicrafts.[3] At this stage, however, the Six were not willing to go beyond these sectoral deals.

From the early 1970s onwards, the EU pursued a more global approach. The Commission's Memorandum on Cooperation an Development Policy (1971) was already the beginning of a policy on a world-wide scale. In practical terms, it meant the introduction of the General System of Preferences (GSP). The UK accession to the EU in 1973 strengthened this tendency because London supported the economic reasons behind this new approach.

However, a complete alteration of the EU's development policy was not possible. During the negotiations prior to the UK entry, the British government tried in vain to obtain guarantees for the developing countries of the Commonwealth similar to those granted to the associated countries. This was unacceptable to the Six, and it became even clearer during the negotiations for the first Lomé Convention (1975) that London could only fully defend the interests of the Commonwealth countries of Africa (and the Caribbean and the Pacific). The Asian Commonwealth nations were left out and an attempt at appeasement was made in the form of a non-binding Joint Declaration of Intent annexed to the Treaty of Accession, which stated that the EU would try 'to extend and strengthen the trade relations' with these countries.[4] The Asian states were pushed aside because of their size. The financial implications of taking them on board would have been too great a burden to carry. But also, it was argued that, for example, India among others had already some superior manufacturing basis which could be in a competitive position with manufacturers in the Union.

Nevertheless, the British accession did set something in motion in the sense that South Asia became a bigger concern for the EU. In 1973 a five-year Commercial Cooperation Agreement was signed between India and the EU, effective from 1974.[5] This agreement set the example for similar negotiations with India's neighbouring countries and with other developing states, both in Asia and in Latin America. The agreement is of a non-preferential character, stating only economic objectives and granting each other most-favoured-nation status. A Joint Commission between officials of both parties was created in order to deal with trade issues on a regular basis. The EU's more global approach was advantageous for India. It could profit from annual agreements under the GSP for finished and semi-finished industrial products and some agricultural products. Important multi-year trade agreements were (since 1977) concluded in textiles under the Multifibre Agreement of GATT. There were also separate agreements on specific Indian export products like coir and jute. In fact, by 1980 about 70 per cent of India's exports were encompassed by one of these agreements. The EU also initiated Trade Promotion Programmes with India in 1976. Initially, they covered mainly India's participation in trade fairs, exhibitions, training programmes and exchanges of delegations. The programmes of the eighties had a much wider range.[6]

However, the Commission did realize that this somewhat complex system of trade arrangements would not be enough to deal with the poverty in India in a satisfactory way. Already, in 1970, it donated some aid through the World Food Programme (Flood I) for the development of the dairy sector, and some emergency supplies were sent for humanitarian aid. With the establishment of the EU aid programme in 1976 for non-associated countries (non-ACP countries), the EC aid to India became institutionalized and took on a more regular character.[7] The aid programme, Operation Flood II, was agreed upon in 1977 and the payments started the following year.

The 1980s and 1990s witnessed a gradual strengthening of the institutional relations between the EU and India. In 1981, a Trade and Industrial Cooperation Agreement between the EU and India was signed. This second-generation agreement prolonged the existing trade arrangements and extended the scope of possible cooperation to all economic sectors, whereby special attention was given to industrial collaboration. It also included the continuation of development aid within the broader EC aid programme for non-ACP countries. Agreements of this type are open-ended in the sense that they include a '*clause évolutive*', which provides for cooperation to be extended into new fields. The newly set up Joint Commission put a stronger focus on economic cooperation and stressed the importance of a stronger involvement of the private sector. But as Grilli points out, this agreement 'contained little beyond good intentions about technical and scientific cooperation and the transfer of technology'.[8]

Moreover, an EC Mission in New Delhi was opened in 1983 which was mainly occupied with the administration of the aid programme.[9] A further intensification started after 1987 as a consequence of internal EU desire to strengthen its external activities in general. A working group for industrial cooperation was installed and at the same time a scheme for the promotion of investments by small and medium-sized European companies in developing countries was worked out (ECIP), in which India was included.

Just as with the creation of 'second-generation' agreements, in the early 1990s more elaborate and ambitious 'third-generation' agreements needed to be concluded, which provide for an ever wider field of cooperation whereby in theory no single sector is excluded. The most recent Cooperation Agreement between the EU and India was finalized in December 1992, but it was only ratified by the EU in July 1994. Once again, it signifies the strengthening of institutional links with India. The agreement stresses the importance of enhancing contacts as equal partners, especially emphasizing the role of the private sector. Its key elements are:

- strong support for the Indian government's economic liberalization programme and structural adjustment;
- stimulation of foreign investment and cooperation in high-technology sectors;
- support for environmental protection;
- support for sustainable development and poverty alleviation (especially rural development);
- granting of MFN status[10] and non-preferential character;
- support for regional cooperation through SAARC;
- respect for human rights and democratic principles;
- the importance of political contacts (the Joint Commission was retained).

This human rights clause was especially difficult to swallow for New Delhi, which insisted that it should be given less prominence in the text (it is inserted in art. 1). The Commission made clear to the Indian government that this clause did not put any conditionality on India and that it was inserted by the EU in order to be consistent in its dealings with third countries, since such a clause figures in all new cooperation agreements. Moreover, the Commission did not want to concede, because 'third-generation' agreements are primarily symbolic, political documents that do not alter the areas in which the EU has competence to cooperate. They neither provide the other partner with more aid nor change the trade status of the partner. The overall competencies are already provided for by the EC rules governing the relations with developing countries in Asia and Latin America.[11] On the other hand, India ensured that the protection of intellectual property rights provisions were rather weak. Overall, this new agreement demonstrates the continuous and increasing interest in India by the EU, at least at the institutional level. Also, it underlines the shift in the approach of the EU towards more commercial and non-aid activities.

ECONOMIC LINKS BETWEEN TRADE AND AID

The economic links between the EU and India are characterized by two main aspects. Firstly, the EU is much more important for India as a trade partner than vice versa. This asymmetry explains the different vested interests of both partners concerning economic relations in general between them. At the same time, one has to point out the imbalance, from the European perspective, between contacts with well-established institutions and those with less developed economies. Secondly, in time the trade aspects of this relationship have become more important than development aid. On the one hand, this implies that the EU regards traditional development aid less and less as the appropriate means to alleviate poverty in India. Rather, it stresses the need for growth in the Indian economy. At the same time it considers this 'Indian tiger'[12] more and more as a potential competitor.

The last twenty years have seen a steady growth of trade between the EU and India (for example EU–India trade rose from a total value of 1.64 billion USD in 1973 to approximately 12 billion USD in 1991.[13]) Recent years have witnessed a steady increase of about 20 per cent per annum, to a figure of 13.97 billion ecu in 1994. For India, the EU is the largest trading partner, accounting for 26 per cent of its exports and 30 per cent of its imports. However, these figures need to be put into perspective. India is of only minor importance for the EU in trade matters, because only 1.29 per cent of EU external commerce is directed towards India, even less than EU trade with Singapore. Hence the difference in importance that has attached to these economic relations. New Delhi is most of the time the partner who wants to strengthen the contacts between the two. The good news for India is that the large trade deficit has had a tendency to diminish of late, mainly owing to a less accentuated growth in imports from the EU.

The EU imports are predominantly and increasingly manufactured goods (around 80 per cent). Other important items are diamonds, textiles, leather articles and carpets. EU exports are mainly manufactured goods, machines and transport material, jewellery and chemical products. The principal European markets for Indian exports are Germany (25 per cent), United Kingdom (24 per cent), Belgium–Luxembourg, Italy and France (around 11 per cent). Approximately the same figures apply for imports into India (although Belgium–Luxembourg accounts for 24 per cent of the imports, because trade in diamonds accounts for this large share).[14]

The main focus of EU activity in India has traditionally been the development aid programme. All EU reports and documents claim that India has been and is the single largest recipient of EU aid in the developing world. Since 1976, when the EU started its development cooperation with India, the country has received over 1.7 billion ecu. This accounts for about 95 per cent of the all EU funds granted to India. To this total sum one needs to add the 55 million ecu loans granted by the European Investment Bank between 1993 and 1995 for projects in the power generation sector. The EU is the second largest bilateral aid donor to India (16 per cent of total)[15] and the largest grant donor (60 per cent of grants). Around 94 per cent of this money has been spent on development cooperation, 4 per cent on humanitarian aid and 2 per cent on economic cooperation. Also, one has to mention that India has been the second largest beneficiary of the GSP after China and before Brazil. Approximately 62 per cent of its trade has been covered by this system.

In the past, development cooperation has concentrated on rural development and the aim of food self-sufficiency (the Flood programmes).[16] The EU–India cooperation strategy up to the year 2000 seems to focus on human resource development as its top priority, and the decision has been taken to fund a primary education programme (150 million ecu) that gives priority to female education; this the biggest EU-run programme of its sort.[17]

That is as far as statistics and strategies go. Some critical remarks can be made concerning EU development aid. As Grilli points out, EU development aid for developing countries has mainly been concentrated on sub-Saharan Africa. Between 1976 and 1988 this region received five times more financial aid from the Union, although South Asia is more than two and a half times larger in population. In fact, aid to India never exceeded 7 per cent of the total aid budget. So, although funds going to India were not marginal in the budgetary aid framework of the EU, they were marginal in relation to the population of the country. At the time, EU aid to India was not higher than 2 ecu per head.[18] Moreover, most EU aid is paid directly by the member states, with Germany, the UK and the Netherlands topping the list. Direct EU funding represents only about 12 per cent of EU assistance to India (1.8 per cent of the total aid), and is only at the same level as aid from the Netherlands. In addition, India has in recent years lost to the Mediterranean region and to Latin America. Analysis has shown that commercial issues have crept into the aid programme, whereby so-called ‘strategic economic ambitions’ are pursued, resulting in a kind of 'I want my money back' policy.[19] The official Indian line confirms this opinion. New Delhi is not seeking aid, although it would always be welcome. In its opinion, foreign aid does not come free. From the Indian perspective, one compromises oneself, has to agree on package deals for a kind of '*juste retour*' and, most importantly, it contributes to the detriment of one's self-respect.[20]

India has quite often complained about the increasing protectionist tendencies of the EU, and it has taken the words 'Fortress Europe' literally. In fact, the EU increasingly regards India with suspicion because it is more and more a competitor in some sectors. The EU finds itself in a rather ambiguous position towards New Delhi. It still stresses the need for development aid, and gives ever greater attention to economic cooperation and sound trading relations between equal partners, but one can nevertheless notice a harder attitude in trade matters *vis-à-vis* its partner. The emphasis is shifting towards reciprocity.

Some examples of this change of policy by the EU are that concessions, such as the preferential treatment of cane sugar exports, have been intermittent. Some anti-dumping measures have been taken against, for example, textile imports. Again, in 1987 India was not offered STABEX coverage for non-ACP countries[21] as were Bangladesh and Nepal, although it has a per capita income not much higher than these two states and lower than of a number of sub-Saharan African states. In recent years, the EU has stressed the importance of the protection of intellectual property rights. India claims it respects its obligations under the IPR regime. Moreover, this is a delicate domestic issue, because although the Indian government tried to get the IPR bill passed in parliament, the opposition (led by the Hindu right-wing nationalist BJP) voted it down. New Delhi fears though that these EU demands, as with the remarks raised concerning labour conditions (including child labour), are put forward out of protectionist interests by the European partner. But a closer look at the parliamentary questions asked by MEPs indicates that on the European side there is also democratic support for this policy.

Arrangements in the textile sector are undergoing drastic changes. Indian exports of textiles and clothing products have for a long time been subject to MFA restrictions and this is still the case. A Memorandum of Understanding was accepted[22] on 26 February 1996 providing from the EU side the removal of its tariffs on handloom and footloom-made articles. It also allowed for more flexibility in the transfer of unused quotas between products and across time. In return, India lowered its own tariffs (from 65 per cent to 20 per cent over 5 to 10 years) and will end non-tariff barriers on textiles and clothes entering the country. This should make it possible for EU manufacturers to compete in the Indian middle-class textiles markets.[23]

This agreement is somewhat different from the progressive phasing out of the MFA over a ten-year period ending in 2005. The 'integration' of textiles and clothes into the WTO started in 1995. Importers agreed on a tariff cut of 16 per cent in 1995, a further decrease of 17 per cent in 1998, 17 per cent in 2001 and the remaining 49 per cent in 2005. India (among other exporters) has been increasingly unhappy with the poor implementation record of the EU (and the USA). It hopes that the EU will change its attitude at the time of the second phase. This reluctance of Brussels can be explained by the Commission's desire to link the MFA liberalization to the opening up of markets in Asia.[24]

The Indian reply to this is straightforward, in pointing out that there is no reverse obligation and that they have already opened substantially their markets last year and are now waiting for a clear positive sign from the EU.

Indian textiles, clothes and leather exports are also potentially damaged by the revision of the GSP in 1995. These two sectors together account for almost half of the EU imports. In 1997 India will lose half of its trade concessions for these exports. In 1999 they will be permanently withdrawn. The EU defends this 'graduation out' because it considers that in this sector India is 'highly competitive'. Furthermore, the Commission points out that New Delhi will gain some benefits in a number of other market segments, as more developed countries (read NICs) are excluded. India, for its part, wants the current situation upheld and desires new agricultural products to be included. Therefore it refers to its development status and also to the EU–Turkey customs union and the loosening of trade restrictions for Russia and the CEECs, because these states have quite a number of competing export products.

One should, however, be careful not to draw too gloomy a picture of EU–India economic relations. Development aid still remains an essential element of the relationship, but in fact it is less important than before. India is being considered as a more mature partner because of its economic success (an average growth of 5 per cent the last ten years) and its huge potential for growth because of the liberalization programme. So far, though, we can only talk about a potential

'Indian tiger'. This, together with the relatively small importance of the Indian market for the EU, explains the somewhat ambiguous attitude of the Union towards Delhi in its 'New Asia Strategy'.

THE NEW ASIA STRATEGY AND THE ROLE OF INDIA

The European Commission launched its document *Towards a New Asia Strategy* in 1994 and the Council adopted it at the Essen summit in December of the same year. Its main objectives are to raise the EU's profile in Asia (and encourage mutual understanding) and to strengthen Europe's economic presence in the region. The economic rationale behind this policy explains why the Commission singled out East Asian and South-East Asian tigers[25] in particular. It also explains why only after a long internal debate South Asia and India were included. The Commission seems to have changed its opinion about South Asia under pressure from the Council, which stressed more the potential of the region and the geo-strategic importance of India.

Even so, India had a number of critical remarks to make on the strategy document, namely that it does not seem adequately to recognize the unique and close affinities (democracy, history, language) that bind the two; that the mutually beneficial nature of current and future economic cooperation and trade has not been fully reflected, nor the significance of the economic reforms programme; that India has been bracketed along with some former centrally managed economies; and that the reference to regional disputes is not comprehensive and could be misinterpreted by some countries (such as Pakistan) to further their own agendas. India's criticism that it was not consulted beforehand might also be relevant as such, except that such seems to have been the general rule.

Towards a New Asia Strategy is a document giving some general reflections and guidelines with the aim of giving a new impetus in EU–Asia relations. The day-to-day implementation has to come afterwards. Therefore, it recommends that a separate focus be given for each country of the region. A communication dealing with EU–China relations was adopted by the Commission in July 1995, and a draft proposal was put forward for a communication on enhancing partnership between the EU and India, which was expected to be adopted during mid-1996.

The EU objectives put forward in its draft proposal are not new. They are:

- to increase trade and investment (the EU share of direct foreign investment in India might have grown in absolute figures from 12.7 million ecu in 1990 to 656.4 million ecu in 1994, but in percentage terms it has decreased dramatically, from 41.4 per cent in 1990 to 18.5 per cent in 1994);
- to use India as a means to get closer to Asian markets;
- to mitigate the impact of structural adjustment;
- to multiply the impact of the European profile in India;[26]
- to promote regional stability and cooperation.

The European Commission has put forward some proposals for better cooperation in three areas: trade and economic relations, development and the human dimension, and international political relations. The Commission proposes a series of sectoral discussions with the aim of removing specific obstacles to trade. This would imply the multiplication of the number of working groups. The aims are:

- to improve trade by multilateral means (Commissioner Brittan in particular is of the opinion that further positive Indian participation in WTO is of great importance for the future relations between the two);
- to eliminate horizontal barriers to trade and investment;
- to remove sectoral barriers;
- to reinforce the liberalization and privatization process;[27]
- cooperation on business awareness, information and research (financed by Asia-Invest programmes);
- South Asia cooperation.

There is also a new approach in development aid policy. Henceforth the EU wants to focus its managed assistance much more than before by directing its support primarily into areas of the new policy framework of the Indian government. Taking into consideration the limited resources available, the EU wants to concentrate its efforts on a limited number of projects. It also wants to complement the activities of the member states, increase the participation of the private sector and encourage local participation.[28] There are four priorities for cooperation:

- the provision of basic services such as primary education and health with emphasis on gender issues;
- employment generation activities (including rural poverty alleviation);

- environmental protection;
- the human dimension (meaning the deepening of local democracy);
- tackling child labour (the EU wants to create a special working group for this purpose).

International political relations can be discussed within the political dialogue framework provided by the EU–India political statement of 20 December 1993 which accompanied the third-generation agreement. In fact there have been annual Troika meetings at ministerial level since 1986. Both sides have ensured that these meetings take place in a friendly atmosphere, that there are no real problems with setting the agenda and that discussions are frank and freely held. Topics put forward by the EU are regional security problems, the Indo-Pak relations, the Kashmir issue, Indo-China relations, the nuclear non-proliferation issue and Conventional Test Ban Treaty, the defence of human rights and democracy, drug trafficking, etc. India demands clarification on the UN reforms and the possibility of a permanent seat in the Security Council, the general direction of CFSP, the EU's policy in Bosnia and towards the Mediterranean and the CEECs. New Delhi is also in favour of strengthening the political dialogue to the level of political directors. The EU is of the opinion that the current institutional provisions, which are less extensive than with Japan, China and ASEAN but more than with Pakistan, are sufficient for the time being. The importance of these meetings has to be put in the right context. They are an interesting forum for exchanging views and addressing opinions, but because of the weak nature of the second (and third) pillar one should not overestimate their importance. There are other meeting points – the UN, bilateral contacts – that are still predominant. The openness on both sides is perhaps just a consequence of the relative negligible character of the political dialogue.

This proposed communication is deemed necessary within the Commission and Council because the possibilities offered by the Cooperation Agreement and by the New Asia Strategy are not fully being used. Also, it should be a sign that the EU considers India as important enough for a stronger involvement from the Fifteen. Why, then, was India not invited for the ASEM summit between the Asia Ten and the EU in Bangkok in March 1996? Officially, the invitations were forwarded by the ASEAN states, and therefore it is difficult to find out how much pressure European diplomacy exerted on the ASEAN to get India (and South Asia) included. What it does show is that EU interest foremost goes out to the Asian Ten. These countries are economically much more important then the South Asian states. The economic liberalization process of Rao (and a similar policy being conducted by the neighbouring states) could change this. They also seem to realize that they will need a stronger commitment to economic cooperation among themselves than what has been shown up to now. The South Asian Association for Regional Cooperation (SAARC)[29] has for years been a sleeping beauty because of the particular political problems between India and Pakistan.

But the other states also fear the possible dominance of India. Furthermore, there are economic problems, since these states are competitors for a number of exporting commodities. Nevertheless, the potential for an increase in intra-regional trade is very large.[30] In December 1995 the SAARC ministers finally signed a Preferential Trade Agreement, which should enhance the trade among their states. The EU takes a positive stand towards these evolutions, especially because the SAARC seems to be interested in strengthening the institutional links with Brussels. The Commission therefore proposed a 'Memorandum of Understanding on Administrative Cooperation', advocating an exchange of information, institutional support and training and technical assistance. Like the Communication, it still needs to be approved but it is another positive sign given by the EU.

CONCLUSION

Institutional links between the EU and India have always been well established and desired by both sides. Economic contacts, however, have always been much more important for India than for the EU. This explains the greater eagerness on the Indian side to strengthen existing ties. For the EU, there are two possible reasons to enhance its contacts with New Delhi. A stronger CFSP profile after the current would strengthen the need for deeper political contacts with the Indian government to enable the EU to discuss second-pillar matters. This is highly improbable, though. The second and real reason would be the economic boom of India. In fact it is the Indian market of middle-class customers that attracts the EU and that is and will be the drive behind stronger EU–India relations. Without this prospect, the EU's interest would be geared towards the Asia Ten. Trade is becoming increasingly more important than development cooperation, which nevertheless still accounts for the overwhelming share of EU funds going to India. However, India is more and more considered as an equal partner and potential competitor, not in a negative light but as an indication of the progress made in general by the Indian economy.

Bibliography

Asian Development Bank, *Annual Report 1994* (Hong Kong, 1995) p. 252.

Commission of the EC, *Fifteenth Annual Report on the Implementation of Financial and Technical Assistance to Asian and Latin American Developing Countries at 31 December 1991*, COM (94) 541 final, p. 31.

Commission of the EC, *Towards a New Asia Strategy*, COM (94) 314 final, p. 32.

Council of EU, *Cooperation Agreement between the European Community and the Republic of India on partnership and development*, OJ, L223/23, 27.8.94.

DAC, *Development Cooperation: 1994 Report* (OECD, Paris, 1995) p. 125.

Delegation of the Commission, *The European Community and India: Partners in Progress* (New Delhi, 1991) p. 17.

Delegation of the Commission, *The European Community and South Asia* (New Delhi, 1993).

Delegation of the Commission, *The European Union and India: A Partnership for Progress* (New Delhi, 1995) p. 28.

EISSEAS, *The Future of the GSP: Implications for the European Community's Partners in Asia* (Brussels, 1990), p. 59 (proceedings of the seminar).

EISSEAS, *Prospects for Cooperation between the European Community and the Developing Countries of Asia* (Brussels, 1991), p. 40 (proceedings of the seminar).

EISSEAS, *Regional Cooperation among Asian Countries: a Role for the European Community* (Brussels, 1992), p. 57 (proceedings of the seminar).

European Parliament, *Motion for a Resolution on Economic and Trade Relations Between the EEC and India,* PE 206.586/fin, 22 February 1994.

European Parliament, *Proposal for a Council decision concerning the conclusion of the Cooperation Agreement between the European Community and the Republic of India on partnership and development*, PE 206.586/fin (A3-0208/94).

European Parliament, *Report on the New Asia Strategy of the Commission*, PE 211.248/fin (A4-0080/95).

European Parliament, *The South Asian Association for Regional Cooperation: Its Origins, Organization and Activities*, PE 212.752, 30 March 1995.

Galtung, J., 'India and the EC Compared,' *Futures*, vol. 24, no. 9 (November 1992).

Ganguly, S., 'The prospects for SAARC,' in Malik, H., *Dilemmas of National Security and Cooperation* (Oxford University Press, New Delhi, 1993), pp. 273–91.

Grilli, E., *The European Community and the Developing Countries* (Cambridge University Press, 1993).

Knall, B. and Veit, W., 'Indo-European Cooperation: An Overview and Analysis,' *Indo-European Cooperation in an Interdependent World* (CEPS, Brussels, 1989) pp. 19–39.
Kumar, G., 'SAARC and its relationship with the European Community', in EISSEAS, *Regional Cooperation Among Asian Countries: A Role For The European Community* (Brussels, 1992) pp. 13–14.
Lall, K. B., Chopra, H. S. and Meyer, T. (eds), *India, Germany and the European Community*, (Sangam, London, 1993a).
Lall, K. B., Chopra, H. S. and Meyer, T. (eds), *European Community and SAARC* (Sangam, London, 1993b), p. 112.
OECD, *Foreign Trade by Commodities* (Paris) various issues.
Pedersen, J. D., 'India and the EC in a New World Order', *Contemporary South Asia*, 1993, vol. 2, no. 3 (1993a) pp. 265–84.
Pedersen, J. D., 'The EC and the Developing Countries: Still Partners', in Norgaard, O., Pedersen, T. and Petersen, N. (eds), *The European Community in World Politics* (Routledge, London, 1993) pp. 139–59.
Pelkmans, J. and Fukasaku, K., *Evolving Trade Links Between Europe and Asia: Towards Open Continentalism?* (OECD, Paris, 1995) p. 12.
SAARC, *Delhi Declaration* (New Delhi, 1995) p. 12.
Rizvi, G., 'South Asian Association for Regional Cooperation: Problems and Prospects,' in *EC–India Perspectives in a Changing International Order* (CEPS, Brussels, 1989) pp. 49–63 (proceedings of a seminar).
Rudner, M., 'European Community Development Assistance to Asia: Policies, Programmes and Performance,' *Modern Asian Studies*, vol. 26, no. I (February 1992) pp. 1–29.
Singh, S., 'India's Economic Reform and Regional Cooperation,' in Fukasaku, K. (ed.), *Regional Cooperation and Integration in Asia* (OECD, Paris, 1995) pp. 21–30.
Soerensen, C., *Les Relations Entre l'Union Européenne et l'Inde: Acquis et Perspectives*, Mémoire, Collège d'Europe (Bruges, 1994) p. 50.
The Economist, A Survey of India (London, January 1995) p. 30.
Vivekanandam, B., 'Britain, the EEC, and the Third World', in Lall, K. B. and Chopra, H. S., *The EEC and the Third World* (Humanities Press, London, 1981) pp. 205–15.
World Development Report, *Workers in an Integrating World* (Oxford University Press, New York, 1995) p. 251.

Notes

1. According to PPP calculations, India is 14th in straight GNP terms.
2. Knall and Veit (1989) pp. 20–6.
3. Kumar (1992) pp. 13–14.
4. Kumar (1992) p. 14.
5. Official Journal of the European Community, L 82, 27 March 1974.
6. Delegation of the Commission (1991) p. 8.
7. Pedersen (1993a) pp. 266–68.
8. Grilli (1993) p. 277.
9. Pedersen (1993a) p. 266.

10. This is a purely symbolical gesture, because both countries are members of GATT.
11. *European Report*, no. 1735 16 June 1993.
12. Perhaps one ought to talk about the 'Indian elephant' instead; this animal has more difficulty in getting itself in motion because of its size and weight but once it reaches full speed it becomes an irresistible force.
13. OECD, *Foreign Trade by Commodities*, Paris, various issues.
14. The source for all these figures is Eurostat.
15. Japan is the largest with about 20 per cent. India has become a major targeting country for the Japanese, undoubtedly for economic reasons.
16. Even the Court of Auditors believes that these programmes were successful.
17. *European Report*, no. 1984, 15 October 1994.
18. Grilli (1993) pp. 278–80 and 287–90.
19. Rudner (1992).
20. Interview between Mr Sachdeev, Counsellor of the Indian Embassy to the EU, and Joost Vandeborre 27 March 1993.
21. The official name of this scheme is Compex. It was initialled for five years but did not get renewed. Export earnings stabilization is now a part of the overall development budget for ALA countries.
22. Portugal was against because it fears the Indian competition for its own manufacturers.
23. *European Report*, no. 2111, 28 February 1996.
24. *European Voice*, 28 March 1996, p. 31.
25. The Asia 10 (ASEAN plus China, South Korea and Japan) account for an steadily increasing share of the world trade. In 1994, 20.6 per cent of all the EU's external imports came from the Asia 10 and 14.4 per cent of its external exports went to that region (source: *European Report*, no. 2116, 16 March 1996).
26. A glance at the Indian press shows how little is known of the EU.
27. The Indian government is pursuing a cautious policy concerning privatization and foreign investment (also because of BJP pressure). It stresses the concept of sovereignty – the final decision should be taken in New Delhi and not in Geneva – and it wants to find a balance between foreign and domestic investment.
28. In reality, there seems to be little co-ordination between the EU and the Member States. One EU professional in New Delhi told me that he only found out during a visit to a project that a Member State was working on the same project. He also said that there is a lot of bargaining involved between the EU and the Indian government in choosing projects. It is the Indian services who put forward a number of shortlisted projects.
29. Founded in 1985 and including Bangladesh, Bhutan, India, the Maldives, Nepal, Pakistan and Sri Lanka.
30. Only 1 per cent of Pakistan exports go to India, but there is a great deal of illegal trafficking.

20 EU–Andean Relations

Karoline Kowald

INTRODUCTION

Despite rhetoric to the contrary it seems to be clear that in the past the EC[1] did not pay great attention to its relations with Latin America, which can be regarded as the periphery of the EC's reach.[2] Other regions in the world always were and still are of much more strategic and economic interest for the Community, such as the USA, Japan or – since 1989 – the Central and Eastern European countries. Even among developing countries, the ACP countries, the Mediterranean region and the South-East Asian countries seem to be favoured over Latin America.

One reason for this is the fact that there are no historical or colonial ties between this region and the founding member states of the EC. Articles 131–6 of the Rome Treaty foresaw an association with the 'overseas countries and territories', the former colonies of the six original EC states. An improvement in European–Latin American relations was expected to be brought about by Spain's accession to the EC in 1986, but despite numerous political declarations – for example in the annexe of Spain's treaty of accession[3] – one must conclude that Spain was more concerned with its own integration into the EC than with promoting Latin American interests within the Community.[4]

Another reason why the EC neglected its relations with this region until the 1970s is the fact that Latin America was considered to be the exclusive sphere of influence of the USA, in which the EC did not want to interfere. Additionally, the geographical distance between the two regions did not make it necessary for the EU to act on a larger scale. In contrast to the Mediterranean countries, where the EU, and Spain particularly has strong strategic and geopolitical interests, there is no fear of mass immigration from Latin America into the EU that would have to be prevented by considerable direct economic aid and investment.

It was only in 1981 that official talks took place between Latin American ambassadors and the Commission. Before, there were only contacts with COREPER, which represents the EC member states, but not with the Commission, which is the organ defending the Community's interests. This so-called 'renewed dialogue' which began in 1981 was interrupted as early as 1982, when the Falklands War between Argentina and the UK broke out and the EC imposed on Argentina the most severe sanctions since its foundation in 1957 which were not lifted until the 1990s.

THE ANDEAN PACT: A LATIN AMERICAN SUBREGIONAL GROUPING

Latin America is made up of several regional groupings for economic integration, whose diversity and interdependence are quite complex and whose success and efficiency vary considerably. At present, the most promising integration grouping is MERCOSUR (Argentina, Brazil, Paraguay and Uruguay), which concluded a framework cooperation agreement with the EC in December 1995.[5]

The Andean Group, also called the Andean Pact, was founded on 26 May 1969 in Cartagena, Colombia, as a subregional grouping within LAFTA (the Latin American Free Trade Organization). The treaty founding the Andean Pact provides for the establishment of a customs union and a mechanism for political cooperation.[6] Its members are Bolivia, Colombia, Venezuela,[7] Ecuador and Peru.[8]

The fact that the Andean Pact duplicated EC institutions and did not take into account the particular problems that affected its member states was one of the reasons for the weak functioning of this integration grouping.[9] The 'Protocol of Quito' of 12 May 1987, which modified the founding treaty, was meant to overcome this crisis. But it was only in January 1992 that the Andean Pact was re-established, at first only as a free trade area (without Peru). Since May 1994 the Andean Pact has been a customs union,[10] although problems still exist between the member states, who have yet to agree on a common external customs tariff.[11] In 1996, the member states of the Andean Group negotiated bilateral free trade agreements with MERCOSUR, which formed a customs union for a number of products in 1995, in order not to be excluded from this market of 190 million consumers.[12]

In 1996, at Trujillo, Peru, the Presidents of the Andean member states agreed on fundamental institutional reforms of the Pact. Its main institutions are now the Council of Presidents, the Council of Ministers for Foreign Affairs, the Commission, the Secretary-General (JUNAC), the Court of Justice and the Andean Parliament.[13] The

Presidents also decided to give the regional grouping a legal personality and agreed on a new name: the Andean Community. Its ultimate objective is to establish a free trade area (ALCAS)[14] including all South American countries.[15]

THE POLITICAL DIALOGUE

It is striking that in its relations with Latin America the EU has always placed much more stress on the so-called 'political dialogue' than on economic cooperation; there are three main ways the EU maintains its political contacts with Latin American countries, and an overview of them is now given as far as they also concern the member states of the Andean Community.

EU Contacts with Latin America: A

The annual so-called 'San José Ministerial Conferences', held between the EC member states and certain Central American states – Costa Rica, El Salvador, Guatemala, Honduras, Nicaragua and Panama – began in San José, Costa Rica, in 1984 in support of the peace and democratization process in Central America. They are attended by a member of the EU Commission and ministerial representatives of the EC member states and of the aforementioned Central American countries, with observers from Colombia, Mexico and Venezuela.[16]

The conferences usually close with the adoption of a political declaration (on peace, human rights and democracy) as well as an economic one.[17] The declaration of the Twelfth San José Conference, in Florence in March 1996,[18] provides for a renewal of this political process.[19] Previously, in November 1995, the Commission had adopted a recommendation for a Council decision on reformulating the objectives of the San José dialogue, adding new objectives (especially more economic cooperation) and adjusting its mechanism, which needs to be redefined.[20] The EC thus responded to Central America's changed need for closer economic and commercial relations with the EC once democracy is consolidated in this region.[21] Nevertheless, the EC Member States have so far not granted Central America's demand for a broader access to the Generalized System of Preferences (GSP), nor have they agreed to increase the amount of credits given by the EIB to this region.[22]

EU Contacts with Latin America: B

The Rio Group consists of eleven countries: Chile, Mexico, Panama, the four MERCOSUR states (Argentina, Brazil, Uruguay and Paraguay) and the five Andean countries (Bolivia, Colombia, Ecuador, Peru and Venezuela). An economic and political dialogue involving the foreign ministers of these countries and of the EC member states was institutionalized in 1990; it takes place annually, alternating between the EC member states and the countries of the Rio Group. The subjects discussed concern the development of democracy in Latin America, political and economic cooperation with the EU, regional integration groupings in Latin America, the large debts of these countries, the fight against drug trafficking, terrorism, environmental protection, economic development in the region, and the impact of the EC internal market on economic relations with Latin American countries. At the third conference between the EC and the Rio Group, in Copenhagen in April 1993,[23] the then twelve member states of the EC signed the new Cooperation Agreement between the EC and the Andean Pact, which will be discussed in more detail later in this chapter.

EU Contacts with Latin America: C

There is, in addition, a variety of interparliamentary contacts between the European Parliament on the one hand and several Latin American parliaments on the other, which were created in the framework of regional groupings. In fact, the EP was the first EC institution[24] to be interested in the establishment of permanent and institutionalized contacts with Latin America.[25] Since the beginning of the 1970s the EP has focused special attention on the problems of this region, such as peace, social justice, democratization or the integration process in Latin America.[26] Above all, the EP supports the democratic component of the different regional groupings, namely the regional parliamentary bodies created within these integration zones, although they are merely consultative organs. It is in fact worth giving a brief account of the interesting and dynamic integration zones in Latin America,[27] The different regional parliaments in contact with the EP are presented in which Andean countries are involved.[28,29]

Parlatino, the Latin American Parliament

Since 1974 there have been interparliamentary conferences attended by deputies of the EP and of PARLATINO, the Latin American Parliament, which at the moment consists of the parliaments of 22 countries in this region. It was created in 1964 as the result of the 'Declaration of Lima' adopted by 160 deputies of 14 Latin American republics.[30] It defined itself as a 'democratic institution, of permanent character, representing all existing political tendencies in the Latin American countries'.[31] The conferences are held every two years, alternating between Europe and Latin America, and mainly promote an exchange of views with the aim of increasing attention on Latin America's problems.[32] Although their importance is mainly political, they support the democratic structure in this region.

Parlandino, the Andean Parliament

Since the creation of the Parliamentary Assembly of the Andean Pact in 1979, the EP has maintained contacts with PARLANDINO. Unlike the interparliamentary conferences held with PARLATINO, there has been to date no regular or institutionalized dialogue. In 1980, during the first official visit of an EP delegation, its president, Mr Klepsch, came to the Andean Parliament's seat in Bogota. In the same year, a delegation of the Andean Parliament, headed by its first president, Mr Echeverri Correa, visited the EP. Since then, several meetings between members of both parliaments have taken place. As a result of this dialogue, joint declarations were signed in 1981, 1982 and 1985. In the last, the presidents of both parliaments emphasized the importance of the first cooperation agreement between the EC and the Andean Pact countries. This had been signed in December 1983 and pointed out the new perspectives for cooperation between both regions opened up by the accession of Spain and Portugal to the EC. Unfortunately, these contacts between the EP and the Andean Parliament have become less frequent of late. Both sides admit that there is a need to modify the current dialogue as regards its frequency, its structure and its institutionalization. The new framework cooperation agreement is expected to give new impetus to contacts between the EP and PARLANDINO.

Parlamento Amazonico, the Amazonian Parliament[33]

In 1978, eight countries (Brazil, Bolivia, Colombia, Ecuador, Guyana, Peru, Surinam and Venezuela) founded the 'Amazonian Pact' (Pacto

Amazonico) based on cooperation in the field of infrastructure, which, after a period of stagnation, was relaunched at the beginning of the 1990s. The Amazonian Parliament, in Caracas, Venezuela, is concerned mainly with protection of the native populations and the environment in the Amazon region. The EP supports respect for the rights of the native populations in this area[34] and pleads for effective measures to protect the rain forest.[35] In 1991, for example, the EP severely criticized the drilling methods used by oil companies in Ecuador because of the enormous harm they do to nature and the Indian population. Yet contacts between the EP and the Amazonian Parliament are rather irregular, and no reference to any recent contacts can be found in the EP's official documents.

The regional Latin American parliaments mentioned above do not have any supranational power. As they lack any competence to adopt legislative regulations, they can only deliver opinions or give recommendations to their respective member states.[36] In order to increase the democratic legitimacy of theses parliaments, the EP particularly supports the holding of direct elections. At present, only the members of PARLACEN (the Central American Parliament) are directly elected.[37]

TRADE RELATIONS

Despite the variety of political contacts which developed during the 1980s, the EC was not willing to grant Latin American countries a level of trade preferences corresponding to its political commitment to this region. A clear sign of this was the fact that the volume of exports from Latin American countries into the EC in ecu terms has been falling since 1985.[38] One reason for this decline was the financial crisis[39] that affected Latin America in the 1980s, the so-called '*decada perdida*', the lost decade. Civil wars, especially in Central America, and dictatorial regimes, e.g. in Chile, Colombia, Peru, Argentina and Uruguay, caused an enormous economic decline throughout the whole region. Additionally the large debts of Latin American countries has disturbed the international financial markets since 1981.

The EC trade balance with Latin American countries, as well as with the Andean Community, has been negative since 1960. In 1993, however, the EC recorded a small surplus.[40] Andean countries export mainly agricultural products, raw materials and some manufactured products, whereas the EC exports machines, transport equipment and finished products. In general, the EC is the second most important trade partner of the Andean Group. Only bilateral trade with the USA is more important.[41] In 1990, 23 per cent of these countries' imports originated in the EC and about 18 per cent of the Andean exports were destined for the EC.[42] From the EC's point of view however the Andean Community is not an important trade partner. Only 1.5 per cent of the total EC imports originate from these countries and not more than 1.2 per cent of the EC exports go to the Andean Community.[43] It is also striking that the share of intra-regional trade in total Andean exports and imports is less than 10 per cent.[44]

This trade structure shows that Andean countries are not important for the EC in terms of trade, and explains why the EC has appeared to show little interest in closer economic cooperation. This may change in the future, if the Andean Community manages to catch up with the emerging markets of the South American countries integrated in MERCOSUR. These economies are strong and developed enough to enter a free trade area with the EC.

Only the GSP represents the comprehensive trade framework for EU–Latin American relations. The EC has, so far, not granted any other trade preferences to these states. This means that Latin America is situated near the bottom of the 'pyramid of trade preferences' that the EC grants to third countries. Latin American countries feel strongly discriminated against in comparison with the ACP countries, which benefit from a wide range of trade preferences within the Lomé Convention.[45] This fact is important, because Latin American and especially Andean export items are mainly agricultural products such as flowers, coffee, cocoa, bananas and meat, fishery products, and raw materials such as mining products, wood and petroleum. All these have to compete with ACP exports to the EC market. The GSP granted to Latin America favours only 15 per cent of its total exports to the EC, and excludes in principle all sensitive agricultural products. Moreover, the EU has established specific tariff quotas and tariff ceilings for individual GSP beneficiaries, as well as administrative constraints such as strict rules of origin and shipping requirements, which have continued to limit the number of items covered by the GSP. Furthermore, the GSP system does not eliminate non-tariff barriers, which are represented mainly by administrative obstacles such as the absence of mutual recognition and the lack of harmonization of standards.

As regards the highly political debate over the EC import regime for 'dollar bananas' from Latin American countries, a framework agreement[46] between the EC and Nicaragua, Costa Rica, Venezuela and Colombia was concluded in order to settle the conflict that had arisen within the GATT. This framework agreement is part of the results of the Uruguay Round. It grants to those Latin American countries a fixed proportion of the quota which the contested Common Market Organization on bananas[47] provides for third-country bananas. The agreement also allows these Latin American producing countries to acquire export licences in order to limit the market power of US multinationals.[48] In addition, the quota for third countries was increased from 2.0 to 2.2 million tonnes per year and the customs tariff was reduced from 100 to 75 ecu per tonne. In 1996, Ecuador, the USA, Guatemala, Honduras and Mexico requested a further GATT panel on the EC import regime for bananas. The EC proposed negotiating a compromise with Ecuador, which was not included in this framework agreement. A final settlement of the banana dispute had not been reached by December 1998.

Statistics show that Andean as well as Latin American countries in general do not make use of all the trade preferences available under the GSP to the same extent as ASEAN countries or China. Only 11 per cent of the total exports from Latin America entering the EC benefit from the GSP;[49] they are only 50 per cent of the products to which the GSP would apply. This suggests that there is a need to simplify access to GSP and to provide Andean exporters with more information on the possibilities offered under the GSP. Another reason why Andean countries make little use of the GSP is the fact that agricultural products that are subject to a Common Market Organization within the EC, such as beef, are not included in the GSP. More processed products need to be exported in order to diversify the range of export products of these countries.

From 1975, the Community allowed regional cumulation of origin for the products of three regional groups, namely ASEAN, the Central American Common Market (CACM) and the Andean Pact,[50] in order to support integration efforts by these developing States. The special rules did allow for general tolerance of non-originating materials, if their value was under 5 per cent of the ex-works price.[51] However, the rules of qualification for regional cumulation were so strict that the CACM has never met them, while ASEAN and the Andean Pact qualified only in 1989 and 1992, respectively.[52]

To assist in the fight against drugs in Bolivia, Ecuador, Colombia and Peru, the Community also decided to drop all tariff quotas and ceilings on all GSP eligible Andean Pact (but not Venezuelan) exports for a period of four years (1991–4), which was later extended to June 1996.[53]

TRADE AND COOPERATION AGREEMENTS

In the 1970s the EC concluded bilateral trade agreements with the countries of the Andean Pact. These first-generation agreements covered specific sectors and were non-preferential; the parties granted each other only the most-favoured-nation treatment that they already had according to art. I of the GATT. The EC, for example, concluded agreements on textiles with Colombia and Peru and agreements on the trade in handicraft products with Bolivia, Ecuador and Peru. Their legal basis was art. 113 of the Rome Treaty.

These first-generation agreements did not really favour the Andean countries, because they were restricted to one small trade sector, and in 1983 they were replaced by a second-generation agreement, which by establishing a joint committee provided a legal basis for broader cooperation in trade, development aid and political contacts.[54] This was a multilateral cooperation agreement between the EC and the Andean Pact and as such the first agreement the EC had concluded with a subregional grouping. This kind of agreement, which was based on arts 113 and 235 of the Rome Treaty, strengthened the integration process and gave the Andean countries as a group more negotiating power *vis-à-vis* the EC.

In 1993 the EC signed a third-generation agreement, giving a new framework for cooperation.[55] An essential part of this is a clause obliging respect for democratic principles and human rights and allowing the EC to suspend the agreement if these rights are violated.[56] The agreement provides for new fields of cooperation, such as environmental protection, tourism and intellectual property rights. The so-called evolutionary clause allows for a tacit renewal of the agreement, which was concluded initially for five years.[57]

The 1993 agreement establishes only a framework, setting up the objectives and fields of cooperation. It provides for the creation of a Joint Committee (consisting of representatives of the EC member states, the Andean countries and the Commission) to decide on the field of cooperation to which priority is to be given. Projects are then to be presented by the Commission or the countries of the Andean Community. These projects concern social development, health, education, the improvement in the situation of women, the development of rural areas, etc. Between 1990 and 1993 the EC spent 429.2 million on development cooperation with the countries of the Andean Community.[58] Among Latin American countries only Central America received more development aid from the EC.

Special emphasis is put on coordinated measures combating drug production, trafficking and abuse. In 1995 the European Community and the countries of the Andean Community signed agreements on the control of drug precursors.[59] At its meeting with the Rio Group in Cochabamba, Bolivia, in 1996, the EU supported a strategy 'based on the principle of shared responsibility and the need for alternative development'.[60]

CONCLUSION

In the past there has been criticism that the volume of trade between the EC and the Andean countries did not increase within the cooperation agreement and that the same degree and kind of cooperation could have been reached without such a legal instrument, because a considerable part of cooperation, such as food aid, emergency aid, financial and technical assistance, is not based on the agreement. Yet the bilateral character of the agreement gives the countries of the Andean Community the possibility of participating in many decisions regarding the fields of cooperation. Additionally, the political and symbolic importance of such agreements should not be underestimated. Nevertheless, the cooperation procedure needs to be strengthened, for example by introducing qualified majority voting instead of a unanimous decision-making procedure within the joint committee. Future development will depend on the Andean Community's capacity to move closer to MERCOSUR in political and economic terms. However, this requires the settlement of the many of social and political conflicts that still exist within and even between the member states, as was shown by the border conflict which broke out between Ecuador and Peru in December 1994.

ANNEXE 20.1 TRADE: EU AND LATIN AMERICA (**in billions of ecu**)

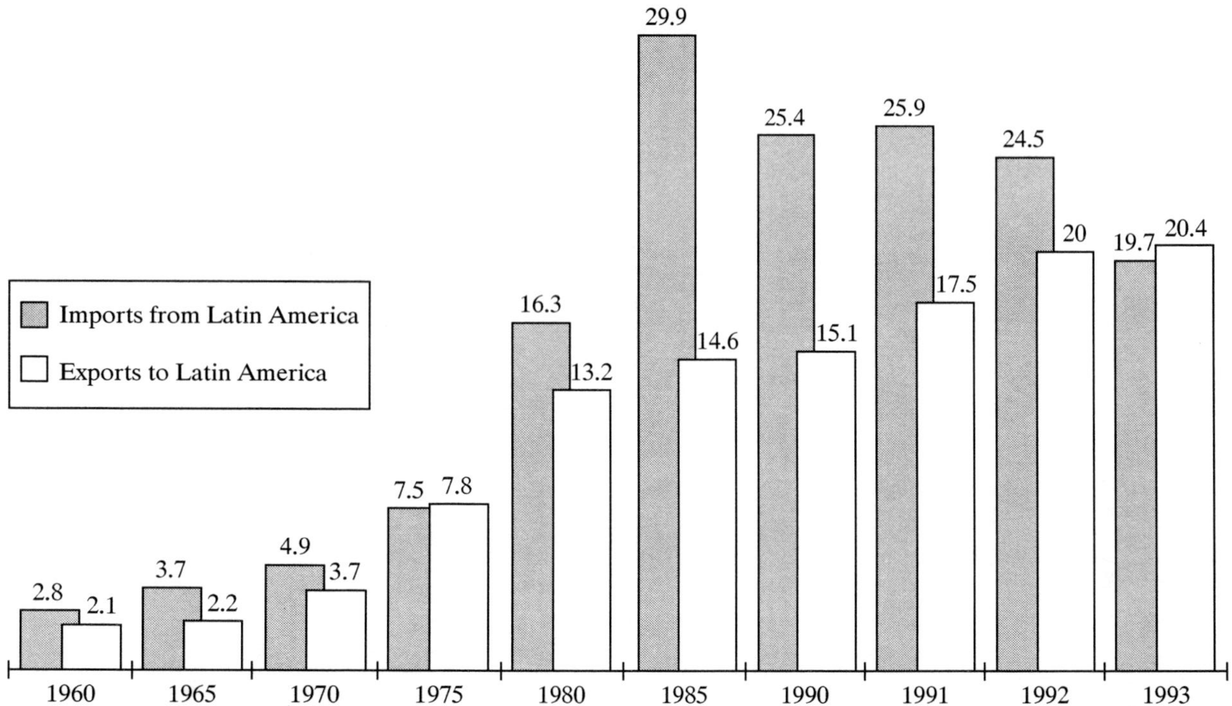

Source: Eurostat, published in *COM* (95) 495 final.

ANNEXE 20.2 TRADE BETWEEN THE EU AND LATIN AMERICA

DESTINATION OF LATIN AMERICAN EXPORTS

	1980			1992		
	1st	2nd	3rd	1st	2nd	3rd
Brazil	EU	LA	USA	EU	LA	USA
Panama	USA	LA	EU	EU	USA	LA
Chile	UE	LA	USA	EU	LA	USA
Peru	USA	EU	LA	EU	USA	LA
Colombia	EU	USA	LA	USA	EU	LA
Ecuador	USA	LA	EU	USA	LA	EU
Mexico	USA	EU	LA	USA	EU	LA
Venezuela	USA	EU	LA	USA	LA	EU
Costa Rica	USA	LA	EU	USA	EU	LA
El Salvador	LA	USA	UE	USA	AL	UE
Honduras	USA	EU	LA	USA	EU	LA
Guatemala	LA	USA	EU	LA	USA	EU
Nicaragua	USA	EU	LA	LA	USA	EU
Bolivia	LA	USA	EU	LA	EU	USA
Paraguay	LA	EU	USA	LA	EU	USA
Uruguay	LA	EU	USA	LA	EU	USA
Argentina	EU	LA	USA	LA	EU	USA

Source: COMTRADE.

SOURCE OF LATIN AMERICAN IMPORTS

	1980			1992		
	1st	2nd	3rd	1st	2nd	3rd
Brazil	USA	EU	LA	USA	EU	LA
Colombia	USA	EU	LA	USA	LA	EU
Ecuador	USA	EU	LA	USA	EU	LA
Mexico	USA	EU	LA	USA	EU	LA
Venezuela	USA	EU	LA	USA	EU	LA
Costa Rica	USA	AL	UE	USA	AL	UE
El Salvador	LA	USA	EU	USA	LA	EU
Honduras	USA	LA	EU	USA	LA	EU
Panama	USA	LA	EU	USA	LA	EU
Guatemala	USA	LA	EU	USA	LA	EU
Nicaragua	AL	USA	UE	AL	USA	UE
Bolivia	AL	USA	UE	AL	USA	UE
Chile	AL	USA	UE	AL	UE	USA
Paraguay	AL	UE	USA	AL	UE	USA
Peru	USA	UE	AL	AL	USA	UE
Uruguay	AL	UE	US	AL	UE	USA
Argentina	UE	USA	AL	AL	UE	USA

Source: COMTRADE, published in COM (95) 495 final.

ANNEXE 20.3 DEVELOPMENT OF TRADE BY SECTOR BETWEEN THE EU AND THE PRINCIPAL REGIONAL LATIN AMERICAN GROUPINGS (in millions of ecu)

REGIONS	SECTORS	EUROPEAN UNION*			
		1985	1990	1993	1994
Latin America	Food products, drink and tobacco	11.285	9.995	10.729	
	Raw materials, fuel, oils, fats and waxes	14.746	8.405	6.751	
	Industrial products	118.364	21.407	27.536	
	Others	1.480	1.462	1.207	
	Overall trade	45.875	41.270	46.223	56.352
Mercosur	Food products, drink and tobacco	7.028	5.438	5.781	
	Raw materials, fuel, oils, fats and waxes	4.573	3.902	3.230	
	Industrial products	6.694	9.041	11.968	
	Others	602	577	386	
	Overall trade	18.897	18.959	21.365	27.692
Andean Pact	Food products, drink and tobacco	1.999	1.557	2.032	
	Raw materials, fuel, oils, fats and waxes	4.665	2.098	1.735	
	Industrial products	4.319	3.687	4.472	
	Others	417	414	376	
	Overall trade	11.400	7.756	8.614	10.011
Central America	Food products, drink and tobacco	1.227	1.212	1.154	
	Raw materials, fuel, oils, fats and waxes	274	180	177	
	Industrial products	1.696	1.174	1.603	
	Others	70	41	36	
	Overall trade	3.267	2.607	2.970	2.438

ANNEXE 20.3 *Continued*

REGIONS	SECTORS	EUROPEAN UNION*			
		1985	1990	1993	1994
Mexico	Food products, drink and tobacco	215	692	583	
	Raw materials, fuel, oils, fats and waxes	4.635	1.632	1.018	
	Industrial products	2.883	4.366	6.423	
	Others	208	136	188	
	Overall trade	7.941	6.826	8.212	9.385
Chile	Food products, drink and tobacco	396	730	639	
	Raw materials, fuel, oils, fats and waxes	380	476	528	
	Industrial products	1.679	2.402	2.477	
	Others	84	167	117	
	Overall trade	2.540	3.776	3.761	4.319

*European Union of 12
Source: IRELA, COMEXT-DATABASE, Bruxellest–Luxembourg; IRELA, published in *COM* (95) 495 final.

ANNEXE 20.4 EC DEVELOPMENT COOPERATION IN LATIN AMERICA

Distribution by sub-regions and periods (commitments in millions of ecu)

	1976–83	1984–9	1990–3
Central America	154.2	447.8	478.1
Andean countries	113.1	361.9	429.2
Mercosur	10.6	63.5	175.5
Others	12.8	112.2	164.5
LA region	24.1	37.4	106.7
TOTAL LA	314.8	1022.8	135.4

Average annual flow by sub-region and periods (in millions of ecu)

	1976–83	1984–9	1990–3
Central America	19.3	74.7	119.5
Andean countries	14.1	60.3	107.3
Mercosur	1.3	10.6	43.9
Others	1.6	18.7	41.1
LA region	3	6.2	26.7
TOTAL LA	39.3	170.5	338.5

Source: Commission européenne, toutes formes d'aides avec les PVD d'Amérique latine et d'Asie. Annexe statistique du 17ème Rapport annuel. Bruxelles, le 20 Octobre 1994, published in *COM* (95) 495 final.

Bibliography

European Commission, *The EU and Latin America* (Brussels, 1996).

European Parliament, *El Parlamento Europeo y America Latina: Relaciones Institucionales y Principales Puntos de Vista*, Working Paper of the EP, Political Series (Luxembourg, July 1995). Also available in English.

Forrester, R. 'EEC Customs Law,' *European Law Review* (1980) pp. 167–87 and pp. 257–86.

Galinsoga Jorda, A., 'La Credibilidad de la ficcion: los acuerdos de cooperacion de la CE con los paises del Grupo Andino y de America Central,' *Revista Cidobd'Afers internacionals,* Barcelona, nos. 23–24 (1992) pp. 61–88.

Grilli, E., *The European Community and the Developing Countries* (Cambridge University Press, 1993).

Huesa Vinaixa, R., 'Incidencia de la adhesion de España a la Comunidad Europea sobre las relaciones de cooperacion con America Latina,' *Noticias/C.E.E.*, no. 45 (October 1988) pp. 95–107.

Hummer, W., 'Integrationszonene als Elemente der politischen, wirtschaftlichenund völkerrechtlichen Wirklichkeit beider Amerika in den neunziger Jahren,' *Lateinamerika Information*, nos. 2/3-95 (Österreichisches Lateinamerikainstitut, Wien, 1995) pp. 2–10.

IRELA (Institute for European–Latin American Relations), *Las Elecciones al Parlamento Centroamericano* (Madrid, 1989).

IRELA, *Economic Relations between the European Community and Latin America: A Statistical Profile, 1991* (Madrid, 1991).

Nuñez, F., 'Las relaciones economicas y comerciales de la Comunidad Europea y Bolivia,' *Revista Cidob d'Afers Internacionals,* Barcelona, nos. 23–25 (1992) pp. 89–114.

Peers, S., 'Reform of the European Community's Generalized System of Preferences – A Missed Opportunity,' *Journal of World Trade*, vol. 129 (1995) pp. 79–96.

Raboy, D., Simpson, T. and Bing, X., 'A Transition Proposal for Lomé Convention: The Case of the EU Banana Regime,' *The World Economy*, vol. 18 (July 1995) pp. 565–81.

Notes

1. The term 'EC' is used to refer to the Community before the Maastricht Treaty as well as to its activities under the first pillar of the Maastricht Treaty. The term EU is used for fields covered by the second and third pillar.
2. See Grilli, (1993), p. 225.
3. OJ, L [1985] 15 November 1985, p. 479.
4. Concerning the impact of Spain's accession to the EC on the relations between Latin America and the EC see Huesa Vinaixa (1988).
5. The text can be found in *COM* (95) 505 Final, 23 January 1995.
6. The Andean Pact is based in Lima.
7. Venezuela was not a founding member. It joined the Andean Pact in February 1973.
8. Chile was a founding member but it left the Andean Pact in 1976.
9. The deep economic crisis, which struck Latin America in the 1980s, made it impossible to meet the ambitious objectives laid down in the founding treaty.
10. Bolivia and Ecuador did not take part in the customs union until the beginning of 1996. Ecuador still applies its own external customs tariff.
11. According to the Commission of the EC, the member states of the Andean Community still apply customs tariffs on a bilateral basis.
12. These trade preferences granted to Andean by MERCOSUR were due to expire at the latest by the end of 1995.
13. *Die Presse*, Austria, 11 March 1996.

14. ALCAS (Area de Libre Comercio de America del Sur). This initiative was launched by Brazil on 9 March 1994.
15. There are also plans for a so called 'Free Trade Area of the Americas' including the whole continent from Alaska to Argentina as it was envisaged by the heads of state and government at their summit in Miami, Florida in 1994. This Free Trade Area would remain until 2005 and would represent the largest integration grouping in the world with 850 million consumers. The nucleus for this pan-American preferential area will be MERCOSUR and NAFTA, whose enlargement to include other Latin American countries (such as Chile) is being discussed.
16. These three countries form the so called 'Group of the Three' (*Grupo de los Tres)*, which was created in February 1989 at the San José conference V in San Pedro, Honduras. Since January 1995 the Grupo de los Tres has been a free trade area.
17. The economic declarations used to be of little substantial importance.
18. Belize represented the six member states of CARICOM, the Caribbean Community.
19. The modifications concern the objectives of the San José process, the mechanisms of the dialogue (Ministerial Conferences only every two years instead of every year) as well as the content and form of future cooperation (a stronger role for the Joint Committee). See *Agence Europe*, 23 March 1996.
20. *Agence Europe*, 30 November 1995, p. 14.
21. The Joint Declaration of the XI Ministerial Conference, in February 1995, took into consideration that, so far, the essential goal had been represented by peace, consolidating democracy and human rights. These objectives had, on the whole, been attained (while of course also remaining valid for the future) and stress is now being placed on substantial economic development (i.e., natural resources and the environment) and strengthening cooperation.
22. Joint Communication adopted at the XII San José Conference in Florence; see *Agence Europe*, 23 March 1996, p. 5.
23. At this conference the Central American States raised the problem concerning the import regime for bananas from Latin America. See *Agence Europe* 23 April 1993, pp. 7–8.
24. The Interparliamentary Conferences have been held since 1974, whereas the San José process, which involves the EC Ministers for Foreign Affairs as well as the Commission, was not created till 1984.
25. The EP disposes of two Interparliamentary Delegations for Latin America: one for South America, the other for Central America and Mexico.
26. This is reflected in the considerable number of resolutions on Latin America adopted by the Parliament.
27. An overview of the different integration zones in Latin America has been given by Professor Waldemar Hummer (1995).
28. European Parliament (1995).
29. Let it also be noted that the EP also maintains a political dialogue with the Parliamentary Commission of MERCOSUR and PARLACEN (the Central American Parliament).

30. Nevertheless, the treaty institutionalizing PARLATINO was only signed in 1987.
31. Declaration of Lima, 7 December 1964.
32. See the Final Act of the XII Interparliamentary Conference held in Brussels in June 1995.
33. Documents also mention a 'Native Parliament' (*Parlamento Indigeno),* whose aim it is to defend the right of Latin America's native population. Nevertheless detailed and confirmed information about the composition, the current functioning or the form of eventual contacts with the EP were not available.
34. See Resolution of the EP of 9 February 1994 on international measures necessary for an effective protection of the native peoples, [1994] OJ, C61.
35. See Resolutions of the EP of 25 October 1990 on the protection of the rain forest and environmental problems in the Amazonian region, [1990] OJ, C295.
36. IRELA (1989).
37. After the respective elections in Honduras, Guatemala and El Salvador, the Central American Parliament was inaugurated officially on 28 October 1991, bringing together members from these three countries and observers from Nicaragua, where direct elections had not yet taken place.
38. Source: Eurostat; see Annexe. The same holds true for the Andean imports from and exports to the EC, which dropped continuously during the 1980s.
39. The last financial shock, which affected Mexico in December 1994, had a harmful impact on the whole region, especially on Argentina.
40. Source: Eurostat; see Annexe.
41. see Annexe. For MERCOSUR the EC is the most important export market. Source: IRELA (1995).
42. Source: IRELA (1991) p. 22.
43. Source: IRELA, (1991) p. 12.
44. Source: European Commission, *The EU and Latin America* (Brussels, 1996) p. 5, 1996.
45. The Dominican Republic and Haiti were included in the Lomé Convention in 1990.
46. Commission Regulation 3224/94 of 21 December 1994, [1994] OJ, L337/72.
47. Council Regulation 404/93 of 13 February 1993, [1993] OJ, L47/1, which entered into force on 1 July 1993.
48. Raboy *et al.* (1995) p. 569.
49. See Huesa Vinaixa (1988) p. 96.
50. See initially (respectively) Commission Regulation 3107/74, 3108/74 and 3109/74, OJ, L336 [1974]. See, in particlar, analysis of the rules by Forrester (1980). Chile was included as long as it was a member of the Andean Pact; it was omitted from Commission Regulation 2968/77, OJ, L350/62 [1977].
51. See initially, art. 1(2) of each regulation.
52. see Peers (1995) p. 84.

53. There are negotiations within the Council of the EC concerning further extension. The original legal bases are: Regulation 3211/90, OJ, L308/1 [1990], extended by Regulation 3835/90, OJ, L370/126 [1990]; special ECSC coverage granted by Decision 90/673, OJ, m L370/151 [1990]. As a further support in the fight against drugs, Central American states, including Panama, were granted tariff-free status for their agricultural exports covered by the GSP from 1992, see Regulation 3900/91, OJ, L368/11 [1991].
54. OJ, L153 [1984] p. 2. Due to ratification problems the agreement did not enter into force before 1987.
55. OJ, C25 [1993] pp. 31–42.
56. See art. 60 of the Vienna Convention on the Law of Treaties.
57. Due to ratification problems in Peru and Ecuador it has not yet entered into force, but is already applied informally.
58. See Annexe.
59. See *COM* (95) 585; *Bulletin of the EU*, No 12, 1995 (Brussels) p. 12, 12–1995.
60. *Agence Europe*, 15–16 April 1996, p. 13.

Part 5

Commercial Instruments of EU Policy

21 Trade Policy and Preferences

Ben Atkinson

INTRODUCTION

This chapter looks at the system of preferences operated by the European Union,[1] with particular emphasis on the General System of Preferences (GSP). The nature of the Common External Tariff (CET) is examined and the importance of tariff escalation noted. The relationship between the World Trade Organisation (WTO) and the EU is reviewed, with a brief summary of the results of the Uruguay Round.

The organization of the EU's new GSP is outlined and the important issues are found to be tariff modulation, the graduation mechanism and rules of origin. A conclusion is reached that the new GSP is an improvement, principally due to its simplified structure and the removal of tariff quotas and ceilings. However, the cumulation of origin restrictions and the existence of a separate scheme for agricultural products are limiting factors.

In an analysis of preferences offered by the EU the nature of preferences needs to be defined. Essentially, a preference can be classified as a reduction in the CET. However, other issues also impact on preferences, including non-tariff barriers (NTBs) such as voluntary export restraints (VERs), import quotas and variable import levies (VILs).

THE PYRAMID OF PRIVILEGES

Trade relations between Europe and the rest of the world have been described as a pyramid of privilege. At the top of the pyramid are the European Economic Area (EEA) and European Free Trade Association (EFTA) countries of Norway, Iceland, Liechtenstein and Switzerland. The Europe Agreements with the Central and Eastern European countries (CEECs) allow for the creation of a Free Trade Area (FTA), albeit with limited coverage for agricultural products.

The hierarchy of privileges also applies to developing countries. The African, Caribbean and Pacific (ACP) signatories of the Lomé Convention receive the most preferential treatment, closely followed by the Mediterranean developing countries. Of the preferential arrangements, the GSP encapsulates the largest number of countries; however, the conditions are less favourable than both the Lomé and the Mediterranean provisions.

Near the bottom of the pyramid are those members of the WTO not entitled to preferential treatment under the agreements mentioned above. These countries receive most-favoured-nation (MFN) status. In 1991 60 per cent of imports to the EU received MFN treatment, with 40 per cent receiving preferential treatment.[2] Finally, there are some countries that are not members of the WTO such as China and Libya. Products from these countries not subject to the GSP receive the least favourable treatment.

Table 21.1 shows recent EU external trade figures. It can be seen that trade with developing countries forms a significant part of external trade.

Figure 21.1 shows the value of imports to the EU for selected developing country groups. The importance of the Asian economies in developing country trade can clearly be seen, whilst, despite the Lomé provisions, ACP countries constitute a small and declining share.

THE EU AND THE WTO

The member states of the EU are contracting parties to the General Agreement on Tariffs and Trade (GATT) and its successor the World Trade Organization (WTO). As a result of the common commercial policy, the European Commission acts as the negotiating body in the GATT and WTO process. The EU is strongly committed to the multilateral trading principles of the GATT and the articles of the GATT form the legal basis of the EU's trade policy.[3]

The Uruguay Round of the GATT was concluded in Marrakesh in 1994 and included agreements on reductions of industrial tariffs and for the first time trade liberalization measures in the agriculture, services and textiles sectors.

The effect of the agriculture agreement will be to convert NTBs into tariffs. The tariffs imposed by developed countries will be reduced by 36 per cent and the volume of subsidized exports will be reduced, thus increasing and stabilizing world agricultural prices. For tropical

Table 21.1 Breakdown of EU trade by trading partners: imports and exports as a percentage of extra-EU trade

	1970		1980		1992		1994	
	Imports	Exports	Imports	Exports	Imports	Exports	Imports	Exports
Industrialized countries	54.6	59.3	59.9	49.6	59.1	55.0	55.6	53.0
EFTA	17.4	25.1	17.0	25.5	22.9	24.7	24.4	22.1
USA	21.7	18.0	16.8	12.8	17.8	16.9	17.1	17.6
Japan	3.4	2.6	4.9	2.2	10.6	4.7	8.96	4.9
Developing countries	38.0	31.0	45.7	41.2	29.8	35.1	29.5	34.0
ACP	8.9	7.6	7.3	7.9	3.7	4.0	3.4	2.8
CEECs	6.4	7.3	7.3	8.0	7.5	8.1	9.0	9.0

Source: Eurostat. Data are for EC12.

Figure 21.1 Imports to the EU from selected developing country groups (1994)

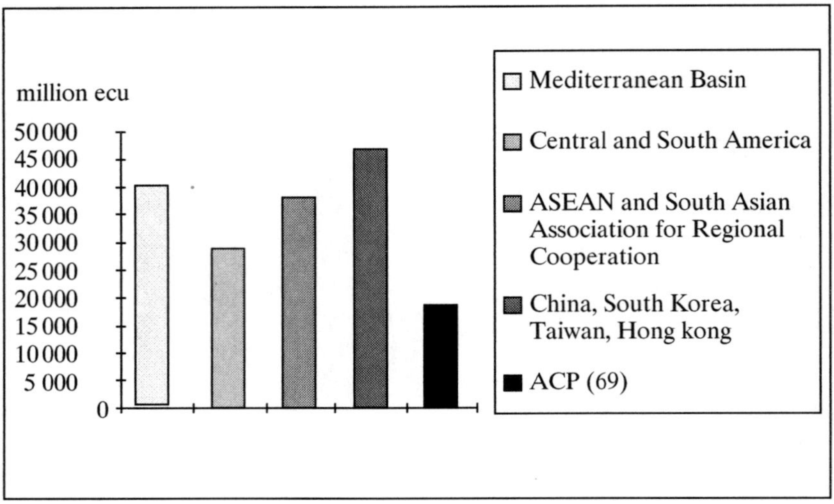

Source: Eurostat data for EC12.

agricultural products, which account for half of the developing countries' exports of agricultural products, a 43 per cent reduction in tariffs will be implemented by developed countries.[4] As a result of the agreement on manufactures industrialized countries will reduce tariffs by 40 per cent and abolish VERs. Trade in textiles, currently controlled by the Multifibre Arrangement, will be liberalized over ten years.

THE COMMON EXTERNAL TARIFF (CET)

A fundamental constituent of the EU is the Common Market. This is essentially a customs union with free movement of factors of production. The customs union[5] entails the elimination of internal tariffs coupled with a CET. To quote Tsoukalis, 'The EC started basically as an incomplete customs union, which meant that the common external tariff constituted the building block of its fledgling international role.'[6] Both tariffs and NTBs are instruments for protection. A motive for protection is that trade between the EU and developing countries has been characterized as being of an inter-industry nature and the result of conventional comparative advantage, with the relative abundance of low-skilled labour in developing countries being one factor determining this comparative advantage.[7]

The European sectors that compete with this trade are typically those that are relatively highly protected, with the demand for protection being politically legitimized by a fear of European job losses. It should be noted that despite protection, European labour-intensive industries with low levels of R&D such as textiles and clothing, footwear and shipbuilding have been characterized in recent years by growing import penetration from developing countries.

An important characteristic of the CET is that it has been significantly reduced following successive rounds of the GATT. Following the Tokyo Round, the CET had an average value of 5 per cent and this figure has been further reduced to a trade weighted average of approximately 3 per cent following the Uruguay Round agreement.[8] However, the reduction in average tariffs obscures higher tariffs and NTBs for certain 'sensitive' products. These sectors include clothing, textiles and agriculture.

An issue of importance is that the sectors with high protection are in many cases those sectors in which developing countries have comparative advantage. Table 21.2 indicates the 1995 CET (or Integrated Tariff of the European Communities – TARIC) for selected products. The examples in Table 21.2 give an indication of the variation and the degree of detail in the CET. It can be seen that agricultural produce, clothing and footwear are subject to higher tariffs than other manufactured products.

Table 21.2 Selected EU MFN tariffs 1995 (percentage *ad valorem*)

Product	Tariff
Onions	19.30
Men's or boys' shirts	12.50
Snowboard boots	18.20
Roller chain used for cycles and motor cycles	3.50
Microphones for use in civil aircraft	0.00
Household refrigerators	2.1
Machine tools	3.6

Source: OJ, L 319 1995.

Tariff Escalation

A second important characteristic of the CET is tariff escalation. This term describes the fact that in general tariffs increase with the degree of processing. Thus tariffs on raw materials are lower than the equivalent tariff for a processed product. Table 21.3 illustrates this phenomenon taking selected MFN tariffs from the CET of the EU. The rates shown are *ad valorem* percentage duties on imports. This is the usual way duties on imports into the EU are calculated.

The existence of tariff escalation discriminates strongly against developing countries. These countries are often producers of raw

Table 21.3 Escalation in the Common External Tariff of the EU (percentage *ad valorem*)

Product [MFN tariff]	1992	1995
Coffee		
Not roasted, not decaffeinated	4	4
Not roasted, decaffeinated	10	10
Roasted, not decaffeinated	12	12
Roasted, decaffeinated	15	15
Cocoa		
Cocoa beans	3	2.5
Cocoa powder	12	9.7
Nuts		
Coconuts, Brazil nuts, cashew nuts	0	0
Roasted ground nuts	12	12
Tobacco		
Unmanufactured	23	23
Cigarettes containing tobacco	90	84.6
Tropical fruit		
Pineapples	9	8.5
Oranges from 16/5 to 15/10	4	3.9
Prepared pineapples	32	32
Orange juice	42	40.6

Source: OJ, C170A 1992 and L319 1995.

materials the processing of which is a fundamental way of achieving value added and a diversified economy. Tariff escalation and high tariffs for processed raw materials indicate the benefit Lomé countries gain from duty-free access. An important aspect of the Uruguay Round agreement is a commitment to reduce the degree of tariff escalation, although no concrete proposals have been forwarded.

PREFERENCES

Multilateralism is one of the founding principles of the GATT. However, the system of preferences operated by the EU clearly runs contrary to this. Article XXIV of the GATT allows for customs unions and free trade areas. These agreements must cover a substantial part of trade, and liberalization should take place within a reasonable length of time. The EU has used a liberal interpretation of this article to justify the hierarchy of trade preferences it offers.[9]

The USA has disputed that the EU agreements with the ACP and Mediterranean countries meet these conditions.[10]

An economic rationale for preferences is indicated below. An issue of concern is whether trade preferences cause trade creation or trade diversion. Trade creation results when production is shifted from a high-cost producer to a low-cost producer, whilst trade diversion occurs if production is diverted from a low-cost to a high-cost producer. From a global economic perspective, trade creation is welfare-improving whilst trade diversion is welfare-reducing.

The Economics of Preferences

In recent years developing countries have significantly diversified their exports with a dramatic expansion of manufactures. However this expansion has been led by a few countries, notably the newly industrialized countries (NICs) of South Korea, Taiwan, Hong Kong and Singapore, as well as China, India, Malaysia and several South American economies. Many developing countries still rely on exports of a few primary commodities. For example, Niger and Zambia rely on three commodities for 99 per cent of export earnings, the same figure being 97.4 per cent for Mozambique and 85.6 per cent for Cambodia.[11]

Reliance on a small number of commodities for export earnings has been characterized as detrimental to economic development. Prices of commodities are notoriously volatile, which causes large fluctuations in export earnings and hence may reduced investment. In addition there is evidence that the terms of trade for primary commodities, particularly agricultural commodities, will decline over time.

Preferences are intended to help developing countries achieve export diversification. An economic rationale for preferences is the 'infant industry' argument. For a number of reasons such as learning curves and economies of scale, new manufacturing industries in developing countries find it difficult to compete with established producers. Thus preferences are intended to act as a temporary advantage, allowing diversification and industrialization.

The Lomé Convention

The Lomé Convention is a trade and aid agreement between the EU and 70 countries in the ACP area. Under the Lomé trade provisions the EU grants, without reciprocity, preferential access for ACP exports to EU markets. About 99 per cent of ACP products enter the EU tariff-free. The Lomé rules of origin allow for full cumulation of origin among the EU and all of the beneficiaries.

Agreements with the Mediterranean Countries

The EU is linked with all Mediterranean countries bar Libya by a number of separate cooperation and association agreements. All the agreements have certain common constituents, including tariff-free access for all industrial products and some concessions for agricultural exports. Full cumulation of origin is allowed between the Maghreb and the EU, whilst bilateral cumulation is allowed for the other countries.

The Barcelona Euro-Mediterranean ministerial conference in 1995 resulted in a declaration which committed the EU and twelve Mediterranean countries to the creation of a free trade area. The partnership is to be based on Euro-Mediterranean association agreements, the majority of which are currently being negotiated.

THE GENERAL SYSTEM OF PREFERENCES (GSP)

The GSP originated at the UNCTAD Conference of 1964. Faced with the problems of developing countries' undiversified and concentrated exports and the prevalence of tariff escalation in developed countries,

Raul Prebisch, the UNCTAD Secretary-General, proposed a single scheme whereby developed countries would admit all developing country exports of manufactures and semi-manufactures duty-free. A major characteristic of the scheme was to be the absence of any reciprocity requirements.

Pressure, largely from the EU, resulted in industrialized countries implementing slightly different versions of the scheme. This allowed the EU to omit products that were of particular interest to its African associates.[12] The USSR implemented the first GSP in 1965, followed by Australia in 1966. The EU introduced its first GSP in 1971.

The GSP requires a derogation from the non-discrimination principle of GATT. The enabling clause was negotiated in the Tokyo Round and provides the legal basis for extension of the GSP without the need for further waivers. The operation of the various GSP schemes is reviewed regularly by the UNCTAD Special Committee on Preferences.

The Functioning of the EU's GSP

In December 1994 the Council of the EU adopted a new GSP for industrial goods, to be implemented from 1 January 1995. The new GSP involves significant changes to the previous system, including some simplifying improvements. Factors influencing the development of the GSP include the erosion of the preference margin as a result of the Uruguay Round and the increasingly heterogeneous nature of developing countries, mainly due to the rapidly developing Asian economies.

The Previous System

The EU's GSP pre-dates the Lomé Convention, so that there was a transfer of ACP countries from the GSP to the more favourable Lomé treatment. In addition, most Mediterranean countries have received more preferential treatment since the 1970s and therefore have not benefited from GSP treatment, although they are still eligible. For these reasons the main GSP beneficiaries are the Asian and Latin American countries. The GSP currently covers imports from 147 independent countries and 25 countries and territories. Recent beneficiaries of the EU's GSP include China,[13] Russia, Ukraine and the other members of the Commonwealth of Independent States (CIS)[14] and South Africa.[15]

Under the initial GSP, the EU established an annual tariff quota for 'sensitive' products, with a flexible tariff ceiling on all other products. Once the tariff ceiling was reached, MFN tariffs were imposed on subsequent imports.

Imports below the tariff quotas and ceilings were tariff-free provided they could meet the rules of origin.

From 1981 tariff quotas were applied on only a small number of products. Tariff ceilings were applicable on semi-sensitive products, whilst non-sensitive products faced no limits, although non-sensitive products were subject to a safeguard clause. The system involved considerable uncertainty for importers and exporters. Exporters needed to ship before tariff quotas or ceilings were reached, and, because of the timing of the regulation's adoption, importers often had to order goods months before they knew whether tariff preferences would be available. Finally, it is important to note that the implementation of the Single European Market in 1993 meant that the previous system of allocating quotas on a national basis had to be replaced by EU-wide quotas.

The New System

Reform of the GSP was overdue and had been delayed until conclusion of the Uruguay Round. A major priority of the new system was to simplify administration, principally through the phasing out of tariff quotas and tariff ceilings. Under the final agreement, the tariff modulation principle established four levels of tariff reductions. A 100 per cent reduction is allowed for non-sensitive products, with a 65 per cent reduction for semi-sensitive products, a 30 per cent reduction for sensitive products and a 15 per cent reduction for very sensitive products. In addition, a number of products were excluded from the scheme. Annexe 1 contains the list of very sensitive products, which consist primarily of textiles.

As a consequence of the abolition of tariff quotas and ceilings, the safeguard mechanism was expanded to take in all products included in the GSP. Article 14 of the regulation allows the reimposition of MFN tariffs if imports cause or threaten to cause serious difficulties to a producer in the EU. Article 14.6 allows emergency reimposition of MFN tariffs in exceptional circumstances without investigation.

Although the safeguard clause clearly has the potential to limit GSP benefits significantly, the system is open to judicial review. It appears that the Commission will have to prove a link between the difficulties and the GSP, and importers and exporters may be able to seek annulment of the decision.[16] The new regulation also contains a clause on the concurrence of anti-dumping duties and GSP preferences, which states that products subject to anti-dumping duties will be exempt from preferences unless the anti-dumping duties are based on a price that takes into account the tariff preference.

Graduation

To prevent the more advanced countries from obtaining the majority of the benefits from the GSP, from 1975 onwards certain countries'[17] shares of semi-sensitive preferences were restricted. The new system further developed this policy, introducing partial graduation for certain sector/country combinations. The graduation mechanism uses a development index, derived by a complex formula, which shows the level of industrial development in relation to the EU, and a specialization index to determine whether sector/country combinations are to be graduated.

For country–sector combinations that are to be graduated from the GSP, there are three possible scenarios. A country receiving over 25 per cent of the GSP benefits for a given sector will lose any preferences for that sector. This principle has been called the 'solidarity mechanism' and appears to be primarily directed at Chinese imports.[18] In those cases where the solidarity mechanism does not apply, for countries listed in Annex VII[19] of the regulation preference margins are abolished for the sector in question, whilst for those countries not listed in Annex VII preferences for the sector concerned were reduced by 50 per cent on 1 January 1997 and abolished on 1 January 1998. To further redistribute the benefits to the least-developed developing countries, the new regulation contains a clause whereby imports from these countries are tariff-free. In addition, the graduation mechanism will not apply to those countries whose exports to the EU of the relevant product do not exceed 2 per cent of GSP beneficiary countries' exports to the EU.

The regulation also includes provision for full graduation from the GSP for the most advanced beneficiaries, beginning in 1998. However, the criteria for full graduation from the scheme have yet to be defined.

Rules of Origin

To be eligible for GSP treatment, goods must satisfy the rules of origin. The GSP rules of origin are more restrictive than those required for countries to qualify for MFN status.[20] At the same time as the adoption of the new GSP regulation, a Commission regulation was adopted including revised rules of origin. An important new element of this regulation is the allowance of bilateral cumulation of origin between the GSP beneficiary states and the EU. However, cumulation of origin between beneficiaries has not been extended beyond the previous concession for the regional groups of the Association of South-East Asian Nations (ASEAN), the Central American Common Market (CACM) and the Andean Pact.

Products are described as originating in a country (or in the regions mentioned above) when they are either wholly obtained in that country or have 'undergone sufficient working or processing'[21] in the country. The regulation defines materials not originating from the beneficiary as being sufficiently worked or processed when the end product is in a different classification. The allowance of bilateral cumulation means that materials defined by the GSP rules of origin as originating in the EU are treated as materials originating in the beneficiary country.

To satisfy the GSP rules of origin an exporter must obtain a certificate of origin Form A, which is issued by the government of the beneficiary country following a written application from the exporter. In order to qualify for bilateral cumulation, producers in beneficiary countries must obtain a proof of EU origin certificate EUR.1, which is issued by the authorities in the EU. Obtaining this certificate may prove an obstacle to taking advantage of the bilateral cumulation provision, particularly for small firms.

Agriculture

A separate GSP regulation has been adopted for agricultural produce. The principal reason for this is the Common Agricultural Policy (CAP) of the EU, although also cited as a reason is the fact that the GSP is intended to promote industrialization. The current GSP regime for agricultural products originating in developing countries was extended until July 1996, pending negotiations on a new scheme. The EU has considered a request from India to provide GSP benefits for at least 25 farm products. These products include shelled walnuts, tobacco and mushrooms. However, the probability of all these products obtaining GSP benefits is remote, because many of them are considered sensitive to the European farm lobby.[22]

Special incentives

The regulation included measures for the imposition in 1998 of incentives in the form of increased preferences for countries fulfilling certain environmental and social standards. The environmental standards relate to the sustainable management of forests, whilst the labour standards are governed by International Labour Organization conventions on the right to form trade unions, the right to strike and the prevention of child labour. The Commission's initial proposal was for concrete preferences of up to 30 per cent of the MFN tariff starting in 1997. However, the Council weakened this proposition and agreed to the possibility of incentives in 1998 following a review of the results of studies on the link between trade and labour rights.

THE EFFECTIVENESS OF THE GSP

There is some debate as to the benefits of the GSP. Langhammer and Sapir[23] conclude that 'after more than a decade of operation, there is not much evidence of the effectiveness of the GSP,' whilst Boormann *et al.* conclude that there are clear signs the GSP has a trade-stimulating effect.[24] Note that the uncertainty resulting from the previous system of quotas and ceilings may have caused EU importers to ignore preferences when pricing imported products. If this were the case then GSP benefits would have accrued to the importer, making the new simplified scheme a marked improvement.

The shift in emphasis of development strategy towards recognizing the complementary role of the agricultural sector in the early stages of development indicates that expansion of the industrial GSP to cover agricultural products would increase the effectiveness of the scheme. Erosion of the preference margin following MFN tariff reductions has served to reduce the advantage GSP treatment confers. This has been exacerbated by the FTA agreements the EU has negotiated with the Central and Eastern European and Mediterranean countries.

CONCLUSION

The nature of the CET of the EU and the preferential treatment it offers to developing countries has been examined. From the nature of the CET it can be seen that despite multilateral trade negotiations, the EU seeks to protect domestic producers in the 'sensitive' sectors through higher tariffs. In addition, tariff escalation, a phenomenon that can only be explained by a desire to keep value-added industries in the EU, discourages diversification of developing countries' economies.

Although the reduction of MFN tariffs as a result of successive GATT rounds has and will continue to reduce preference margins, whilst high tariffs for certain products and tariff escalation exist, preferences can still play a role in offering a temporary advantage to a country in the early stages of industrialization.

The new simplified GSP, which should reduce uncertainty regarding preference eligibility, is to be welcomed. The graduation principle will enable the less advanced developing countries to gain a larger share of the benefits and will increase the competitive advantage preferences offer. However, the lack of full cumulation provisions regarding the origin of products from developing countries is a factor limiting the effectiveness of the new scheme. Inclusion of agricultural products in the main GSP would be a major improvement which would significantly benefit developing countries.

ANNEXE 21.1

Very Sensitive Products (Council Regulation (EC) no. 3281/94)

Combined Nomenclature Code	Description of goods
Chapter 50	Silk
Chapter 51	Wool, fine or coarse animal hair; yarn and woven fabrics
Chapter 52	Cotton
Chapter 53	Other vegetable textile fibres; paper yarn and woven fabrics of paper yarn
Chapter 54	Man-made staple fibres
Chapter 56	Wadding, felt and non-wovens; special yarns; twine, cordage, ropes and cables and articles thereof
Chapter 57	Carpets and other textile floor coverings
Chapter 58	Special woven fabrics; tufted textile fabrics; lace; tapestries; trimmings; embroidery
Chapter 59	Impregnated, coated, covered or laminated textile fabrics; textile articles of a kind suitable for industrial use
Chapter 60	Knitted or crocheted fabrics
Chapter 61	Articles of apparel and clothing accessories, knitted or crocheted
Chapter 62	Articles of apparel and clothing accessories, not knitted or crocheted
Chapter 63	Other made-up textile articles; sets; worn clothing and worn textile articles; rags
7202	Ferro-alloys

Bibliography

Boormann, A., Boormann, C., and Stegger, M., *The EC's Generalized System of Preferences* (Nijhoff, London, 1981).

Colman, D. and Nixson, F. *Economics of Change in Less Developed Countries* (Harvester-Wheatsheaf, London, 1994).

Commission of the European Communities, *Europe in a Changing World,* (1993).

Commission of the European Communities, *Official Journal of the European Communities*, OJ, C170A (1992), OJ, L348 (1994) and L319 (1995).

Eurostat, *External Trade*, various years.

Evans, P. and Walsh, J., *The EIU Guide to the GATT* (Economist Intelligence Unit, London, 1994).

GATT, *Trade Policy Review, European Communities, General Agreement on Tariffs and Trade* (Geneva, 1993).

Grilli, E., *The European Community and the Developing Countries* (Cambridge University Press, 1993).

Inama, S., 'A Comparative Analysis of the Generalised System of Preferences and Non-Preferential Rules of Origin in the Light of the Uruguay Round Agreement', *Journal of World Trade*, vol. 29, no. 1 (February 1995). pp. 35–50.

Krueger, A. O., *Trade Policies and Developing Nations* (Brookings Institution, Washington, 1995).

Langhammer, R. J. and Sapir, A., *The Economic Impact of the Generalised System of Preferences* (Gower, London, 1987).

Lebullenger, J., 'La Rénovation de la politique communautaire du Développement', *Revue trimestrielle de droit européen*, no 4 (October–December, 1994). pp. 101–125.

Matthews, A., *EC Trade Policy and the Third World: an Irish Perspective* (McGill, 1991).

Peers, S., 'Reform of the European Community's Generalised System of Preferences: A Missed Opportunity', *Journal of World Trade*, vol. 29, no. 6 (December 1995).

Stevens, C. and Verloren Van Themaat, J. (eds), *Europe and the International Division of Labour* (Hodder & Stoughton, London, 1991).

Tsoukalis, L., *The New European Economy* (Oxford University Press, 1993).

UNCTAD, *Operation and effects of the Generalized System of Preferences* (United Nations, Geneva, 1989).

UNCTAD, *Commodity Yearbook* (United Nations, Geneva, 1990).

Vainio, M., 'Quantifiable Impact of the Uruguay Round on Poverty', *Development Policy Review*, vol. 14, no. 1 (March 1996).

Waer, P. and Driessen, B., 'The New European Union Generalised System of Preferences', *Journal of World Trade,* vol. 29, no. 4 (August 1995) pp. 52 –65.

Weston, A., 'Who is More Preferred? An Analysis of the New Generalised System of Preferences', Stevens, C., (ed), *EEC and the Third World: A Survey; 2, Hunger in the World* (Hodder & Stoughton, London, 1982) pp. 75–93.

Wood, A., *North–south trade, Employment and Inequality: Changing Fortunes in a Skill Driven World* (Clarendon Press, Oxford, 1994).
WTO, *Trading into the Future* (World Trade Organization, Geneva, 1995).
Yamazawa, I. and Hirata, A., *Trade Policies towards Developing Countries* (St. Martin's Press, New York, 1993).

Notes

1. Strictly speaking, trade preferences come under art. 113 of the European Community (EC) Treaty, part of the Common Commercial Policy (CCP). However, for simplicity and to reflect public perceptions, the EU will be referred to, of which the EC is part.
2. GATT (1993) p. 37.
3. Commission of the European Communities (1993) p. 20.
4. Krueger (1995), and the WTO internet page [http://www.unicc.org/wto].
5. The EC92 Internal Market programme also involved the elimination of all non tariff barriers to intra-community trade.
6. Tsoukalis (1992) p. 278.
7. Wood (1994).
8. Evans and Walsh (1994).
9. It should be noted that the GSP has an enabling derogation from the GATT non-discrimination rule.
10. Matthews (1991) p. 103.
11. UNCTAD *Commodity Yearbook* 1990.
12. Matthews (1991) p. 105
13. 1993.
14. 1993.
15. South Africa was added to the GSP in 1994, although the scheme contains certain exclusions.
16. Peers (1995) p. 88.
17. Notably the Asian 'tigers' South Korea, Singapore and Hong Kong.
18. China has been a major beneficiary of the GSP and in 1994 obtained almost 25 per cent of the total GSP. Under the solidarity mechanism, China lost its GSP benefit for chemicals, apparel and clothing, glass and ceramics from the beginning of 1996. Tariff preferences will be phased out by 1998 for leather, furs and footwear.
19. Hong Kong, Singapore, South Korea, Saudi Arabia, Oman, Brunei Darussalam, Qatar, United Arab Emirates, Kuwait, Bahrain, Libya and Nauru.
20. European Court of Justice case 385/85 (1986) ECR 2929.
21. Article 67 Commission Regulation (EC) no. 3254/94.
22. The Hindu Business Line on the internet, p. 22 February 1996.
23. Langhammer and Sapir (1987) p. 69.
24. Boormann *et al.* (1981).

22 EU Textiles Policy and Developing Countries

Marc Lemaître

INTRODUCTION

Over the past fifty years, the most populated region in the world has managed to expand its economy at a pace never observed before. Countries like Taiwan or South Korea have attained levels of development comparable to those of Southern Europe. One of their main common features, apart from the well-publicized very high savings rate they have sustained over the whole period, is that they have concentrated on low-skill and labour-intensive production as a first step towards industrialization. Among the industries best filling these criteria is textiles. This activity seems to have been the first key to rapid and lasting economic development.

Unfortunately, it is also well known that trade in textiles is among the most distorted in the international economy, along with trade in agricultural products. In that respect, the successful conclusion of the Uruguay Round in 1994, which includes an agreement on textiles, has given birth to the hope of a future world treating this essential product in a fairer and more liberal way. This chapter examines the way in which the EC has played its part in regulating international trade in textiles. After a historical review of the main international agreements impeding trade in textiles since the Second World War, the focus moves to the economic consequences of the Multifibre Arrangement (MFA) , the furthest reaching and longest lasting of them. In the second part, the future is examined, presenting the changes agreed upon in GATT 1994, making an assessment after one year of implementation, and evaluating the economic consequences for both developed and developing countries, with genuine liberalization and without it.

HISTORY OF THE MFA

Since the 1950s trade provisions in textiles have been among the least liberal. The first restrictions date back to 1955. In that year, the USA persuaded Japan to agree to a voluntary export restraint (VER) scheme for cotton textiles. The protection it provided was relative, as other exporters like Hong Kong filled the gap. Hence, additional VERs had to be negotiated with other suppliers.

The Short-Term Arrangement on Cotton Textiles

To obtain acceptance of its bilateral VER agreements from the GATT, the USA was the instigator of the 1961 Short-Term Arrangement on Cotton Textiles (STA). This agreement obtained a 'waiver' from the GATT council. A 'waiver' is permission to breach general principles of GATT. One condition to obtain it is that the agreement is only temporary. This was the case with the STA, as it had a period of validity of one year only.

But what GATT principles did the STA offend? One was the fundamental prohibition of quantitative restrictions on imports and exports, stated in art. XI of the General Agreement. Clearly, the bilateral restrictions negotiated within the STA were not compatible with art. XI. The second principle of the GATT is the prohibition of any form of discrimination in the establishment or application of import restrictions (art. XII-1), i.e. quantitative restrictions must apply equally to all third countries. The STA, in spite of its multilateral character, was in fact discriminating, because in essence it constituted a framework for bilateral restrictions in trade in cotton products. It also introduced the notion of 'market disruption', describing a situation under which additional short-term restrictions could be imposed upon specific suppliers.

The Long-Term Arrangement on Cotton Textiles

Continuity was ensured through the Long-Term Arrangement on Cotton Textiles (LTA) of 1962. This agreement, which was extended twice to disappear only in 1974, concerned all textile and clothing products with a minimum cotton content (in value) of 50 per cent. It was more restrictive than the STA in several other ways. First, more efficient restrictions could be imposed in cases of market disruption. Second, although these restrictions could not reduce the quota level under that of the preceding year, they could in effect impose zero growth on them. Third, the normal rule that quotas should increase by a minimum of 5 per cent per annum mostly led to a growth rate that did not exceed this figure. On top of that, the LTA was asymmetric in the sense that countries affected by export restrictions were stripped of their right under the General Agreement (art. XIX) to seek and to receive compensatory concessions or to retaliate.

MFA I

The STA and LTA had perverse effects because they only covered products with a minimum of 50 per cent content of cotton. This led exporting countries to switch their production inputs to synthetic fibres and wool to escape quantitative restrictions. The tolerance of industrialized countries, especially the USA but also increasingly the EC, was short-lived. Under pressure from their national textile industries screaming for protection and experiencing a lower growth period, the first Arrangement regarding International Trade in Textiles (better known as the Multifibre Arrangement, henceforth MFA) was agreed upon and came into effect in 1974.

The MFA, like its predecessors, was a multilateral arrangement providing a framework indicating the circumstances under which trade in textile products could be restricted and the nature of the permitted restrictions. But, unlike the STA and LTA, the agreement was applicable to all textiles, wool and man-made fibres as well as cotton. Its initial period of validity was four years.

The first version of the MFA looked more promising for exports from least developed countries (LDCs) than its predecessors. Its 'basic objectives' were described as being 'to achieve the expansion of trade, the reduction of barriers to such trade and the progressive liberalization of world trade in textile products.' (art. 1, s. 2). Furthermore, its 'principal aim' was 'to further the economic and social development of LDCs and secure a substantial increase in their export earnings from textile products and to provide for a greater share for them in world trade in these products.' (art. 1, s. 3).

In concrete terms, the much more precise definition given to the notion of 'market disruption' limited the scope for abusive interpretation by importing countries. Secondly, the quotas of products under restraint had to grow as a rule by a minimum of 6 per cent per annum. Thirdly, these quotas had to be managed flexibly, allowing for 'swings,' 'carry-overs' and 'carry-forwards'. Lastly, compliance with the

Arrangement provisions was to be supervised internationally by a Textile Surveillance Body (TSB).

However, there were some less positive features of the MFA. For a start, the general rule of a minimum 6 per cent growth rate had many exceptions, especially concerning the most sensitive products. As for products originally not subject to export restrictions, they could be hit by quotas through the so-called 'basket exit mechanism' if the growth of exports in these products was too rapid. Articles 3 and 4 especially were considered of the utmost importance by developed countries. On the basis of their provisions, it was possible for them to impose restrictions unilaterally on grounds of either market disruption or real risks of market disruptions, without being obliged to take account either of the opinion of the restricted country or of that of the TSB.

MFA II

Renewal of the first MFA was negotiated in 1977 under difficult circumstances. Protectionist pressures in the USA and especially Western Europe had increased dramatically in the meantime. An obvious reason was the much-deteriorated economic climate following the recession of 1974–5. Secondly, the EC, because of its internal divisions, had failed to reach restrictive bilateral agreements quickly enough under the first MFA. On top of an increasing import penetration came a rapid growth in productivity through new technologies, contributing considerably to job losses in the European textiles industry. This transformed the EC into the leading protectionist negotiator in 1977, which thereby took over the role previously held by the USA. The EC's tough stand, soon endorsed by the other developed countries, resulted in a second MFA, which was much less favourable for exporting LDCs.

The first MFA framework was renewed subject to the condition that bilateral agreements 'could include the possibility of jointly agreed reasonable departures from particular elements in particular cases,' as long as these departures 'would be temporary and that participants concerned would return in the shortest possible time to the framework of the arrangement.' This of course meant opening Pandora's box and a serious dilution of the MFA discipline, as it failed to define what was to be considered reasonable regarding both the nature of the departure and its duration. As if this protection had not been enough, the new concept of 'cumulative market disruption' was introduced into the MFA. Whereas, under MFA I, measures to curb imports from a particular country could only be taken if that country was the clear cause of market disruption, from MFA II onwards it was sufficient to prove that global imports from 'low-cost' countries caused or risked to cause market disruption to impose restrictions across the board. More generally, the 6 per cent minimum growth rule laid down in the first Arrangement became the exception rather than the rule.

MFA III and IV

Since the second MFA was also valid for four years, negotiations for a second renewal of the Arrangement took place in 1981. Again, circumstances were difficult, owing to a bad economic climate. As a consequence, importing countries imposed yet another restrictive concept to be included in the MFA. The so-called 'anti-surge' clause made it impossible for exporters to fulfil underutilized quotas in a 'sudden and substantial' manner, on the ground that this was a major cause of market disruption. A second concession to importing countries was the possibility of actually reducing quotas for dominant suppliers. Again, the EC was among the toughest negotiators. The Commission described the results achieved as follows:

> Following the practically non-stop negotiations held during the latter half of the year within the GATT Textiles Committee, in which the Community played a particularly active role, a Protocol was adopted by consensus extending the MFA from 1 January 1982 to 31 July 1986. The Protocol ... takes into account many of the points of concern expressed by the Community throughout the negotiations.[1]

The single concession made to exporters was the deletion of the 'reasonable departures' clause. In 1986, a third extension of the MFA came into force. Thanks to a softening of the EC position no major changes from MFA III occurred. MFA IV was prolonged thrice, for 1992, 1993 and 1994.

General Remarks

What seemed to be a benign departure from the principle of quota-free trade in 1955 developed into a very complex and durable system of quota-ridden trade. As a general trend throughout the period since 1950, trade restrictions on textiles grew in terms of countries and of products, as well as in terms of effectiveness. Only in the period 1986–94 was there just a consolidation of trade barriers. A system meant to be temporary (at least in the minds of exporters) finally offered increasing protection for more than thirty years. Overall, the textiles industry in industrialized countries gradually became the second most protected economic sector after agriculture. This of course had considerable economic consequences for both importing and exporting countries.

THE ECONOMICS OF THE MFA

A few figures can give a first broad idea of the importance of the textiles industry in the EC. On the production side, the clothing and footwear industry represented 4.1 per cent of manufacturing employment and 1 per cent of total employment (or slightly more than 1 million jobs) for the EC in 1993. In some member states, however, that share was considerably higher. For Italy, the respective figures were 11 per cent and 3 per cent, for Greece 18.6 per cent and 3.8 per cent and for Portugal 15.5 per cent and 4.3 per cent. As regards consumption, an average of 7.4 per cent of household expenditure went to clothing and footwear in the EC in 1992. It is significant that these figures show that textiles seem to be of greater importance to consumers than to the economy as a whole. As in the field of agriculture, EC policy has failed to reflect this reality.

Geographical Coverage

As mentioned above, at the heart of the MFA there are numerous bilateral arrangements negotiated between exporting and importing countries. The EC has been responsible for negotiating bilateral agreements on behalf of its member states. By 1993, 21 exporting countries[2] had bilateral agreements with the EC under the MFA. On top of that, MFA-comparable agreements had been concluded with the 12 countries of the Community of Independent States (CIS), Latvia and Lithuania. For six Central and Eastern European countries[3] a protocol on textiles providing for the abolition of all restrictions in seven years was included in their Europe Agreements with the EC. Of the Mediterranean countries, five have preferential treatment in that they benefit from quota growth rates 50 per cent higher than under the normal MFA regime. To summarize, all main exporters (bar Turkey, which has had a customs union with the EC since the beginning of 1996) have some sort of restriction imposed upon them. Among LDCs, only the ACP states have benefited from generally unrestricted access to the EC market thanks to the Lomé Conventions. With the notable exception of Mauritius, they have not been able to take full advantage of that concession, because among their main exports to the EC only uncarded cotton (the lowest-value product related to textiles) registers in a poor tenth place.

Basic Arguments for Trade Restrictions in the Textiles Industry

Developed countries (or rather lobbies from the textiles industry) have been extremely inventive in producing allegedly commonsense reasons for shielding the textiles industry from normal international competition. Here are some of them.

The most straightforward argument invoked is that low-cost exporters threaten the survival of a major industry. It is important here to remark that international trade is based on comparative advantage, and thus on relative differences in costs, and that the textiles industry is not that 'major' any more.

A fairer point is that the textiles industry is concentrated in backward regions and employs low-skilled labour which could not easily be re-employed in other economic activities. The social costs of a surge in imports, therefore, could be considerable.

A third argument concerns social dumping and unfair competition through exploitation of the LDC labour force, subsidization, pollution and so on. The reader may judge the soundness of this argument.

Finally, there is an argument that the clothing industry is a matter of national security. 'What would we wear during the next war if our textiles industry had disappeared?' lobbyists ask.

Economic Effects of the MFA

Bilateral agreements in the MFA framework were agreements between an exporting and an importing country about what maximum quantity (or quota) per product category could be exported annually from the former to the latter. Importing countries have also called these agreements voluntary export restraints (VERs), which is not entirely false in the sense that exporters stood to gain something as well from them.

A quota limits the cheap supply of a product to the importing country's domestic market and therefore increases the equilibrium price of the product. If the licence system managing the quota is in the hands of the exporting country (which is the case for the MFA), then it is the exporting firms that can capture a so-called economic rent coming from the difference between the equilibrium price and the normal perfect competition price. In this way, exporting countries are compensated somewhat.

A second advantage for exporters was the secure market share that they had through the negotiated annual increase in quotas. This was especially appreciated by less-efficient producers, who would otherwise have gradually lost ground to more competitive suppliers. Consequently, the MFA system penalized the most efficient producers because of the rigidity of the system. This system was particularly tough on new entrants, as they had to rip away quotas from pre-established exporters to break into the market. Conversely, countries with a high initial quota faced a very enviable and cosy situation.

In addition, the granting of quotas was a highly politicized decision, especially in the case of the USA. The best example is the easy terms accorded to China in the early 1980s for evident ideological reasons, while at the same time Bangladesh, a country poorer than China, was effectively barred from the US market.

What then was the cost, if any, of the MFA for LDCs? Most studies dating back to the 1980s have shown that LDCs' textiles exports to the industrialized world would globally have been twice as big had trade merely been restricted by tariffs. This means that the textiles industry would have spurred economic growth even further in most countries and would have provided many more jobs to extremely poor populations, helping them to improve their lot considerably. Because of intense competition on the world market there would have been no rent to capture for favoured exporters and so the benefits of exports would have been more broadly distributed. Productivity would have improved more rapidly, as no market share would have been secure for a long time. And, last but certainly not least, the least developed countries would have had a chance to set up a textiles industry as well, because they would not have been kept out of the market by percolated quotas.

Of course, some places like Hong Kong would have needed to diversify more quickly into new industries (which would have been beneficial in the long term), while on the other hand others like Bangladesh would have had the opportunity to go down the road of industrialization earlier.

For producers in importing countries, the MFA has proved to be a very effective protection against competition from LDCs. Tariffs would have had to be extremely high to achieve broadly the same result without VERs. But the desegregated effects would have been different because countries and products couldn't have been targeted in the same way. With the MFA, the weakest parts of the textiles industry could be quickly protected. But this did not secure jobs. In fact, job cuts were massive during the 1970s and 1980s, and there were two main, connected reasons for this evolution. First, productivity gains were high because of technological change. Not only were jobs cut as a consequence but the nature of the remaining jobs had totally changed. Low-skilled workers were not employable any more. Second, competition from the most productive developed countries was fierce. As no quota system existed between industrialized countries, countries like Italy could take advantage of limited access granted to LDC exports to increase strongly their own market penetration in the OECD area. In economic jargon, this is known as the trade diversion effect.

So job losses, although they would certainly have been somewhat bigger had the MFA not existed, resulted mainly from rapid technological change and competition from high-cost countries. It is therefore not wrong to say that, certainly from the early 1980s onwards, the MFA was more directed at protecting huge capital investments and high-skilled jobs, rather than (as always pretended) poor and vulnerable low-skilled workers, as the latter had already largely been swept aside by automation.

Finally, it is important that any analysis of the economic consequences of the MFA reflects its impact on the biggest but least organized interest group, i.e. consumers. As mentioned, there were two main causes for high clothing prices. The first was straightforward; import volumes from cheaper suppliers were limited. The second was that quotas were allocated by country, which meant that less-productive LDCs also had a share of developed countries' domestic markets. Studies trying to quantify the total effect on final retail prices in clothing concluded to prices approximately 50 per cent higher than they otherwise would have been. One could simply conclude that these higher prices were a justified and equitably distributed burden to 'save' jobs. But in fact the burden was disproportionately borne by the most underprivileged sections of the population. There are two reasons for this.

The first is that poorer people spend a greater part of their incomes on basic necessities such as food and clothing than the better-off. So proportionately they pay more of the hidden tax induced by trade protection; it is regressive, just like VAT. The second reason is that poor people do not buy the same kind of clothes as the rich. While the poor would typically buy cheap basic clothes which LDCs are particularly good at producing, the rich tend to acquire fashionable and high-quality clothing, products in which developed countries have kept a competitive edge. This means that the rich nearly totally avoid paying for protection by buying low-tariff textiles from the OECD. Seen from a different angle, each single allegedly saved job has cost the poor, above all, between 42,000 USD and a staggering 145,000 USD, depending on the studies.

To sum up, it can be said that, on the whole, the LDCs lost, although some possibly benefited; that producers in the OECD won (some very much so, because they took advantage of the trade diversion effects) and that consumers lost substantially.

THE URUGUAY ROUND AND ITS EFFECTS ON TRADE IN TEXTILES

The Uruguay Round negotiations started in 1986 with a view to liberalizing trade in agricultural products, of integrating services into the GATT framework and of reintegrating fully trade in textiles. Until 1991, this last objective was the most sensitive of all and poisoned all the talks. The reason was simple. Spain and Portugal, still in an adjustment phase following their accession to the EC, did not want to confront even stronger competition in a sector that remained strategic in their eyes. They were strongly supported by Italy and Greece in their opposition. From 1992, attention focused more on agriculture. As the conclusion of the Uruguay Round looked more and more like a 'take it or leave it' package deal, and as the transition period for the abolition of the MFA was particularly generous, southern European reluctance faded away, paving the way for a successful conclusion of the talks.

The Agreement on Textiles and Clothing (ATC)

The ATC is a ten-year agreement that entered into force on the day the WTO was set up, i.e. on 1 January 1995. It settles the way in which the MFA is to be phased out. Four phases are provided for. The first started immediately and imposed an exit from MFA of 16 per cent of imports in volume on the basis of 1990 trade figures. The second commenced in 1998 and requires the exit of a further 17 per cent. The third, starting in 2002, will see an additional 18 per cent included in the normal WTO framework. In the fourth and final phase, beginning in 2005, the concluding 49 per cent of textiles products will have been freed from the MFA and the latter will have ceased to exist.

For remaining quotas during the three first stages, improvements on the old MFA treatment are provided for. Annual growth rates of these quotas are scheduled to be 16 per cent higher in the first stage than they otherwise would have been, another 25 per cent higher in the second stage and finally yet another 27 per cent higher in the third stage. As an example, if the normal annual growth rate of a product were fixed at 6 per cent, it would have been 6.96 per cent in 1995–7, 8.7 per cent in 1998–2001 and 11.05 per cent in 2002–2004. Very small suppliers would have better treatment.

A transitional safeguard mechanism can be used for the products not yet integrated into GATT 1994. This permits the imposition of an export restraint if 'it is demonstrated that a particular product is being imported ... in such increased quantities as to cause serious damage, or actual threat thereof, to the domestic industry producing like and/or directly competitive products.' The export restraint can be imposed in spite of disagreement on the part of the exporter and even the Textile Monitoring Body (TMB, successor of the TSB), which only has the power to make recommendations. The temporary quota cannot be smaller than the actual exports in the twelve previous months and cannot last longer than three years. In addition, importing countries may take measures in case of 'circumvention by trans-shipment, re-routing, false declaration concerning country or place of origin and falsification of official documents.'

The ATC, having being signed by all GATT 1994 parties, is applicable to all of them. This means that developed and less developed countries alike, be they signatories of the MFA or not, must scrap all quantitative restrictions by 2005.

Immediate Consequences and Prospects for the Future

The first thing to note is the pernicious effect that the ATC will have on certain countries. Because the ATC concerns all products that are mentioned in any one bilateral agreement under the MFA as well as all GATT 1994 signatories, the MFA and all the products it covers will *de facto* be extended to any member of the WTO. This means that it is possible that countries will face new quotas during the transition period because they export products that would not yet have been liberalized.

The second remark concerns the liberalization process itself. The basis for trade liberalization is total volume of trade in 1990, meaning that imports from developed countries as well as developing countries are taken into account. Because trade between OECD countries was never durably affected by quantitative restrictions and did not fall under MFA regulations, the liberalization of 51 per cent of trade by 2002 will mean practically nothing, because about half of developed countries' imports are already free of non-tariff barriers (NTBs). In fact, real market-opening will only come in 2005. To compensate somewhat for this concession made to the rich world, it was imposed that liberalization should occur in each of four broad categories (tops and yarns, fabrics, made-up textiles products and clothing). But it is not specified what share of each group should be freed from NTBs.

Furthermore, during the validity of the ATC, measures may already be taken under art.s VI (anti-dumping) and XIX (import surges damaging local industry) of the GATT. This was not the case under the MFA, as it already had its own more stringent protection mechanisms. Adding the transitional safeguard mechanism, importing countries in fact have two protection instruments at their disposal during the ATC.

There is not too much room for optimism concerning respect for the letter and the spirit of the ATC. The next few years will certainly be packed with tension, confrontations and unresolved disputes. But assuming that in the end, i.e. by 2005, trade in textiles will be liberalized to the extent that all NTBs will have been scrapped, how will trade relations be likely to evolve?

If liberalization is completed on schedule, both LDCs and industrialized countries stand to gain substantially. Economic gains from the Uruguay Round as a whole have been estimated to be of between 200 billion and 500 billion USD for the world, over two-thirds thereof for the USA and the EC alone. A substantial part of these huge gains is to come from the textiles sector.

Consumers from the OECD and whole economies in LDCs can expect to reap these benefits as trade grows considerably.

However, these happy prospects could evaporate if OECD governments do not play fair. Remaining instruments after 2005, such as art. VI and XIX, could be powerful tools to hinder normal trade expansion. If governments listen to the inevitable pleas of their domestic industries having a hard time restructuring (but do not forget that they already had 35 years to get themselves into shape), consumers will not see their lot improve and LDCs will see theirs worsen considerably, for the simple reason that they will not be able to capture the rents linked to VERs any more.

CONCLUSIONS

The MFA was a very restrictive and distortive protection mechanism. It favoured old suppliers among LDCs as well as the most efficient OECD producers on the back of both the poorest LDCs entering the textiles industry later and OECD consumers with the lowest purchasing power.

The GATT 1994 and the ATC promise sweeping changes in the right direction. By 2005 they should lead to a trade system that provides producers with a level playing field, although with relatively high tariff barriers. This favourable outcome will however depend exclusively on the goodwill of the countries of the industrialized world, as some potentially powerful weapons will still remain at their disposal. The temptation to use and abuse such weapons could prove irresistible, at least in a first phase, for the simple reason that OECD countries will have postponed genuine liberalization until the last minute. It is easy to guess that textiles lobbies will be particularly active in 2005.

The least that can be said is that a lot of uncertainty remains as to whether the letter as well as the spirit of the ATC will be respected. A lot is at stake both for consumers and for LDCs. One thing should always be present in the minds of decision-makers. If they really want to help LDCs they should let them export their way out of poverty. No transfers, however large they might be, could achieve the same result as opening markets. In this respect, the increasingly tolerant stand the EC has taken on textiles in the last ten years is a welcome development. This new approach could prove very useful to the EC if the USA continues playing tough, for it would then become a natural ally of LDCs.

Let us hope that all the world leaders are serious about lending a helping hand to the most underprivileged and that they will translate their fine speeches into courageous acts.

Bibliography

Babarinde, O., *The Lomé Conventions and Development: An Empirical Assessment* (Avebury, London, 1994).

Bensch, A. and Paemen, H., *Du GATT à l'OMC: La Communauté européenne dans l'Uruguay Round* Leuven (Leuven University Press, 1995).

Choi, Y.-P., Chung, H. S. and Marian N., *The Multi-Fibre Arrangement in Theory and Practice* (Pinter, London, 1995).

Commission of the European Communities, *General Report on the Activities of the European Communities in 1973* (Office for Official Publications of the European Communities, Brussels, 1974).

Commission of the European Communities, *General Report on the Activities of the European Communities in 1977* (Office for Official Publications of the European Communities, Brussels, 1978).

Commission of the European Communities, *General Report on the Activities of the European Communities in 1981* (Office for Official Publications of the European Communities, Brussels, 1982).

Commission of the European Communities, *General Report on the Activities of the European Communities in 1985* (Office for Official Publications of the European Communities, Brussels, 1986).

European Study Service, *Textiles and the EC* (DRT Europe Services, Brussels, 1994).

Howse, R. and Trebilcock, M., *The Regulation of International Trade* (Routledge, 1995).

Khavand, F., *Le Nouvel Ordre commercial mondial: du GATT à l'OMC* (Nathan, 1995).

Messerlin, P., *La Nouvelle Organization mondiale du commerce* (Institut Français des Relations Internationales, Paris 1995).

Nehmé, C., *Le GATT et les grands accords commerciaux mondiaux* (Editions d'Organization, Geneva 1994).

Pelkmans, J., *Opening Up the Euro-Market for Textiles*, CEPS Paper no. 54 (Brussels, 1993).

Prométhée, *Annuaire 1994 des accords textiles de l'Union Européenne* (Prométhée, Paris 1994).

Van Houtte, H., *The Law of International Trade* (Sweet and Maxwell, London, 1995).

World Trade Organization, *Trading into the Future* (Geneva, 1995).

Notes

1. Commission of the European Communities (1982) p. 230
2. Bangladesh, Brazil, China, Colombia, Guatemala, Haiti, Hong Kong, India, Indonesia, Macao, Malaysia, Mexico, Peru, Philippines, Singapore, South Korea, Sri Lanka, Taiwan, Thailand, Uruguay, Yugoslavia (suspended).
3. Bulgaria, Czech Republic, Hungary, Poland, Romania, Slovakia.

23 The EU and the World Trade Organization

Cathryn Costello

INTRODUCTION

The World Trade Organization (WTO) is:

> the legal and institutional foundation of the multilateral trading system. It provides the principal contractual obligations determining how governments frame and implement domestic trade legislation and regulations. And it is the platform on which trade relations among countries evolve through collective debate, negotiation and adjudication.[1]

This chapter will discuss the innovations and potential shortcomings of the WTO as the regulatory structure of the multilateral international trading system, focusing on its role as the framework for EU trade relations with developing countries. Firstly, the background to the WTO will be outlined, followed by an assessment of the new institutional dispute settlement mechanism. Changes in traditional trade policy will be discussed, particularly in the light of their impact on EU trade preferences. Finally new agreements in the areas of agriculture, services and intellectual property will be outlined.

BACKGROUND

The WTO came into existence on 1 January 1995, as a result of the Uruguay Round (UR) of multilateral trade negotiations. The creation of permanent institutional structure for international trade relations was long overdue. Original plans for such an organization were dashed in 1947, when the US Congress rejected the Havana Charter and its creation, the International Trade Organization. Only the part of the Charter on tariffs and trade came into force, as the General Agreement on Tariffs and Trade (GATT).

However the GATT system had serious shortcomings. Important GATT rules and procedures were ignored by the members.[2] Many regulations were unclear, allowing leeway for their abuse.[3] Furthermore, several economic areas were effectively excluded, including agriculture and textiles. The selective nature of codes negotiated in subsequent trade rounds threatened the multilateral aspirations of the system. In particular, the Tokyo Round codes on various forms of non-tariff barriers (NTBs) were signed by less than a third of GATT members, but those countries which had not signed still benefited from the agreements because of the operation of GATT's most-favoured-nation (MFN) clause. Thus the free-rider problem was seen as acute.

In order to remedy this situation, the WTO system extends and strengthens multilateral trade rules. The central principle of the system is that it forms a single undertaking, to be accepted as a whole by each contracting party. In all the WTO Agreement contains some twenty-nine individual texts, which form part of this single undertaking.[4] While the old GATT applied to trade in merchandise goods, the WTO has a wider ambit, also covering trade in services and trade-related aspects of intellectual property.[5] They include GATT 1994, the amended and updated reincarnation of GATT 1947, which continues to regulate international goods trade.

DISPUTE SETTLEMENT

Weaknesses in the original Dispute Settlement Mechanism (DSM) added to the problems in the old GATT system. The old DSM allowed for the evasion of dispute settlement altogether by blocking the establishment, terms or reference or composition of the dispute settlement panel. Moreover, the previous rule of adopting panel reports by consensus meant that an offending GATT member could block the findings of a dispute settlement panel. Other deficiencies in the old DSM included the lack of stringent time limits, the possibility of 'forum shopping'[6] and the lack of rules on the implementation of rulings.

The new DSM seeks to remedy these deficiencies.[7] Art. 23(1) of the Dispute Settlement Understanding (DSU) lays down that the system shall be compulsory. Members commit themselves not to take unilateral action against perceived violations of the trade rules but to seek recourse in the multilateral dispute settlement system. Similarly the tactic of preventing the establishment of a panel is no longer possible. Articles 16(4) and 17(4) reverse the old rule regarding adoption of the panel report. Now there must be a consensus vote *against* the report for it not to go through. Furthermore all the major steps in the deadline now have clear deadlines. The creation of an appellate body (AB) is another innovation. The AB is to hear appeals on legal issues, which should enhance the rules-based nature of the system. The system is an integrated one, so that a panel can interpret any of the WTO agreements bearing on the dispute at hand, thus avoiding forum shopping. Another major improvement is the drafting of detailed rules on implementation (arts 22 and 23).

It is widely accepted that this more robust DSM could be beneficial to developing countries, by serving to restrict unilateral measures against them and allowing them to pursue their rights independently of their power in the international trade environment.[8] However, the mechanism remains untested and whether it will truly contribute to the international rule of law in trade issues remains to be seen.[9] If successful the developing countries will benefit from more consistent rules, but they nevertheless remain more vulnerable to retaliatory action. For example, the WTO can authorize the withdrawal of MFN treatment from an offending country, a sanction that would have drastic effects were it directed against a typical developing economy heavily dependent on a large developed economy.[10] Another worry of developing countries concerns the possibility of cross-retaliation,[11] resulting from the integrated nature of the DSM.[12] The impact on the EU is best appreciated in the light of its approach to previous adverse panel reports.[13] A good example concerns the trade preferences granted under the Lomé Convention for bananas originating in ACP countries. These were condemned by GATT panel report but under the old system the EU was able to block the findings against it. In essence, the new DSM means that the EU can no longer employ its traditional pragmatic approach to such legal problems, exploiting the grey areas of the old GATT, implausibly invoking its loopholes (e.g. art. XXIV on free trade areas and customs unions in the banana dispute) or simply political imperatives.[14]

TARIFFS, GREY AREA MEASURES AND ANTI-DUMPING

The Uruguay Round brought a commitment to overall tariff reductions. The cut is comparable to those achieved in the Kennedy and Tokyo Rounds. The EU committed itself to widespread tariff reductions on manufactured goods, bringing the average rate down by 38 per cent. Furthermore, tariffs on tropical products have been abolished altogether.[15] Further trade liberalization is signalled in the Safeguards Agreement, which contains a phased prohibition of so-called grey area measures, which include voluntary export restraints, orderly marketing arrangements and the like. Such measures, although technically based on the consent of the exporting country, are generally recognized as resulting from threats of unilateral restriction on those imports.

The overall prospect for liberalization of trade in goods resulting from the Round has met a cautious response. The Anti-Dumping (AD) Code failed to achieve any fundamental reform of the existing Tokyo Code, leaving this favourite protectionist weapon essentially intact.[16] Indeed it has been suggested that the AD Code thwarts the liberalizing achievements of other aspects of the WTO.[17] Although some commentators have observed a policy tendency against the use of AD measures in the EU context, the point is nevertheless accepted that the abolition of grey area measures may be premature, as long as AD measures remain as an easy alternative.[18] Some developing and newly industrialized countries have expressed similar worries.

The extension of liberal market access is an issue of concern for ACP countries, who see the UR liberalization as eroding their preferential access to their most important export market, that of the EU, under the Lomé Convention.

The extent to which the erosion of ACP preferences would directly affect their economies depends on their export profile. Some studies suggest that those ACP states with the highest proportion of value-added exports will be most seriously affected, i.e. Kenya, Cameroon, Côte d'Ivoire and Mauritius.[19] However, there are as yet no precise estimates of net losses.[20]

In any case, it is clear that the value of trade preferences is diminished as trade barriers are liberalized on a multilateral basis. Furthermore, non-reciprocal trade preferences are prima facie incompatible with GATT. Trade preferences generally infringe the cardinal principle of the MFN clause. The grant of such preferences is only permissible in a free trade area or customs union. However, for GATT compatibility, two conditions must be fulfilled: 'substantially all' trade within the area must be liberalized,[21] and the common external tariffs of the area must not 'on the whole' be more restrictive than was the case before the block was formed.[22] EU trade policy continues to focus on such regional liberalization.[23] However, such agreements are subject to strict scrutiny under the WTO[24] and by no means represent an easy alternative.[25]

THE AGREEMENT ON AGRICULTURE

Developing countries were anxious to see this issue dealt with in a multilateral framework, given the high degree of protectionism in the agricultural sector of developed countries, through elaborate systems of market intervention. An alliance of developed and developing countries adversely affected by this protectionism, the Cairns Group,[26] was instrumental in the UR negotiations. The EU's Common Agricultural Policy (CAP) exemplifies this protectionist approach and the adverse effects of the CAP on international prices and markets had long been a cause for concern.[27]

GATT rules did not effectively deal with these issues,[28] either granting agriculture special treatment (e.g. permitting the use of import quotas under art. XI and export subsidies under art. XVI) or even ignoring the issue.

The Agreement on Agriculture (AA) deals with three main issues: domestic support, market access and export subsidies. As regards domestic support, WTO members agreed to a 20 per cent reduction in the total aggregate measure of support over six years. In the area of market access, all NTBs are to be converted to tariffs (tariffication) and then reduced by an average of 36 per cent. All tariffs are to be bound by the end of the implementation period. Agricultural export subsidies still receive exceptional treatment, in that existing export subsidies are allowed but capped at a base period (1986–90) levels in terms of volume and expenditure. Subsidized export expenditure is to be reduced by 36 per cent and subsidized export volume by 21 per cent over six years, in each of 22 product categories. Perhaps the most apt description of the AA is the it effects a reregularization of agricultural trade, rather than a genuine liberalization.[29]

The EU maintains that the 1992 CAP reform[30] fulfils the requirements of the AA. Although doubts have been expressed about this assertion, it is generally accepted that the agreement does not entail any drastic modifications to CAP.[31] In addition the suggestion has been made that omission of compensatory payments from the agreement would allow such payments to be used instead of the subsidies, thus leaving a loophole which would allow circumvention of the agreement's purpose.[32]

Overall world agricultural prices are predicted to rise by 10 per cent to 30 per cent as a result of the AA.[33] Thus the implications for the developing world vary from country to country. Positive outcomes are anticipated for developing countries involved in agriculture-related export activities such as Argentina, Brazil, Thailand, Malaysia and the Philippines. However, the AA is expected to have a negative impact on agricultural net importers, especially in Africa. Countries such as Nigeria, Angola, Mozambique, Senegal and Côte d'Ivoire are expected to suffer.[34]

TRADE IN SERVICES

The WTO contains the first set of multilateral and legally enforceable rules on trade in services, the General Agreement on Trade in Services (GATS). This marks a considerable widening of the scope of international trade rules. Negotiations revealed a conflict of interest between developed and developing countries. Developed countries were primarily interested in the right to establish a commercial presence in other countries. Developing countries objected, on the basis that such liberalization could thwart attempts to foster important domestic services, such as banking and insurance.[35] Those countries were, on the other hand, anxious to secure liberalization of labour-intensive services exports.

The outcome is an agreement that reflects the resulting compromise, based on the principle of progressive liberalization.[36] The scope of the agreement is all internationally traded services, defined according to mode of delivery.[37] National treatment does not apply as an automatic right and wide exceptions to MFN are allowed. Thus GATS is best seen as an incipient step towards international liberalization of trade in services. The crucial issue of the movement of labour was addressed in an annexe to the GATS. This provides that although labour at managerial and technical level is not restricted, GATS does not apply to measures affecting the movement of individuals providing services or residence on a permanent basis.

The effects of GATS on developing economies are extremely difficult to assess, given the nature of the agreement and the lack of models for determining trade in services in general.[38]

It is likely that the Council for Trade in Services will maintain pressure for liberalization in this sector, although its long-term impact is uncertain.

INTELLECTUAL PROPERTY RIGHTS

During the Uruguay Round negotiations, industrial countries, especially the USA, insisted that an agreement on intellectual property rights (IPR) be drawn up. It was argued that a strengthening of IPR was necessary to encourage innovation. This desire is explained by the shift in world trade patterns over the last decade or so, whereby apart from most African countries, LDCs are no longer predominantly exporters of primary products but of manufactured goods. Newly industrialized countries (NICs) have gained competitiveness in innovative product markets, often through a strategy of imitation.[39]

The resulting agreement on Trade Related Aspects of Intellectual Property (TRIPs) seeks to establish broad international minimum standards of protection in the areas of patents, trademarks and copyright, based on existing international conventions on IPR protection. These are supplemented where no international agreement existed previously. There is also a call for international harmonization. In addition there is a general national treatment commitment and an MFN clause. Notably the level of patent protection is relatively high, reflecting the conception of the industrial nations. The agreement allows a transition period for implementation by LDCs. Developing countries tend to regard TRIPs as an attempt by the industrial nations to avoid competition from imitating LDCs.[40] However it is argued that TRIPs can be seen as an incipient step towards a global competition policy, which, while admittedly allowing innovative companies in industrial countries to secure their pioneer profits by securing a sufficiently long imitation-lag, nevertheless benefits developing countries by rewarding innovation and removing uncertainty as to IPR.[41] This argument has been disputed, on the basis that it ignores implementation costs and variations in levels of development. It has been suggested that developing countries are likely to implement the Agreement selectively in sectors where they have comparative advantages, citing the example of India's early grant of copyright protection to computer programs.[42]

CONCLUSION

This chapter has highlighted particular aspects of the WTO agreements that will regulate global trade relations into the next century. Overall, the agreements constitute a considerable liberalization of world trade, although only time will tell whether this tendency will prevail over protectionist impulses. Moreover, the strengthening of the multilateral trading system, brought about by the wider ambit and greater detail of the agreements, should not be underestimated. Together with the robust DSM, the rule of law in international trade relations is enhanced.

The WTO now forms the framework for EU trade relations with developing countries. It is time for a fundamental rethink of the EU's use of preferential trade agreements and its 'hierarchy of preferences' to reflect the increasing integration of developing countries into the global economy. Ultimately, the use of trade preferences is incompatible with the rules and aspirations of a multilateral trading system. The challenge for the EU lies in accommodating its relations with developing countries in this system.

Bibliography

Berrod and Fournier, 'The Common Institutional Framework of the New World Trade System,' in Bourgeois, Berrod and Fournier (eds), *The Uruguay Round Results. A European Lawyers' Perspective* (College of Europe, Bruges, 1995) pp. 25–32.

Bourgeois, P., 'The Uruguay Round of GATT: Some General Comments from an EC Standpoint', in Emiliou and O'Keeffe (eds), *The European Union and World Trade Law – After the GATT Uruguay Round* (1996) pp. 81–90.

Bronckers, 'WTO Implementation in the EC. Anti-Dumping, Safeguards and Intellectual Property,' *Journal of World Trade*, vol. 29, no. 5 (1995) p. 73.

Cosgrove, C. A., 'Has the Lomé Convention Failed ACP Trade?', *Journal of International Affairs* vol. 48 (Summer 1994) pp. 223–49.

CTA, *EEC Trade Preferences and ACP Exports. Report to the European Commission* (Reading, 1989).

Davenport, N., Hewitt, A. and Koning, A., *Europe's Preferred Partners? The Lomé Countries in World Trade* (ODI and ECDPM, London and Maastricht, 1994a).

Davenport, N., Hewitt, A. and Koning, A., *The Impact of the Uruguay Round on ACP States* (ODI and ECDPM, London and Maastrict, 1994b).

ECDPM, *Lomé 2000* (Maastrict January 1996).

Evans, P. and Walsh, J. (eds), *The EIU Guide to the New GATT* (Economist Intelligence Unit, London, 1994).

Fisch and Speyer, 'TRIPs as an Adjustment Mechanism in North–South Trade,' *Intereconomics* (March/April 1995) pp. 65–9.

Fournier, 'GATS. Introductory Note', in Bourgeois, Berrod and Fournier (1995).

Grilli, E., *The European Community and the Developing Countries* (Cambridge University Press, 1993).

Grilli, E., *Creativity of Europe's Trade Policies towards Developing and Eastern European Countries* (Netherlands Economic Institute, The Hague, 1994).

Grossmann, Koopmann and Michaelowa, 'The New World Trade Organisation: Pacemaker for World Trade?' *Intereconomics* (May/June 1994) pp. 107–15.

Hamilton and Whalley, 'Evaluating the Impact of the Uruguay Round Results on Developing Countries,' *The World Economy*, vol. 18, no. 1 (January 1995) pp. 31–51.

Hartmann, M., 'New Developments in International Agricultural Trade. A Threat or a Chance for LDCs and CEECs'?, *Intereconomics* (March/April 1995) pp. 59–65.

Horlick, 'How the GATT became Protectionist? An Analysis of the Uruguay Round Draft Final Anti-Dumping Code,' *Journal of World Trade*, vol. 27, no. 5 (1992) pp. 5–17.

Hudec and Robert, 'Legal Issues in US–EU Trade Policy: GATT Litigation 1960–1985,' in Baldwin, Robert, Hamilton and Sapir (eds), *Issues in US–EU Trade Relations* (University of Chicago Press, 1988) p. 245.

Ingersent, Rayner and Hine 'Ex-post evaluation of the Uruguay Round Agriculture Agreement,' *Economic Journal*, vol. 103, no. 421 (November 1993).

Ingersent, Rayner and Hine (eds), *Agriculture in the Uruguay Round* (Macmillan, London, 1994).

Kappel, R., 'Africa's Marginalization in World Trade. A Result of the Uruguay Round Agreements,' *Intereconomics* (January–February 1996) pp. 33–42.

Kuyper, P-J., 'The New WTO Dispute Settlement System: The Impact on the Community,' in Bourgeois, Berrod and Fournier (eds), *The Uruguay Round Results. A European Lawyers' Perspective* (College of Europe, Bruges, 1995) pp. 87–114.

Pelkmans, J., 'The Economic Significance of the Round,' in Bourgeois, Berrod and Fournier (1995) pp. 43–58.

Rasmussen, H., 'The Institutions of the World Trade Law after the WTO confronted with some Legacies of the Past', in Bourgeois, Berrod and Fournier (1995) pp. 135–40.

Roessler, 'The Agreement Establishing the World Trade Organisation,' in Bourgeois, Berrod and Fournier (1995) pp. 67–86.

Scott, J., 'Tragic Triumph: Agricultural Trade, the Common Agricultural Policy and the Uruguay Round,' in Emiliou and O'Keefe (eds), *The European Union and World Trade Law* (1996) pp. 165–80.

Swinbank, 'CAP Reform, 1992,' *Journal of Common Market Studies* vol. 31 (1994) pp. 359–72.

Tyers, 'The Cairns Group Perspective,' in Ingersent *et al.* (1994) ch. 5.

Watkins, *Fixing the Rules: North–South Issues in International Trade and the GATT Uruguay Round* (Catholic Institute for International Relations, London, 1992).

World Trade Organization, *Trading into the Future* (Geneva, 1995a).

World Trade Organization, *Trade Policy Review: European Union* (Geneva, 1995b).

Zeeb, 'Intellectual Property Protection and the Globalization of the World Economy,' *Intereconomics* (January/February 1996) pp. 21–6.

Notes

1. World Trade Organization 1995a.
2. Infra, on the Dispute Settlement Mechanism.
3. For example, the rules on anti-dumping, countervailing duties and subsidies.
4. There are also four other agreements, originally negotiated in the Tokyo Round, which have a selective group of signatories and are known therefore as 'plurilateral agreements'. They relate to trade in civil aircraft, government procurement, the dairy sector and bovine meat. The agreement on government procurement is potentially of great importance, especially for developing countries, but as it remains merely plurilateral in nature, is outside the scope of this chapter.
5. There are also agreements, *inter alia*, on trade related investment measures (TRIMs), sanitary and phytosanitary measures, rules of origin, and technical barriers to trade but they fall outside the scope of this chapter.
6. In the old GATT system, the GATT and various codes were separate treaties and a panel could only interpret that Agreement or Code under which it was established. This led to the practice of 'forum shopping' whereby complainants brought cases under that Agreement/Code which served their purposes.
7. Kuyper (1995).
8. Davenport *et al.* (1994b) Hamilton and Whalley (1995).
9. Rasmussen (1995).
10. Davenport *et al.* (1994b) p. 53.
11. For example, retaliation in goods trade in a dispute about services.
12. Hamilton and Whalley (1995) p. 39.
13. Hudec and Robert (1988). The authors describe the EU approach as viewing the old GATT DSM as one based on negotiation, rather than adjudication.
14. Grilli (1993).
15. World Trade Organization 1995b.
16. The new AD Code does clarify central concepts, including that of normal price, which should lead to greater transparency and predictability. However there is a unique deferential standard of review for the DSM in AD cases, which could undermine these clarifications.
17. Horlick (1993).
18. Bronckers (1995).
19. CTA (1989).
20. Davenport *et al.* (1994b) Kappell (1996).
21. This means that sectoral FTAs and CUs are GATT-incompatible. In the EU context CAP presents a major stumbling block in this respect.
22. Article XXIV of the GATT.
23. For example, the proposed customs union with South Africa; long-term plans for a Mediterranean Free Trade Area.
24. The UR contains an agreement on the interpretation of art. XXIV, which attempts to clarify how the effects of FTAs and CUs are to be calculated. Furthermore, such agreements must cover at least 90 per cent of trade with full reciprocity being introduced within ten years.

25. The negotiations on the FTA with South Africa are instructive in this respect. See Chapter 12 in this book on EU–South African relations.
26. The Cairns Group consisted of Australia, Argentina, Brazil, Canada, Chile, Colombia, Hungary, Indonesia, Malaysia, New Zealand, the Philippines, Thailand and Uruguay. One estimate is that agricultural protection in industrial countries, particularly in the EU and US, was responsible for reducing the value of agricultural exports from these countries by more than half. See Tyers (1994).
27. For example, Watkins (1992) the author describes the practice of international dumping of agricultural surpluses by the US and EU.
28. Scott (1996).
29. Hartmann (1995).
30. Swinbank (1992).
31. Ingersent *et al.* (1993).
32. Scott (1996) p. 177.
33. Hamilton and Whalley (1995).
34. Kappell (1996) p. 40.
35. Cosgrove (1994) p. 239.
36. Fournier (1995).
37. GATS identifies four such modes of delivery:
    - services supplied from one country to another;
    - services supplied in one country to consumers from another;
    - services provided through the presence of a commercial entity of one country in the territory of another;
    - services provided in one country by individuals from another.
38. See Pelkmans (1995) p. 50.
39. Fisch and Speyer (1995).
40. Ibid., p. 68.
41. Ibid.
42. Zeeb (1996).

24 Globalization: the EU and Developing Countries

Carol Cosgrove-Sacks

The EU is frequently cited as the most advanced form of regional integration currently in existence. The structure of EU relations with developing countries similarly reflects the regionalist dynamic: relations with Africa are at the core of EU policies towards developing countries, while regionally based networks of relations complement the core in the Mediterranean, Asia, and Latin America. The EU's focus in the 1990s on Central and Eastern Europe serves to highlight yet another regional preoccupation and further emphasizes the essentially regionalist approach that to date has characterized EU external relations. But is this a sustainable approach in the era of globalization? To what extent are EU policy makers able to respond positively to the challenge of globalization for the benefit not only of their own electorates but also for the benefit of the developing countries whose interests the various sets of EU regional arrangements are supposed to serve? What are the likely implications of globalization for EU–developing country relations?

This concluding chapter addresses these issues and attempts an admittedly provisional assessment of prospects for the future of EU relations with developing countries. It is divided into three parts. The first examines the so-called challenge of globalization, analysing briefly its driving forces and its effects, and assessing its impact on the network of EU commitments to developing countries. The second part focuses on the EU's response to globalization, looking at the formal policy goals, the inherent difficulties of creating a consistent response, and the special problems posed in the context of EU–ACP relations. Finally, the third part looks ahead to the emerging shape of EU relations with developing countries in the twenty-first century and the importance of enterprise development.

THE CHALLENGE OF GLOBALIZATION

Globalization, hand in hand with breathtakingly rapid technological change, is bringing about 'tectonic' shifts in the world economy.[1] The increasing globalization of the international economy is creating interdependencies that tend to undermine established national and regional structures. The rapid expansion of world trade in goods and services, and the transformation of capital and money markets onto a global scale prompted by new technologies in communications and data processing, is in the process of prompting a homogenization of production and consumption, which is in turn stimulating the emergence of international technical and quality standards and similar economic regulations and institutions throughout the world. Competitiveness in world markets is an increasingly common goal. The costs of research, development and commercialization to global markets are high and as the product life cycle shortens with the advent of new technologies, so the entry costs to worldwide markets becomes ever higher. In turn, the threat of marginalization increases for those countries and enterprises which cannot surmount these entry barriers. As the former President of the European Commission, Jacques Delors, has asked, who will gain from competitiveness and who will be the victims of the associated precariousness of production structures? What will be the place of Europe (and its relations with developing countries) in future economic production in a globalized economy?[2] 'The inequalities in the global economy and the assymetries of interdependence influence the relations between globalization, growth and development in many ways.'[3]

Professor Simai charted the scale of global production, amounting to some 24 000 billion USD in 1995, of which more than 80 per cent was accounted for by only 24 high income countries, and about 5 per cent of global GDP being derived from 45 low income countries that together accounted for more than 55 per cent of the world population. These gaps in income, production, consumption and savings between the high income countries (including the EU) and the less developed countries represent a compelling challenge. The establishment of the WTO, which has become a symbol of globalization, has fixed the spotlight on trade as the core factor to overcome these inequalities. The liberalization of world trade is the principal goal of the WTO, but many developing countries do not yet belong to the new organization and the latter is also challenged by existing regional trade arrangements, many based on discriminatory preferences. The

Director-General of the WTO, speaking to EU trade ministers in 1996 in Dublin, called for coherence between the multilateral trading system and regional trade blocks, pointing to

> the great new wave of regional trade initiatives, some spanning continents and oceans, impelling us to look closely at the systemic implications of regionalism in order to reinforce the m.f.n. principle and ensure that regional and multilateral systems converge around it.[4]

The impact of globalization on developing countries has been uneven. Much depends on their ability to attract international investment and to stimulate their services sector. Asia has to date proved to be much stronger in this respect than Latin American, Mediterranean or African countries. World trade in services was estimated to exceed 1100 billion USD in 1995 compared with trade in goods worth some 4000 billion USD, and while the WTO calculated that trade in goods increased by 8 per cent in value terms in 1995, trade in services rose by more than 10 per cent. Moreover, foreign direct investment grew much faster than international trade and sales of foreign affiliates of multinational corporations were estimated to exceed the value of trade in goods and services.[5] However, the member states of the United Nations gathered at the Ninth UN Conference on Trade and Development (UNCTAD IX) recognized that developing countries, particularly in Africa, are unable to participate fully in the world economy and that they are increasingly marginalized by the process of globalization. The UNCTAD Midrand Declaration stressed that the impact of globalization and liberalization is uneven, and that a mutually beneficial trading system in which the developing countries could enjoy a productive partnership with high income countries must be a high priority. To what extent do the various regional arrangements between the EU and developing countries add up to an effective framework, based on long-term commitments and effective actions? The evidence presented in this volume suggests that only the Lomé Convention fits this requirement, but that the EU–ACP relationship is unlikely to equip the ACP states with the means necessary to overcome their increasing marginalization. The driving forces of globalization may be characterized as the emergence of horizontal markets, international finance, acceleration of innovation and new technologies, and the development of intra-firm and industry supply chains across the world. Horizontal markets, which extend the concept of niche marketing on a global scale, generate a degree of demand that only the largest firms can meet and entail the application of international technical and quality control standards that many developing countries cannot sustain. International finance has probably contributed dramatically to globalization, and financial markets have themselves become global. New technologies, particularly in communications and manufacturing control systems, make it easy to transfer investment and shift production. Electronic data interchange and increasingly cheaper data transmission systems make it possible for both goods and services to be produced far from the consumer and delivered 'just in time' to the door. But in turn they depend on adequate infrastructure in terms of telecommunications, power generation and transport networks, all of which are less than reliable in most developing countries, and especially in Africa. These new technologies accentuate knowledge-based products and have prompted a strategic shift in the higher income countries, where more than 50 per cent of GDP is estimated to derive from activities requiring high levels of education, e.g. software, telecommunications, pharmaceuticals, and the media.[6] While information technology permits previously untradable services to be traded internationally (such as back office services and accounting for banks and airlines, software design, and long-distance learning schemes), such out-sourcing also depends on adequate infrastructure. The absence of the latter also limits access for developing country firms to intra-firm and intra-industry supply chains, such as the automotive sector where components come from many sources. The 1996 World Investment Report by UNCTAD showed that foreign direct investment inflows to Africa were significantly less than to other regions in 1995. In contrast, record levels of investment flowed into Central and Eastern Europe, contributing to the integration of these countries in transition into the global economy.[7]

A significant result of foreign direct investment has been to reduce the dependence of many developing countries on the export of commodities. In East Asia it fell from 69 per cent in 1970 to 26 per cent in 1992; in South Asia from 53 per cent to 27 per cent; in Latin America from 88 per cent to 62 per cent. In Africa the drop was much less marked, from 88 per cent to 76 per cent. Even more significantly, average commodity prices between 1973 and 1992 showed marked regional variations, with African commodities performing badly. Over this period, average African commodity prices declined by around 50 per cent, whereas Latin American prices rose by 5 per cent; in Asia, they grew by more than 60 per cent.[8]

While globalization is a remarkable feature of the closing years of the twentieth century, there are other, often contradictory forces at work that also influence the framework for EU relations with developing countries. Regionalism persists, not least in the burgeoning free trade areas of North America (NAFTA), East Asia (APEC) and Europe itself (the EEA).

THE EU RESPONSE

The EU has responded rather slowly to the challenge of globalization as it affects relations with developing countries. First, the Maastricht Treaty, itself negotiated in 1991–2, recognized the growing dynamic of globalization and recorded the goal of integrating developing countries fully into the world economy. Second, by the mid-1990s the logic of the completion of the Single European Market and the establishment of the WTO prompted more concerted action on the part of the EU. Compliance with the Uruguay Round agreements, which required reform of the general system of preferences (GSP), the Multi-Fibre Arrangement (MFA) and significant adjustments to the common external tariff and the common agricultural policy, coincided with the need to revise arrangements for the common organization of markets and public procurement rules in the aftermath of the establishment of the Single European Market. These in turn focused the attention of EU policy makers on the need to secure access for European goods and services to global markets and to promote reciprocity in trade deals with third countries, even those with far lower income and at a significantly lower level of industrialization. Third, these principles were partially applied in the context of the revision of EU–ACP cooperation during the mid-term review of the Lomé Convention. The ACP states were to some extent protected by their privileges under the Lomé Convention, at least until the expiry of Lomé IV in 2000 but have been warned, in the words of J. Deus de Pinheiro, the EU commissioner for development, that 'this is the last of the Conventions as we have come to know them.'[9]

The Maastricht Treaty defined European development policy in Title XVII as an autonomous area of EU policy and committed the member states and the European institutions to coordinate their actions and to achieve coherence with other policies. This far-reaching commitment has yet to be achieved, but the EU's response to the globalization process has spurred the European Commission services and the relevant ministries of the member states to greater awareness of the existing contradictions of EU relations with developing countries.

The Maastricht Treaty requirement of coordination was the basis of the European Commission's 1995 paper, *Complementarity Between the Development Policies and Actions of the Union and those of the Member States*. Pressure on public budgets, including overseas development assistance, rather than a rational evaluation of the best outcome for the recipients of development cooperation, prompted the EU to conclude that there should be clearer specialization of tasks between common and national development programmes, that the EU programme should complement national priorities and that the whole process should be subject to respect for the principle of subsidiarity, as set out in art. 3b of the Maastricht Treaty. This suggests that problems of overlap, duplication and even of conflicting actions are likely to persist and to dissipate the impact of the total EU development effort. The EU is certainly still far from effective coordination of national programmes, the definition of joint regional and sectoral priorities and the elaboration of strategies for assistance to specific countries. On the global level, greater contact is now made between the EU and the World Bank and IMF, but there is little real coordination between the bilateral and multilateral donor agencies with the goal of ensuring integrated action on the ground. It is, perhaps, important to note that development cooperation is an area where EU institutions and the member states enjoy 'mixed competence', unlike the common commercial policy where the European Commission represents the member states and negotiates on their collective behalf. The EU member states control some 40 per cent of votes in the World Bank, so a united effort could produce effective results.

Greater coherence of EU development cooperation as a constructive response to globalization and the need to make limited resources more cost-effective should start within the European Commission itself. Currently five commissioners and four directorates-general have active policy responsibilities for development cooperation in various forms. João de Deus Pinheiro and DG VIII deal with ACP countries and South Africa; Manuel Marin and DG IB deal with the southern Mediterranean, Asia and Latin America; Hans Van Den Broek and DG IA deal with those Mediterranean applicants for EU membership and the successor states of the Soviet block; Emma Bonino and the agency ECHO deal with humanitarian aid; and Sir Leon Brittan and DG I are responsible for all aspects of the common commercial policy, including the GSP, MFA and the EU's position in WTO and international economic organizations. Allegedly, the commissioners meet every 'two to three weeks' but rarely are they all present, and they have little time to consider common foreign policy options.[10] Moreover, the policy coherence required by the Maastricht Treaty also involves cooperation in the context of the Common Foreign and Security Policy (CFSP), which is in turn subject to the provisions of the 'second pillar' of the Treaty, where the member states retain the right of initiative and decision. The European Parliament has criticized this fragmentation of policy-making but its power to effect substantive change is limited. Finland and Sweden are new member states whose aid administrations in the 1980s and the 1990s were frustrated in trying to obtain coordination and coherence with the EU in recipient countries. They may have the combined capacity, alongside Denmark and the Netherlands, to insist that this situation is no longer acceptable, not least to their electorates but also to beneficiaries. It is ironic that those member states, especially Germany and the UK, whose representatives call most frequently for cost reductions in international agencies to deal with what they allege is wasteful duplication, have so far failed to secure coordination of their national programmes with those of the EU.

The pressures to globalize EU development cooperation have been most effective regarding food aid, which amounted to almost 1.3 billion USD in 1995. During 1995–6 the member states agreed the basis for coordinated food security programmes, the European Commission working closely with the World Food Programme, the Food and Agriculture Organization, the International Committee of the Red Cross, the UNHCR and the UNRWA together with a wide range of non-governmental organizations active in relief and development work. They agreed criteria to establish country priorities and have proceeded to define groups of recipients (e.g. the highest-priority group defines those with the highest incidence of food insecurity and lowest income per head, including Eritrea, Haiti, Mozambique and Bangladesh) as well as country food security strategies to be implemented by bilateral and multilateral agencies. Common guidelines within the EU as such have also been agreed regarding development cooperation for health, and education and pilot projects are in the process of being implemented. Overall, however, structured coordination and policy coherence remains a goal rather than an achievement.

Market access strategies were the centrepiece of the EU's response to the debate on the globalization of international trade.[11] This communication from the European Commission to the Council and other EU institutions set out the basic goal of EU policy to achieve open markets worldwide. It emphasized the contribution of the Single European Market to the liberalization of international trade and confirmed the commitment of the EU to the WTO and compliance with the Uruguay Round. In autumn 1996 these policies were affirmed by the EU, especially in the context of preparations for the December 1996 Ministerial Session of the WTO held in Singapore. The principal policy instruments prescribed to respond to globalization were both multilateral and bilateral. Multilaterally, the EU advocated consolidation of the Uruguay Round agreements and their extension to such 'new areas' as: trade and investment and trade and environment; ensuring that adequate pressure to open their markets would be exerted on applicant countries for WTO membership; and the extension of the WTO regime to the General Agreement of Trade in Services (GATS) and public procurement. Bilaterally, the EU committed itself: to push for reciprocity in trade negotiations; to proceed with free trade area agreements, such as those negotiated with Mediterranean states like Turkey and Tunisia and on a block-to-block basis with MERCOSUR in Latin America; and to introduce adjustments in the EU's GSP regime to secure greater access for European exports. Significantly, no reference was made to the Lomé Convention or to the need for special measures to protect the weakest economies. The preparation for implementing the second round of textile trade liberalization as agreed in the Uruguay Round will, according to the EU commissioner responsible, Sir Leon Brittan, reflect the degree of access enjoyed by European exporters to such textile supplier countries as Brazil, India, Indonesia, Pakistan, and Thailand. This type of policy stance may be interpreted as signalling a threat of protectionism in EU trade policies. Any move in this direction would be catastrophic for developing countries in the process of adopting more outwardly oriented development strategies based on tariff liberalization – for instance, as is the case in India. The EU has lowered its tariffs in accordance with the GATT-negotiated reductions, but some analysts argue that protectionism has increased regarding such products as steel, textiles and consumer electronics.[12] The EU responses to globalization do not augur well for the future of the Lomé Convention. To quote Mr Pinheiro, the EU is

> at a turning point ... We are witnessing trends towards liberalization in the world and this will be deepened, so that any system based on preferences and trade barriers is condemned. We have to find new ways of helping ACP countries.[13]

The mid-term review of the Lomé Convention reaffirmed the aim to ensure that the ACP could be fully integrated in the global economy, and recognized that the tariff benefits they have enjoyed for more than twenty years in the EU market are being significantly eroded by the implementation of the Uruguay Round deal. Strengthening ACP capacity in trade development is a high priority of Lomé IVB and the trade concessions in the EU market were extended and enlarged. However, the EU stopped short of recognizing that the ACP as the weakest trade partner deserved unrestricted access to the European market for all their exports. At the same time the EU failed to confront the reality that there are countries in other parts of the world, notably Asia, where levels of poverty are as extreme but who are excluded from the privileges of the Lomé Convention despite high levels of dependence on the EU market.

There seems little room for doubt that the ACP in general and Africa in particular have slipped down the EU agenda. EU–ACP trade is relatively small and trade preferences for the African states do not advance strategic EU interests in the aftermath of the Cold War, the collapse of the Soviet Union and donor fatigue and impatience with dictatorial regimes and countries torn apart by faction fighters. Despite the fact that there are significant success stories among the ACP, e.g. Botswana, Senegal, Mauritius and most of the Caribbean countries to name but a few, the prevalent view among European policy-makers is that the Lomé Conventions since 1975 have not delivered sufficient benefits to justify their extension in the next century. Indeed, there is little evidence that the European Commission, which has long been a staunch ally of the ACP, would relish trying to defend a renewed convention in the WTO after the current arrangement expires. Defence of special preferences for the ACP would doubtless prejudice the EU's advocacy of open markets and liberalization based on non-discrimination, not least in the eyes of the USA and Japan.

In its Green Paper on relations between the EU and the ACP countries on the eve of the twenty-first century,[14] the European Commission declared that the EU must make its presence felt in all regions of the world. The EU's primary concern is to integrate the poor into economic and social life and the ACP countries into the global economy. The Green Paper did not frame any formal proposals but presented options for the future.

The goal, as stated by the European Commission, was to revitalize ACP–EU relations and open new horizons. The link between the ACP and the EU is still a 'key part of the Union's identity.'[15] The Green Paper set out four options:

1. The *status quo*.
2. An overall EU–ACP convention supplemented by special bilateral agreements.
3. Splitting up the Lomé Convention into separate regional African, Caribbean and Pacific arrangements.
4. A specific agreement for least developed countries, *not* restricted to current ACP. It would recognize the special circumstances of the least developed countries.

Overall, the Green Paper stated that the EU should give priority to a consistent and coherent approach. Moreover, the EU should commit itself to formulating an overall strategy for the ACP, embracing both EU and national policies, plus better coordination machinery on the ground. A sustainable relationship between the EU and the ACP will need to be based on new principles:

The regional emphasis of EC development policies, embedded in the Treaty of Rome, continued with the Yaoundé Conventions and extended to its maximum by the Lomé Agreements, has in many ways become both an anachronism and a straightjacket.[16] Nevertheless, for most ACP states the EU is still their major market and their links to Europe via the Lomé Conventions have represented at least partial participation in the globalization process. The ACP faced the challenge of the Single European Market with great trepidation and were deeply sceptical that they could benefit from what the European Commission described as the exciting opportunities for the ACP deriving from the dynamic growth and expansion of European markets in the 1990s. Even if these opportunities really existed, the ACP states were doubtful that their exporters would be sufficiently robust to take advantage of them.[17] Some three years or so later, the prospects for the majority of the ACP exporters to benefit from the much stronger competitive pressures of the global trade environment seem even more bleak.

CONCLUSION

EU development cooperation faces a legitimacy crisis. Throughout the EU, aid budgets are under pressure as part of public spending cuts. The concept of the welfare state is threatened in Europe, and aid dependency is being challenged from both within and beyond the Union. European policy-making focuses on the short-term goals of meeting the so-called Maastricht criteria for participation in economic and monetary union, and there is only very limited energy remaining for redefining longer-term common interests between Europe and developing countries. The protracted and cumbersome policy-making process within the EU in itself limits the scope for innovation and flexibility. The relatively disappointing results so far evident from the Intergovernmental Conference (IGC) on the likely reform and future enlargement of the Union, and especially its institutions, indicates the pressures to maintain the *status quo* and the great difficulties encountered in building a consensus for change. Indeed, the lessons from the IGC during 1996–7 suggest that EU policies towards developing countries will continue to be dictated by *ad hoc*, essentially short-term interests and that underlying inconsistencies and conflicts between various groups of EU member states will not be resolved. Rather, the contentious issues are likely to be sidelined and the special sensitivities of the least developed countries are unlikely to command significant attention. In short, the marginalization of developing countries' interests has become part of the *status quo*.

Wider obligations, especially those imposed by the Uruguay Round agreements, the WTO agenda and the combined G7 and OECD pressures for a multilateral investment agreement, all emphasize these trends. The EU initiative to promote a common Market Access Strategy will direct attention to the barriers faced by European exporters in foreign markets. The European Commission is developing a database to list technical and other barriers to trade by sector and by country, and will monitor third country legislation to remove these barriers. Developing countries are likely to face increasing pressure to open their markets in the context of negotiations for development assistance from the EU.

Moreover, there is a definable shift in public policy attitudes throughout the EU towards the so-called 'payback' from development cooperation, not just in terms of export market access but also in terms of financial flows. The EU–ACP *Courier* quoted European Commission estimates that for every 100 ecu granted in aid, the EU 'gets back' 48 ecu as jobs, supplies and technical assistance contracts.[18] These figures do not take account of secondary business opportunities, such as future sales of spare parts, maintenance contracts and other deals financed by non-EU agencies, which could be part of the same overall development programme. There is evidence throughout the EU member states that governments seek a 'return on aid', which in turn prompts further debate on the practice of 'tying' aid (or limiting access to aid-financed contracts on the basis of nationality), which deserves much more attention than is feasible here. Suffice to state that this debate is indicative of a fundamental change in perspective and philosophy, to the possible detriment of developing countries' interests.

At the same time, it is important to stress that many European companies still retain a competitive edge over those from USA or Japan in many developing country markets. Their extensive and established trade links, their degree of specialization and their technological skills already adapted to African, Asian and Latin American markets represent a significant advantage. The challenge is for EU links with developing countries to construct sufficiently dynamic and innovative relationships which will strengthen this competitive position but still be compatible with the WTO.

The globalization process has highlighted the role of the private sector in engineering economic growth and competitiveness. EU links with developing countries need to be conducive to enterprise development. EU assistance to trade development, whether for the benefit of the ACP states, the member countries of the Andean Group, or the so-called partners in the Mediterranean, should concentrate on encouraging and assisting the private sector in its efforts to create market share, and if possible increase it. Cost-effective assistance to the private sector, however, is not easily designed or delivered. Indeed, the evidence shown in this book regarding the ECIP and the role of the private sector in Asia and Latin America suggests that to date the EU has had only limited success. It is important to recall that while all the most prosperous countries in the 1990s have market economies, we should not conclude that the introduction of a market economy will automatically lead to prosperity. The evidence from the transition process in the former communist economies of Central and Eastern Europe, and the chronic social problems associated with structural adjustment programmes in Africa and Latin America, demonstrate that it is extremely difficult to achieve an appropriate public sector partnership with the private sector. Effective management of the impact of globalization, especially on fragile economies, requires strong public and private sector institutions jointly committed to enterprise development.

Trade rather than aid and private investment rather than development assistance are now perceived as the most effective engines for economic growth and prosperity. Economic development and the modernization of a weak economy are likely to be faster when trade flows freely and permeates the economy with new sources of knowledge, skill, enterprise and capital.[19] Thus the principal challenge to the EU in re-shaping its network of relations with developing countries in the twenty-first century is to define structures that will enable and stimulate enterprise development. These structures, whether based on reciprocity or on asymmetrical free trade areas, need to provide predictable frameworks for investment decisions. This would in turn encourage the further development of what can still be termed an international division of labour between Europe and developing countries, to the mutual advantage of both groups.

Bibliography

Cosgrove, C., 'Autonomous Development or Participation in World Trade? Reflections on the ACP–EEC Experience,' in Cosgrove, C., and Jamar, J. (eds), *The European Community's Development Policy: The Strategy Ahead* (De Tempel for the College of Europe, Bruges, 1986) pp. 217–28.

Cosgrove C., 'The Impact of 1992 on EC–ACP Trade and Investment,' in Zartman, I. W., *Europe and Africa – The New Phase* (Rienner, Boulder, 1993) pp. 63–75.

Cosgrove, C., 'Has the Lomé Convention Failed ACP Trade?,' *Journal of International Affairs* vol. 48 (summer 1994) pp. 223–49.

Cosgrove Twitchett, C. *A Framework for Development: the EEC and the ACP* (Allen & Unwin, London, 1981).

Cosgrove Twitchett, C., *Europe and Africa: from Association to Partnership* (Saxon House, Farnborough, 1978).

The Courier, ACP–EU (March–April 1995) no. 145.

The Courier, (November–December 1996) no. 160.

CTA, *EEC Trade Preferences and ACP Exports*. Report to the European Commission (Reading, 1989).

Davenport N., A. Hewitt and A. Koning, *Europe's Preferred Partners? The Lomé Countries in World Trade* (ODI and ECDPM, London and Maastricht, 1994).

Delors, Jacques, *Our Europe* (Verso Press, London 1992).

The Economist, Survey of the World Economy, 28 September 1996.

The European, 14 July 1995 p. 17.

The European, 14 July 1996.

European Commission, DG VIII/I, Brussels, November 1996.

European Union, *The Global Challenge of International Trade*, COM(96) 53,14.02.96.

GATT, *Trade Policy Review, European Communities, General Agreement on Tariffs and Trade* (Geneva, 1993).

Grilli, E., *The European Community and the Developing Countries* (Cambridge University Press, 1993).
Helleiner, G. K., *Trade, Trade Policy and Industrialization Reconsidered* (United Nations World Institute for Development and Economic Research, Helsinki, 1995).
ODI, *Commodity Markets: Options for Developing Countries*, Briefing Paper London (5) 1995.
OECD, *The Knowledge-Based Economy* Paris (1996).
Roarty, M. J., 'Trade Policy in the EU,' *European Business Review*, vol. 96, no. 1, 1996.
Simai, M., *Globalization, Multilateral Cooperation and the Development Process* (Institute for World Economics, Budapest April 1996).
UNCTAD, *World Investment Report 1996* (Geneva).
World Trade Organization, Press Release no. 56 (Geneva, 18 September 1996) p. 1.

Notes

1. *The Economist* (1996).
2. Delors (1992) p. 71.
3. Simai (1996) p. 14.
4. *World Trade Organization* (1996).
5. Ibid.
6. OECD (1996).
7. UNCTAD (1996) p. 8.
8. ODI (1995) p. 1.
9. Quoted in *The Courier* ACP–EU no. 145 (1995).
10. *The European* (1996).
11. European Union (1996).
12. Roarty (1996) p. 3.
13. *The European* (1995).
14. European Commission (1996).
15. Ibid.
16. Grilli (1993) p. 343.
17. Cosgrove (1993) p. 63.
18. *The Courier* (1996).
19. Ibid.

Index